D0151472

Asian Development

Asian Development
Economic Success and Policy Lessons

William E. James
Seiji Naya
Gerald M. Meier

The University of Wisconsin Press

The University of Wisconsin Press
114 North Murray Street
Madison, Wisconsin 53715

The University of Wisconsin Press, Ltd.
1 Gower Street
London WC1E 6HA, England

5   4   3   2   1

Printed in the United States of America

Library of Congress Cataloging-in-Publications Data
James, William E.
   Asian development.
   Bibliography: pp. 225–272
   Includes index.
   1. Asia—Economic conditions—1945–   . 2. Asia—
Economic policy.   I. Naya, Seiji.   II. Meier, Gerald M.
III. Title.
HC412.J33   1988   338.95   88-40191
ISBN 0-299-11780-4
ISBN 0-229-11784-7 (pbk.)

Contents

Tables

Figures

Authors' Note

This book appraises the unprecedented economic development record of the countries of Asia. It focuses on the extraordinary performance of the Asian "newly industrializing countries" (Hong Kong, Korea, Singapore, and Taiwan), the four resource-based countries of the Association of Southeast Asian Nations (ASEAN-4—Indonesia, Malaysia, the Philippines, and Thailand), and the low-income countries of South Asia (Bangladesh, Burma, India, Nepal, Pakistan, and Sri Lanka). Of prime interest is why the records of development performance have differed among these countries. In answer, we place major emphasis on the differential success in devising and implementing appropriate policies in the countries themselves.

The success of so many countries in such a diverse region as Asia is surely one of the most significant accomplishments in economic history. A dynamic process of growth appears to be at work in Asia whereby countries at varying levels of development are able to accelerate their progress and begin catching up with the leading countries. The process is best exemplified by the newly industralizing countries (NICs) following Japan. It is possible that the ASEAN-4 countries will in turn grow fast enough to gain on the NICs. Whether South Asia will eventually begin to catch up remains problematic, though the growth rates of some—Pakistan, Sri Lanka, and India—have improved. In South Asia, higher growth and employment generation are prerequisites for lessening abject poverty.

The Asian success story that is documented in this study is very clearly based on the adoption of appropriate policies by Asian governments since the 1960s. Even during the period of sharp changes in the international economy during the 1970s—oil shocks, world inflation, recessions, external debt crises, new technologies, new products, and new industries—the Asian countries have shown exceptional flexibility in responding to change. Their ability to adjust to changing external conditions in closely related to the type of policies they have implemented.

Development strategies and policies have differed from country to country in Asia. The general policies followed range from the open, market-oriented policies of the NICs and ASEAN-4 to the more inward-looking interventionist policies of South Asia. But the direction of policy change in Asia has increasingly been toward a more open, outward-looking, market-oriented approach.

The growing interdependence of the Asian less developed countries (LDCs) with each other and with the more advanced economies of Japan, the United States, Canada, Australia, and New Zealand is reflected in the rapid expansion of trade and investment in the Asia-Pacific region. The positive record of economic development of the Asian LDCs has contributed greatly to the ascendancy of the Pacific over the Atlantic. In the past, growth in the United States and Japan pulled up the growth rates of the smaller economies of the Asia-Pacific region. In future, it seems likely that, increasingly, it will be the growth of the Asian developing countries that acts as a catalyst to growth in the more advanced economies. China's emergence and modernization efforts are likely to reinforce this trend.

In this book we emphasize the empirical record of growth and development performance of the Asian LDCs. Behind the statistics of differential development performance among the countries of East, Southeast, and South Asia lie effective domestic economic policies. A country's course of development is determined not by its "initial conditions," but by the quality of its national economic management. As the chapters in this book explain in detail, what matters most are appropriate policies that promote industrial development based on comparative advantage (chapter 2), relax the savings constraint and allocate investible funds most productively (chapter 3), make the best use of external capital in overcoming the foreign exchange constraint (chapter 4), provide incentives and technologies to develop the agricultural sector (chapter 5), and promote development of the human resources (chapter 6).

The Asian countries provide an excellent opportunity for assessing the role of policy in determining development performance. This volume presents cross-country comparisons and an assessment of secular trends in specific countries and subgroups (NICs, ASEAN-4, South Asia) with regard to macroeconomics, trade, and sectoral policies. It also emphasizes the changing international economic environment and the influence of external events and trends.

The study originated from research initiated at the Economics Office of the Asian Development Bank (ADB) in Manila, where from 1980 to 1984 Seiji Naya served as chief economist, and William James served as economist. The ADB monograph *Developing Asia: The Importance of Domestic Policies* prepared in 1982 outlines some of the basic ideas we have been able to develop more fully as part of the Development Policy Program of the East-West Center's Resource Systems Institute over the past few years.

This book is intended to serve a wide audience of economists and non-economists. We have tried to make the analysis accessible to noneconomists by keeping technical and theoretical discussion to a minimum. Students of development theory and Asian studies will find the book useful as an empirical complement to more theoretical studies. It should also be useful as a source book for business and social science majors concerned with Asian and Pacific affairs. Policymakers and development practitioners may gain a wider perspective from the overview that this book provides. Instead of having to rely on numerous individual country reports, the reader may gain a synthetic summary from this book.

In initiating and carrying out the research necessary to complete the study, we have been fortunate that two remarkable regional institutions, the Asian Development Bank and the East-West Center, strongly supported us. The research we conducted at the Economics Office of the ADB was instrumental in beginning the study. President Victor Hao Li of the East-West Center saw the need for the completion of this study, and his encouragement is deeply appreciated. We must also acknowledge our debt to Theodore Morgan and Roger Ernst, who gave us detailed comments and suggestions on various drafts. Pearl Imada, Clarita Barretto, Janis Togashi, and Eric Ramstetter provided outstanding support in preparing the study. The untiring secretarial help of Ann Takayesu, Jeni Miyasaki, and Cynthia Nakachi in preparing the manuscript is gratefully acknowledged.

Any remaining errors and omissions are the authors' responsibility.

Abbreviations

ADB	Asian Development Bank
ASEAN	Association of Southeast Asian Nations (also ASEAN-4)
DAC	Development Assistance Committee
DFI	direct foreign investment
EEC	European Economic Community
EPR	effective protection rate
EPZ	export processing zone
FTZ	free trade zone
GATT	General Agreement on Tariffs and Trade
GDP	gross domestic product
GNP	gross national product
IDA	International Development Association
IMF	International Monetary Fund
LDC	less developed country
M2	broad money supply
MDC	more developed country
MITI	Ministry of Industry and Trade
MRT	marginal rate of transformation
NGO	nongovernmental organization
NIC	newly industrializing country
NPR	nominal protection rate
ODA	official development assistance
OECD	Organization for Economic Cooperation and Development
OPEC	Organization of Petroleum Exporting Countries
SEZ	special economic zone
SFI	specialized financial institution
SITC	Standard International Trade Classification
SMI	small- and medium-scale industrial firms
TI	total inflows

Asian Development

1 Development Performance
An Overview

Before the 1960s, world economic activity was concentrated in and around the North Atlantic. Europe and the United States were the major centers of industrial growth and trade. But a quarter century of spectacular economic growth in the Asia-Pacific region has shifted the center of the world economy from the Atlantic to the Pacific. The dynamic economic performance of Japan in the 1960s and the East and Southeast Asian countries in the 1970s has reshaped the global economy. Since 1960 real economic growth rates in the Asian less developed countries (LDCs) have been among the highest in the world (table 1.1).

The rapid economic growth of the LDCs in the Asia-Pacific region is one of the most significant events of the past 25 years, leading to predictions of the coming of a "Pacific Era." Four countries—Hong Kong, the Republic of Korea (henceforth Korea), Singapore, and Taiwan—in particular have been so successful in terms of both economic growth and social development that they are now used as models of development. Numerous articles and books have been written about the "four little tigers," the "gang of four," or the "newly industrializing countries" (NICs), as they are often called, and the benefits of the outward-looking, market-oriented policies they adopted. The four large members of the Association of Southeast Asian Nations (ASEAN-4)—Indonesia, Malaysia, the Philippines, and Thailand—followed the lead of the NICs toward more outward-looking policies and rapid growth in the mid-1970s, while the South Asian countries and the People's Republic of China (henceforth China) enacted policy reforms in this direction more recently.

The last 15 years have generally been filled with difficulties for developing countries. Developing countries have had to contend with a rapidly changing world economy. Table 1.1 shows that growth of world output slowed in the 1970s and even further in the 1980s. The two oil shocks and prolonged recessions led to balance-of-payments problems for oil-importing countries, and the

3

Table 1.1. Annual Rate of Growth of Real GDP (percentages)

	1960–70	1970–80	1980–86
World	4.9	3.5	2.5
Industrialized countries	4.8	3.0	2.4
United States	3.8	2.8	2.2
Japan	11.5	5.4	4.2
Developing countries	5.5	5.3	2.3
Africa	4.9	3.8	0.6
Asia	4.5	5.1	6.1
Middle East	7.9	6.1	1.3[a]
Latin America[b]	5.7	5.9	1.2

Sources: International Monetary Fund (IMF), *International Financial Statistics*, Yearbook 1986, June 1987; World Bank, *World Development Report*, 1984 and 1986; Asian Development Bank (ADB), *Annual Report*, 1986; Republic of China, Council for Economic Planning and Development, *Taiwan Statistical Data Book* (hereafter by title only), 1985.

Note: Regions are given as defined by the IMF.

[a] 1980–85.

[b] Countries in the Western Hemisphere with a population of less than 1 million are excluded.

softening of the oil market in the 1980s created difficulties for even the oil-rich countries. High interest rates in the early 1980s increased the debt-servicing burden and contributed to the repayment difficulties of many developing countries. Commercial banks reacted by drastically reducing the flow of private external funds to developing countries. At the same time, problems in industrialized countries led to decreasing trends in official flows. Thus despite falling interest rates in the mid-1980s, external sources of funds were not readily available to developing countries. World trade (especially exports of developing countries) fluctuated widely and generally stagnated in the 1980s, declining in nominal terms in almost every year since 1981 (table 1.2).

Most developing countries, including the Asian developing countries, have been negatively affected by these changes in the world economy. The spectacular growth rates of the NICs in the 1960s and 1970s, averaging 8 to 10 percent, have slowed significantly in the first half of the 1980s (table 1.3). The ASEAN-4 countries also had slower growth, but South Asian countries have generally improved their economic performance. Asian LDCs as a whole, however, continued to grow faster than other regions. It is the only developing region growing at about 5 percent per year.

The key to the success of these countries has been the adoption and implementation of domestic policies that promote efficient use of resources and encourage private sector initiative. The worsening of external conditions in the

Table 1.2. Growth of Merchandise Exports[a] (percentages)

	1960–70	1970–80	1980–86	1981	1982	1983	1984	1985	1986
NICs	*12.2*	*28.2*	*9.6*	*11.8*	*–1.0*	*8.1*	*16.7*	*1.7*	*13.9*
Hong Kong	13.8	22.9	10.3	9.5	–3.9	4.4	22.5	6.2	14.8
Korea	38.1	35.6	12.1	17.6	2.7	10.6	16.4	3.4	12.8
Singapore	3.2	28.7	2.5	7.6	–0.9	4.8	9.3	–5.5	–1.4
Taiwan	24.6	29.6	12.3	12.4	–1.8	11.6	17.5	0.9	22.3
ASEAN-4	*4.0*	*26.3*	*–1.8*	*–0.8*	*–1.0*	*0.6*	*8.9*	*–11.6*	*–8.3*
Indonesia	2.8	34.8	–6.3	1.6	0.2	–5.4	3.4	–17.8	–25.4
Malaysia	3.6	22.6	1.2	–10.0	2.2	14.7	14.4	–6.8	–11.3
Philippines	5.3	18.6	–3.0	–1.5	–13.8	–1.6	7.3	–14.5	3.4
Thailand	5.6	24.8	5.2	7.5	–1.2	–9.1	14.1	–4.1	19.0
South Asia	*2.2*	*16.6*	*2.0*	*0.7*	*2.6*	*3.1*	*2.8*	*–9.9*	*11.2*
Bangladesh	NA	14.3[b]	2.5	4.2	–2.9	–6.2	22.8	6.8	–13.5
Burma	–7.0	15.9	–7.3	1.1	–21.1	–4.2	0.3	–14.9	–10.4
India	4.3	15.5	1.4	–3.5	11.4	–2.3	3.1	–18.0	14.4
Nepal	1.4[c]	6.7	10.0	42.9	–59.1	6.4	26.6	20.0	–12.7
Pakistan	0.1	20.8	4.4	9.2	–20.3	22.1	–20.3	6.6	19.0
Sri Lanka	–1.2	12.0	2.3	2.4	–5.5	3.0	27.5	–10.1	–9.7
World	9.2	20.6	0.8	–1.8	–7.8	–2.8	5.5	0.8	9.8
United States	7.7	17.7	–0.3	5.5	–10.1	–5.9	8.0	–2.2	1.9
Japan	16.9	21.0	8.3	13.9	–9.5	5.8	13.4	4.2	15.9
Developing countries	6.5	24.9	–4.4	–2.3	–12.9	–6.7	3.5	–5.3	–4.4

Sources: IMF, *International Financial Statistics*, Yearbook 1987; *Taiwan Statistical Data Book*, 1987.

Note: NA = Not available.

[a]Compounded annual growth rate in current prices.   [b]1972–80.   [c]1963–70.

5

1980s make appropriate policies even more important if Asian developing countries are to overcome problems without disruption to long-term development. It will not be easy, but the record of the Asian developing countries leaves us very optimistic about their future.

This introductory chapter provides an overview of development strategies and the performance record in the various Asian countries. The process of development in the region might be best understood by examining the constraints on development and the appropriate policies that can relax these constraints. In so doing, we shall place Asian development in a wider context by viewing it as a good testing ground for development theory. We shall also be able to

Table 1.3. Growth of Real GDP and GDP Per Capita (compounded rates)

	Real GDP				Real GDP Per Capita
	1960–70	1970–80	1980–85	1986	1960–85
NICs					
Hong Kong	10.1	9.8	4.2	11.2	6.3
Korea	9.5	8.2	7.5	11.9	6.4
Singapore	9.2	9.3	6.0	1.9	6.7
Taiwan	9.6	9.7	6.1	9.9	6.4
ASEAN-4					
Indonesia	3.8	8.0	3.6	3.2	3.0
Malaysia	NA	7.9	5.1	1.2	4.2[a]
Philippines[b]	5.2	6.3	−0.9	1.1	1.6
Thailand	7.9	6.9	5.3	3.5	4.2
South Asia					
Bangladesh	NA	5.8	3.9	4.4	2.5
Burma	2.8	4.2	5.2	3.7	1.8
India	3.9	3.2	5.4	5.0	1.6
Nepal	2.2	2.0	3.9	4.0	0.1
Pakistan	NA	5.6	6.3	7.5	2.7[d]
Sri Lanka	5.8	4.7	5.0	4.3	3.2
Other Asian LDC					
China	4.0	5.8	9.8	7.9	3.9

Sources: IMF, *International Financial Statistics*, Yearbooks 1986 and May 1987; ADB, *ADB Annual Report*, 1986 and 1987; World Bank, *World Tables*, 1980 and 1983; Republic of China, *Statistical Yearbook of the Republic of China*, 1986; People's Republic of China, State Statistical Bureau, *Statistical Yearbook of China*, 1986.

Note: NA = Not available.

[a]1970–85.   [c]1973–80.

[b]GNP.   [d]1973–85.

draw some more general conclusions for developing countries—especially regarding the need for a set of appropriate governmental policies and the recognition of the interrelationship between trade and structural transformation. Subsequent chapters will then explore more intensively some particular features of the development process in these Asian countries—industry, agriculture, employment, savings mobilization, trade and foreign investment, human resources, balance-of-payments adjustment, and external debt.

Comparative Analysis

Three main groups of Asian LDCs can be distinguished by income level and economic structure and by overall economic performance over the past quarter century. Included in this study[1] are four newly industrializing countries: Hong Kong, Korea, Singapore, and Taiwan; four middle-income Southeast Asian nations: Indonesia, Malaysia, the Philippines, and Thailand; and six low-income South Asian countries: Bangladesh, Burma, India, Nepal, Pakistan, and Sri Lanka. The groupings are based on certain common characteristics shared by the countries: per capita income, structure of economy, openness to trade, and policy orientation. There are, however, differences among countries within each group. These are taken into account whenever it is important to do so. We recognize that statements made in relation to a group of countries may not apply with equal force to each country of that group.

In the 1950s, development economists might have plausibly referred to a "representative poor country" that had fairly standard characteristics. But over the past three decades, diversity among the LDCs has increased greatly, and it is difficult to select a set of characteristics that would be common to all LDCs. Sharp differences exist in the availability of natural resources, structure of production, degree of participation in world trade, political stability, importance of private enterprise, population size, and quality. Income-level differences between LDCs have been recognized formally by multilateral lending institutions like the World Bank. "Middle-income" LDCs are distinguished from "low-income" LDCs, and loan terms are adjusted accordingly. Because of these differences, it is not easy to generalize about the economic performance of a group of countries.

Initial conditions of the Asian developing countries varied greatly. The countries encompass a wide range of cultures, religions, ethnic groups, and languages. Resource endowments, size, and terrain are strikingly different (table 1.4). Indonesia and Malaysia export oil and natural gas; Indonesia belongs to the Organization of Petroleum Exporting Countries (OPEC). Countries like Taiwan and Korea are highly dependent on external sources of oil and other natural resources.

Per capita real gross domestic product (GDP) growth in the NICs was sus-

Table 1.4. Size of Asia-Pacific Countries in 1985

	Population (millions)	Area (1,000 km²)	GDP US$ Millions	GDP US$ Per Capita	Merchandise Exports (US$ millions)
NICs					
Hong Kong	5.4	1	34,081	6,288	30,184
Korea	41.1	99	86,180	2,099	30,283
Singapore	2.6	1	15,970	6,238	22,812
Taiwan	19.1	36	59,141	3,095	30,688
ASEAN-4					
Indonesia	165.2	1,919	86,445	523	18,590
Malaysia	15.7	330	33,360	2,128	15,441
Philippines	54.7	300	32,789	600	4,607
Thailand	51.3	542	38,572	752	7,121
South Asia					
Bangladesh	98.7	144	14,208	144	1,000
Burma	36.6	678	6,812	186	304
India	750.9	3,288	193,125	254	8,003
Nepal	16.7	147	2,280	137	160
Pakistan	96.2	804	30,029	322	2,740
Sri Lanka	15.8	66	5,823	368	1,333
Other Asian LDC					
China	1,042.9	9,561	232,302	223	27,759
Developed countries					
Australia	15.8	7,682	155,585	9,847	22,759
Canada	25.4	9,971	348,854	13,751	90,781
Japan	120.8	372	1,325,208	10,970	177,164
New Zealand	3.3	269	23,506	7,233	5,720
United States	239.3	9,363	3,957,000	16,537	213,144

Sources: ADB, *Key Indicators of Developing Member Countries of ADB*, July 1986; Far Eastern Economic Review, *Asia 1986 Yearbook*, 1986; IMF, *International Financial Statistics*, May 1987.

tained at an average rate of more than 6 percent for more than two decades (1960–85). Because of this rapid growth, Hong Kong and Singapore, with per capita incomes of US$6,288 and $6,238, have almost graduated from the ranks of LDCs. Korea and Taiwan are larger, with populations of 41 and 19 million, and per capita incomes of $2,099 and $3,095, respectively.

Per capita income for the ASEAN-4 ranged from $523 for Indonesia to $2,128 for Malaysia in 1985. Malaysia is classified as an upper-middle-income country by the World Bank. The other three are classified as middle-income countries. Indonesia is the third largest of the Asian LDCs after China and India, in terms of both land area and population. With 165 million people, it is the fifth most populous country in the world. The Philippines and Thailand have populations of approximately 50 million people. Both are endowed with considerable natural and human resources, but in the Philippines, political tensions and economic mismanagement have held back growth. Thailand is still primarily an agrarian-based economy, but its manufacturing and services sectors have been fast expanding. Malaysia is a resource-rich country with a smaller population of approximately 16 million.

The South Asian countries are all low-income countries, with per capita GDPs in 1985 ranging from $137 in Nepal to $368 in Sri Lanka. India is the second largest Asian LDC and one of the largest countries in the world in terms of both land area and population. In addition to India's 751 million people, populations of approximately 100 million each are in Bangladesh and Pakistan, 37 million in Burma, and 16 million each in Nepal and Sri Lanka. These countries are still predominantly agricultural, though large industrial sectors exist in India, Pakistan, and Sri Lanka.

The region's diversity is striking. Asia includes extremely large and populous India and the tiny island city-state Singapore. Nepal is a mountainous, landlocked country; Indonesia and the Philippines are vast archipelagic nations. Malaysia is thinly populated; Bangladesh has one of the highest rural population densities in the world.

In many Asian LDCs, over half the population still relies on small-scale peasant agriculture, but in others the industrial sector has grown so much that their exports are more than 90 percent manufactured goods.

The countries in Asia differ politically as well. Some struggled for national independence—Indonesia, Korea, India. Some were more or less granted independence—Malaysia and the Philippines. Others were never successfully colonized—Thailand—or never achieved full independence—Hong Kong. Many of the countries in the region have strong authoritarian regimes, although India is the world's largest democracy.

Despite these differences, there are enough common characteristics in levels of income, structure of production, and development strategies and policies to give coherence to the analysis of the three groups.

The combined GDP in 1985 of the 14 Asian countries included in our analysis was less than half that of Japan. India has the largest GDP (excepting China) among the Asian developing countries, yet with a population of 751 million its 1985 per capita GDP was $254. The combined 1985 GDP of the ASEAN-4 was about 14 percent of Japan's, and that of the NICs was barely 15 percent of Japan's (table 1.4).

Despite the relatively small size of their economies, the Asian developing countries have a far greater impact on the regional economy than GDP estimates would imply. The total merchandise exports and imports of these countries in 1985 were of almost equal value to those of Japan. The NICs, with only 30 percent of the three groups' combined GDP, accounted for 67 percent of their merchandise exports.

The more trade-oriented countries have attained the highest rates of economic growth and have also achieved faster rates of structural transformation from agriculture to industry and services. The quality of economic growth has been higher in the NICs than elsewhere because it has been accompanied by full employment and improved opportunities for a larger share of the population. Poverty incidence declined steadily in the NICs. The distribution of income has been more even in the NICs than in other LDCs. Income distribution in Taiwan is at least as equitable as that in any other market economy, including Japan.

The type of economic development that has occurred in the NICs has attracted attention out of proportion to the small size of these countries. Other less developed countries regard their performance as exemplary. However, the conditions faced by the ASEAN-4 and South Asian nations are different from the NICs in several major aspects. The ethnic and religious heterogeneity of the populations is much greater in these countries than it is in Taiwan, Korea, or Hong Kong. And despite the racial mix in Singapore, it has a small, entirely urban population and never had to face the enormous regional disparities of countries like India, Indonesia, or Pakistan. Because of the differences in internal conditions, development strategies in ASEAN-4 and South Asia have to be adjusted accordingly. Nevertheless, some general policy lessons and guidelines can be extracted from a comparative assessment of the economic performance of the three groupings of Asian developing countries.

Newly Industrializing Countries

The Asian NICs—Hong Kong, Singapore, South Korea, and Taiwan—have achieved economic growth rates virtually without historical precedent. Only Japan charted a similarly rapid path of growth in the 1960s. The speed with which the NICs have industrialized is astonishing. Nineteenth-century development in Europe and North America and the later achievements of the Soviet Union pale in comparison with the record of the NICs.

Hong Kong and Singapore have very little agriculture; more than 60 percent of their GDP is contributed by the service sector. The agricultural sector is more important in Korea and Taiwan, but the share of the agricultural sector in the GDP of both countries has declined sharply. In 1985, agriculture was down to 14 percent of the GDP for Korea and only 6 percent for Taiwan. For the NICs, the policy emphasis on labor-intensive exports made the manufacturing sector more important in terms of both total output and labor force (tables 1.5 and 1.6). In the 1980s, manufacturing activities made up about 30 percent or more of GDP and the labor force.

Southeast Asian Countries

Three resource-rich Southeast Asian nations—Indonesia, Malaysia, and Thailand—also demonstrate strong economic growth. In the 1960s, real growth of GDP ranged from 4 percent for Indonesia to nearly 8 percent

Table 1.5. Structure of Production (percentage of GDP)

	Agriculture			Industry			Services		
	1960	1970	1985	1960	1970	1985	1960	1970	1985
NICs									
Hong Kong[a]	4	2	1	38	37	30	55	56	68
Korea	37	27	14	20	30	41	43	44	45
Singapore	4	2	1	18	30	38	79	68	61
Taiwan	29	16	6	29	41	50	43	45	44
ASEAN-4									
Indonesia	54	47	25	14	18	36	32	35	39
Malaysia	36	31	20	18	25	37	46	44	43
Philippines	26	28	27	28	30	33	46	43	40
Thailand	40	28	17	19	25	30	42	46	53
South Asia									
Bangladesh	58	55	48	7	9	15	36	37	37
Burma	33	38	48	12	14	13	55	48	39
India[a]	47	43	35	19	20	27	28	28	38
Nepal[b]	NA	68	58	NA	11	14	NA	21	27
Pakistan	44	33	25	15	20	28	36	37	47
Sri Lanka	32	27	24	20	23	27	48	46	50
Industrial market economies									
Australia[c]	12	6	6	40	41	35	48	54	59
Canada	6	4	3	34	32	24	60	65	72
Japan[a]	13	6	3	45	47	41	43	47	56
United States[b]	4	3	2	38	35	32	58	62	66

Sources: ADB, *Key Indicators of Developing Member Countries of ADB,* July 1986; Organisation for Economic Cooperation and Development (OECD),*National Accounts Statistics 1972–84;* World Bank, *World Development Report,* 1980, 1982, 1984, and 1986; World Bank, *World Tables,* 2d ed.

Note: NA = Not available.
[a]1984.   [b]1983.   [c]1982.

Table 1.6. Structure of Labor (percentage of labor force)

	Agriculture			Industry			Services		
	1960	1970	1981	1960	1970	1981	1960	1970	1981
NICs									
Hong Kong	8	4	3	52	55	57	40	41	40
Korea	66	50	34	9	17	29	25	33	37
Singapore	8	4	2	23	30	39	69	66	59
Taiwan	50	37	19	21	28	42	29	35	39
ASEAN-4									
Indonesia	75	66	58	8	10	12	17	24	30
Malaysia	63	56	50	12	14	16	25	30	34
Philippines	61	53	46	15	16	17	24	31	37
Thailand	84	80	76	4	6	9	12	14	15
South Asia									
Bangladesh	87	86	74	3	3	11	10	11	15
Burma	NA	70	67	NA	8	10	NA	22	23
India	74	74	71	11	11	13	15	15	16
Nepal	95	94	93	2	2	2	3	4	5
Pakistan	61	59	57	18	19	20	21	22	23
Sri Lanka	56	55	54	14	14	14	30	31	32
Industrial market economies									
Australia	11	8	6	40	37	33	49	55	61
Canada	13	8	5	34	32	29	52	60	66
Japan	33	20	12	30	34	39	37	46	49
United States	7	4	2	36	34	32	57	62	66

Sources: World Bank, *World Tables*, vol. 2, 3d ed.; World Bank, *World Development Report*, 1985 and 1986; *Taiwan Statistical Data Book*, 1984.
Note: NA = Not available.

for Thailand (table 1.3). Although lower in Southeast Asia than in the NICs, GDP growth rates of these countries were much higher than the average for LDCs. Growth of real income per capita, at 4 to 5 percent annually, has been impressive in Southeast Asia.

The lone exception has been the Philippines. The Senator Benigno Aquino assassination, of course, triggered the political crisis, but the Philippine problem began much earlier than 1983. Economic growth has slowed since the late 1970s. Per capita income growth over 1960–85 averaged less than 2 percent, comparable to that of South Asian countries.

These four Southeast Asian countries, together with Singapore and Brunei, have established the most successful regional grouping in the entire third world—the Association of Southeast Asian Nations (ASEAN).[2]

Significant structural transformation has also occurred in the ASEAN-4 (tables 1.5 and 1.6). During the 1970s, the share of industry in GDP rose while the share of agriculture fell. In Indonesia, the share of industry in GDP increased from a low base of 14 percent in 1960 to 36 percent in 1985, but much of this gain was due to the petroleum boom. The Philippines started at the highest base, 28 percent in 1960, and experienced a slower rate of structural change through the 1970s. Industry accounted for less than 20 percent of GDP in 1960 for Malaysia and Thailand, increasing to 37 and 30 percent, respectively. Industrial employment, however, did not increase as rapidly. In the 1980s, it comprised approximately 10 percent of the total labor force in Indonesia and Thailand, and a little more than 15 percent in the Philippines and Malaysia.

South Asian Countries

Average annual rates of growth of real GDP have been lower in the South Asian countries (Bangladesh, Burma, India, Nepal, Pakistan, and Sri Lanka) than they have in the NICs and ASEAN-4 throughout the 1960s and 1970s. Real economic growth rates began to accelerate in the late 1970s. In the 1980s, economic growth rates in South Asia have converged with those of other Asian countries.

Real GDP per capita has grown very slowly in large parts of South Asia—India, Burma, and Nepal. In Bangladesh, Pakistan, and Sri Lanka, per capita real growth has averaged better than 2 percent per year.

Overall, industrial development has been relatively slow in South Asian countries. By 1960, the industrial sector comprised 15 percent of GDP in Pakistan and approximately 20 percent in India and Sri Lanka (table 1.5). This was similar to Malaysia, Thailand, and Singapore. Industry's GDP share increased slowly to approximately 25 percent in all three South Asian countries by 1985, but labor absorption by industry has been minimal. Agriculture remains the major source of income and employment for most of the population of South Asia.

This section has emphasized the diversity within the region as a whole as well as commonalities within the three groups of countries. Despite differences, the countries have all confronted the same economic challenge of having to relax a number of constraints on their development in order to absorb their large labor forces and achieve a structural transformation of their economies so as to raise the level of per capita real income. The most prominent constraints that have been common to the Asian developing countries are (1) the savings constraint, (2) the foreign exchange constraint, (3) the agricultural constraint, and (4) the human resource constraint.

Constraints

The attainable rate of development in a country is limited by its ability to mobilize sufficient domestic resources—by its ability to relax the savings constraint. An increase in the ratio of savings to national income is generally a necessary—if not sufficient—condition for making resources available in order to accelerate a country's development. Even though labor may be abundant, the output of an LDC remains limited by a shortage of capital. If any one factor has been emphasized as the major factor governing the rate of development, it has been capital accumulation. When presenting his model of a dual economy in the early 1950s, Sir Arthur Lewis contended that

> the central problem in the theory of economic development is to understand the process by which a community which was previously saving and investing four or five percent of its national income or less, converts itself into an economy where voluntary saving is running at about 12 to 15 percent of national income or more. This is the central problem because the central fact of economic development is rapid accumulation (including knowledge and skills with capital).[3]

The second constraint—the lack of foreign exchange—will obviously limit a country's development when its growth of gross national product (GNP) depends on some increase in imports. The capacity to import will be determined by the country's growth in exports, commodity terms of trade, net inflow of foreign capital, and access to foreign exchange reserves. To the extent that a passive balance on current account cannot be financed, the country must reduce its rate of growth as it becomes impossible to fulfill import requirements.

The "two gap" model focuses on both the savings constraint and the foreign exchange constraint.[4] An increase in savings will not relax the foreign exchange constraint, even though it releases resources for investment, if the country is unable to substitute domestic resources for imports or if there are limitations to exports on the demand side. An inflow of foreign capital is more growth promoting when a country's development is constrained by the shortage of foreign exchange rather than by the shortage of domestic savings.

The lag in agricultural production constitutes another bottleneck in the course of the country's development. Agriculture contributes to the development process in a number of ways: it provides inputs of raw materials and foodstuffs that are used in the industrial sector; a marketable surplus from agriculture also gives rise to a demand for industrial products; an investable surplus of savings and taxes may be tapped from the agricultural sector; balance-of-payments improvement may depend on the export or import substitution of primary products; and the containment of labor in more productive agriculture may be necessary to stem the excessive rural-urban migration. Successful industrialization thus depends on a prior or parallel agricultural revolution.

If, as Marshall observed, "the part of nature in production may show a tendency to diminishing returns, but the part of man shows a tendency to increasing returns," then the ultimate constraint on development can be said to be limited human resources.[5] Time series and cross-sectional studies of the sources of growth based on aggregate production functions reveal that an increase in the inputs of labor, capital, and natural resources over time can account for only 50–60 percent of the realized increase in output.[6] The unexplained residual of the additional 40–50 percent of growth in output must be attributed to technical progress, improved quality of the inputs, and improved ways of combining the inputs to produce goods and services. The development of human resources must account for a large part of unexplained residual. Economists have therefore reduced their emphasis on physical capital and have given more attention to human capital. This is reflected in the emphasis on human capital theory,[7] redistribution with growth,[8] and fulfillment of basic human needs.[9]

The progress in a country's course of development can be interpreted in terms of the relaxation of the foregoing constraints. As the constraints become less binding, the country succeeds in absorbing more labor from the traditional sector and in undergoing a structural transformation in the pattern of production, employment, and demand. The labor absorption process has been analyzed in the classic dual-sector models of Lewis and of Fei and Ranis.[10] Extensive quantitative analyses of the structural transformation process have been provided in studies by Chenery and associates.[11] From these studies it can be concluded that the sources of growth come from both the supply side of the economy through increases in capital and labor and technical change—and from the demand side through the effects of reallocation of resources to higher productivity activities, and through changes in demand and trade as income rises.[12] But if a country is to achieve its potential rate of development, it is necessary that it pursue appropriate domestic policies, and the international environment must also be sufficiently favorable to allow the country to take fuller advantage of the sources of growth.

Economic Growth Factors and Domestic Policies

Recently, a proliferation of books and articles examining the factors behind the success of Japan and the NICs have appeared. Some economists point out that the initial conditions have been a crucial element in the success of these countries and thus this feat cannot be duplicated.[13] Some suggest, for example, that small size and lack of resources helped the NICs perform much better than the resource-rich ASEAN countries. This conforms to the adage "A country's development prospects are inversely proportional to its natural resource endowment."[14] One economic explanation of the paradox refers to the sudden increase in export earnings and the inflow of external funds induced by a natural resource boom.[15] This would lead to an upward pressure on the real exchange rate and to a squeeze on other traded goods. Although the so-called Dutch disease (referring to the discovery of petroleum in the North Sea) describes a short-run condition, a long-term equivalent of the disease is commonly found in countries with abundant natural resources. An abundance of natural resources leads to a comfortable balance-of-payments position and a strong national currency. This discriminates against exports of manufactures. Countries with no natural resources, on the other hand, must make the most of their human resources. The NICs used their large and skilled labor force and emphasized exports of labor-intensive manufactures. The rapid growth of these industries led to increasing wages and improvements in income distribution.

A second explanation of the paradox stems from the nature of resource development. Resources (especially minerals) tend to have concentrated ownership and require capital-intensive technology. These traits encourage rent-seeking activities rather than efforts to improve productivity. These explanations, however, are suggestive at best—some countries have done well with resources while other countries without resources have not. The declining terms of trade in the 1980s have forced the ASEAN-4 countries to attempt to diversify their economic and export structure. Exports of light manufactures which use their abundant labor have become increasingly important.

There is also a hypothesis that the success of the Asian countries, including Japan, can be attributed to their Confucian heritage and other so-called characteristics of Asian ethics which encourage hard work, loyalty, and diligence.[16] There can be no doubt that the quality of the labor force and entrepreneurial talent have played a major role. But these factors cannot be attributed solely to cultural heritage. The provision of opportunities for educational advancement and market activities have contributed to the development of human resources and institutions in the successful Asian countries. Counterexamples indicate that such cultural preconditions are not a sufficient condition of industrialization and they may not even be necessary.[17]

Other economists emphasize several fortuitous events in the world economy, including large foreign aid and a relatively unchallenged market for light manufactures, as the most important factors behind the NICs' rapid growth. External factors indeed play an important role; a relatively open international trade environment is crucial for the continued growth of these countries. Yet export growth as well as economic growth continued in the 1970s despite turbulent events and slower world trade.

Thus although special conditions were important, we contend that the key is the outward-looking development strategies adopted by these countries. These policies have led to long-term development and dynamic gains in technology, economic organization, and management. The next question to ask then is: Will this strategy continue to work in the future, and is it transferable? We believe the answer is yes.

The distinguishing feature of industrialization in Asian developing countries is that they have opted for an export-oriented strategy. As will be discussed in chapter 2, all of the Asian developing countries have moved away from import substitution policies to export orientation. Export orientation has involved dismantling or offsetting previously imposed protection measures that discriminate against exports, e.g., redemption of duties on imported inputs, ending of multiple exchange rates, and correction of overvalued currencies. Promotional measures in favor of exports, especially cheap bank loans and tax concessions for exports, were implemented to neutralize import protection. Generally, the countries moved toward more neutral policy stances, reducing distortions caused by import substitution policies. In other words, policy incentives for firms to produce for the domestic and external markets became more balanced. Hong Kong and Singapore have long been virtually free trade economies, while Korea and Taiwan substantially reduced tariffs and corrected exchange rate misalignments in the 1960s. The ASEAN-4 countries have not been as outward-looking as the NICs because of a number of economic and political constraints. They have generally followed more restrictive trade policies, designed to foster industries producing for the domestic market. But in the 1970s they followed the NICs and began to adopt an export-oriented approach. South Asian countries, especially Sri Lanka and India, have also moved in this direction.

The countries that pursued an export-oriented strategy were able to relax their foreign exchange constraint. Exports in the NICs grew at an average of 20 and 30 percent in the 1960s and 1970s. The ASEAN-4 countries were also able to expand exports in the 1970s, while other countries that continued with import substitution suffered balance-of-payments difficulties. Countries following export-oriented policies also enjoyed high rates of real economic growth.

Overall Development Strategy

The outward-looking development strategy adopted by the NICs, however, involved more than export orientation, though openness to world trade and investment is a crucial element. Export-oriented strategies will not succeed without a good macroeconomic environment. Several aspects of the overall development strategy of these countries should be highlighted:

1. Outward-looking development strategies also involve a market- or private-sector-oriented approach. Business activities are mainly left to the private sec-

tor, and the allocation of resources is basically left to the market. Governments strive to provide a stable economic environment in which the private sector can flourish. The market mechanism is effective in providing information at minimum cost, and the greater competition allowed under such a system intensifies the search for innovations that increase efficiency of production.

Countries that tried to replace the market through direct controls have generally had inferior records of development.[18] For governments to overrule or replace the market, governments must have the knowledge, foresight, and administrative capacity to undertake complex intervention. In practice, however, administrators are often not able to accomplish this task. Governments overextend themselves when they attempt to take over decision making in areas best left to the market. The difficulties of planning and the misallocation and corruption resulting from numerous regulations and controls have been underestimated, and good effects have been overestimated.

The role of the government, however, does not necessarily have to follow the textbook laissez-faire model. Government planning and regulation are still required. In more successful developing countries, the emphasis on direct controls has been reduced; government decrees have become less important. Rather, government policies are effected primarily by indirect controls that work through the price mechanism.

The governments of the Asian developing countries have all (with the possible exception of Hong Kong) been a determining force in economic development. Yet there are major differences in the degree and quality of government involvement. The NICs have been especially successful in selecting appropriate policies. They have used financial policies to reduce uncertainties and encourage investment in new industries. Industrial and trade policies were adopted to shift the structure of production in line with changing comparative advantage. Even Singapore, which generally adopted a policy of noninterference in trade, has used other policies to stimulate certain industries, though perhaps to excess in some areas. Yet governments did not try to overwhelm the market, and were flexible enough to adjust policies when necessary.

In contrast with the relatively market-oriented policies of the governments in the Asian NICs and to a lesser extent the ASEAN-4, the governments in the South Asian countries have regulated their economies more directly and more extensively, with less reliance on the market price system and private enterprise. Although the South Asian countries have recently taken steps to expand the role of private enterprise, they clearly have further to go in liberalizing their economies. If the quality of their national economic management rises, the South Asian countries will also raise their economic performance closer to their potential.

2. Price distortions in the national economies have to be reduced to corre-

spond to conditions in the world economy. Price distortions usually take the form of wage rates being too high for unskilled labor (given the abundance of that labor), too high an exchange price for domestic currency (given the foreign exchange shortage), too low for interest rates (given the scarcity of capital), and too low for farm products (given the need to increase farm production).

The correction of price distortions so as to establish honest prices reflecting the true scarcity or abundance of a commodity or factor (equating supply and demand) achieves a more efficient allocation of resources. Specifically, it increases employment, stimulates production of scarce goods, avoids arbitrary bureaucratic decisions, and averts delay, ideological bias, and corruption in those decisions.

Although "getting prices right" does not ensure development, "getting prices wrong" frequently blocks growth.[19] A World Bank study found a high correlation between price distortions and low growth rates.[20] The same study reported that the Asian developing countries have a lower composite index of distortions than developing countries in other regions do. Less developed countries with big price distortions and slower export growth were also more likely to experience debt-servicing problems. Many LDCs with serious price distortions in the 1970s had to undergo debt rescheduling in the 1980s.

The outward-looking policies of the NICs integrated national economies into the world market. Price distortions were lessened, near-equilibrium exchange rates stimulated exports, positive real interest rates stimulated domestic savings and investment, wage levels kept in line with productivity stimulated employment, and agricultural price policy stimulated larger supplies. An outward-looking approach tends to set bounds on how far an economy can stray from the market. In an economy subject to competition, the costs of supporting an inefficient industry and the strain this puts on the government budget are more readily apparent than they are in a closed and heavily protected economy.

3. Openness requires cautious financial management. The Asian developing countries have generally adopted prudent macroeconomic policies to control budget deficits and restrain excessive demand and inflation. Even those with serious bouts of inflation (e.g., Korea, Indonesia, and the Philippines) continued to keep the average rate below that of other middle-income countries.

Prudent demand management has gone hand in hand with promotion of financial development. An Asian Development Bank study on resource mobilization found that saving is positively related to the real interest rate, the availability of financial institutions and instruments, and investment efficiency.[21] The Asian developing countries have opted for financial liberalization and deregulation of the interest rate. Financial development, combined with low rates of inflation and rapid growth, encouraged high rates of resource mobilization and increasing saving rates.

The NICs and ASEAN-4 countries have generally been very successful at mobilizing domestic resources and have for the most part relaxed the savings constraint to development. Savings-to-GNP ratios increased or maintained high levels through the 1970s, especially in the NICs (see chapter 3). By the 1980s, domestic saving averaged over 30 percent of GDP in the NICs, financing most of the gross domestic investment. Some of these countries have emerged as capital surplus countries. The ASEAN-4 countries have also improved their savings and investment performance, though not as dramatically as the NICs.

Of the South Asian countries, only India increased its saving ratio to 20 percent by the 1980s. Other South Asian countries have not been able to overcome the vicious circle of poverty, low growth, and low savings, though Burma and Sri Lanka now save more than 10 percent of GNP.

Despite their remarkable domestic resource mobilization, investment continues to exceed saving in most cases. Korea, Indonesia, Malaysia, Thailand, and the Philippines have accumulated large foreign debts, though only the Philippines has had a debt-servicing crisis.

4. The NICs and ASEAN countries gave priority to economic growth over social welfare spending; active redistributive policies played a minor role except for policies to help the indigenous people who make up the majority in Indonesia and Malaysia. But the outward-looking policies encouraged the use of the abundant factor of production—labor. Therefore, the NICs in particular gave considerable resources to education primarily to promote future growth. The increased demand for labor and emphasis on human resource development helped to spread the benefits of growth widely. Such policies have helped the NICs to overcome the human resource constraint (see chapter 6).

As a result, the NICs are among the most egalitarian countries in the world, far more so than Latin American and South Asian countries that have stressed redistributive policies. Thailand, Indonesia, and Malaysia have also made great strides in reducing the incidence of poverty. These countries have made significant gains in health, life expectancy, literacy rates, and other social indicators (chapter 6). People in the ASEAN-4 countries, for example, could expect to live 10 years longer in 1985 than in 1970. The probability of infant survival doubled during the same period.

Asian countries demonstrate a high positive correlation between economic growth and social indicators.[22] Countries with the highest economic growth rates since 1960 have also had the greatest improvement in general living standards, poverty amelioration, and income distribution. In Korea and Taiwan the incomes of the poorest 40 percent grew as fast or faster than GNP in the 1960s and 1970s. Urban-rural income differences were reduced in both countries.

5. The combination of outward-looking, market-oriented policies and cautious macroeconomic management gave the Asian developing countries a great

deal of flexibility. Policymakers learn from past mistakes and are thus able to change inappropriate policies. Korea, for example, chose to concentrate on the development of heavy industries in the late 1970s, but recently slowed its movement in this direction. Singapore also reversed its high-wage policy that was meant to move its economy to higher skill and technology industries but only eroded its competitive position.

Summary: Comparative Development Performance

This chapter has emphasized the pursuit of appropriate domestic policy measures in order to relax the constraints on a country's development and thereby lead to better development performance, as measured by real economic growth and various social indicators.

Behind the statistics of differential development performance among the countries of East, Southeast, and South Asia lies the importance of appropriate policies. A given country's course of development appears not to have been limited by its "initial conditions," but to have been determined by the quality of its economic policies. The outward-looking strategy has had a pervasive influence on all policies. Monetary and fiscal policies have been affected; agricultural policies and the development of human resources have been influenced. And in less obvious but important ways, the policies have strengthened the organizational framework of the economy and have intensified learning rates, that is, the ability of individuals, households, and firms to respond to changes in markets, technology, and other conditions.

The following chapters reason that what matters the most are appropriate policies that stimulate trade, industrial growth, and employment (chapter 2), raise the savings rate and allocate funds to the most productive investments (chapter 3), maintain equilibrium in the balance of payments (chapter 4), provide incentives to accelerate agricultural development (chapter 5), and develop human resources (chapter 6). The final chapter brings together the key lessons of successful development strategies for Asian countries and looks to the future.

2 Industrialization and Trade Policies

Introduction

Raising the general standard of living is the goal of development, but countries diverge on the best methods of achieving this goal. Historically, the growth of the now developed nations was accompanied by a shift from agricultural into industrial activities. This process of structural change, as noted first by Kuznets and later by Chenery, has occurred without exception.[1] It is not surprising, therefore, that present-day LDCs consider industrialization as a key to higher levels of income and living standards.

In the 1950s and 1960s, many developing countries undertook policies to promote industrialization. The conventional wisdom at that time supported industrialization that initially aims at replacing imports of consumer goods in the domestic market.[2] It was felt that the special characteristics of developing countries (e.g., imperfections in the factor markets) and other dynamic factors (e.g., external economies resulting from learning by doing and economies of scale) mitigated the optimality of laissez faire and the doctrine of comparative advantage, thus warranting intervention. As a result, many developing countries adopted highly protective trade policies and built high tariff walls around their industrial sector. But in practice, import substitution strategies have conferred a short spurt of growth, after which most countries have not been able to continue rapid industrial growth.

Most of the Asian developing countries followed import substitution strategies, at least initially. The NICs, however, after the first stage of import substitution, shifted to a more export-oriented strategy in the 1960s, with spectacular results. They did not share the export pessimism expressed by many development economists in the 1950s and 1960s.[3] Because of the limited size of their domestic markets, the NICs quickly recognized that import substitution was a self-limiting process. Korea and Taiwan, like Japan in the 1950s, dramatically increased growth rates of GDP, industry, and exports after the strategy change. The NICs have become among the most trade-oriented countries in the world, their exports and imports comprising between nearly 40 and more than 100 percent of their GDPs (table 2.1).

Other Asian developing countries began to follow the lead of the NICs. The ASEAN-4 began to liberalize trade in the 1970s, while the South Asian countries shifted their policies in this direction even more recently. Growth of exports and output increased rapidly in the ASEAN-4 throughout the 1970s. Export-to-GDP ratios increased to more than 20 percent in Indonesia, the Philippines, and Thailand and 55 percent in Malaysia. Export-to-GDP ratios and growth rates of South Asian countries also increased in the 1980s over

Table 2.1. Export and Import Ratios (percentage of GDP at current prices)

	Exports			Imports		
	1970	1978	1985	1970	1978	1985
NICs						
Hong Kong	101.1	98.9	105.8	95.7	102.2	99.4
Korea	14.3	31.1	36.4	24.1	35.1	35.9
Singapore[a]	77.1	122.8	124.8[b]	122.7	154.9	147.2[b]
Taiwan	29.7	52.4	55.1	29.7	45.9	44.1
ASEAN-4						
Indonesia	12.8	21.9	22.7	15.8	20.8	21.0
Malaysia	40.5[c]	49.1	54.9	39.0[c]	43.5	49.8
Philippines	19.1	18.2	20.8	19.3	23.2	17.8
Thailand	16.7	21.5	26.3	21.5	25.5	27.5
South Asia						
Bangladesh	6.0[d]	5.5	6.5	5.0[d]	14.0	14.5
Burma	5.6	5.8	4.6	8.2	10.1	8.6
India	4.4	7.3	6.8[b]	4.5	7.6	8.5[b]
Nepal	4.9	10.6	11.0[b]	8.3	15.5	20.0[b]
Pakistan	14.9[d]	9.3	10.9	14.3[d]	18.3	21.1
Sri Lanka	17.0	33.3	26.0	19.2	37.9	38.8
Developed countries						
Japan	10.7	11.2	16.5	9.5	9.5	12.7
United States	5.7	8.3	7.0	5.5	9.7	10.1

Sources: ADB, *Key Indicators of Developing Member Countries of ADB*, April 1984, April 1985, and July 1986; Government of Hong Kong, Census and Statistics Department, *Monthly Digest of Statistics*, August 1986; IMF, *International Financial Statistics* 40, no. 5, May 1987; World Bank, *World Tables*, 3d ed., 1983; World Bank, *World Development Report*, 1986.

[a]Merchandise exports only.   [c]1971.
[b]1984.   [d]1973.

averages of the past two decades. These countries have shown that trade policies have a profound effect on industrialization and growth.

This chapter reviews trade and industrialization strategies pursued by the various countries, discusses changing economic conditions, and examines the options available for promoting export growth and further industrial and employment expansion. Within each group, industrial and trade performance is related to differences in the level of development, resource endowment, internal social and economic dynamics, and policies pursued. This chapter will focus on the effect of a country's industrial and trade strategies on the structure and growth of output, employment, and exports.

Conceptual Issues in Industrialization Strategies

For 30 years, developing countries have made explicit policies to promote industrialization. The experience of these 30 years has shown us that although the pace of industrialization depends in part on initial conditions—factor and resource endowment, size, location, and social mores—and on the international environment, policy is the main determinant of the rate of industrial growth and structural change.

The two major approaches to industrialization are frequently described as import substitution or export promotion.[4] By *import substitution* policies, we do not mean the natural process of import replacement that occurs as more financing, technical knowledge, and skilled labor are made available with economic development. Under this natural process, new industrial activities will tend to first supply domestic markets. Production for the domestic market was a major source of industrial expansion in all Asian countries including those, like Korea, that followed an export-led growth path.[5] Moreover, as other industries reach a more advanced stage of maturity, they begin to compete in international markets. Naturally occurring import substitution and export diversification take place simultaneously.

In this chapter, *import substitution* refers to deliberate policies by the home government aimed at increasing the share of domestic producers in the home market at a greater speed and to a higher level than would occur in the natural process of import replacement. Export promotion policies, on the other hand, refer to policies used to compensate export industries for the discrimination resulting from the preferential treatment granted to import substitutes. Because such policies do not usually entail net subsidies to exports, and are often implemented in conjunction with import subsitution policies, however, the term *export promotion* can be misleading.[6] Throughout this chapter, export-oriented policies shall refer to all policies that reverse the discrimination against exporters and allow for more balanced incentives rather than policies that grant exports higher net subsidies than are granted to production for domestic markets.

Import Substitution as an Industrialization Strategy

As was mentioned in the introduction to this chapter, import substitution strategies rest on the assumptions of external economies resulting from learning by doing, imperfect markets for information and for capital, and with some qualifications, the existence of factor market distortions (e.g., the prevailing wage is higher than the social opportunity cost of labor). Because of these conditions, it is argued that trade protection is necessary for infant industries until they can compete internationally. An import substitution strategy is often appealing to developing countries because it is believed that replacing previously imported goods with domestic production will ease the balance-of-payments situation and at the same time fulfill the countries' aspirations toward industrialization. Import substitution policies are often a manifestation of economic nationalism; establishing protected enterprises, often state owned, is seen as a means of developing indigenous productive facilities and entrepreneurs

In the first phase, import substitution usually covers nondurable consumer goods industries. After the initial filling of market demand for these goods, industrial growth inevitably slows down to the rate of expansion of domestic demand, unless the growth can be sustained by penetrating foreign markets. Most often, the import substitution process must be pushed into a second phase: domestic production of consumer durables and intermediate and capital goods. The second phase does not necessarily reflect a greater maturity of the economy or a changing factor endowment. It results from the necessity of opening up additional markets for industrial output, even while artificially high profits and production inefficiencies become embedded in the already established industries.

The strategy includes a wide variety of government interventions into product and factor markets which artificially raise output prices and factor demand in the industries promoted. It also allows a country to maintain a stronger domestic currency than would otherwise be the case. Import substitution policies discriminate against export-oriented industries and agricultural activities through higher factor costs (because of resource flows into protected industries), higher prices of other inputs, and less competitive prices for exports.[7]

The difficulties associated with these policies have become apparent in recent years. In practice, as protected infant industries grow, their unit costs fail to decline. Even if costs do decline, deliberate import substitution often leads to entrenching of business and labor groups more interested in retaining monopoly privileges than in raising productive efficiency. Moreover, import substitution policies may not even save foreign exchange because imports of machinery, other equipment, and intermediate goods must increase in the initial period.

One indicator of how the structure of protection affects the production pattern is the effective protection rate (EPR).[8] The EPR differs from the nominal protection rate (NPR): NPRs measure the difference between domestic and border prices of commodities brought about by protection, while EPRs measure the extent to which domestic value added exceeds international value added. Despite some criticism on both theoretical and empirical grounds, EPRs offer some insight into the effect of protection structures on resource allocation.[9] EPRs are important in evaluating incentives given by government policies because they tell us the extent of production subsidy being offered to each sector by the whole system of protection. As such, it is a useful measure of the degree of distortion brought about by various taxes and subsidies on tradables.

Import substitution strategies usually result in a wide variation in EPRs across industries. Tariffs on capital and intermediate goods tend to be lower than tariffs on final products, a difference frequently resulting in large positive subsidies on "final touch" production. Since exportables are usually not protected and inputs used in the production of exportables are often subject to duties (thus constituting a tax on exports), the EPR for exportables is often below average or even negative. The escalation of EPRs (rates increase with the degree of processing) common in most countries adopting inward-looking strategies indicates that protection schemes provide the least protection for capital goods and, in fact, subsidize the use of imported capital goods.

A number of policies associated with import substitution regimes artificially encourage the use of (scarce) physical capital relative to (abundant) semiskilled labor. Direct interventions by government in factor markets—minimum wage laws, interest rate controls, tariff concessions on imported capital inputs, and tax concessions on investment in capital equipment—have been commonly used. Tariff and nontariff barriers usually provide greater protection to industrial activities intensive in the use of skilled labor and capital equipment. Firms in all industries are often given incentives to choose techniques using less low-skilled or semiskilled labor than otherwise, and investment is distorted toward heavy capital outlays per employee and per unit of output.

The Role of Small- and Medium-Scale Enterprise

Import substitution policies favor the development of larger, well-established firms. Yet most industrial firms in developing countries are small in size. The numerical importance of small enterprises and their role in generating employment are recognized throughout Asia. The potential contributions to growth of small- and medium-scale firms have not been realized, particularly in countries following import substitution strategies.

The small-scale sector is frequently emphasized as a means of promoting industrial employment, because the production process in small-scale industries tends to be more labor intensive than those of larger firms.[10] Small- and medium-scale industrial firms (SMI) can also make substantial contributions toward capital formation, the development of entrepreneurs, and the generation of off-farm employment in rural areas. In developed and developing countries, a large proportion of the labor force in the manufacturing sector is employed in SMI. In Japan, for example, SMI are an essential part of the industrial structure; they provide parts to larger firms in a subcontracting system and in the mid-1950s exported more than 50 percent of their total output.[11] In Taiwan, SMI provide rural employment opportunities and have contributed to improvements in the distribution of income.[12] However, the development of healthy, economically viable small- and medium-scale enterprises has been hampered by policies favoring large-scale, capital-intensive enterprises in many developing countries.

One study of the ASEAN countries found that even at prevailing prices, uncorrected for possible distortions in favor of large-scale industry, SMI were more efficient than large-scale enterprises in about half of all industrial subsectors.[13] The fact that the smaller firms could compete effectively in nearly half of the industries indicates that they could contribute even more if distortions biasing competition for scarce factors in favor of large-scale firms were reduced.

But a caveat is in order here: an industrialization and employment strategy based predominantly on small-scale firms may encourage the establishment of many small inefficient firms using more capital per unit of output than do larger firms. Such policies may lead to an extremely dualistic industrial structure—many small, traditional firms and a few large firms with no middle-sized, modern firms. The general conclusion to be drawn here is that industrial activities should be evaluated in terms of their use of scarce and abundant factors before their potential contribution to economic development is judged.

Export-Oriented Industrialization Strategies

In general, export-oriented strategies tend to involve fewer and smaller departures from free trade and markets than do import substitution strategies. The superior performance of countries on an export-oriented growth path is caused by the more efficient allocation of resources brought about by these countries' participation in world trade. Traditional international trade theory explains this as being the result of specialization in accordance with comparative advantage. Optimal resource allocation (in static analysis) under competitive conditions is achieved when the marginal rate of transformation (MRT) for domestic production equals that for international production. When the domestic and international MRTs of x:y are equal, no additional national product can be had by shifting resources out of product x in order to produce more of y. Empirical evidence generally supports this notion and strongly links trade and efficiency as well as trade and growth.[14]

The dynamic benefits of export-oriented policies are crucial: exploitation of economies of scale in the wider export market, fuller utilization of capacities, exposure to more competition, better quality controls, and enlarged technological and social capabilities. Economies of scale from higher potential export volume encourage new industries to start up much earlier than they would if they were confined to the domestic market. Exports also enlarge technological capability by facilitating technical transfers and by stimulating technical effort.[15]

According to Allyn Young, the learning rate of an economy is highly dependent on people's aptitudes and attitudes, and their social institutions and political arrangements.[16] The country's "social capability" to incorporate change is enhanced greatly by participation in international exchange. As the success stories of Taiwan and Korea indicate, the most important induced effects of trade and foreign investment are likely to be in the acceleration of the economy's learning rate when the outward-looking policies are combined with reliance on the market system and selective government interventions.

Moreover, relaxation of the foreign exchange constraint through exports improved the creditworthiness of these countries. Export earnings facilitated the importation of capital and intermediate goods necessary to sustain the capacity for high growth. The expansion of exports even increased demand for intermediate inputs from other industries, and the rising incomes from exports increased consumer demand. Because exports tended to be labor intensive, they increased employment and the earnings of labor for the NICs.

Experiences of Asian Developing Countries

The rapid industrial growth of many of the Asian developing countries compared to the growth of other developing regions reflects the different types of policies they have adopted. During the 1970s, industrial sectors (manufacturing, mining, construction, and public utilities) made substantial contributions to economic development in Asian less developed nations by accelerating their total income growth, by expanding opportunities for productive and remunerative employment, and by easing balance-of-payments problems. The success of many Asian countries in promoting industrial expansion is shown in high average growth rates of industrial and manufacturing output during the 1970s. Manufacturing GDP, on average, grew more than four times as fast in the NICs and ASEAN-4 (more than 10 percent) as it did in Latin America and over three times as fast as it did in Africa between 1973 and 1984 (figure 2.1).

Because of the rapid growth, the shares of the industrial and manufacturing sectors in GDP have grown, while by contrast the share of agriculture in GDP

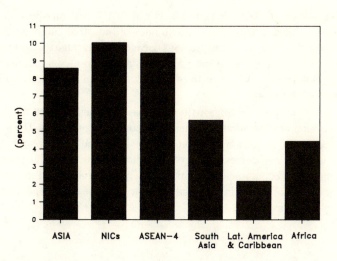

Figure 2.1. Average Annual Growth of Real Output in the Manufacturing Sectors of Developing Regions, 1973–84
Sources: World Bank, *World Development Report*, 1986; ADB, *Key Indicators of Developing Member Countries of ADB*, July 1986.
Note: Regional figures are simple averages of growth rates of the countries in each region. See table 2.A1 for a list of countries in each region.

has been continuously declining in nearly all Asian countries.[17] The progress made in shifting the labor force out of agriculture into industrial jobs varied widely among the regions, however. In the NICs, the high rates of industrial growth have led to rapid growth of employment. In the ASEAN-4 countries, the rate of growth of industrial employment barely exceeded that of the labor force as a whole, and the share of industrial employment remained low. Although the larger South Asian countries had a substantial industrial base by the 1970s, the performance of the industrial sector as a whole was below the average for the Asian region both in terms of output growth and employment generation.

Rapid Asian rates of manufacturing and industrial growth were achieved despite severe international disturbances in the 1970s. Before adjustment to the first oil price shock of 1973–74 had been completed in many oil-importing countries, however, oil prices surged further up in 1979–80. The second oil price increase plus prolonged recession in many of the Organization for Economic Cooperation and Development (OECD) countries had a more severe negative impact on Asian industrialization than the first oil shock-recession sequence. Table 2.2 shows that growth rates of industrial and manufacturing GDP fell in the 1980s from the previous decade-long average in all of the NICs and ASEAN–4 countries. In most South Asian countries, on the other hand, GDP growth rates and the growth of the industrial and manufacturing sectors improved in the 1980.

The next three subsections will review the policies adopted by the three groups of countries to adjust for changing economic conditions. The ability of Asian countries to sustain or improve their industrial performance depends mainly on their own domestic efforts and policies. Structural adjustment to the changing world economic environment may require substantial investment to open new lines of industrial production and to increase the competitiveness of existing industries.

Table 2.2. Growth of Industrial and Manufacturing Real Output (compound annual rates in percentages)

	Industry			Manufacturing		
	1960–70	1970–80	1980–85	1960–70	1970–80	1980–85
NICs						
Hong Kong	NA	10.3	NA	NA	10.4	NA
Korea	16.5	14.0	8.8	16.8	15.4	8.4
Singapore	14.3	9.9	4.7	14.5	10.9	1.3
Taiwan	13.2	12.5	5.9	14.7	12.7	6.5
ASEAN-4						
Indonesia	6.5	11.3	4.6[a]	4.6	13.6	6.5[a]
Malaysia	NA	9.6	7.2	NA	11.4	6.2
Philippines	5.9	8.3	−2.9	6.5	7.0	−1.4
Thailand	11.5	9.2	4.9	11.6	10.0	5.4
South Asia						
Bangladesh	7.9	4.4	4.8	6.5[b]	6.3[b]	2.5[b]
Burma	3.4	5.1	7.3	4.1	4.0	6.4
India	5.5	3.8	5.2[a]	5.2	4.3	5.5[a]
Pakistan	10.8	5.2	8.8	9.9	4.3	10.1
Sri Lanka	6.6	4.0	4.0	6.2	2.0	4.2

Sources: World Bank, *World Tables*, 3d ed., 1983; ADB, *Key Indicators of Developing Member Countries of ADB*, July 1986.
Note: NA = Not available.
[a]1980–84.   [b]Including mining.

The Newly Industrializing Countries[18]

Nowhere in the world has the growth of trade and the industrial sector played as critical a role as it has in the NICs of Asia. The economies of Taiwan and Korea, in particular, underwent fundamental structural changes in a remarkably short time. These countries are now so thoroughly identified as exporters of manufactured goods that it is hard to remember that only a couple of decades ago they were predominantly agricultural. In 1960, primary goods, mainly agricultural, accounted for 86 percent of Korea's exports and 73 percent of Taiwan's. At that time, exports were less than 10 percent of the GNP in Taiwan and 5 percent in Korea. But industrial sector growth in the NICs was generally in excess of 10 percent per year (table 2.2) and accounted for more than 40 percent of the total growth of GNP in the 1960s and 1970s, and by 1970, manufactures accounted for over 70 percent of total exports. Manufactured exports led the high growth of the industrial sector in the NICs (table 2.3).

The NICs' success is of course due to many factors,[19] but there is no doubt that the outward-looking industrialization strategy applied in these countries is an essential component. Hong Kong was from the outset virtually a free trade economy and experienced exceptionally high export growth in the 1950s. Singapore, after it was forced out of the Federated States of Malaysia in 1965, had a brief import substitution phase, but shifted to export orientation in 1967. In the 1950s, Korea and Taiwan entered the first phase of import substitution. However, a major policy change in the late 1950s and early 1960s reduced tariffs substantially and provided more equal incentives for the expansion of all economic activities. The biases against exports resulting from import barriers were offset by subsidy schemes (mainly tax and credit preferences), and export preferences compensated for a slight overvaluation of home country currencies, so that exporting remained as profitable as domestic sales. Exporters were not handicapped vis-à-vis foreign competitors. This "balanced" incentive system facilitated the shift from production for domestic markets to production for export, and encouraged the use of semiskilled and unskilled labor in light consumer goods manufactures and other labor-intensive industries. With the lifting or reducing of tariffs and other trade restrictions, profit rates in export-oriented, labor-intensive manufacturing rose sharply.[20]

Korea and Taiwan continued to provide protection for selected industries even as they moved toward an export-oriented growth path. They appear to have followed Japan's pattern of export-oriented industrialization. Japan in the 1950s shielded several of its infant industries from foreign competition; some of these industries have grown to become the most efficient producers of various manufactures in the world.[21] It appears that the degree and duration of protection afforded to an industry is a significant factor in its subsequent development. High rates of protection for prolonged periods usually result in in-

Table 2.3. Growth of Manufactured Exports

	Value (US $ millions)		Compounded Growth Rate (percentage)
	1970	1985	
NICs			
Hong Kong	1,940	15,773	15.0
Korea	621	25,825	28.2
Singapore	415	11,474	24.8
Taiwan[a]	1,037	21,902	26.4
ASEAN-4			
Indonesia[b]	12	2,191	44.9
Malaysia[c]	121	3,471	32.3
Philippines[a]	68	1,205	24.8
Thailand[b]	30	2,386	36.6
South Asia			
Bangladesh[d]	216	641	10.4
Burma[e]	2	6	22.8
India[f]	908	4,609	15.9
Nepal[d]	7	76	25.0
Pakistan	398	1,657	10.0
Sri Lanka[b]	5	382	36.9
Total LDCs[b]	8,929	139,740	21.7
World[b]	172,868	1,067,938	13.9

Sources: United Nations Conference on Trade and Development, *Handbook on International Trade and Development Statistics*, supplement 1986 (1987); Republic of China, Department of Statistics, Ministry of Finance, *Monthly Statistics of Exports and Imports*, December 1986.
[a]1970 and 1983.   [c]1971 and 1983.   [e]1970 and 1976.
[b]1970 and 1984.   [d]1974 and 1985.   [f]1970 and 1981.

efficient, monopolistic industry. Moderate protection for infant industries was coupled with export incentives to encourage them to become competitive in Japan, Korea, and Taiwan. The overall structure of protection in the NICs and Japan was relatively neutral.

Average nominal and effective tariff rates were lower, and nontariff barriers and quantitative restrictions were used less widely, in the NICs than they were in most other developing countries (table 2.4). The effective rate of protection for all manufacturing averaged 13 percent for Korea (1968), 4 percent for Singapore (1967), and 14 percent for Taiwan (1969).[22] The protection structure left little room for excess profits or inefficiencies in Hong Kong, Singapore, and Taiwan. In Korea, high profits were generally reinvested by Korean entre-

Table 2.4. Average Tariff Rate

	Simple Average Tariff Rate (percentage)
NICs	
Korea	23.5
Singapore	6.4
ASEAN-4	
Indonesia	32.6
Malaysia	25.0
Philippines	29.2
Thailand	30.7
South Asia	
Bangladesh	74.7
India	65.7
Pakistan	71.0
Sri Lanka	44.2

Sources: Data were computed by the Philippine Tariff Commission from the following sources: *Korea Douanes*, 1982–83; *Singapore Trade Classification and Customs Duties*, 1983; *Indonesia's Customs Tariff*, 1980; *Malaysian Practical Guide to Customs Duties Order*, 1982; *Philippine Tariff and Customs Code*, 1982; *Customs Tariff of Thailand*, 1983; *India Douanes*, 1979–80; *Pakistan Douanes*, 1979–80; *Sri Lanka Douanes*, 1983–84. For Bangladesh, United Nations Conference on Trade and Development, *Trade Information System*, computer tape, 1984, was used.

preneurs.[23] The Korean government encouraged investment, particularly in export and import substitution industries, through credit and tax incentives, control of foreign exchange, and informal pressure. Taxation on undistributed profits invested in new technology was kept low.[24]

An important feature of protection in the NICs was that for the most part, international competitiveness was emphasized. This meant that domestic prices were not allowed to exceed international prices for prolonged periods. In fact, industries receiving protection were pushed to rapidly become internationally competitive in the NICs. Firms were expected to produce goods comparable to imports in quality and price and to begin exporting within a few years. The requirement to produce at world market prices prevented the proliferation of excessively capital-intensive activities.

The overall industrialization strategy supported an output mix that conformed to domestic factor endowments. The resources available had a strong influence on the pattern of industrial development. Because of Singapore's proximity to the ASEAN-4, petroleum refining and other resource-processing industries along with labor-intensive manufactures contributed to industrial growth. Its geographical position in Southeast Asia enabled Singapore to use its considerable marketing talents and advanced service sector to trade intensively with its ASEAN partners. The large percentage share of primary commodity exports reflects Singapore's role as an entrepôt.

For the other NICs, their comparative advantage lay in their abundant and well-educated labor force. Traditional labor-intensive products (clothing, textiles, resource-based manufactures, and miscellaneous manufactures) comprised more than 50 percent of total exports in 1970 (table 2.5). Policies were used to enhance this advantage. Into the 1970s, government intervention in labor markets remained moderate. It took the form of wage ceilings rather than minimum wages in excess of equilibrium wage rates. Average wage rates for unskilled labor were low and stable during the 1960s and began to rise when surplus labor was largely absorbed and labor productivity increased in the late 1960s and early 1970s.[25]

Because of their emphasis on labor-intensive manufactures and their highly elastic supply of low-cost semiskilled labor, two-thirds of the NICs' industrial expansion was generated through added industrial employment. In Korea and Taiwan, the industrial sector absorbed all the annual rise in the labor force, and also drew labor from other sectors. From the 1970s, there was no longer a labor surplus. The increase in industrial employment has allowed workers to share the benefits of rapid economic growth, especially in Taiwan.

The increase in overall industrial employment corresponded with the decrease in employment shares of small- and medium-scale industrial firms from about 50 percent in Taiwan and Korea in the 1960s to 37 percent and 26 percent, respectively, in the 1970s.[26] The large employment share of SMI in Taiwan is due in part to the fact that unlike the Korean government, Taiwan did not actively pursue policies aimed at deliberately encouraging large enterprises.[27] The SMI in Taiwan contributed to a more even income distribution and a wider regional distribution of manufacturing activities (see chapter 6).

SMI (establishments with 5–99 employees) play a significant role in the NICs' manufacturing sectors. Excluding cottage industry (firms with 4 or fewer employees), SMI accounted for over 90 percent of the total number of manufacturing firms and produced between 17 and 23 percent of manufacturing value added in Korea, Singapore, and Taiwan in the 1970s.[28] In Singapore and Taiwan, where price distortions are minimal, SMI are highly efficient, contribute strongly to exports, and serve as subcontractors for large firms.[29] In Korea, however, subcontracting and exporting are not prevalent among small-scale firms. A survey in 1975 found that less than 20 percent of the sales of

Table 2.5. Exports of NICs by Principal Commodity Groups (percentage of total exports)

	Hong Kong		Korea		Singapore[a]		Taiwan	
	1970	1983	1970	1984	1970	1984	1970	1983
Primary commodities	7.5	8.3	24.9	15.8	70.3	45.5	29.9	12.8
Raw materials	3.7	4.4	15.3	11.4	53.9	36.9	9.6	6.5
Agricultural and food products	3.7	3.9	9.6	4.4	16.4	8.6	20.3	6.3
Manufactured goods[b]	92.2	90.9	75.1	84.1	26.7	47.7	70.0	87.2
Chemicals	4.0	3.7	1.4	2.9	2.7	5.0	2.3	2.5
Resource-based manufactures	5.8	3.5	12.5	4.0	3.0	2.2	9.2	7.1
Textiles	10.9	9.3	10.2	8.9	3.5	1.4	13.3	7.3
Metal manufactures	2.4	2.4	1.5	4.8	1.3	1.0	1.9	4.8
Electrical machinery	9.2	14.8	5.3	13.8	4.0	16.9	11.9	16.1
Non-electrical machinery	1.5	6.4	1.0	3.1	4.0	10.5	3.3	6.3
Transport equipment	0.7	1.6	1.1	18.9	3.0	3.4	0.8	3.8
Precision instruments	0.0	8.9	0.0	1.4	0.0	1.5	0.4	2.1
Clothing	27.8	24.2	25.6	15.4	2.0	2.2	14.3	11.9
Furniture	0.6	0.5	0.0	0.2	0.0	0.3	0.2	2.3
Footwear	2.0	0.9	2.1	4.6	0.3	0.1	1.9	7.2
Miscellaneous manufactures	27.2	14.6	14.6	6.0	2.9	2.3	10.4	15.8
Total exports[c] (US$ billions)	2.5	22.0	0.8	29.3	1.6	25.7	1.5	25.1

Sources: United Nations, Commodity Trade Statistics, various years; United Nations, 1983 Yearbook of International Trade Statistics, 1985; Republic of China, Department of Statistics, Ministry of Finance, Monthly Statistics of Exports and Imports, February 20, 1986.
[a]Singapore records no values for trade with Indonesia. Singapore exports to Indonesia are derived from Indonesian imports from Singapore using Singapore conversion factor CIF/FOB for the respective year. (The CIF/FOB conversion factor takes into account the costs of insurance and freight [CIF] that are included in Indonesian import values in order to derive Singapore's exports to Indonesia on a free-on-board [FOB] basis.) Total exports are adjusted to include exports of Singapore to Indonesia that are not reflected in the original source.
[b]The categories of manufactured exports do not necessarily add up to the total of manufactured exports since not all categories are listed. Manufactured plus primary commodities may not add up to 100 because SITC 9 (commodities and transactions not classified elsewhere) is excluded.
[c]Total includes re-exports.

35

SMI were contract sales to other firms in Korea. Like exports, the percentage of sales to other firms increased with size.[30]

The incentive systems applied in the NICs, however, were not entirely free of bias. Intermediate and engineering goods industries enjoyed heavily protected domestic markets. Traditional consumer goods industries suffered: they had to pay higher prices for protected inputs. Yet, such biases were not strong enough to affect either the profitability or the international competitiveness of labor-intensive manufactures.

Beginning with the mid-1970s, the prospects for future industrial development in the NICs became less favorable. At the same time that higher labor costs tended to reduce the international competitiveness of some traditional exports (even though productivity gains acted to offset this), rising balance-of-payments deficits, inflation, and unemployment led Europe and the United States to impose additional (mostly nontariff) trade barriers, discriminating against the exports of newly industrializing countries. Before the NICs were significantly affected by these changes, the governments started new policies aimed at diversifying industrial exports.

These policies were based on the judgment that the effects of the new protectionism in more developed countries and the loss of competitiveness because of rising domestic wages could best be countered by shifting industrial production toward technology-intensive and heavy industrial activities. The NICs were also concerned about their own balance-of-payments positions. If some imported raw materials and machinery could be produced domestically, foreign exchange would be saved. The strategy is clearly shown in the changing composition of industrial output and exports in these countries. Capital- and technology-intensive goods increased, while light manufactures decreased.[31] In Korea and Taiwan, incremental output shifted to machinery, basic metal industries, and chemicals, though light consumer goods maintained an important share.

In the NICs, the share of traditional labor-intensive manufactured exports in total exports declined, although it remained large enough to keep these products among the top individual export items. During the 1970s, the factor content of NIC exports increasingly shifted into human and physical capital-intensive products and services. In Taiwan and Hong Kong, by the 1980s, the shares of electrical machinery in total merchandise exports were larger than those of primary products. Similarly, the shares of nonelectrical machinery, precision instruments, and transportation equipment showed significant gains. These changes indicate the enhanced competitiveness of the Asian NICs in sophisticated manufacturing industries.

The industrial policies aimed at shifting the output mix toward more skill- and capital-intensive manufactures had varying degrees of success. Korea embarked on an industrialization policy emphasizing heavy industry by providing credit for selected industries at artifically low interest rates, and introducing import controls plus selective tariff protection.[32] Korean exports of iron and steel increased from less than 2 percent of the total exports to almost 10 percent in the 1970s. But Korea had only mixed success in its promotion of heavy industrial exports. This strategy encouraged private investment to reach an unprecedented level in 1979. However, a downturn occurred in 1980, when there was social and political unrest, a poor harvest, and rising prices of food, oil, and other necessities. Domestic inflation accelerated during a time when output growth slowed down and even turned negative. The crisis led the Korean government to review critically the heavy-industry strategy. Subsequent policy changes have de-emphasized heavy industries and moved to develop exports that are smaller in scale, are less import intensive, and encourage the development of technology.

Taiwan and Singapore chose a different adjustment path, aimed at export-led growth with standardized product cycle goods (e.g., radios, color televisions) and selected heavy engineering goods. Taiwan did not directly intervene in capital markets and foreign trade to promote high-technology sectors. Instead, it established a science-based industrial park to facilitate the inflow of advanced technology. The Singapore government chose to intervene in the labor market. Legal wages were raised in several successive increments by a total of about 80 percent in 1979–81. At the same time, measures were taken to upgrade the skills of the labor force. The wage increases were meant to induce a shift from unskilled to skilled labor-intensive activities, in which higher labor productivity would permit higher wages without conferring any advantage to capital-intensive industries. Many workers have little education; therefore, making such a transition is very difficult in a short period of time.

The government of Singapore continued to pursue a high-wages policy into the mid-1980s. Between 1981 and 1984, hourly wages of production workers were raised by 61 percent. This increase made wages in Singapore in 1984 almost 70 percent higher than those in Hong Kong and Korea and 25 percent higher than those in Taiwan. In 1981, Singapore wage rates were about the same as those in Hong Kong, and a third higher than those in Korea.[33] The higher wages led to the contraction of traditional labor-intensive export manufacturing in Singapore, a change causing resources to shift to capital-intensive industries—shipbuilding, machinery, petroleum refining, chemicals, and the like. Singapore's industrial export base narrowed; its share of traditional manufactured exports in total manufactured exports fell below the shares of the other NICs. The mistaken wage policies contributed to the drop in economic growth rates in the mid-1980s. Negative growth occurred for the first time in over two decades. Singapore's mid-1980s economic crisis forced the government to revise its strategy. New policies aimed at reducing labor costs and other costs of production were quickly adopted.

Hong Kong was hit hard by the prolonged world recession that sent exports and growth plummeting in 1982, and also by a crisis of confidence over the territory's future. The September 1984 Sino-British agreement calmed the nerves of the business community, but it failed to rekindle investment to expand manufacturing capacity. A sharp drop in exports to the United States and the continued slow growth of domestic demand and construction contributed to a less than 1 percent real growth rate in 1985. Unlike other NICs, however, Hong Kong has not dramatically changed the composition of its manufactured exports. Instead it has developed a highly competitive services sector that contributes to foreign exchange earnings. Increasing protectionism in more developed countries (MDCs), and uncertainties over the intentions of the government of China over the long run, could reduce growth prospects in Hong Kong. On the other hand, China's modernization opens up vast new opportunities for Hong Kong. This has already resulted in a tenfold increase in Hong Kong's exports to China in 1980–85.[34] Investment by Hong Kong residents in China's special economic zones (SEZs) has also grown dramatically.

Slower real economic growth has accompanied the new industrial strategy of the NICs. Some of the policy changes had the effect of reducing economic efficiency even as the external economic environment became more hostile. The NICs' industrial development will continue to be export oriented because of the limited size of their domestic markets and their poor natural resource endowments, which cause a high dependency on imported raw materials and energy. Whether the NICs can sustain high rates of export growth in the face of growing protectionism (particularly in Europe, Japan, and the United States) and slower real growth of world trade depends on other possible changes. Long-run industrialization in the NICs depends on the future expansion of world and regional markets, and on the products for which the NICs can gain a comparative advantage. Protectionism against their traditional labor-intensive and semiskilled products, increasing wage rates as a result of full employment of the labor force, and emerging competition from more labor-abundant countries will probably check further export growth in products such as textiles and clothing.

Structural shifts in MDCs can open up new, less protected markets for more sophisticated exports from the NICs. But such opportunities will be limited if economic recession and rising unemployment continue to slow down adjustment processes in MDCs. There appears to be little reason for optimism that rapidly growing, open world trade will revive in the late 1980s. Nonetheless, the Asian NICs may to some degree be able to circumvent barriers to their exports by export diversification toward more skill-intensive products as they have done in the past. The markets for these products are less distorted by trade barriers, and retaliatory measures are less likely than they are in traditional labor-intensive sectors.

Another option, however, may lie in trade between the NICs and other LDCs. In the 1970s, trade channels were established successfully between NICs and Middle Eastern oil exporters, while trade with other less developed countries inside and outside the region grew fast enough to maintain average shares of about 20 percent and 12 percent since 1970. Declining oil revenues are likely to slow export growth to the Middle East, however. Moreover, trade with other LDCs is hampered by protection. Progress depends on the willingness of LDCs to cooperate with one another through mutual access to each other's markets.

Development of the NICs' domestic markets for consumer durables, housing, and discretionary spending could increase demand for many new products and services. Such expansion seems to be inevitable in the 1980s because incomes and consumer spending power have risen substantially, while the quality of housing and ownership of durables such as automobiles, color televisions, video cassette recorders, and refrigerators have lagged. For example, Koreans owned fewer than 14 automobiles per 1000 persons in 1980, even though per capita income was close to that of Japan in 1968, when automobile ownership there was 170 per 1000 persons.[35]

Domestic market development need not imply more protection for domestic producers. In fact, high tariff and nontariff protection has slowed growth in consumer durables buying in Taiwan and Korea. Reducing high rates of protection in the auto, housing, and durables sectors can spur greater domestic efficiency and boost consumer demand without threatening the overall viability of domestic industries.

As income continues to grow in the larger NICs, domestic industrial growth in sophisticated sectors, e.g., microcomputers, electrical appliances, and home furnishings, can expand and strengthen overall industrial growth. Hong Kong and Singapore cannot rely much on domestic market expansion because of their small size. But both may continue to boost their industrial sectors by capturing a share of the expanding China market.

ASEAN-4

Industrial expansion was also a major source of growth for the ASEAN-4 countries in the 1960s and 1970s (table 2.2).[36] But exports of primary products continue to account for the greater share of the total exports of the ASEAN-4. In 1970 the share of primary commodities in total exports exceeded 90 percent; it declined sharply to average less than 80 percent in the early 1980s (table 2.6). The reliance on primary exports is highest in Indonesia

Table 2.6. Exports of ASEAN-4 by Principal Commodity Groups (percentage of total exports)

	Indonesia		Malaysia		Philippines		Thailand	
	1970	1984	1970	1984	1970	1983	1970	1984
Primary commodities	98.6	89.2	90.9	73.5	93.5	49.9	89.5	65.7
Raw materials	79.0	82.0	77.4	54.2	49.5	19.5	39.0	15.0
Agricultural and food products	19.6	7.3	13.5	19.2	44.0	30.5	50.5	50.7
Manufactured goods[a]	1.1	10.0	8.2	26.4	6.3	24.1	5.2	32.9
Chemicals	0.5	2.4	1.1	1.1	0.5	1.7	0.4	1.0
Resource-based manufactures	0.2	3.9	2.9	1.9	4.5	3.9	2.1	6.1
Textiles	0.0	0.9	0.4	1.0	0.5	0.9	1.2	5.4
Metal manufactures	0.0	0.0	0.3	0.3	0.0	0.2	0.2	0.6
Electrical machinery	0.0	0.6	0.4	15.7	0.0	4.3	0.0	5.6
Nonelectrical machinery	0.3	0.4	0.9	1.6	0.0	0.3	0.0	1.4
Transport equipment	0.0	0.0	0.8	1.5	0.0	0.5	0.0	0.3
Precision instruments	0.0	0.0	0.0	0.0	0.0	0.3	0.0	0.6
Clothing	0.0	1.4	0.5	1.8	0.0	6.4	0.1	7.4
Furniture	0.0	0.0	0.0	0.1	0.0	1.7	0.0	0.6
Footwear	0.0	0.0	0.2	0.1	0.0	1.1	0.0	1.1
Miscellaneous manufactures	0.0	0.3	0.6	1.2	0.8	2.8	0.5	2.7
Total exports[b] (US$ billions)	1.1	21.9	1.8	16.5	1.1	5.0	0.7	7.4

Sources: United Nations, *1983 Yearbook of International Trade Statistics*, 1985; United Nations Conference on Trade and Development, computer tapes, 1983, 1984.

[a]The categories of manufactured exports do not necessarily add up to the total of manufactured exports since not all categories are listed. Manufactured plus primary commodities may not add up to 100 because SITC 9 (commodities and transactions not classified elsewhere) is excluded.

[b]Total includes re-exports.

(89 percent) and Malaysia (74 percent); but was still substantial in Thailand (66 percent) and the Philippines (50 percent).

The large share of primary exports reflects the comparative advantage of these countries and differentiates them from the NICs. The presence of natural resource wealth in the ASEAN-4 countries, however, is a mixed blessing. Although it has contributed substantially to the foreign exchange earnings of the ASEAN-4, resource wealth often results in rent-seeking behavior as various interest groups try to capture a share of the wealth that natural resource development promises. Moreover, resource development often requires large amounts of capital and requires skills that are in short supply—such projects create little employment. Logging and other extractive industries may produce environmental problems and diseconomies to traditional agriculture. In addition, as was discussed in chapter 1, the appreciation of the effective exchange rate often brought about by natural resource wealth may deter exports from manufacturing and agriculture as well. Finally, the ability to generate exports from natural resources reduces the drive of policymakers and the business community to develop labor-intensive manufactured exports.

The policy package used to accelerate industrial growth in the ASEAN-4 was selective protection of domestic producers against foreign competition by raising domestic output prices above world market prices. To achieve this, tariffs were frequently used along with import quotas and surcharges. Because protection was typically introduced on an ad hoc basis and the protective structure was frequently changed, however, it is difficult to assess its impact. Nevertheless, a cascading structure of protection was created: typically the highest levels of protection were granted to finished goods, the lowest to raw materials and primary products.[37] This has led to the wide dispersion of EPRs across individual industries as well as between manufacturing and agricultural subsectors. Effective protection of capital-intensive, import-competing industries producing final consumer goods tended to be high, while EPRs for exportables were often negative. Sectors with a comparative advantage often faced heavy discrimination, and some sectors producing a negative domestic value added were strongly promoted.

Although the experience of the ASEAN-4 with import substitution policies had many commonalities, the degree of government intervention varied. Indonesia, the largest ASEAN country in population and land area, has had the most inward-looking policy. Indonesia has a history of widespread government intervention, ownership, and regulation. Though the present government has partially dismantled the import licensing and exchange controls of the Sukarno regime's "guided economy," it still makes much use of nontariff trade barriers and price controls. Even without considering nontariff barriers, estimates of nominal and effective protection rates for consumer goods manufacturing industries in the 1970s were generally higher for Indonesia than they were for any other ASEAN nation. One study of Indonesia's trade policies found negative EPRs for over one-third of the sectors that export, but for only one-eighth of the sectors that import.[38] The simple average of nominal tariffs, 1978 data, was lower than it was in the Philippines (table 2.7), but the 1980 data show Indonesia with a somewhat higher average tariff level than the other ASEAN-4 countries.

In contrast, Malaysia has had few nontariff trade restrictions. The overall simple average tariff rate is quite low, though there is a wide dispersion of individual tariffs. EPRs for manufactured goods are also low. One explanation of the limited protection is that it was generally believed that Chinese-run businesses would be major beneficiaries of protection.[39] A motive for state involvement in the industrialization process for Malaysia (and also for Indonesia) was the desire to promote indigenous businesses vis-à-vis Chinese-run firms. Malaysia has included indigenous ownership and employment requirements as part of its overall economic plan since the late 1960s. Malaysia has among the largest public enterprise share in industry and manufacturing in ASEAN. The Philippines and Thailand are intermediate cases—though in the 1970s Thailand's tariffs were significantly lower than those of the Philippines (table 2.7). Both countries resorted extensively to nontariff barriers, with fairly high nominal tariff rates for manufactures. EPRs are also high, particularly in capital-intensive, import-competing industries.

Import substitution policies led to an initial period of rapid growth followed by a slowdown as the domestic market became saturated. Typical industrial enterprises overbuilt in the optimism engendered by initial rapid import substitution growth eventually operated far below capacity. Rescue through expansion into export was not possible, since protection tolerated inefficient production and low quality by international standards.

The movement into the next stages of import substitution in the early 1970s became the main source of the continued industrial growth experienced by Indonesia, Thailand, and Malaysia. In the Philippines, however, industrial expansion was stifled by the exhaustion of some of the markets for consumer durables and capital goods and by the increasing scarcity of investible funds. The inability of firms to import needed intermediate goods and equipment contributed to negative growth rates as industry operated far below capacity. The exhaustion of the domestic market revealed a second effect of continued high import protection: the more inward-looking industrialization is, the greater is the need for imported capital and technology.

The increased import dependence accompanying import substitution industrialization caused severe balance-of-payments problems for the oil importers during the 1970s. Until then, their rich natural resource endowments allowed

Table 2.7. Comparison of Simple Averages of Tariff Rates in ASEAN (percentages)

SITC Code	Product Group	Indonesia		Malaysia		Philippines		Singapore		Thailand		ASEAN	
		1978	1980	1978	1982	1978	1982	1978	1983	1978	1983	1978	1983[a]
0	Food and live animals	42.9	47.9	10.7	13.7	67.2	40.6	1.3	0.6	42.6	50.6	33.0	30.7
1	Beverages and tobacco	46.0	61.9	346.8	1361.6	82.5	55.2	458.2	593.2	62.4	52.6	199.2	424.9
2	Crude materials, inedible	14.2	14.5	2.8	4.0	27.4	21.6	0.0	0.1	18.4	16.7	12.6	11.4
3	Mineral fuels	15.2	8.5	7.1	4.9	14.9	17.0	9.0	0.8	14.2	15.5	12.1	9.4
4	Animal and vegetable oils and fats	30.0	28.8	0.3	1.0	43.9	28.1	0.0	0.0	24.7	23.6	19.8	15.5
5	Chemicals	26.8	10.6	19.2	8.1	41.1	18.0	37.2	1.5	28.1	20.7	30.5	11.8
6	Manufactured goods	37.9	42.2	14.9	16.7	52.0	33.2	0.4	0.1	32.0	32.4	27.4	24.9
7	Machinery and transportation equipment	18.0	20.0	10.7	10.2	23.0	21.9	1.4	0.5	18.0	24.0	14.2	15.3
8	Miscellaneous manufactured goods	49.9	49.8	19.0	12.5	68.9	35.0	3.4	0.8	37.8	39.9	35.8	27.6
9	Miscellaneous	21.7	28.5	7.7	7.2	62.5	36.7	0.0	0.0	20.8	22.1	22.5	18.9
	Overall	33.0	32.6	15.3	25.0	44.2	29.2	5.6	6.4	29.4	30.7	25.5	24.8

Sources: Philippine Tariff Commission, *Tariff Profiles in ASEAN: An Update*, 1985; Philippine Tariff Commission, *Tariff Profiles in ASEAN*, 1979.
[a] ASEAN 1983 data reflect average tariff rates of member ASEAN countries in the years noted.

them to keep trade deficits within reasonable limits through agricultural and raw materials export earnings that financed the imports of capital and technology necessary for continued import substitution industrialization. Since the ability and willingness of outside lenders to finance ever-increasing balance-of-payments deficits are constrained by their estimates of debt-servicing capacity, governments in the Philippines and Thailand tended to control foreign exchange and ration imports. Such measures had a destabilizing effect on the investment climate in general, and especially on industries depending on imported inputs. As government administrative decisions are increasingly relied upon, the energies of the business community are spent lobbying for special privileges rather than for production and innovation. The Philippine experience has provided repeated examples of both of these effects.

Strong incentives were given in all Southeast Asian countries favoring the use of physical capital. The most frequently used and most powerful means was government intervention in capital markets, to artificially lower the user cost of capital below equilibrium, often even to negative real rates of interest.[40] In addition, fixed capital investment was promoted by preferential credits, tax holidays, special depreciation allowances, and tariff exemptions for capital goods not available domestically. These preferences were 15–45 percent of total capital costs in the Philippines, and exceeded by a considerable margin the mostly indirect subsidies granted to the employment of labor (like the deductibility of training expenses).[41] The prevailing incentive structure thus promoted the expansion of physical-capital-intensive industrial activities and the introduction of labor-saving technologies. The effect was reinforced by the underpricing of public utilities and energy inputs—all too often overlooked when we evaluate incentive structures. Capital-intensive production processes use large amounts of oil, coal, electricity, and water; hence price controls on these products subsidize these processes and discriminate further against labor use.

Labor market policies artifically increased wage and nonwage labor costs, favoring the employed, and discriminating against the underemployed or unemployed by reducing employment growth. Minimum wage and other social policies raising wage costs above the shadow wage rate place at a disadvantage firms that primarily employ unskilled labor and scarcely use (subsidized) capital.[42] Moreover, in times of inflation, governments often respond to growing social tension caused by the erosion of real wages by increasing the nominal minimum wage in excess of productivity increases. For example, between 1973 and 1975, the government granted four consecutive minimum wage hikes in Thailand, and these resulted in a more than 100 percent rise in the minimum wage rate.[43] Such drastic changes in the price of labor—and uncertainty with respect to future erratic wage policy decisions on the part of the government—

discourage the employment of labor in all enterprises and give an artificial advantage to capital-using technologies and products.[44]

Unlike the NICs, therefore, about two-thirds of industrial output growth in the ASEAN-4 countries came from higher output per worker and only one-third from more employment in the 1970s. Employment in manufacturing grew at less than 5 percent annually in the 1970s except for Malaysia. The increments to employment were not sufficient in most countries to ease the burden of either rural or urban surplus labor.

The emphasis on capital-intensive, large-scale industries has also negatively affected the development of small-scale enterprises in Indonesia, the Philippines, and Thailand, despite policies in all of these countries promoting small-scale industry. The development of modern, middle-sized firms that serve as subcontractors or exporters has been retarded by policies (e.g., preferential credit schemes, import licensing, and tariff exemptions) favoring established large-scale firms. Many of the unemployed resorted to activities in the informal sector; cottage industries (establishments with fewer than 5 employees) accounted for more than 75 percent of the total number of establishments in these countries.[45] But profits were concentrated in large-scale privileged firms that had higher shares of value added than they had of employment. As a result, income distribution worsened, particularly in Indonesia, where almost 80 percent of the manufacturing labor force remains in cottage industries.[46] In Malaysia, in contrast, SMI comprise a smaller proportion of the total number of enterprises and a higher proportion of value added, a reflection of the relative efficiency of SMI in Malaysia. SMI seem a more effective means in Malaysia than establishment of large-scale public enterprises.

The above overview of industrialization strategies in Southeast Asia explains major forces shaping the pattern of industrial development up to the mid-1970s. When domestic forces still provided room for expansion, industrial output grew at respectable rates (as it did in Indonesia, Thailand, and Malaysia), but output growth slackened when these markets were exhausted, and lack of competition, and discrimination against exports, prevented a spillover into export markets (as it did in the Philippines).

In the second half of the 1970s, in an effort to adjust to the increases in the oil import bill, the governments of the oil-importing countries (Philippines and Thailand) tried to increase manufactured exports. Export controls were relaxed, and export taxes abolished or reduced. Governments granted duty-free importation allowances for necessary inputs to exporters, introduced special rebates on income and turnover taxes, and opened new (mostly short-term) export credit facilities. Overall simple average tariff rates decreased sharply in the Philippines (table 2.7).

The Philippines made a cautious attempt to reduce the overvaluation of its currency; but because domestic inflation rates remained above those of its major trading partners, real exchange rates soon returned to their former levels.[47] Thailand, a country that studiously avoided devaluation in the 1970s, took a bold step in devaluating the bhat substantially in 1984. With the help of the World Bank's structural adjustment loan programs, Thailand and the Philippines have tried to provide more balance to their incentive systems in order to promote more efficient and resilient industrial growth.

The oil exporters, Indonesia and Malaysia, also undertook similar reviews of their trade and industrial policies in the late 1970s and mid-1980s with the aim of promoting more vigorous manufacturing export growth. Indonesia's 1978 rupiah devaluation was designed to prevent erosion of incomes in the nonoil sectors of the economy, and of smallholders in agriculture in particular. It gave a surprisingly strong stimulus to manufacturing exports, which surged until the inflation differential and a boom in the domestic economy cut back growth of manufactured exports.[48] The second oil price bonanza of 1979 and 1980 had the unfortunate effect of casting aside any concern regarding the need to diversify the sources of foreign exchange earnings until oil prices fell and current account deficits mounted after 1982. It then became plain that Indonesia would have to expand nonoil exports greatly if it was to attain acceptable economic growth without an unacceptable foreign debt. As a result, a second major devaluation occurred in March 1984, and a third followed in September 1986.

Changing from inward- to outward-oriented industrialization is a lengthy process. It is premature to make a final judgment on the long-term effects of these policy changes, but some general conclusions are possible.

The new policies favoring manufactured exports were adopted with some tariff cuts, but did not substantially reduce nontariff barriers and other preferences promoting production for domestic markets. In Indonesia, more nontariff barriers have been erected, so that tariff reductions have done little to reduce the average EPR or to reduce dispersion of EPRs. Export incentives thus had little net impact on the sectoral pattern of incentives. Hence discrimination against exports was only partly mitigated by the new measures; even subsidized exporters were still at a net disadvantage vis-à-vis producers of import-competing goods. The incentive structure favoring capital-using industrial activities remained basically unchallenged.

Malaysia, however, seems to have been more successful with its industrial promotion policies to encourage industrial employment and exports. A major part of the change was the setting up of several free trade zones (FTZs), also called export processing zones (EPZs), in which production of textiles and electronic goods rapidly expanded. Scattered evidence suggests that added industrial employment was created mainly in the FTZs. By 1982 over half of

Malaysia's manufacturing exports originated in the FTZs. Hence, the notable overall performance of Malaysia's manufacturing was based to a considerable degree on footloose production in the FTZs, where multinational corporations dominate.

Despite their success to date, the long-term viability of the FTZs is debatable. For example, FTZs attract subassembly types of activities with little linkage to the domestic industrial sector and may impede the transfer of technology and the accumulation of marketing expertise usually gained from exports. A more serious criticism of the FTZs is that by establishing them, governments may feel less pressure to pursue more open, outward-looking policies, in general. Recent studies,[49] however, conclude that the benefits of FTZs have exceeded their costs. Efforts to better integrate FTZ firms into the economy have been hindered by the failure of domestic industries to make reliably available to FTZ firms good-quality locally processed materials and equipment. And regulations that limit the sale of FTZ goods in domestic markets on an equal footing with imports have also prevented integration.

Despite various programs and measures to promote manufacturing exports and industrial efficiency, government planning in ASEAN-4 continues to favor import substitution and investment in skill-intensive and capital-intensive heavy industries.[50] Yet the number and share of manufactured exports has increased in each ASEAN-4 country. In the Philippines, Malaysia, and Thailand, manufactured exports by 1984 were as great as 24 to 33 percent of total exports. For Indonesia, manufactured exports were smaller (10 percent in 1984) despite the high 1970s growth rate. The oil price hikes of the 1970s brought about huge increases in oil export earnings in Indonesia, thus reducing the incentive to develop manufactured exports. The high growth rate of manufactured exports in the ASEAN-4 during the 1970s (table 2.3) indicates that further reductions in distortions that discriminate against exports could substantially enhance their competitiveness in labor-intensive goods.

The ASEAN-4's expansion of manufactured exports was accompanied by some diversification into new export products, but to a lesser degree than was the case in the NICs (table 2.6). Exports of the "classical trio"—clothing, textiles, and miscellaneous manufactures—grew fast. In the 1970s, the share of clothing exports rose from 4 to nearly 15 percent of manufactured exports. Together, the share of the "trio" increased from 21 to 28 percent of manufactured exports. Exports of electrical machinery (primarily microchips) in Malaysia also grew rapidly.

The processing of primary goods and the production of manufactures using locally available materials and large labor input would seem to be an area of continuing strong comparative advantage in ASEAN. Processing industries tend to be physical capital intensive but not skill intensive and, in many cases, have strong backward linkages to the rural sector. Although the share of these resource-based manufactures declined to about one-fifth of all manufactured exports over the 1970s, more recently, the export subsitution of processed raw materials and resource-based manufactures for unprocessed primary goods is gathering momentum in the ASEAN-4. For example, canned fish products in Thailand and the Philippines have rapidly become major exports. Malaysia has also sought to enhance its commodity exports' value added through down-stream processing. But most of its nontraditional exports have been generated by footloose assembly operations (electronics especially) in export-processing zones.

Nonetheless, there are problems with attempting to achieve export substitution through quantitative restrictions on exports of raw materials and subsidization of processors. The emphasis on processing raw materials for export has led to restrictions on log exports in Malaysia, the Philippines, and Indonesia. Each of these countries now exports plywood and other processed timber products. Indonesia has become the largest supplier of plywood in the world since 1984. But Indonesia's export earnings from plywood, veneer, and processed wood in 1984 were barely 60 percent of its 1980 export earnings from logs and sawn wood.[51] The ban on the exports of logs led to a rapid proliferation of plywood and sawmill firms. Many were operated inefficiently, and when world prices fell during the recession, there was excess capacity and many mills were forced into bankruptcy. The transition to resource-based manufacturing exports based on comparative advantage would allow maximal foreign exchange, productivity, and employment gains.

In addition, Indonesia and Malaysia have tried to upgrade and expand their petroleum refineries, and they have reduced imports of refined products (mainly from Singapore). These are high risk and capital intensive; and worldwide over-capacity in petroleum refining has already put pressure on efficient refiners in the United States, Japan, and Singapore. Competition with low-cost Middle Eastern refiners may be difficult; hence caution should be exercised in any further domestic refining investment.

In the past, the ASEAN-4 countries' manufacturing exports have not been closely linked with their strong and diverse agricultural and mineral resources. In part, this is because some of these require huge investments and management skills that are in very limited supply in the ASEAN-4. Foreign investment has helped overcome these bottlenecks in some cases (see chapter 4). Future growth of resource-based manufactured exports should be rapid provided appropriate policies to encourage investment and increase the supply of skilled manpower are adopted. It will also be necessary to reverse the existing discrimination against agricultural and mineral exports inherent in the existing trade and industrial policies.

The sharp and prolonged decline in the prices of primary products in the 1980s emphasizes the importance of export diversification. Declining oil revenues have forced Indonesia and Malaysia to adopt austerity measures to solve current deficits and debt-servicing requirements. Although falling oil prices are welcome news to oil importers like the Philippines and Thailand, falling prices for rubber, tin, timber, and other commodities have necessitated similar measures even in nonoil primary exporting countries. The weak commodity prices reflect not only a weak cyclical demand due to the slower growth of output in the more developed countries, but also some longer-term subsitution factors. Technological improvements have reduced the need for primary inputs, and the shift toward higher technology and service-oriented industries may indicate a long-run trend toward a lower demand for commodities.

If these natural resource-rich countries are to continue their successful growth performance and increase employment in their industrial sectors, they must continue with major reforms to improve the efficiency of resource use and international competitiveness. The reforms require the correction of an artificially distorted price structure through tariff cuts and trade liberalization, the junking of disincentives to export, and the redesign of investment incentives (which now favor large-scale, capital-intensive projects). At the firm level, the changes require a new output mix, new production technologies to conserve energy, and higher product quality standards.

Some of these policy revisions are now being worked out and implemented. If properly executed, the structural adjustments should lead to more balanced industrial production, both geographically and in the relationship of the industrial sector to other sectors; and to an increased supply of consumer goods and manufactured exports. There will probably be stiff opposition to the policies from vested interests within these countries. The opposition is partly based on the expectation that trade liberalization plus higher interest rates will result in bankruptcies of existing firms and rising unemployment, because the export potential is too limited or because internationally competitive firms cannot be established rapidly enough. This pessimistic expectation in fact describes the transition problem, for which painless solutions are not available.

The prospects for larger manufactured exports from Southeast Asian countries look favorable, even if existing trade barriers remain. As the NICs lose their comparative advantage in unskilled labor-intensive goods because of rising wage levels, countries at lower levels of industrial development can gradually replace the NICs in exporting to countries within Asia and to the more developed countries. And high wage rates in MDCs encourage the relocation of labor-intensive parts of production to countries with low wage levels plus a work force sufficiently skilled to ensure reasonable labor productivity. These conditions exist in Southeast Asia and in some South Asian countries.

South Asia

Growth rates of income, industrial output, and employment in South Asian countries have been somewhat better than the performance of non-Asian low-income countries. But industrial performance in the countries of South Asia has lagged behind that of the other Asian countries.[52] In the 1970s, in South Asia, industrial performance helped neither output growth nor employment creation (table 2.2). In Bangladesh, Nepal, and Burma, industrial development is still in its infancy; the expansion of manufacturing was constrained to varying degrees by a lack of entrepreneurs, financing, and technological know-how and a weak infrastructure.

India, Pakistan, and Sri Lanka have a long history of industrial development and experience with heavy industrial production. During the 1960s, industrial growth in these countries was much like that of Southeast Asia. But industrial growth slowed down considerably during the 1970s. In Sri Lanka and Pakistan there was a steep drop in the growth rates of manufacturing, though in India the decline was less pronounced (table 2.2).

Pakistan in the mid-1960s was widely regarded as a successful case of import substitution industrialization strategy.[53] However, the highly uneven distribution of the benefits of industrial growth between East and West Pakistan (in favor of the latter) and the capital-intensive pattern of industrial development led to social unrest, high unemployment, and stagnation in the late 1960s and early 1970s. Industrial production did not recover until the late 1970s in Pakistan, when a more export-oriented strategy was initiated.[54]

The 1970s' experience of South Asia is in sharp contrast with that of the NICs and ASEAN-4, where growth rates of manufacturing were maintained or even accelerated. The divergence in growth rates results from differing industrialization strategies, plus internal constraints.

In most South Asian countries, policy-caused price distortions and direct government interventions adversely affected industrial development. These policies aimed at industrial self-sufficiency (particularly emphasizing basic industry, e.g., chemicals, metal products, machinery) under close government supervision and largely disregarded the countries' factor endowments and the bottlenecks to industrial development (like insufficient infrastructure, energy shortages, and lack of organizational and managerial skills). The South Asian countries added another dimension to import subsitution. They tried to coordinate closely the activities of private enterprise with national development plans, using a tight net of regulations that affected almost every step of production and distribution. They have maintained the highest average tariff rates in Asia, along with extensive bureaucratic controls on imports (table 2.4).

The existing impediments to industrial growth were reinforced, not mitigated, by inefficient public enterprises, burdensome administrative and licensing procedures, and government policies aimed at industrial self-sufficiency at any cost. The consequences were negative for economic development: debt accumulation, discouragement of private domestic and foreign investors, little expansion of industrial employment, underuse of productive capacity.

The government of India viewed state control of industry as a crucial means for redressing income inequalities and rapidly establishing a modern industrial economy. Soon after independence the influence of economic planning became pervasive. Under the direction of Professor P. C. Mahalanobis, India's public enterprise sector was substantially expanded in an inward-looking direction. The Indian government adopted a policy of taking over numerous firms, such that it developed a monopoly in several industries or became one of the few oligopolists in others.[55] At the same time, private industry faced elaborate controls. Industrial entrepreneurs were hindered by licensing requirements for the initial investment and any subsequent expansion of capacity. Import allotments were based on a rated capacity. Thus, the licensing system encouraged businesses to begin with an excess capacity. It also made it more lucrative to lobby politicians and bureaucrats for license approvals than to set up and operate efficient production facilities. Strong barriers were erected against imports; protection was given to a large number of industries without regard for relative costs or quality. Imports of intermediate and capital goods were allowed only if no domestically produced counterpart was available. Importers were sometimes required to export a percentage of their output, but the overvalued rupee and the high cost and low quality of inputs made this difficult.[56] Extensive bureaucratic controls also constrained competitive exports which were already suffering from negative rates of effective protection. Minimum wage laws, price controls, and the omnipresent threat of nationalization further inhibited the growth of the private sector.

Small-scale industrial development was promoted in India by reserving production in specific industries for the small-scale sector and by giving substantial financial and fiscal incentives. However, these incentives discouraged the growth of new, more efficient small- to medium-scale firms. Rather, they kept the existing small firms in business, even though these tended to be technologically stagnant and inefficient in using scarce capital.[57]

A pattern of inward-looking, autarkic industrial development became widespread in South Asia in the 1950s, 1960s, and even through the early 1970s for some countries. Public enterprises were believed to be better agents for government policies than were private enterprises. That conviction was also strong in Bangladesh, Burma, and Sri Lanka. Hence, industrial development in these countries came to be mainly controlled by large, state-owned corporations. The private sector mostly consists of cottage and small-scale traditional industries. Privately owned industrial enterprises have been discouraged; subsidized credit and other privileges are granted first and often, exclusively, to firms in the public sector.

The performance of public enterprises has all too often been unsatisfactory.[58] They have suffered from management inefficiencies and bureaucratic impediments, and have been burdened with executing too many government policies. They have been simultaneously used as vehicles for employment policies, for supplying essential consumer goods at artificially low prices, for executing ambitious government plans for heavy industry, and for achieving foreign exchange savings or earnings whether or not they were competitive. Such varied tasks undermined the economic viability of public enterprises. Heavy expenditures were often needed to sustain them.

A main rationale for extensive controls has been the desire of government policymakers to protect the poor. But a recent study of economic development and political change in South Asia finds that populist governments asserting poverty amelioration and greater income equality as objectives had distinctly poorer performance even with regard to the poor than regimes seeking higher rates of economic growth through pro-growth policies.[59] The electoral success of pro-growth governments was usually assisted by the higher employment made possible by growth and the substantial effect employment creation had toward reducing poverty. But structural problems from external trade deficits plus the inability to attract foreign investment often disrupted growth and brought populist governments back into power.

In sum, inefficient public enterprises, distorted prices, and bureaucratic rigidities have led to high-cost, low-productivity industry and reluctance to invest by private domestic and foreign investors. In fact, they have often led to capital flight by the private sector. The resulting limited foreign capital inflow, lack of international competitiveness, and overvalued currencies cause recurrent foreign exchange shortages that limit supplies of necessary inputs.[60] Adjustment of the industrial structure has been impeded by government policies favoring large-scale, physical-capital-intensive, and technology-intensive industries and by artificially increased wage costs and employment guarantees to employees of public enterprises. Overall, the industrialization strategy followed in South Asia has placed heavy demand on scarce factors (skills and capital) and has made little use of unskilled labor. The result has been predictable: slow growth of output and industrial employment.

The inward orientation of industrial policies has constrained the ability of South Asian countries to diversify exports, and pressing food and population problems have until recently diverted resources from export-oriented agriculture. The policy direction of South Asia has begun to change, and government policymakers have indicated their desire for more market-oriented policies to boost exports and sustain higher growth. In pursuit of more efficiency and more employment, discrimination against private enterprise is being reduced, and more efficient management of public industrial enterprises is being sought. Sectoral priorities are being reconsidered. More emphasis is being given to production for export and to unskilled labor-intensive manufactures.

The Sri Lankan government has taken major steps to rationalize the incentive system and ease restrictions on private enterprise. Removal of import restrictions helped to spur manufacturing and industrial production in the late 1970s, while export subsidies and the unification and devaluation of the domestic currency increased incentives for the production of exports. Sri Lanka's exports were still dominated by agricultural products and food and raw materials, but manufactured exports rose from under 2 percent to 28 percent between 1970 and 1983 (table 2.8). Clothing exports made the strongest gains, accounting for almost 70 percent of Sri Lanka's manufactured exports by the 1980s. Sri Lanka is the only South Asian country with trade-to-GDP ratios comparable to those of the ASEAN-4 countries (table 2.1).

After the major reform in 1977, however, the exchange rate was allowed to appreciate in real terms, and high tariffs protecting domestic manufacturing industries created large profit opportunities in the domestic market. Steps taken in 1985 toward tariff reform aimed at reducing the variance of EPRs and discussions of privatization of the generally poorly performing public enterprises show the Sri Lankan government's resolve to improve resource allocation and economic efficiency. Yet the future development of Sri Lanka, despite the improved policy direction, is uncertain because of intensifying political and social unrest.

India has also moved toward liberalization of its economy, continuously since the late 1970s and more rapidly in recent years. Licensing requirements for large firms and import restrictions have been loosened. India has achieved much in the way of export diversification. In fact, India has done better than most Asian LDCs in both the number of products exported and the index of concentration of exports.[61] The value of India's exports, however, remained very small for an economy of such large size. Exports comprised less than 7 percent of GDP in the mid-1980s, less than that of the United States (table 2.1). In a sense, India exports a little of everything, but not much of anything. It has good prospects for expansion in areas such as machinery (electrical and nonelectrical), certain types of transport equipment, and some engineering and consumer goods. But balance-of-payments problems arising from swiftly expanding imports and political realities may force the government to slow down the implementation of liberalization policies.

In Pakistan and even in socialist Burma, more freedom to private entrepreneurs has produced an upswing in private investment and in industrial growth. Bangladesh plans a return to private ownership for jute mills and other enterprises that were poorly managed by the public sector. Export-to-GDP

Table 2.8. Exports of South Asian Countries by Principal Commodity Groups (percentage of total exports)

	Bangladesh		Burma		India		Nepal		Pakistan		Sri Lanka	
	1975	1983	1970	1976	1970	1980	1976	1981	1970	1983	1970	1983
Primary commodities	31.9	38.3	98.5	97.0	54.2	42.2	67.0	48.0	41.2	37.1	98.6	71.9
Raw materials	24.7	19.2	32.7	32.9	24.7	14.1	37.4	35.8	30.9	16.1	26.0	25.4
Agricultural and food products	7.2	19.0	65.8	64.2	29.5	28.1	29.6	12.2	10.2	21.0	72.6	46.5
Manufactured goods[a]	67.7	61.0	1.5	2.9	45.4	57.5	32.8	51.9	58.8	61.6	1.4	28.0
Chemicals	0.6	1.3	0.1	0.5	2.3	4.2	0.4	0.5	0.8	1.0	0.3	0.6
Resource-based manufactures	6.9	9.5	1.5	2.3	8.6	14.5	1.1	14.8	4.4	4.6	0.6	5.4
Textiles	59.5	44.9	0.0	0.0	22.7	15.2	25.6	17.3	45.1	42.7	0.0	0.6
Metal manufactures	0.0	0.0	0.0	0.0	1.6	2.9	0.0	0.0	0.0	0.5	0.0	0.0
Electrical machinery	0.0	0.6	0.0	0.0	1.1	1.5	0.0	0.0	0.0	0.5	0.0	0.0
Nonelectrical machinery	0.0	1.0	0.0	0.0	1.9	3.4	0.0	0.0	1.1	0.5	0.0	0.3
Transport equipment	0.0	0.6	0.0	0.0	2.3	3.2	0.0	0.0	2.8	0.4	0.0	0.4
Precision instruments	0.0	0.0	0.0	0.0	0.0	0.4	0.0	0.0	0.0	0.0	0.0	0.0
Clothing	0.0	2.6	0.0	0.0	1.8	7.8	0.7	2.1	0.7	7.4	0.4	18.9
Furniture	0.0	0.0	0.0	0.0	0.0	0.0	0.0	0.0	0.0	0.0	0.0	0.0
Footwear	0.0	0.0	0.0	0.0	0.8	0.6	0.0	0.5	0.0	0.5	0.0	0.0
Miscellaneous manufactures	0.6	0.3	0.0	0.0	2.3	3.5	4.9	16.8	3.5	3.8	0.1	1.3
Total exports[b] (US$ billions)	0.3	0.8	0.1	0.2	2.0	7.5	0.03	0.1	0.7	3.1	0.3	1.1

Source: United Nations, *1983 Yearbook of International Trade Statistics*, 1985.

[a]The categories of manufactured exports do not necessarily add up to the total of manufactured exports since not all categories are listed. Manufactured plus primary commodities may not add up to 100 because SITC 9 (commodities and transactions not classified elsewhere) is excluded.

[b]Total includes re-exports.

ratios rose in these three countries in the 1980s, but have not increased enough to overcome large trade deficits. Economic growth rates, however, have generally increased in the 1980s.

These examples indicate that national policies can enhance industrial development, despite the substantial hurdles that South Asian nations face from deficiencies in infrastructure, administration, entrepreneurial capabilities, and scarcity of foreign exchange and domestic savings. Poor economic performance can be seen to be more the result of inappropriate policies than a consequence of a low level of economic development.

In South Asia, the industrial sector will probably make only a modest contribution to economic growth and direct employment creation during the late 1980s. Problems of industrial development remain formidable, and internal ethnic and political conflicts along with declining concessional aid are likely to add to the problems. But national policies can do much to facilitate the shift of resources from agriculture to industry, to increase the efficiency of industry, and to strengthen the linkages between economic sectors so that industrial and agricultural development reinforce one another.

Industrialization can make an indirect contribution to employment through creating linkages with the primary sector and through increasing the demand for services. If industrial production is to have more linkages and be more labor absorbing in years to come, there is a need for (1) diversifying industrial outputs among traditional consumer goods and manufactures using domestic raw materials; (2) improving industrial infrastructure, and streamlining customs procedures, to reduce wastage and delays; (3) directing the priorities of public sector corporations so that productivity and profitability become the main goals; and (4) dismantling direct controls, and restructuring incentive systems to make them more economically rational.

What is appropriate differs widely between large countries with well-established industrial sectors like India and much less developed economies like Bangladesh. Everywhere there is scope for more efficient use of domestic resources. India has given priority to its science-based engineering industries and has developed new nontraditional exports. It is unlikely that the other South Asian countries can repeat India's achievements in technology-based industries. But they can benefit from increased foreign investment and joint ventures in order to produce resource-based products and selected nondurable consumer goods, which can become significant foreign exchange earners. This is already beginning with ready-made garments.

Issues for Future Industrial Development

Structural change will be an important issue in the industrial development of the Asian countries for years to come. Sustained high growth in agriculture is important, but in every country the size of primary commodity production will decline in comparison with industry and services.

Structural changes in response to shifts in comparative advantage—as old opportunities close and new opportunities open—require flexibility in resource allocation. Reforms of macroeconomic and sectoral policies that influence investment decisions, choice of technique, product mix, and marketing are needed in most of the Asian countries. A dismantling of trade barriers and lessening of restrictions on private enterprise and markets would increase flexibility. The policy reforms toward freer trade and less distorted incentive systems will encourage a transition toward new internationally competitive lines of manufactured commodities. But the transition will not occur easily or quickly. The industrial restructuring schemes that now are being formulated and reviewed in all Asian countries will demand of their governments political determination and administrative skills of a high order. But the flexible reaction of many of these countries to the external shocks of the recent past has shown that it is possible to maintain the momentum of economic development despite adverse external conditions, if there is sufficient social consensus and political support to carry out the necessary policy changes. Such policy changes are likely to cause political and social friction: the threat of these will delay and discourage adoption of the needed changes. During the transition time ahead in South and Southeast Asia, labor and capital market problems are likely to be conspicuous.

If Asian countries continue to dismantle their protectionist trade regimes and to support more export-oriented industrialization, the emerging international division of labor may at a minimum create scope for increased intraregional trade. Countries move up the ladder of comparative advantage—beginning with specialization in primary products and moving to unskilled-labor-intensive manufactures, skilled-labor-intensive products, capital-intensive goods, and finally knowledge-intensive goods. As one group of countries moves up the ladder, another group can take their place. A large part of the NICs' exports replaced Japanese exports in the world market and did not depend only on increases in import demand. Malaysia, Thailand, and Sri Lanka have begun to make their presence felt in the world market for textiles, clothing, and electronics, as the NICs move into more skill-intensive products. A "multiple catching up process" could be seen in world trade.[62] With slower growth in trade in the 1980s, this process has become more difficult. Countries find it harder to move up the ladder. Structural adjustments become more painful, and pressures to protect declining industries grow. The new protectionism may limit trade expansion in manufactured goods between more and less developed nations.

Because of more difficult external conditions, adjustment will be required not only at the margin; adjustment will require redeployment and, in some cases, renewal of major parts of each country's capital stock.

Summing up, all of the Asian developing countries will have to achieve major industrial reforms to improve their efficiency of resource use and the international competitiveness of their manufacturing industries. The means are, first, making better use of each country's current and prospective comparative advantage in industrial production; second, promoting regional dispersion of industries and developing efficient small-scale and medium-scale industries; third, improving domestic resources—increasing domestic savings and allocating it better, and increasing education, on-the-job training, and the development of entrepreneurial skills; and finally, dismantling administrative obstacles to industrial expansion, particularly overly restrictive trade and investment regulations.

The task requires changes in incentive systems in many of these countries in order to achieve a more effective combination of market forces and government intervention than was achieved in the past. Emphasis on market mechanisms does not imply that government intervention cannot play an important role in industrial expansion. The point is simply that government intervention, instead of creating distortions in prices and resource flows, should instead work to shrink distortions resulting from economic problems like sluggish flows of information, external economies or diseconomies, rigidities in technology, and excessive rigidity or volatility of prices.

Appropriate macroeconomic, financial, and labor market policies are crucial. To the extent that they allow factor prices to measure marginal contributions to production, an optimal allocation of resources is promoted. A critical review of interest rate subsidies, overvalued currencies, minimum wage rates, and administratively fixed nonwage labor costs is a necessary condition for successful structural adjustment. Some of these policies may be justified, or partially justified. Most will not and should be removed.

The envisaged readjustment of prices and output structures will tend to result in a larger supply of consumer goods (at lower prices), and will encourage an overflow from domestic markets to exports.

The benefits from industrial development will be larger and more widespread if industrial structures are adapted to comparative advantage. More open, and so more competitive, industrial development in both South and Southeast Asia and less government control on the private sector can help to restructure the economy toward comparative advantage more readily than can bureaucratically determined investment priorities.

The dismantling of policy-induced distortions suggested in this chapter is an urgent, though difficult task. Import liberalization may increase imports before export performance can be improved, and may add to balance-of-payments difficulties for some time. If exchange rates are revised to correct for the overvaluation of national currency, the prices of imports will rise, including prices of food and other products that figure heavily in the consumption of low-income groups. In both private and public enterprises, entrenched interests that have long been protected will protest, pleading the infant industry case, the need to preserve existing jobs, and nationalist arguments for continuing protection against foreign competitors.

Most Asian less developed countries will need assistance from foreign donors to see them through the short-run problems inherent in the adjustments of major parts of their industrial sectors. Such lending has a high rate of return: the alternative is import compression and slowed economic growth. The need also exists to improve domestic saving during the transition to a more open and competitive industrial sector (chapter 3).

Governments cannot afford to postpone policy reform. Policies to maintain the status quo will be progressively more costly through income forgone and increased unemployment and underemployment. Poorer countries are less able to bear such waste than are more developed countries.

As to petroleum, the favorable impact of the oil price decline in the 1980s on the economic prospects for the oil-importing Asian developing countries is obvious. Oil-importing developing countries should have breathing room for at least the remainder of the 1980s: the pressure of oil prices on their balance of payments should decrease. Energy prices—particularly those of oil and gas—are likely to rise in the 1990s. Most Asian countries have not done very well in the conservation of energy use in their industries.[63] These countries' concern for appropriate energy policies should continue.

Asian less developed countries should be able to realize further gains in output and employment growth from industrial specialization and trade, despite the uncertainties of future capital flows and energy costs.

Table 2.A1. Developing Countries in Regional and Subregional Groups

Region	Country
NICs	Korea, Singapore, Taiwan
ASEAN-4	Indonesia, Malaysia, Philippines, Thailand
South Asia	Burma, India, Pakistan, Sri Lanka
Latin America and Caribbean	Argentina, Bolivia, Brazil, Chile, Colombia, Dominican Republic, Ecuador, El Salvador, Guatemala, Haiti, Honduras, Jamaica, Mexico, Nicaragua, Panama, Paraguay, Peru, Venezuela
Africa	Cameroon, Ethiopia, Ghana, Ivory Coast, Kenya, Liberia, Sierra Leone, Sudan, Zaire, Zambia, Zimbabwe

3 Domestic Savings and Financial Development

Introduction

Early theories of economic development emphasized capital accumulation. W. Arthur Lewis formulated the central problem of economic development as that of raising the proportion of national income saved and invested from 4–5 percent to 12–15 percent.[1] In contrast to the affluent countries where the growth problem was viewed in Keynesian terms—too much saving, too little spending—in the newly emerging countries, investment and hence economic growth were constrained by the insufficiency of saving.[2] Domestic savings were in many developing countries barely enough to maintain the existing capital stock. The rate of domestic savings would not permit enough investment to sustain economic growth at a rate high enough to employ the rapidly growing labor force, let alone to uplift the general standard of living. To overcome the savings constraint initially, foreign capital inflows were essential, but in the longer term, sustained economic growth would require increased domestic savings.[3]

There are three steps in the process of capital accumulation. First, the volume of real savings must increase so that additional resources become available for investment. Second, a means of collecting and channeling the savings to make them available to investors is necessary. Third, savings must be transformed into productive capital by an act of investment.

The first step, mobilizing additional real savings, is fundamental to increasing investment and thereby initiating higher economic growth. The increase in savings can come from internal or external sources. Internally, additional savings may be generated voluntarily by reducing consumption or involuntarily through higher taxation, compulsory lending to the government, or inflation. Savings from external sources can be generated by reduced imports of consumption goods, foreign capital inflows, improvements in the terms of trade, or earnings from factors employed overseas (remittances).

The increase in real savings necessary for growth in low-income countries is unlikely to result from self-imposed cuts in consumption. Nor is such an

59

approach compatible with increased economic growth and development. Consumption by the poor must increase if economic development is to occur.[4] Taxation of luxury consumption is warranted, but can hardly be relied on to much increase savings.

What is needed is to initiate a process of higher growth and to raise the marginal saving rate of the community as a whole. Positive interactions of growth with saving and investment can be promoted by appropriate policies, particularly those that encourage financial development.

However additional savings are generated, they must then be collected and channeled to investors. This can be done by three channels or mechanisms: self-finance, government appropriation, or financial intermediation. The efficacy of the three channels varies. This is a crucial point because numerous studies of economic growth have shown that increased inputs of capital and labor explain only part of the increment in output; much growth must be attributed to residual factors of technology, improved quality of labor (human capital), and economies of scale. In short, not just the size of investment but also its efficiency determines growth. Unless increased savings are channeled to the most productive investments, growth will not be as high as it otherwise would be.

Savings can be accumulated as real assets (gold, land, livestock, jewelry, inventories or goods) or financial assets (stocks, bonds, savings deposits, currency). In the less developed Asian countries, much saving and investment takes place in nonfinancial form, particularly in rural communities. Farm households save and invest by making improvements in their land and buildings, making simple tools, or accumulating inventories of commodities they produce (e.g., rice). Their investments are limited to what they can make themselves. Even when money is used, it is often the case that it is used to purchase real assets (gold, jewelry, land) that protect the saver-investor from inflation but add nothing to the nation's productive capacity. Self-finance reduces the farm household's dependence on outside funds, but represents, in most cases, a socially suboptimal use of scarce savings.

Informal finance involving direct lending by the saver to the investor is also quite common in the Asian LDCs. Relatives, acquaintances, and neighbors often engage in reciprocal lending and borrowing, but again this limits the efficiency with which savings are allocated to investment. Primary lending is restricted to small amounts insufficient to permit capital improvements of even modest scale.

Government appropriation is a second channel by which public savings or the surplus of current revenue over current expenditure is directed to investment. Government may also gain access to private savings through the imposition of regulations and controls on financial institutions.[5] In countries with large public enterprise sectors, budgetary appropriations are a more important means of channeling saving to investment than they are in countries where private enterprise is predominant.

Financial intermediation, the remaining channel, has significant advantages over self-finance and primary lending. Cole and Patrick summarize the role of financial intermediation in economic development:

> Practically every kind of productive activity—in agriculture, manufacturing, infrastructure, domestic and foreign trade, and by large units and small—requires some form of finance. The financial system provides the medium of exchange; it allocates resources to investment; it provides a return on and presumably affects the level of savings; it pools, transforms, and distributes risk; it is an important locus for the implementation of stabilization policy.[6]

Financial institutions or other intermediaries attract savings by offering assets that are safe and convenient and provide additional income. The intermediaries lend these financial savings to borrowers on the basis of a careful assessment of their creditworthiness. The financial institutions can attract many small deposits that together provide a large fund that can be lent for investment projects of substantial size. Through the law of large numbers, these institutions can provide owners of savings deposits with convenience and liquidity and still finance long-term investments. Banks are the most important intermediary institutions in Asia, but nonbank intermediaries (finance companies, post office savings, investment trusts, insurance companies) as well as stock exchanges (in which private companies raise funds through share issues) and organized bond markets (trading in government debt instruments) also play a significant role in the more developed financial systems.

Throughout Asia, financial intermediation is the main channel for mobilizing domestic savings and financing investment. Governments have been active in promoting and establishing new financial institutions in order to develop the financial sector. However, government control has also been used extensively to direct finance to those investments deemed to have priority by government. The imposition of controls has often made it more difficult to attain the objectives of increasing domestic savings and the development of an efficient financial system. In this chapter, we examine the record of Asian countries in saving, investment efficiency, and financial development. Before turning to this, we review the policy issues pertinent to choosing among alternative techniques for mobilizing savings and allocating investment. The specific saving-investment techniques chosen are closely related to the broader macroeconomic policies and development strategy of each developing country.

Financial Repression and Macroeconomic Policy

The three channels outlined earlier for mobilizing savings for investment are alternative techniques, or substitutes for one another. Gurley and Shaw distinguish government appropriation (taxation) and self-finance as "internal financial processes"; whereas foreign aid (considered in the next chapter) and financial intermediation are "external financial processes."[7]

External finance, in the Gurley-Shaw sense, involves decentralized decision making, market organization, and relative prices that guide behavior. Private savings are drawn into intermediary institutions and securities markets for use by government and private investors. Investment decisions are based on market criteria and are strongly influenced by market interest rates. The financial markets operate most efficiently and grow faster in a macroeconomic environment that is conducive to the development of private enterprise. Trade restrictions limited to modest indirect measures (tariffs), relatively undistorted markets for goods and factors of production, absence of rampant inflation, equilibrium foreign exchange pricing, and freedom to invest and operate business without excessive taxes or regulations are components of this type of macroeconomic environment.

Internal finance, in contrast, involves greater centralization, less specialization, and more government control. Means of mobilizing savings to meet government plan objectives include "scissors pricing" that turns the terms of trade against agriculture, overvaluation of domestic currency, heavy taxation of foreign trade, and inflation, which acts as a tax on money balances and transfers real resources from creditors (holders of money) to debtors (issuers of money, i.e., the government). The government almost always will have a strong incentive to reduce the price of capital. Interest rates charged by financial institutions (owned or regulated by government) are suppressed to below equilibrium levels, even to negative real rates. This exacerbates economic dualism by forcing would-be borrowers who are rationed out of the formal sector to seek funds from the informal sector at much higher rates of interest. It also creates an incentive for capital-intensive production techniques and favors capital-intensive activities among enterprises with access to cheaply priced loans. In short, internal finance requires "financial repression." The financial system is prevented from developing and expanding. This type of savings-investment technique is compatible with a highly regulated, inward-looking economic development strategy. Extensive distortion of macroprices usually accompanies this approach (see pp. 70–72).

Most of the Asian developing countries have imposed numerous controls on financial intermediaries, and these have inhibited the ability of financial institutions to mobilize savings deposits and allocate funds to the most productive investments. The extent of controls varies according to the overall macroeconomic and development strategy of each country. The market-oriented NICs, Hong Kong and Taiwan in particular, have fewer controls, and financial institutions have functioned in a highly efficient manner. Though most banks in Taiwan are government owned, private cooperative financial institutions are widespread and have increased their share of the market. Competition for funds has kept interest rates honest. Korea and Singapore and the ASEAN-4 countries have more regulations and sizable government involvement alongside private financial institutions. The South Asian countries have tended to have the most regulated and least developed financial systems. Government ownership and control is pervasive. But changes and reforms in the financial sector have accompanied efforts to spur economic development. Before reviewing the financial policies, we examine domestic saving performance in the Asian LDCs.

Domestic Saving Performance
In 1960, Asian domestic saving and investment rates were generally below what was thought necessary for adequate economic growth (table 3.1). Domestic savings in the Asian LDCs, other than Malaysia, Indonesia, and the Philippines, financed on average only slightly over half the gross domestic investment. Hong Kong, Korea, and Singapore had among the lowest saving rates in Asia. Indonesia, Pakistan, Nepal, and Sri Lanka had domestic saving rates of under 10 percent. Domestic saving rates rose impressively during the 1960s throughout developing Asia, but for most countries a gap remained between investment and savings as investment rates also rose (table 3.2).

Saving and investment rates increased sharply throughout Asia during the 1970s (table 3.1). By 1985, over 80 percent of gross domestic investment was financed by domestic savings in the Asian LDCs. Domestic saving rates averaged nearly 30 percent of GDP in the NICs and ASEAN-4. The rates averaged only about 11 percent in South Asia, varying widely among the countries. Through great effort, India raised its domestic saving rate to 20 percent in the 1980s. Sri Lanka tried to improve its saving performance after the huge resource gaps it suffered in the late 1970s, but with only limited success.[8]

Insofar as domestic saving was less than investment, the gap was filled by foreign capital inflows (table 3.2). Taiwan was an exception: domestic saving exceeded investment.

The means through which Asian countries increased domestic saving rates varied considerably. The largest part of domestic savings was generated by the private sector, especially by households. In the 1970s, government saving (the excess of current revenues over current expenditures) in less developed Asian countries averaged less than 3 percent of gross domestic savings. Substantial fiscal efforts raised tax revenue as a percentage of GDP, but in most cases,

Table 3.1. Domestic Savings and Investment 1960, 1970, 1980, and 1985 (percentage of GDP)

	Gross Domestic Savings				Gross Domestic Investment			
	1960	1970	1980	1985	1960	1970	1980	1985
NICs								
Hong Kong	6	25	31	27	18	21	36	21
Korea	1	15	23	31	11	25	31	30
Singapore	−3	21	38	42	11	39	45	43
Taiwan	13	26	33	31	20	26	34	18
ASEAN–4								
Indonesia	8	11	29	26[a]	8	14	21	23[a]
Malaysia	27	22	31	35	14	21	28	34
Philippines	16	20	25	13	16	20	31	16
Thailand	14	22	21	19	16	26	27	23
South Asia								
Bangladesh	8	9[b]	3	3	7	10[b]	13	11
Burma	11	9	18	14	12	12	22	17
India	14	18	20	20[a]	17	18	25	23[a]
Nepal	NA	2	11	11	NA	3	18	18
Pakistan	5	9	7	7	12	16	17	18
Sri Lanka	9	19	12	12	14	21	34	24

Sources: ADB, *Key Indicators of Developing Member Countries of ADB*, July 1986; World Bank, *World Development Report*, 1984.

Note: NA = Not available.

[a] 1984.   [b] 1973.

expenditures by governments increased almost as much, so that the contribution of governments to domestic saving remained small (see pp. 85–88).

Of the NICs, Taiwan had by the early 1960s achieved significant growth in its domestic saving rate, after receiving large inflows of foreign aid in the early 1950s. Personal (household) savings rose from 3 percent of disposable income in 1952 to 21 percent in 1980. Improved incentives to save were established at the same time as household real incomes, particularly those in rural areas, increased. Among the key elements inducing more saving were ready access to depository institutions and positive real returns to financial savings (see pp. 00–00).

By the mid-1960s, Korea and Singapore instituted major policy reforms aimed at raising domestic savings. The Korean effort focused on raising interest rates on time deposits. Korea maintained high deposit rates into the early 1970s and, in the space of only a decade, 1960 to 1970, Korea's domestic saving rate rose from 1 percent to 15 percent. Singapore, with negative domestic saving

Table 3.2. Saving and Investment Gap (period
averages in percentages)

	Saving–Investment Gap/GDP	
	1961–70	1971–80
NICs		
Hong Kong	5.4[a]	−0.6
Korea	−9.6	−5.9
Singapore	−11.0[b]	−9.3
Taiwan	−0.4[c]	1.4
ASEAN–4		
Indonesia	−2.3	4.3
Malaysia	4.8[b]	4.9
Philippines	NA	−4.4
Thailand	−1.2	−4.5
South Asia		
Bangladesh	NA	−7.8[d]
Burma	−4.2[e]	−2.2
India	−1.5[f]	−3.4
Nepal	NA	−3.4[g]
Pakistan	−6.5	−9.5
Sri Lanka	0.1[h]	−8.3

Sources: ADB, *Key Indicators of Developing Member Countries of ADB*, various years; World Bank, *World Tables*, 1980; World Bank, *World Development Report*, 1981; IMF, *International Financial Statistics*, various months; IMF, *Government Finance Statistics Yearbook*, 1980.

Notes: NA = Not available. The savings-investment gap was computed by subtracting investment from savings in the same year. Since the period averages presented for savings and investment do not always cover the same number of years, the resource gap given here is not just the mere difference between the two average ratios.

[a]1970.   [d]1973–80.   [g]1975–80.
[b]1965–70.   [e]1964–70.   [h]1966–70.
[c]1969–70.   [f]1968–70.

in the mid-1960s, had by 1970 attained a domestic saving rate of over 20 percent (table 3.1).

By 1970, in all of the NICs the government budget was making its own contribution to savings. But the main emphasis was placed on raising household saving through financial incentives, including positive real rates of return on savings deposits. Structural change factors, including the rising share of industry and manufacturing as well as exports in GNP, also made it easier for the NICs to mobilize domestic saving than it was for more agrarian, less trade-oriented economies.[9]

In South Asia, domestic resource mobilization efforts varied widely. India and Sri Lanka had higher domestic saving rates than the other South Asian countries by the 1970s. Both countries inherited strong fiscal institutions from the British. Subsequently, tax performance was notably stronger than elsewhere in South Asia. For example, India raised the ratio of tax revenue to GNP from 6 percent in 1950 to 16 percent in 1980. Both countries have also had success in reducing population growth and, hence, dependency ratios. Some argue that relatively stable political environments have also encouraged savings in these two countries.[10] South Asian policies in the 1960s generally aimed at increasing tax revenues. Some efforts were made to extend branch banking and so make deposit institutions more accessible, but little attention was given to improving financial incentives.

Government controls often included holding nominal interest rates down at low levels to facilitate cheap government borrowing. This policy made it difficult for banks to provide attractive incentives to depositors: domestic saving rates stagnated or rose only slowly.

ASEAN-4 countries made rapid strides in mobilizing domestic savings in the 1960s, and except for Indonesia, domestic saving rates exceeded 20 percent by 1970. Indonesia had saved only 8 percent of GDP in 1960; when oil prices surged in the 1970s, however, incomes rose and domestic savings achieved impressive growth. The financial sector was vibrant in the other ASEAN-4, where private and government banking were both strong. Incentives created by rapid economic growth, and the presence of large mineral, plantation, and commercial sectors, tended to produce substantial saving rates in ASEAN-4. In the countryside, growth of smallholders' incomes was higher in ASEAN-4 than South Asia, and the rural income growth contributed to higher saving rates in the ASEAN-4.

Throughout the 1970s, domestic saving rates continued to rise in the NICs and ASEAN-4, as well as in Burma, Nepal, and India. However, the rates of domestic saving fell in Thailand and the Philippines in the 1980s and fell or remained low in much of South Asia. Investment rates varied less in Asia than domestic saving rates because of the availability of foreign savings during the 1970s and early 1980s.

Remittances from workers employed in the Middle East became an important new source of savings for oil-importing Asian countries. These remittances augmented domestic incomes and savings, and also foreign exchange and government revenue. National saving rates in Pakistan and Bangladesh are far higher than domestic saving rates, mainly because of the savings out of remittances.

Within each subgroup of countries, differences in real GDP growth were not due to differences in saving and investment rates. Other influences on incremental output—the types of investments made, changes in other inputs, skills, and organizational improvements—often are dominant in determining growth. For example, in South Asia, India, which saved and invested a higher proportion of GNP than any other country, had at best a mediocre growth performance. In the late 1970s and early 1980s, Pakistan achieved a real GDP growth rate nearly twice that of India's, with an investment rate that was only two-thirds as high.

The recent rapid growth of output in Pakistan was accompanied by increasing productivity in agriculture and industry. Agricultural productivity gains were derived through the use of higher-productivity farm inputs (e.g., seed, fertilizers, and tube wells). Reorganization, management improvement, and consolidation of public sector enterprises resulted in higher industrial capacity utilization. The share of private investment in total investment increased from only one-third to over half between 1970 and 1984, an increase leading to further efficiency gains.

A sharp rise in India's incremental capital-output ratio (ICOR) offset the improvements in the rate of saving.[11] The Philippines had saving and investment rates higher than Thailand's, but still grew more slowly from 1970 to 1980.

The efficiency with which savings from domestic and foreign sources are allocated among alternative investments is limited by the efficiency of capital markets. As the financial system develops, it becomes better able to attract domestic and foreign funds and to allocate them efficiently. Strong links exist between financial development, the saving rate, and investment efficiency, on the one hand, and the rate of economic growth on the other.

The development of financial markets and institutions, in conjunction with effective macroeconomic policies and competitive markets for factors and goods, has positive influence on the efficiency of overall investment allocation. Policies to promote financial development have helped to increase saving rates in the Asian LDCs, but much remains to be done.

Financial Markets and Financial Development

Financial development varies greatly within the Asian region. Hong Kong and Singapore have emerged as international financial centers in their own right. At the opposite extreme, some rural areas in South and Southeast Asia remain essentially nonmonetary economies, most transactions being made in kind. In between, there are mixes of formal financial institutions and informal curb markets, monetary and nonmonetary contracts and transactions, and private and public ownership of firms selling financial services.

The gap between interest rates in formal and informal credit markets is often astonishing.[12] Farmers owning large parcels of land may obtain loans to purchase tractors or mechanical harvesting equipment at rates of interest of 6 to 12 percent from commercial banks. In some cases, mechanization of planting and harvesting displaces labor and imposes greater social costs than benefits. Small farmers may borrow only small amounts from village moneylenders or in the case of tenants—their landlords. Working capital (for purchases of seed, fertilizer, feed) loans often carry interest rates of 50 percent or more in rural Asia. Market segmentation also occurs in urban areas and in the industrial sector. Large firms, in general, have access to relatively cheap credit from banks. Small- or medium-scale establishments are often rationed out of formal credit markets and must borrow funds in the curb market at interest rates of 20 to 30 percent or more. The segmentation of urban credit markets can hinder the expansion of relatively efficient labor-intensive firms and industries. Government policies have often increased segmentation and have exacerbated interest rate differences paid by various groups of borrowers.

In analyzing the policy issues associated with financial development, one should distinguish "organizational dualism" from policy-induced dualism.[13] The problem of organizational dualism is inherent to economically less developed societies. It will not disappear simply by eliminating government-caused price distortions. Fragmentation exists even within informal and formal financial markets—there are often large differences in interest rates offered various types of borrowers. Similarly, credit rationing by modern financial institutions occurs with or without government intervention in setting interest rates and allocating funds.[14] But government policies can speed the pace of financial development, or may cause increased fragmentation.

The informal sector often is more efficient and more equitable in mobilizing and allocating funds than is a highly repressed formal financial sector.[15] In the informal sector, interest rates are set by market forces; competition is usually substantial among lenders, as entry is unrestricted (except by poorly enforced government prohibitions). The informal sector provides a mechanism through which formal credit can be allocated to more efficient uses than it otherwise would have been. It plays a role complementary to that of the repressed formal sector. Attempts to abolish the informal market by law would reduce economic well-being and growth. A better approach would be to gradually absorb the informal sector into the regulated financial system through a process of liberalization and reform of the repressed system.

The extent of organizational dualism depends in part on the information and transactions costs faced by financial intermediaries. Formal institutional lenders, usually commercial banks, prefer to lend in fairly large amounts to the small number of established creditworthy big business firms. The administrative cost of such lending tends to be rather low; so is risk. Transactions costs of lending the same amount in small loans to many small and new firms would be substantially higher, even without the costs of assessing the creditworthiness of many small borrowers and the higher risk involved. Informal sector lenders must gradually acquire information about various small farms or businesses, and vary interest rates charged according to risk assessment, collateral offered, and the competition in lending that they face. Formal financial institutions may not find enough business to justify setting up branches in rural areas or small towns, and the total amount of deposits they can attract may be small, because of low income levels and absence of the "banking habit" in households engaged in small-scale farming or business.

Financial Deepening versus Financial Repression

Financial deepening, the growth of financial assets faster than the growth of nonfinancial assets, involves the monetization of an economy, the increasing use of financial intermediation by savers and investors, and the rise of specialized financial institutions (SFIs). Formal institutions gradually absorb or displace informal finance. Savings are increasingly held in financial forms rather than in nonfinancial assets.

A rough index of financial deepening, but the best available, is the ratio of money (defined as currency in circulation, demand, savings, and time deposits [M2]) to GDP. This ratio has been rising in most countries, but at uneven rates (table 3.3).

The Asian LDCs are still far behind the United States and Japan in the degree of financial development. Countries with higher levels and faster growth in the M2-to-GDP ratio tended also to have higher saving, investment, and real rates of economic growth. Between 1961 and 1984, financial deepening was most rapid in Taiwan. The M2-to-GDP ratios of Taiwan, Singapore, and Hong Kong exceeded 0.70 by the 1980s (table 3.3). The demand for money is strongly influenced by the real deposit rate of interest. Countries with negative real deposit rates had among the lowest M2-to-GDP ratios. In Pakistan and the Philippines negative real deposit rates were associated with stagnation or decline in the M2-to-GDP ratio.

Some government policies inhibit the growth of the financial sector. Government interventions that hold nominal interest rates down to low levels under inflationary conditions restrict demand for financial assets as real rates of return are low or even negative. Savers invest in real assets that provide some protection from inflation. Financial savings are discouraged; loanable funds are in short supply. The financial sector then remains "shallow." The real rate of growth of financial markets and the real size of the financial system relative to nonfinancial magnitudes are reduced by financial repression.[16] Financial in-

Table 3.3. Financial Deepening

	M2/GDP[a] (percentage)			Real Deposit Rate[b] (percentage)
	Average 1961–70	Average 1971–80	Average 1981–84	Average 1961–81
NICs				
Hong Kong	89.3[c]	85.7	112.4	1.8
Korea	19.0	33.7	37.8	1.0
Singapore	59.8[d]	61.7	70.6	2.8
Taiwan	34.1	58.1	79.9	4.1
ASEAN–4				
Indonesia	7.5[e]	16.1	19.3	− 35.4
Malaysia	29.4	44.2	59.9	3.0
Philippines	22.0	19.8	22.4	− 0.7
Thailand	26.0	35.8	46.0	2.6
South Asia				
Bangladesh	NA	19.9	23.4	1.5
Burma	27.6	23.3	32.9	1.0
India	24.0	31.2	43.9	− 1.1
Nepal	9.3[f]	16.6	26.8	− 0.9
Pakistan	49.5[e]	44.2	45.6	− 1.0
Sri Lanka	25.5	23.1	30.2	0.3

Sources: ADB, *Key Indicators of Developing Member Countries of ADB*, October 1985, various issues; IMF, *International Financial Statistics*, Yearbook 1985, various issues; ADB, *Domestic Resource Mobilization through Financial Development* 2, February 1984.

Note: NA = Not available.

[a]Currency and demand, savings and time deposits (M2) divided by GDP in current prices.

[b]The real deposit rate is represented by the continuously compounded nominal 12-month deposit rate of interest minus the expected rate of inflation (i.e., continuously compounded rate of change in GNP deflator).

[c]1965–70.   [d]1963–70.   [e]1966–70.   [f]1968–70.

stitutions, other than a few dominant banks, are unlikely to be very successful, if they are even established.

Financial repression aggravates financial dualism. The supply of loanable funds is smaller than demand (at the low or negative real interest rates); hence credit is ever more tightly rationed by commercial banks and other lending institutions. The banks' preference for low-risk lending, usually to large-scale enterprises with strong credit ratings or government backing, makes it difficult or impossible for smaller firms to obtain bank credit. They must go to informal markets or do without. Would-be entrepreneurs are not able to gain term financing sufficient to set up new businesses.

The structure of interest rates is one set of prices that is nowhere left entirely to the free play of market forces. Yet it is important to recognize an underlying equilibrium (or "natural") interest rate structure that would equate the supply of savings with the demand for loanable funds at the full capacity output in each developing country.

The practice of setting interest rate ceilings at levels far below those that are consistent with underlying market conditions has not been as widespread in Asia as it has in other less developed areas.[17] There are, however, few Asian LDCs that have not, at one time or another, been adversely affected by interest rate controls and selective credit policies. Below equilibrium interest rate ceilings reduce economic efficiency in a number of ways. Project selection becomes suboptimal, incentive is given to the selection of capital-intensive production processes, and disincentive to the selection of labor-intensive ones.

Controls on interest rates are usually accompanied by policies aimed at directing funds to government-determined "priority" sectors. High reserve requirements have often been used to channel funds into government coffers or to borrowers in priority sectors at lower interest rates than those faced by "non-priority" borrowers. High reserve requirements reduce bank profits and diminish the amount of discretionary lending through the financial system. As the size of the financial system is reduced, so is the amount and growth of financial saving. The extent of public sector involvement varies in Asia. Government's share of domestic credit appears to be negatively related to income levels. For example, in 1977, the public sector absorbed 70 percent of domestic credit in Bangladesh, 60 percent in Nepal, 48 percent in Pakistan, 42 percent in Sri Lanka, 20 percent in Thailand, and 13 percent in Korea. The countries with a higher share of private sector absorption of domestic credit also have tended to attain higher rates of economic growth in Asia.

Edward Shaw stresses that "financial repression has its typical complements in development strategy. It is part of a package."[18] The package generally includes an overvalued domestic currency, low or negative real interest rates, inflationary monetary-fiscal policies, artificially cheapened prices for food and industrial raw materials, imposition of minimum wage laws in the protected industrial sector, high tariffs on imported goods (other than imported inputs for protected industries), and high taxation of traditional exports. Shaw concludes that financial repression

> is an inferior strategy under the best of circumstances and a self-defeating strategy in the usual case: the excess demands or "gaps" that it generates on

some markets and the excess supplies that occur especially in markets for labor and for products of capital-intensive industry prove impossible to close at desired or acceptable growth rates of income and consumption.[19]

The case for financial development through liberalization of policies rests on the need for more financial saving and more efficient investment. Although the details of policy depend on the circumstances of each country, enough theory, practice, and evidence exist to arrive at policy implications for the Asian LDCs.

Financial Institutions and Development Experience

All of the Asian countries have over the past three decades expanded their financial sectors, and diversified the array of financial institutions. The rate of expansion of the financial sector has varied greatly across countries and subgroups. In almost all Asian countries, governments to a greater or lesser degree have intervened in the allocation of credit in the belief that market forces alone would not satisfy development priorities.

Interventions have almost always included the establishment of state-owned financial institutions. Some governments have gone as far as nationalizing private banks. Only in Hong Kong has intervention been confined to purely regulatory functions.

The financial policies adopted by governments have been very different. Since the 1960s in the NICs and Malaysia, government policies provided incentives to depositors. Inflation rates were low; interest rates were high enough to provide a positive real return on deposits. Financial institutions, public and private, grew and became more efficient. Investment increased in amount and quality as government policies encouraged term lending to industrial enterprises. In short, government interventions strengthened financial markets and helped promote financial development.

In other countries, government policies during the 1960s and 1970s often held interest rates at unrealistically low levels. There was less success in mobilizing savings deposits. Financial institutions were used to provide large established private business groups and the government with cheap credit. Shortages of funds and the preference of financial institutions for low-risk lending made it difficult for smaller or newer enterprises and farmers to obtain bank credit. Financial dualism worsened as government policies amounted to financial repression.

To correct this, governments set up new institutions. But a major shortcoming of these financial development efforts in most countries of South Asia and ASEAN-4 was the one-sided emphasis given to improving the financial sector's ability to disburse credit. Little attention was given to measures aimed at encouraging growth of private savings deposits. The NICs were exceptions; the experiences of Korea and Taiwan are particularly instructive.

Taiwan and Korea

Accelerated growth in Taiwan coincided with marked increases in household (personal) savings rates and with a steady rise in the ratio of domestic savings to GNP. Taiwan government officials placed great emphasis on controlling inflation. The experience of hyperinflation during the civil war on the Chinese mainland convinced the government that inflation had to be restrained. High interest rates were adopted in order to prevent inflation in the 1950s. The government of Taiwan, with some hesitation, broke with the generally accepted LDC policy of keeping interest rates low in order to encourage investment. Interest rates paid to savers and charged to borrowers were upped to levels far higher than elsewhere. The high interest rates had the then unexpected effect of speeding up capital accumulation and growth. As Scitovsky notes: "High deposit rates raised both the saving rate and the proportion of savings channelled into bank deposits, however, lending rates apparently were not high enough to reduce businessmen's demand for investible funds to below the rate at which funds became available."[20]

Financial development was not limited to urban areas in Taiwan. Rural households were encouraged to join saving schemes at the same time that farm credits were being made available through rural banks and cooperatives. When productivity and income gains took hold in agriculture, household savings rose remarkably. The financial system served effectively to encourage savings and allocate them efficiently. The strong incentives to save provided by positive real deposit interest rates were reinforced by favorable tax treatment of interest income.

Government intervention figured heavily in Korea's financial development. Korea lagged behind Taiwan partly because of the ravages of the Korean war, but partly because of its policies. In the 1950s, Korea's household saving rate was only slightly less than Taiwan's. The two nations' saving rates diverged sharply until September 1965. Then Korea's low interest rates on savings deposits were doubled. The result was, by the early 1970s, a sharp rise in the saving rate and a sevenfold rise in bank deposits.

As part of its strategy, the Korean government also established a number of SFIs. The government was the main owner of larger commercial banks; local banks and branches of foreign banks were in private hands.

Several features of the Korean government's role in the financial system stand out. First, the SFIs have been active in attracting savings, unlike their counterparts in some other Asian countries. Their funds, raised from deposits and sales of debentures, provide over 50 percent of loans. Emphasis on deposit taking favored their expansion. Second, private local banks were allowed to flourish, catering to the needs of local businesses. Local banking institutions have also been effective in attracting funds and in gaining a rising share of total deposits. Third, there has been an active policy to incorporate traditional lending and saving into modern institutions. As early as 1972, mutual savings and finance companies were set up to attract funds from informal money markets into the formal sector. These companies make small unsecured loans and discount bills for holders of installment savings accounts. They also operate mutual credit societies in the manner of the traditional rotating savings and credit associations, called *kyes* in Korea. Funds from small private savers are available as loanable funds for small private borrowers and are not monopolized by government. Hence, while the informal money markets continue to operate, an even greater number of small savers and borrowers are using the financial institutions. In the late 1970s, the formal sector of both Korea and Taiwan provided about 60 percent of total agricultural credit (table 3.4).

The Korean domestic saving rate remained substantially below that of Taiwan. From 1965 to 1981 the average difference was 10 percent. This large difference is mainly because Taiwan's private household saving rate was more than double that of Korea. The household saving rate (as a percentage of GNP) in Taiwan was 12.1 percent; in Korea it was only 5.4 percent. The explanation for this enormous gap is clearly related to Taiwan's consistent policy of keeping real interest rates on deposits positive. Korea, on the other hand, had large fluctuations in real interest rates, sometimes they were negative, sometimes positive.

Households save for various reasons, but essentially saving can be viewed as one among several alternative means of providing for one's old age. In Korea the wild fluctuations in deposit rates were a disincentive to changing the traditional reliance on one's children in favor of financial savings. In Taiwan, accumulating personal savings became a more cost-effective means of old-age security because of the steady positive returns.[21] High personal saving rates also make it possible for people to start their own business. In Taiwan the growth in the number of small- and medium-sized enterprises has been much higher than it has in Korea, where industry is dominated by large corporate conglomerates called *chaebol*. The rapid expansion of small manufacturing enterprises in Taiwan both in terms of number and contribution to manufacturing output is also related to financial policies. In Korea, the government directed concessional credits to already established firms—discouraging newcomers. Taiwan's system made credit available to small and large, new and established alike. The perception that it was feasible to start one's own business in Taiwan helps explain the higher personal saving rates as well. Scitovsky states: "Growth Taiwanese style kept business firms small and encouraged personal saving by

Table 3.4. Percentage Distribution of Agricultural Credit by Source

		Institutional Loans (IL)		Noninstitutional Loans
		Percentage of Farmers with IL	Percentage of Agricultural Credit	Percentage of Agricultural Credit
NICs				
Taiwan	1974	40	34	66
	1979	NA	65	35
Korea	1974	95	65	35
	1977	NA	59	41
ASEAN–4				
Indonesia	1979	NA	5	95
	1983	9	49	51
Malaysia	1974	2	NA	NA
	1979	NA	18	82
Philippines	1974	28	42	58
	1979	NA	61	39
	1981–82	25	29	71
	1983–84	8	13	87
Thailand	1974	7	8	92
	1981	NA	64	36
South Asia				
Bangladesh	1974	15	14	86
	1981	NA	15	85
India	1974	20	30	70
	1974–75	NA	33	67
	1981		61	39
Nepal	1974	NA	25	75
	1976–77	NA	43	57
Pakistan	1956	NA	29	71
	1970–71	5	40	60
Sri Lanka	1974	14	20	80
	1978–79	NA	22	78

Sources: World Bank, *Bank Policy on Agricultural Credit*, 1974, annex tables 2 and 3; Asian Productivity Organization, *Farm Credit Situation in Asia*, 1984, p. 19; International Labor Office, *Group-based Savings and Credit for the Rural Poor*, 1983, p. 106; A. K. Bandyopadhyay, *Economics of Agricultural Credit*, 1948, p. 121; R. J. G. Wells, "The Rural Credit Market in Peninsular Malaysia, December 1979, p. 20; S. L. Floro, "Credit Relations and Market Interlinkage in Philippine Agriculture," 1987, p. 209; O. Sacay et al., *Small Farmer Credit Dilemma*, 1985, pp. 6–8.

Notes: NA = Not available. All estimates of types of lenders are based on sample surveys except for India, where a national credit survey was available. Estimates of farmers getting institutional loans are usually nationwide, but some are from sample surveys; in a few cases they represent potential rather than actual borrowers in a given year.

the newly entering or about-to-enter small businessmen; growth Korean style discouraged new entrants and their savings and made it easy for established firms to grow without generating their own savings."[22]

The difference in domestic saving performance had significant macro-economic implications. The gap between investment and domestic saving in Korea (between 1965 and 1981 averaging almost 8 percent of GNP) had to be filled by foreign capital inflows (also see table 3.2), and an enormous foreign debt resulted. Taiwan avoided the accumulation of foreign debt and even had a small and growing capital surplus. Since the early 1980s, Korea has succeeded in controlling inflation. Savings deposits have been encouraged by consistently positive real returns. Consequently, by the mid-1980s, Korean domestic saving was sufficient to finance domestic investment (table 3.1), and thus to curtail the growth of foreign debt (see chapter 4). In 1983, in Korea the five major government-owned commercial banks were sold to private owners. The government reduced its involvement in bank operations in order to create a more competitive banking sector that would draw funds away from the unregulated financial markets.

Financial policies in the ASEAN-4 and South Asian countries have been supportive of development strategies based on import substitution industrialization. However, in the late 1970s, financial reforms accompanied efforts to promote more outward-looking development strategies in a growing number of Asian LDCs.

South Asia and ASEAN-4

At independence, the financial sectors in South Asia and ASEAN-4 were dominated by a small number of private commercial banks that provided finance mainly for commerce. Little was left for investment in agriculture or industry. Informal sources of credit provided most of the working capital for rural enterprises and manufacturing. The commercial banks were reluctant to lend in accordance with government development priorities. In particular, private banks were averse to making medium- or long-term loans to industrial enterprises. As a result, governments in South Asia nationalized existing commercial banks, and also set up new government-owned banks. Nationalization of commercial banks took place in the 1950s and 1960s in Nepal, Burma, Sri Lanka, and India; and in the 1970s in Pakistan and newly independent Bangladesh.

In the ASEAN-4, more private participation was permitted in banking and the nonbank financial institutions, though government-owned banks were also established. In Thailand, private commercial banks retained a dominant role in the financial sector. Private finance and securities companies proliferated in the 1960s and 1970s; but few new commercial bank licenses were granted.

Indonesia's financial sector came to be dominated by state-owned commercial banks and development finance institutions. The private banks in operation there mainly served the Chinese business communities in urban centers. The Philippines and Malaysia had an intermediate mix of private and government banks. In both ASEAN-4 and South Asia, more often than not, state-owned commercial banks operated unprofitably and contributed little to attracting savings or increasing capital formation.

State-owned institutions were viewed as a means to promote indigenous businesses and to attain other nationalist economic objectives in Southeast Asia. As Myrdal noted:

> The financial institutions created since independence in Asia are mostly state owned. Each country in the region has established a Central Bank to create an independent money and investment supply that can be regulated to serve its own development goals. But all countries have also expanded the private banking systems inherited from their colonial predecessors. In the whole region there has also been frequent government intervention in trading and commerce, with the establishment of state export-import institutions. This intrusion in commerce and business has often been motivated by prejudice against foreigners, particularly the Chinese and Indian middlemen who are present to some degree in all the Southeast Asian countries.[23]

In predominantly Muslim nations like Malaysia and Indonesia, religious beliefs prevent indigenous people from becoming moneylenders. Traditionally in Southeast Asia, Chinese and Indian businessmen have been the moneylenders. Protective laws and expansion of state-run rural banks have only partially replaced informal sector creditors. The relations between the Chinese and indigenous populations remain tense in parts of Southeast Asia but have improved considerably since the 1950s and 1960s in Thailand, the Philippines, and Indonesia. The particular role of the state in promoting indigenous economic control was greatly expanded in Malaysia under the New Economic Policy (NEP) during the 1970s and 1980s. The philosophy behind government involvement in finance and, more broadly, commerce and industry in South and Southeast Asia has strong nationalistic and redistributive elements. This contrasts with the growth-oriented motives for government intervention in the NICs, where such ethnic rivalries are minimal or nonexistent (except, perhaps in Singapore).[24] The establishment of a class of indigenous entrepreneurs in most Southeast Asian countries somewhat lessened this motive for expanded state control over the economy since the late 1970s.

The thrust toward rapid industrialization through import substitution led South and Southeast Asian governments to establish SFIs aimed at providing medium- and long-term credit to industrial firms, which were themselves often state-owned. Until the introduction of modern rice and wheat varieties in the middle to late 1960s, little was done to expand agricultural credit facilities. During the 1960s and 1970s, commercial banks were encouraged to expand by setting up numerous branches in rural towns and communities—somewhat indiscriminately and at high cost. They did, however, create a network: these banks were in a better position for lending to farmers and small-scale rural industrial firms than were other government institutions. The commercial banks were required to push out a large volume of small loans as quickly as possible to meet the requirements of farmers. But they had little experience or administrative skill in this area. Serious problems of loan recovery arose in most rural credit programs. As late as the mid-1970s, institutional credit seldom reached more than a fraction of rural households in South Asia and ASEAN-4 and generally provided only a small share of total agricultural credit (see table 3.4).

This is so even though throughout developing Asia since 1960 there has been a great increase in the number of depository offices. Table 3.5 shows that population per branch has fallen rapidly in both urban and rural areas. There is still much room for improving access, especially in rural areas of Nepal, Bangladesh, India, Sri Lanka, and Thailand. Successful rural development in Taiwan and Korea has been accompanied by greatly improved access of rural people to depository institutions.

Agricultural credit is by and large in the hands of the informal lenders. In the mid-1970s, about 80 percent of total agricultural credit came from non-institutional sources in South Asia and ASEAN-4, and only about 20 percent was accounted for by institutional sources. By the late 1970s and early 1980s, although moneylenders still provided more than half of total agricultural credit, Bangladesh, Nepal, and Sri Lanka experienced a slight increase in the proportion of agricultural borrowing from the formal sector. In Thailand and the Philippines, institutional credit provided a greater share of total credit, but the distribution of funds was concentrated in favor of large farmers. The reasons for the widespread preference for moneylenders over banking institutions as a source of credit can be traced to the rural borrower's distrust and dislike of institutions and bureaucratic procedures. The extensive paperwork and stiff collateral requirements of formal lenders contrasts with the convenience and personal touch of village moneylenders.

The policy emphasis in South Asia during the 1970s was on increasing the financial sector's capacity to disburse credit to activities given priority by planners. To spur investment and to provide inexpensive credit to government enterprises, interest rates were kept low. This depressed the rates of interest the banks could offer to depositors. Positive real deposit rates were rarely offered to savers in South Asia during the 1960s and 1970s. Chronic credit shortages arose; the

Table 3.5. Population per Depository Institution Branch (thousands)

	1961	1965	1970	1975	1980	1982
NICs						
Korea						
Urban	29.1	26.3	17.7	13.3	11.3	10.5
Rural	121.1	118.4	109.0	51.0	9.7	9.6
Total	63.4	54.4	35.1	21.8	10.5	10.1
Taiwan						
Urban	26.0	21.6	21.6	19.9	20.8	20.4
Rural	10.8	10.4	9.6	6.2	4.5	3.7
Total	15.0	14.5	14.2	11.2	10.0	9.2
Southeast Asia						
Thailand						
Urban	24.0	19.1	16.7	15.4	12.9	12.5
Rural	43.8	46.3	42.4	37.9	27.9	26.6
Total	39.7	39.1	35.2	31.5	23.9	22.9
South Asia						
Bangladesh						
Urban	NA	NA	NA	8.5	10.2	8.0
Rural	NA	NA	NA	98.4	30.8	27.5
Total	NA	NA	NA	50.0	23.5	20.7
India						
Urban	18.5	17.5	14.3	9.7	8.4	8.4
Rural	484.1	415.8	114.9	64.6	31.3	25.1
Total	87.4	78.7	48.2	29.5	19.5	17.2
Nepal						
Urban	23.2	25.5	12.7	13.1	10.3	10.1
Rural	919.5	521.2	233.4	141.5	79.4	68.8
Total	412.9	310.9	139.4	98.7	59.3	52.7
Sri Lanka						
Urban	31.9	21.1	14.6	10.7	7.2	6.5
Rural	8,284.3	1,119.2	108.2	16.1	16.1	38.5
Total	171.8	98.8	45.0	14.3	12.1	16.4

Source: ADB, *Domestic Resource Mobilization through Financial Development* 2, February 1984.
Note: NA = Not available.

private enterprise sector faced very strict credit rationing; public enterprise had the first claim on loanable funds. In addition, financial institutions gave only limited consideration to raising the efficiency of their own operations. Credit for new private businesses was rarely available through the banking system. A shallow system of finance evolved.

An Asian Development Bank study of financial development in four South Asian countries (Bangladesh, Nepal, Pakistan, and Sri Lanka) states:

> Except for spreading the network of bank branches in rural areas, little was done during most of the 1970s in any of these countries to enhance banks' capacity to attract deposits. Efforts to meet targets for agriculture and other mandatory types of loans were not matched by sustained efforts to promote the banking habit and to mobilize rural savings. . . . Banks were not under any pressure to compete for deposits. . . . Taken overall the performance of domestic commercial banks as mobilizers of savings has not been all that impressive.[25]

Sri Lanka allowed a number of foreign banks to set up branches in the late 1970s, and this created competition for deposits with domestic banks. As a result, a wider range of financial instruments and services became available, and the domestic saving rate began to increase.

Nonbank financial institutions are generally less developed in low-saving countries of South Asia than elsewhere in the region. Governments have established insurance companies, provident funds, savings banks, and related schemes; but their coverage is limited and their contribution to savings mobilization small. Similarly, stock exchanges and securities trading institutions that attract savings for private investment have remained small because of the thinness of markets, risks, and hence illiquidity of equity instruments and bonds.

Nearly all the deposits taken in by nonbank institutions go to the government coffers. Private savings are also diverted to the government through reserve requirements placed on deposits with the commercial banks. The government therefore ends up with control over most private savings in addition to its own revenues.

The governments of South Asian countries have in the 1980s proclaimed a change in development strategy in favor of greater private sector participation. Financial resources must be made available if private business is to play a larger role in economic development. Significant reforms will be needed to allow financial institutions to attract greater savings. Greater freedom in allocating funds and setting interest rates in accordance with market conditions will also be necessary for financial development in South Asia.

In the ASEAN-4, private banking and nonbanking financial institutions by the 1970s comprised significant shares of the financial sector. Government-operated provident funds are still limited in coverage, but they, and savings banks and securities exchanges, are more developed than in South Asia. The broad range and diversity of financial institutions contributed strongly to the growth of domestic savings.

The existence of private banks, other financial institutions, and securities markets in the ASEAN-4 provided some competition to the government financial institutions. Banks and other depository institutions aggressively have sought to increase savings deposits by offering a variety of financial instruments and, within the government-imposed interest rate restrictions, providing favorable incentives. Interest rate controls in the 1980s were relaxed in the Philippines and Indonesia (Malaysia generally pursued antiinflationary, pro-saving interest rate policies), but remained at restrictive levels in Thailand. Thailand's domestic saving rate declined from 22 percent in 1970 to only 19 percent in 1985. Government involvement in banking is minimal. Private banks were used more as a cheap source of loans for powerful business interests than as effective institutions for mobilizing private savings. Introducing more competition and providing positive real deposit and lending rates in the financial sector in Thailand and Indonesia have been advocated by the World Bank and the Asia Development Bank as a means of improving savings mobilization and investment allocation. The Philippines' financial sector, however, since the early 1980s has been hamstrung by bad loans and the loss of confidence by depositors. The negative macroeconomic environment created by external debt and internal political crises make it first necessary to consolidate and stabilize the financial sector there before renewed expansion can take place.

Singapore and Hong Kong

In Hong Kong and Singapore, the rapid growth of financial sector institutions from the 1960s to the early 1980s contributed enormously to mobilizing savings, and was a main cause of rapid economic growth. The divergent approaches—in Singapore with strong government control, in Hong Kong with near-complete absence of government regulation and intervention—demonstrate that there is no single path to follow.

No formal control on interest rates exists in Hong Kong, though the largest commercial banks are known to have an informal "interest rate cartel." Real deposit rates have been consistently maintained at positive levels in Singapore, less consistently in Hong Kong. In neither city-state have interest rate structures been seriously out of line with market conditions for long, as both wish to avoid capital flight. The macroeconomic environment in the city-states has been favorable to savers and investors. Financial deepening has accompanied outward-looking trade and industrial policies.

Both city-states are now significant exporters of financial services and expect rapid financial sector growth to be a major force in their future development. Singapore has enacted a universal provident fund scheme that has raised compulsory savings and allowed the government to undertake ambitious infrastructural development. In Singapore, compulsory contributions to the central provident fund did not deter private voluntary saving much: since the early 1970s,

Singapore's domestic saving rate has been the highest in Asia.

Financial development in Singapore and Hong Kong has been associated with strong foreign bank participation. Sound monetary management, particularly in Singapore, has held inflation down and enhanced the demand for financial assets. Malaysia, among the ASEAN-4 countries, has also had strong foreign bank participation and noninflationary monetary policy. It also has had high rates of saving and investment, and a stable and convertible currency.

Financial Sector Growth and Change

In Asian countries, the growing reach of the financial system during the 1970s and 1980s led to substitution of financial for nonfinancial forms of saving. Greater availability of facilities and more choice of financial instruments over the past two decades have been powerful stimuli to increased saving. Some of the changes include: (1) the spread of commercial bank offices, post office savings banks, cooperatives, credit unions, savings and loan associations, development banks, investment and unit trusts; (2) an increase in the volume and variety of financial assets available to savers; (3) a rise in the degree of monetization of the rural economy associated with the spread of commercial agriculture; and (4) greater access to credit from formal sector institutions.

This widening and deepening of the financial system allowed greater and more productive investment to occur. Financial intermediation increased greatly. The change is most noticeable with the household sector and with private business corporations. Government investment has also been routed through the financial system in Korea, India, and Sri Lanka, though the uses of funds have not always been efficient.

Increased financial intermediation leads to a virtuous cycle of higher saving, improved investment efficiency, and higher real economic growth.

Financial Liberalization: Policy Issues

The financial sectors of nearly all Asian countries face new stresses and new opportunities in the 1980s. There is more awareness among the governments that financial policy has a major effect on a country's ability to mobilize loanable funds, and hence domestic resources, and to allocate them effectively. Difficulties in collecting more government revenues through taxation, the slowdown in growth of foreign development assistance and commercial bank lending, and lower remittances from emigrant labor in the Middle East—all these make financial reform imperative. The case is much the same for countries with low saving rates and for those with domestic saving rates of 20 percent or more. More efficient financial intermediation can spur economic growth in both groups of countries.

The interrelationships between saving rates, financial intermediation, and economic growth have been topics of research conducted by the Asian Development Bank (ADB). The ADB's econometric study shows that higher real deposit rates of interest, economic growth, per capita real income, and improved terms of trade all increase the saving ratio in the Asian developing countries. A larger population dependency ratio reduces the saving ratio. Access of the population to depository branches also increases the saving rate.[26]

The positive effects of increased financial saving and intermediation on economic growth are found to result from improved efficiency, not just larger amounts of investment. Financial development reduces dualism and fragmentation in financial markets. It broadens the access of businessmen, farmers, and new entrepreneurs to funds.

Financial development policies are likely to succeed when they accompany reforms that reduce or eliminate price distortions in markets for foreign exchange, labor, and goods. Allocation of credit by financial intermediaries is then likely to facilitate investments in activities a country has comparative advantage in. Techniques are chosen that make use of relatively abundant local resources like labor. Broader access to loanable funds encourages about-to-enter entrepreneurs to launch new enterprises.

A number of modifications are needed to further develop the financial sector in the Asian LDCs. Greater freedom in setting interest rates and reforms in other operational aspects of the financial system are among the most pressing. Restrictive policies designed to place the lion's share of funds at the government's disposal (or to direct them to activities favored by planners) have impeded the financial system's development.

In rural areas of Asia that are now undergoing rapid change, improved access to financial institutions that are responsive to the particular requirements of rural communities (timely provision on a seasonal basis of credits for working capital) can help mobilize rural savings, raise farm productivity, and spur the creation of rural nonfarm businesses. In more remote or less developed rural communities, use of satellite offices, mobile banking units, or other arrangements requiring less overhead than a branch bank should be considered. Low-cost arrangements have proven effective in a number of developing countries. Establishing a complete network of rural banks that serve the needs of village communities in Asia involves far more than setting up bank offices or branches. To attract deposits, rural banks will have to provide security and convenience to small savers. Operational efficiency will have to be improved greatly if institutions are to replace informal credit arrangements. Timely lending to farmers without extensive red tape and delay is essential. Government policies will have to be modified so that rural banks can charge interest rates commensurate with the costs of their operations. High interest rates do not deter cultivators from borrowing as long as credit is available in sufficient amounts at the time it is demanded.

In the informal market, making a deposit often entitles one to receive credit when it is needed. With formal institutions, cumbersome loan approval processes are common. When institutions are able to make credit available on short notice and in adequate amounts, they bind customers and their savings to them.

Small savers in urban areas also are a potential source of greater savings. The informal services sector's credit needs, now met mainly by curb-market lenders, could likewise be served by financial institutions, were they to have sufficient flexibility in setting interest rates and other loan terms. Small savers are influenced by the size of the minimum deposit accepted, required minimum balance, ease of deposit and withdrawal procedures, charges for checking, and prizes or bonuses for opening deposits in varying amounts or of varying maturities. Attractions such as regular, periodic compounding of interest, conversion to negotiable certificates of deposit, access to charge accounts or overdraft privileges, and linking to insurance or annuities can also be important to more sophisticated customers.

The uniformity of instruments and practices imposed on branch offices often limits the freedom of local managers and discourages aggressive marketing and deposit seeking. Within reasonable guidelines, local managers could have greater latitude in deposit-taking incentives and marketing techniques. When interest rates and conditions on types of deposits are set by the government, initiatives by financial institutions are handicapped. Even when government or central bank control is not inhibiting, the absence of competition among private institutions leads to sluggish performance.

New savings instruments other than bank deposits are important for savers in higher income brackets, and to more educated, urban middle-income groups. Such savers are sensitive to yield and liquidity differences and are often willing to undertake risk to obtain higher expected yields. An increase in the supply and variety of financial assets like bonds, shares, debentures, mortgages, and certificates of deposit—all readily tradable in organized markets—could generate additional saving. In almost all of South Asia and ASEAN-4, such financial claims constitute a much smaller proportion of "money" than currency, time, and demand deposits.

In a number of Asian countries, a sizable fraction of private saving is in the form of contractual payments into provident, life insurance, or social security funds. Much of this contractual saving is used by governments to finance their expenditures. The motive for contractual saving is mainly risk coverage rather than yield maximization. It is likely in most countries that the contribution of contractual saving to overall financial saving could be expanded by broadening the coverage offered. The impact on the national saving rate depends on the extent to which contractual saving cuts into voluntary saving by newly covered groups. Evidence from several Asian countries indicates that compulsory saving can be increased without substantially reducing other private saving.[27]

An area of common concern in Asia is the supply of all types of credit to small- and medium-scale industrial firms (chapter 2). Financial institutions prefer to lend to larger industrial borrowers, since they provide a substantial amount of business at low administrative cost. Traditionally, bankers in Asia have viewed larger, established business houses as less likely to default than new, smaller establishments. Governments have therefore tried administrative measures to allocate credit to smaller-scale firms. But establishment of institutions catering to small- and medium-scale enterprises is by itself no solution: if lending to such borrowers is unprofitable, no administrative guidelines or new financial institutions will help much. If, on the other hand, such lending is made profitable (when the borrowing firms themselves become viable), then no new financial institutions are necessary. Technical and marketing assistance, and some equity participation, is where new institutions can help most.

An alternative approach, adopted in parts of India with some success, is the offer of guarantees on credit. A fee is paid for insurance cover; there is a ceiling on the liability of the guarantor, so this facility adds to the willingness of financial institutions to lend to small firms. The guarantees have in large part obviated the need for more new institutions to serve the small-scale industrial sector.

In South Asia the lack of private banking and other financial institutions has led to a complacent, noncompetitive financial system. With monopoly government banks come high operating costs, large margins between saving and borrowing rates, and costly bureaucratic procedures. Complacency means that technological advances in financial services are not adopted, and deposit mobilization is given low priority. Licenses for private financial firms and invitations to foreign banks to establish branches and provide technical assistance would improve the situation. Increased competition can produce long-term efficiency gains, encourage cost-effective operations, and stimulate efforts to attract deposits.

Government Resource Mobilization

How can governments through their budgets mobilize resources for development? Among the considerations are the ratio of tax revenue to GNP, the "buoyancy" or elasticity of tax revenues as income grows, and government saving.

We focus on government saving, which depends formally in the statistics on current and capital expenditure and the treatment of public enterprises. We measure government saving as the difference between current revenues and current expenditures (table 3.6). In the 1970s and 1980s a few countries in South Asia had chronic deficits. In others, surpluses in current budgets financed part of the public investment. The percentages financed varied considerably.

In the NICs, government current budget surpluses contributed to higher rates of domestic saving. In some countries the contribution of government saving to economic growth was blunted by inefficient investment: there were low rates of return and rising capital-output ratios (as in the Philippines).

The two main factors that depress the contribution of governments to domestic saving are pressures on politicians to increase current expenditures and the difficulties faced in raising tax and other revenues.

Table 3.6. Government Saving and Investment (percentages)

	Government Saving[a] as Percentage of GDP			Government Saving as Percentage of Government Investment		
	1970–75	1975–80	1980–85	1970–75	1975–80	1980–85
NICs						
Hong Kong	3.7	4.2	3.0	88.4	74.2	50.3
Korea	1.9	2.7	3.1	60.4	150.6	122.8
Singapore	7.1	7.3	11.0[b]	74.0	57.9	66.1[b]
Taiwan	6.2	6.4	3.1	105.9	89.6	80.8
ASEAN–4						
Indonesia	5.3	8.3	8.3	63.0	67.2	68.1
Malaysia	0.8	1.1	0.5	10.6	10.9	4.2
Philippines	1.9[c]	2.8	2.9[b]	101.7[c]	75.5	66.1[b]
Thailand	1.6	1.0	−0.0[b]	41.1	25.1	—
South Asia						
Bangladesh	0.0[d]	2.2	2.6	3.9[d]	25.0	21.1
Burma	−2.6[e]	2.6	4.5[b]	—	118.3	128.5[b]
India	0.6	0.1	−1.7[b]	8.9	1.1	—
Nepal	2.2	3.0	3.1[f]	43.4	39.4	29.0[f]
Pakistan	−0.5	−1.4	1.9[f]	—	—	—
Sri Lanka	−7.7	−1.6	−0.6	—	—	—

Sources: ADB, *Key Indicators of Developing Member Countries of ADB*, April 1986; IMF, *International Financial Statistics*, Yearbook 1986, May 1987.

Note: A dash indicates that the government runs a deficit or incurs dissaving.

[a]Government current revenue minus government current expenditure. A negative sign indicates government dissaving.

[b]1980–84.   [d]1973–75.   [f]1980–83.
[c]1972–75.   [e]1971–75.

Much of government expenditures on public goods like health, education, and the dispensation of justice are essential and complementary to physical investment for development. Still, there is evidence of government expenditures in Asian countries that subsidize the production or consumption of goods and services with little or no economic justification. Tighter controls against government waste, including the elimination of unnecessary subsidies and cutting back of low-priority expenditure programs, could do much toward generating additional budget savings in most South Asian and ASEAN-4 nations. The excellent overall saving performance of Taiwan is due, in part, to a tight fiscal policy that generated substantial government saving. By encouraging the flow of private savings to the banking system, noninflationary government finance therefore increases the importance of financial intermediaries and raises their earnings.

The obstacles to raising tax collections are many in countries with low income per capita, weak administrative systems, and social attitudes unconducive to compliance with tax laws. Nonetheless, much can be done to bridge the huge gap in performance between countries such as Singapore and Malaysia at one end of the spectrum and Nepal and Bangladesh at the other. In many Asian developing countries the tax system is overcomplex and cumbersome, and inelastic with respect to levels and changes in income. Indirect taxes, including taxes on international trade, are still the main source of government revenue in most of Asia.

Simplification of tax regulations could improve collection and compliance. Very much needed are the political will and the administrative and legal capacity to override vested interests and to halt the erosion of the tax base through evasion and corruption. The adoption of taxation measures that do not unduly penalize work effort and entrepreneurship, but that do levy charges on nonproductive activities and conspicuous wealth (e.g., urban real estate, private luxury automobiles) could enhance growth.

One kind of government performance not usually considered, but warranting close scrutiny, is public enterprise. Often state enterprises are a drain on government savings because of their pricing of services below costs, bureaucratic overstaffing, poor management, and nepotism and corruption. An International Monetary Fund (IMF) survey of 64 public enterprises in developing countries showed that the average rate of return before tax was negative 4.8 percent![28] In South Asia and ASEAN-4, government enterprises operate inefficiently, and require continual budgetary transfusions to stay afloat. The losses of public enterprises represent a serious wastage of potential saving in some Asian countries. The financing of government and quasi-government enterprises could often advantageously be shifted from budget to commercial channels, thereby forcing the question of whether the enterprise is able to pay its own way. A

market-based evaluation of costs and returns would encourage wiser investments and greater efforts to recover costs.

Conclusion

Government commitment to better domestic resource mobilization for growth
through financial development has increased throughout Asia. Since 1980,
programs of financial reform have been initiated in Sri Lanka, Bangladesh,
Indonesia, Thailand, the Philippines, and Korea. In some cases, liberalization
has meant greater scope for private banking and finance. For example, the
Bangladesh government has issued licenses for six private commercial banks,
and announced that two of the six nationalized commercial banks will be returned to their original shareholders, and 49 percent of the shares in the other
four will be offered to private investors. In Indonesia, interest rates have been
adjusted to reflect more accurately the market situation and scarcity of funds,
and to make financial institutions more competitive and efficient.

The excellent saving performances of the NICs, ASEAN-4 countries, and
India have been a major ingredient in raising the investment rate. More efficient
financial intermediation will be important in supporting further rapid growth
in Asia.

The need for improved efficiency in financial institutions is recognized and
is being acted upon in different ways by different countries. The outlook is for
greater reliance on market forces and private initiative. The emphasis on domestic saving is partly a reaction to harder external financial conditions and to
external debt problems.

4 External Financial Flows and External Debt

Introduction

Inflows of foreign capital can relax savings and foreign exchange constraints on development. Whether or not foreign capital infusions result in greater and more productive investment, higher economic growth, and improvements in general living standards depends largely on the internal policy environment and institutions of the country in question.[1]

There are few industrialized nations that have not in the past made substantial use of external finance. Net flows of capital into less developed countries unable to finance investment (and imports) from domestic savings (and exports) alone may increase economic welfare in capital surplus and deficit countries alike. In the former, returns on investment would be lower in the absence of foreign lending opportunities. In the latter, without external funds, some domestic resources would lie idle or would be used less effectively, and development programs would have to be cut. In Asia, additional real resources supplied through external financial inflows helped sustain economic growth rates during the 1970s, especially after the first oil crisis.

The colossal expansion of LDC foreign debt since the early 1970s and the eruption and spread of debt reschedulings in the early 1980s have rekindled debate on the role of foreign capital in economic development. Remarkably, the Asian developing countries avoided (with the exception of the Philippines) external debt crises in the first half of the 1980s. This was so despite the exposure of the trade-dependent Asian countries to the external shocks of the past decade. Their experiences indicate the positive role foreign capital can play in a country's development.

Since 1970, substantial current account deficits have been the rule in the developing Asian countries, except Taiwan. In 1976–78, temporary surpluses occurred in India and Malaysia (table 4.1), but except for Taiwan, deficits were incurred throughout the 1970–85 period by all countries. In almost all cases,

Table 4.1. Ratio of Current Account Balance to GNP (percentages)

	1970–75	1976–78	1979–82	1983–85
NICs				
Korea	−7.4	−1.2	−6.4	−1.6
Singapore	−18.0	−6.6	−9.9	−3.4
Taiwan	−0.7	4.3	1.2	12.2
ASEAN–4				
Indonesia	−2.0	−1.8	−0.7	−4.1
Malaysia	−3.3	2.9	−5.8	−6.6
Philippines	−1.1	−4.7	−6.1	−4.1
Thailand	−2.0	−4.6	−5.9	−5.6
South Asia				
Bangladesh[a]	−5.3[b]	−4.0	−5.1	−2.8
Burma[a]	−1.7	−2.7	−6.6	−4.0
India	−0.2	1.4	−1.1	−1.1[c]
Nepal[a]	NA	−0.2	−1.9	−5.3
Pakistan	−7.5[b]	−4.6	−3.5	−2.4
Sri Lanka	−2.5	−2.4	−11.3	−6.0

Sources: ADB, *Key Indicators of Developing Member Countries of ADB*, various issues; IMF, *International Financial Statistics*, Yearbooks 1986 and May 1987.
Note: NA = Not available.
[a]Ratio to GDP instead of GNP.
[b]1973–75 instead of 1970–75.
[c]1983–84 instead of 1983–85.

current account deficits were lower than overall deficits in the trade balance (goods and services) because of positive current transfers (only Singapore and Malaysia are exceptions). The deficit on current account was financed mainly by borrowing, except in Singapore, where direct foreign investment was exceptionally large.

Current account deficits in most Asian developing countries resulted in part from the large oil price shocks that occurred in 1973–74 and 1979–80.[2] There is also evidence that booming investment, particularly in the late 1970s, played a substantial role in explaining current account deficits.[3] In some cases (e.g., the Philippines), public expenditures grew much faster than revenues, and widening fiscal deficits were financed by foreign borrowing.

Foreign Capital, Investment, and Growth

External capital inflows can be used to augment domestic savings and so raise the investment rate; or to smooth out consumption and so avoid drastic changes in the well-being of a country's population; or to do some of both. As long as foreign capital inflows do not cause a reduction in overall savings and investment, they may contribute to economic development. In low-income countries, foreign assistance targeted specifically for consumption by the poor can be as productive as investment.[4] In most instances, foreign capital inflows are intended for investment purposes. To the extent that they entail an obligation to repay, foreign inflows must be used primarily to build up the productive capacity of an economy.

An inflow of foreign savings augments the total resources available to a country. The contribution foreign capital inflows ultimately make to economic growth and development, however, hinges on the relationship such inflows have with domestic savings and the quality of investment. Early planning models frequently neglected the potentially large negative impact that inflows of foreign savings could have on the domestic saving rate.[5] They also failed to consider the possible adverse impacts on the efficiency of investment.[6] In some cases, rapidly increasing foreign savings inflows appear to be associated with premature increases in the capital intensity of production and with declines in the output (value added) per unit of capital.[7] However, it is difficult to generalize, since in other cases, especially in Taiwan and Korea, foreign capital inflows seem to have bolstered savings, investment, and growth.[8]

The increases in the investment rate that occurred in Asian developing countries during the 1970s coincide with increases in foreign savings in most cases. Taiwan had a surplus of domestic savings over investment during most years (corresponding to its current account surpluses). The rise in the saving rate relative to the investment ratio there and in Hong Kong reflect the transition these economies have made from dependence on foreign capital to self-sustained growth.

In the oil-exporting ASEAN-4 countries, Malaysia and Indonesia, foreign savings declined in importance (relative to domestic savings) during the years of high oil prices (and therefore, high domestic savings). But in the early 1980s, foreign savings rose sharply as domestic savings were insufficient to finance investment. In the other ASEAN-4 countries and South Asia, increased foreign inflows undoubtedly allowed investment to be higher than it otherwise would have been.

The impact of various types of foreign financial inflows on domestic saving, capital formation, and long-term economic development can be quite different. There is considerable heterogeneity in types of external finance. Despite the fungibility of finance, various types of inflows are not perfect substitutes for one another. For example, inflows of foreign economic assistance are usually tied to specific projects and imports of specific goods and services. Direct foreign investment is thought to have much different effects on long-term economic development than do borrowings from capital markets (bond issues and syndicated commercial bank loans).[9] The terms and conditions of loans from different sources vary substantially, and therefore, where a country gets its funds may have significant effects on the cost of servicing its external debts.

The composition of external finance, of course, varies according to each country's specific circumstances and changes over time. In the following section, the composition and trends of external financial flows of the Asian developing countries are examined.

Composition and Trends in External Financial Flows

External financial flows by type are summarized in table 4.2. IMF data from the balance-of-payments accounts of the Asian LDCs allow some disaggregation of capital flows.

Total net flows (table 4.2) are defined as *minus* the trade deficit or, conversely, the sum of unrequited transfers, direct and portfolio investment, other long-term capital, other short-term capital, errors and omissions, exceptional financing, counterpart items, liabilities constituting foreign authorities reserves, and changes in reserves.

For the Asian developing countries as a whole, net capital flows were relatively high during the periods coinciding with the first and second oil shocks, 1973–75 and 1979–82, but relatively low during 1976–78 and 1983–85. The patterns differ between countries, however. For example, Thailand and the Philippines had large increases in capital movements and net inflows in 1976–78, as did Indonesia (see table 4.A1). These inflows correspond to the higher domestic investment rates that these ASEAN countries had during the late 1970s. For the South Asian countries, inflows increased most during 1979–82.

The composition of the capital inflows changed, particularly after 1979. Most notable is the jump in the size of short-term capital between 1979 and 1982.

Long-term capital (more than one year maturities) was the most important type of external finance for the Asian LDCs. Unrequited transfers, direct investments, and official transfers were next in size, respectively. However, unrequited transfers have exceeded long-term capital in South Asia. In Singapore, direct investment and short-term borrowings were more important than long-term capital or transfers.

Long-term capital as defined in table 4.2 covers a wide range of debt-financing instruments from various sources (official and private) and under differing terms and conditions (concessional and commercial). Short-term capital includes trade finance and accommodating finance. Major differences in the composition of external finance between the subgroups are in the relative size of direct and portfolio investment and short-term borrowings. Direct and portfolio investment tends to be much smaller in South Asia than it is in the NICs or

Table 4.2. Total Net Capital Flows and Net Investment Income by Recipient Group and Type (annual averages, US$ millions)

		Net Capital Flows					Net Investment Income	
Group	Period	Total Net Flow[a]	Unrequited Transfers	Direct and Portfolio Investment[b]	Other Long-Term Capital[c]	Other Short-Term Capital	Direct Investment Income[d]	Other Investment Income
13 Asian LDCs	1973–75[e]	7,049	2,368	1,454	3,280	927	−1,610	−650
	1976–78	5,441	3,540	1,923	6,394	−60	−2,514	−1,236
	1979–82	22,915	7,847	3,838	11,444	4,203	−4,591	−4,040
	1983–85	20,681	9,290	4,736	12,574	917	−5,284	−7,172
Three NICs[f]	1970–72	1,157	180	231	442	244	−13	−70
	1973–75	2,680	192	675	1,298	751	−102	−298
	1976–78	254	301	838	1,853	−806	−128	−689
	1979–82	5,161	271	1,280	3,984	3,175	−195	−2,640
	1983–85	−4,744	229	1,916	1,189	−1,129	−247	−2,270
ASEAN-4	1970–72	828	199	277	522	289	−422	−36
	1973–75	1,540	434	776	983	102	−1,510	33
	1976–78	2,599	352	1,070	2,711	786	−2,382	−215
	1979–82	6,669	685	2,434	5,169	1,044	−4,379	−1,287
	1983–85	9,484	742	2,914	6,437	−401	−4,992	−4,057
South Asia	1973–75[e]	2,828	1,743	3	999	73	3	−385
	1976–78	2,588	2,887	15	1,830	−40	−5	−332
	1979–82	11,086	6,892	124	2,291	−15	−17	−113
	1983–84	11,906	8,254	87	3,662	600	−31	−914

Sources: IMF, *International Financial Statistics*, Yearbooks 1979 and 1980; various monthlies; IMF *Balance of Payments Statistics Yearbook*, various years; Republic of China, CBC, *Balance of Payments, Taiwan District, Republic of China*, 1958–82 summary various monthlies.

[a]The total net flow is defined as minus the balance of trade (merchandise and other goods, services, and income) and equal to the sum of the components listed plus the following: net errors and omissions, counterpart items, exceptional financing, liabilities constituting foreign authorities' reserves, and total change in reserves.

[b]For 1970–72, direct investment only.

[c]For 1971–72, includes portfolio investment. For 1970, portfolio investment is not available.

[d]Data not available for Singapore, Burma, and India; aggregates exclude these countries.

[e]Excludes Nepal.　　[f]Korea, Singapore, and Taiwan.

93

ASEAN-4 countries. Short-term borrowings exhibit no clear pattern between subgroups, except for the previously mentioned bulge in the relative share of short-term borrowings during 1979–82. Short-term capital was large in earlier years in two heavily indebted countries—the Philippines and Korea—and in Thailand (1976–78) and became higher in India and Pakistan after 1982.

Investment income flows in table 4.2 include interest and dividend payments and receipts on debt and equity, but exclude amortization payments. A negative sign indicates negative investment income or a net outflow. The investment outflows for Asian LDCs increased on average, becoming more than half the size of the net capital flow during 1976–78 and again in 1983–85. Until 1983–85, the majority of this income was that earned by foreign investors from direct investment in the Asian countries. However, because of rising debt repayments made by Korea and the ASEAN-4 countries, the outflow of "other investment income" has risen rapidly, exceeding outflows of direct investment income by a substantial margin in 1983–85. Thus a smaller portion of net capital inflows has been available for purposes of increasing domestic investment in recent years. Taiwan is an exception. By 1983–85, it had positive net investment income, in addition to its substantial current account surplus. India in 1979–82 and Nepal in 1976–85 also had positive investment income, but both had substantial current account deficits. These two countries had relatively light interest payments to make on the borrowings they undertook in the 1970s.

Flows by Source

The OECD provides data on external financial flows to less developed countries by source: private and official. The OECD data also permit a breakdown of official financial flows from bilateral and multilateral sources. From the OECD data, it can be seen that total external financial flows to Asian LDCs rose substantially during 1970–78 though at a lower rate of growth than those for all developing countries (tables 4.3 and 4.A2). From 1979 to 1982, the period coinciding with the second oil shock, inflows to Asia grew faster than did inflows to all developing countries. And in 1983–85, total inflows fell less in Asia than elsewhere. The real value of financial flows increased greatly through 1979–82 even though the dollars were eroded by inflation. The sources of external financial flows to Asia, however, changed drastically. The share of official flows (divided between bilateral and multilateral sources) declined in 1979–82, even though a sharp decline in the share of bilateral assistance was partially offset by a large increase in multilateral assistance. Private flows, especially commercial bank lending, increased much faster than official flows in this period.

The share of official flows in Asian developing countries declined from over 70 percent of total inflows in 1973–78 to only a little over 60 percent in 1979–82, but rebounded to 68 percent in 1983–85. Private inflows increased as a share of total inflows in Asia between 1973–75 and 1979–82, but fell back in 1983–85. The relative importance of private inflows rose steadily in the NICs, but fluctuated more in ASEAN-4 and South Asia.

The share of multilateral flows increased more steadily than the share of private flows as a whole. The fastest growing components of multilateral flows were those of the ADB.[10] Lending from the ADB and World Bank continued to grow rapidly between 1980 and 1984. But in 1985 the growth of multilateral flows fell sharply.[11]

Since rapid increases in flows from multilateral sources helped offset a decline of Asian countries' share in bilateral official flows to less developed countries, a slowdown in future flows from multilateral sources could be damaging to the region and could lower its share in global aid flows. The ADB and the World Bank met strong resistance from some donor countries during capital-replenishment exercises in the early 1980s. Other multilateral agencies also faced constraints on their resources. The OPEC fund activities were severely affected by sharp declines in oil prices between 1982 and 1986. United Nations agencies and the IMF faced increasing demand on their limited funds from heavily indebted Latin American countries, and donor countries were reluctant to contribute more.

The Baker Plan, announced in Seoul in 1985, offered one positive sign that the donor countries were becoming more favorably disposed to increasing the resources of multilateral agencies. The difficult budgetary positions of the United States and a number of European countries may place obstacles in the way of increasing official flows. Japan and West Germany with their large balance-of-payments surpluses could step up their levels of assistance. On the demand side, the Asian countries themselves became less willing and less able to absorb new inflows in the mid-1980s. The alarming increases in the current account deficits of major borrowers like Malaysia, Indonesia, Thailand, and India in 1983–84 caused these countries to delay investment and cut government spending in the mid-1980s.

Within Asia, the distribution of flows between regions varied. The NICs' share of total inflows declined sharply during the first oil shock–recession period (1973–75), but rose afterward until a large decline in 1983–85. ASEAN-4 countries had a roughly constant share of total inflows, but then in 1983–85 had a sharp increase. South Asia's share rose and then gradually fell. The NICs had a very sharp decline in the share of official inflows for the period 1970–85. The shares of ASEAN-4 countries in official and private flows fluctuated considerably. South Asian countries had a sharp rise in their share of official flows in 1973–75, and throughout the period (1970–85) received over half of the official flows to Asia but only a small share of the private flows. Multi-

Table 4.3. Financial Flows from OECD, OPEC, and Multilateral Institutions (US$ millions)

Group	Period	Total Flows	Official Flows			Private Flows[a]			
			Subtotal	Bilateral	Multilateral	Subtotal	Direct Investment	Portfolio Investment	Export Credits
All LDCs	1970–72	16,326	NA	NA	NA	NA	NA	NA	NA
	1973–75	33,077	NA	NA	NA	NA	NA	NA	NA
	1976–78	59,577	28,774[b]	20,280[b]	8,494[b]	36,327[b]	10,704[b]	16,220[b]	9,402
	1979–82	88,193	42,116	29,408	12,709	46,077	13,298	23,191	9,588
	1983–85	69,655	43,787	28,104	15,684	25,868	9,014	13,065	3,367
14 Asian LDCs	1973–75	6,732[c]	4,814	3,363	1,451	1,918	NA	NA	NA
	1976–78	8,852	6,226	3,985	2,241	2,626	1,050	442	1,135
	1979–82	14,777	8,952	4,876	4,076	5,825	2,543	1,183	2,084
	1983–85	13,332	9,118	4,319	4,799	4,214	1,435	2,073	706
NICs	1970–72	1,087	621	493	128	466	NA	NA	NA
	1973–75	1,492[c]	805	542	263	687	NA	NA	NA
	1976–78	2,048	905	533	372	1,143	403	78	661
	1979–82	3,979	1,141	714	427	2,837	1,322	520	996
	1983–85	2,070	417	77	340	1,654	1,071	724	−142

ASEAN-4								
1970–72	1,194	837	726	111	356	NA	NA	NA
1973–75	2,513[c]	1,238	884	354	1,274	NA	NA	NA
1976–78	3,267	1,806	1,122	685	1,460	624	380	456
1979–82	5,509	2,898	1,516	1,382	2,611	1,120	622	869
1983–85	6,036	3,841	2,034	1,807	2,195	323	1,136	737
South Asia								
1973–75	2,727[c]	2,771	1,936	835	–44	NA	NA	NA
1976–78	3,537	3,515	2,330	1,184	23	23	–17	17
1979–82	5,289	4,913	2,646	2,267	376	101	41	219
1983–85	5,225	4,860	2,209	2,652	365	41	213	111

Sources: OECD, *Geographical Distribution of Financial Flows to Developing Countries*, 1976–79 through 1982–85 issues; ADB, *Key Indicators of Developing Member Countries of ADB*, April 1984, April 1985, and July 1986.

Note: NA = Not available.

[a]DAC countries only; no private flows were recorded from other countries or agencies.

[b]1977–78.

[c]Sum of components; does not add up to total given in source (1975 only).

lateral flows became particularly important to South Asian countries. In 1983–85, inflows from multilateral sources exceeded those from bilateral and private sources combined.

In Asia, as was the case in other developing regions, international capital market borrowings became increasingly important after the first oil shock of 1973. The main form these borrowings took was that of syndicated loans from commercial banks; bond issues also rose sharply. Most of these capital market borrowings went to the NICs and ASEAN-4 countries judged to be more credit-worthy than the low-income nations of South Asia.[12] The concentration of capital market borrowings in the NICs and ASEAN-4 is evident (table 4.4). Increased reliance on world capital markets worsened the debt-servicing burdens of these countries. Some South Asian countries that directly borrowed little from the capital markets experienced much less of a hardening of the average terms and conditions of their external debts.[13]

In South Asia and ASEAN-4, Malaysia is the only country to which multilateral flows grew more slowly than overall flows (table 4.A2). The ADB, as we have noted, had the highest rate of expansion of the multilateral agencies in funding Asian LDCs. Though ADB financing is not dominant, it did help maintain Asia's share in total official flows. ADB lending to India began only after 1985, and so ADB lending was more important for the other Asian LDCs, particularly in South Asia, than the total figures suggest. Among the NICs, only Korea showed faster growth in multilateral official flows than it did in total flows.

The pattern of external financial flows to South Asia during the 1970s conforms to their low levels of economic development and persistent poverty. Yet this pattern has begun to change. India borrowed small amounts from the capital markets through bond issues in the early 1970s (table 4.4). By the early 1980s, India, Sri Lanka, and Pakistan were active in borrowing from commercial sources. India and Sri Lanka issued bonds. Pakistan undertook short-term borrowing from foreign banks to shore up its foreign exchange reserves.

Concessional official development assistance (ODA) will have to continue to be the major source of funds, particularly for the poorest South Asian countries: Bangladesh, Nepal, and Burma. Since 1980, India and Sri Lanka have sharply increased the share of private sources in the external funds they receive. Of their total outstanding public and publicly guaranteed debt, the share owed to private sources by India rose from under 5 percent in 1970 to 9 percent in 1980 and to 20 percent in 1984.[14] Of Sri Lanka's outstanding debt, the percentage owed to private sources was 27 percent in 1984, and over half of that carried a variable interest rate.[15] Pakistan was careful to keep its share of debt owed to private sources low—since 1970, it has remained less than 10 percent.

There has been an overall hardening of terms on external financial inflows

Table 4.4. Concentration of Gross Borrowings in International Capital Markets

| | Amount (US$ millions) | | | | | | | | | Distribution (in percentages) | | |
| | Gross Borrowings | | | Eurocurrency Credits | | | Bonds | | | Gross Borrowings | | |
	1972–75	1976–80	1981–85	1972–75	1976–80	1981–85	1972–75	1976–80	1981–85	1972–75	1976–80	1981–85
NICs	*2,173.8*	*14,857.1*	*34,913.2*	*1,890.4*	*13,981.3*	*29,127.1*	*283.4*	*875.8*	*5,786.1*	*33.8*	*45.9*	*52.8*
Hong Kong	910.1	3,143.7	8,415.8	759.1	3,015.4	7,037.5	151.0	128.3	1,378.3	14.2	9.7	12.7
Korea	792.5	8,419.0	22,705.0	773.6	8,125.9	18,937.8	18.9	293.1	3,767.2	12.3	26.0	34.4
Singapore	93.5	1,109.5	2,006.1	—	729.9	1,650.5	93.5	379.6	355.6	1.5	3.4	3.0
Taiwan	377.7	2,184.9	1,786.3	357.7	2,110.1	1,501.3	20.0	74.8	285.0	5.9	6.7	2.7
ASEAN-4	*4,233.0*	*16,738.6*	*25,427.5*	*4,105.9*	*14,933.9*	*18,049.5*	*127.1*	*1,804.7*	*7,378.0*	*65.9*	*51.7*	*38.5*
Indonesia	2,322.1	4,264.7	6,987.9	2,304.6	4,052.0	6,112.6	17.5	212.7	875.3	36.1	13.2	10.6
Malaysia	543.1	3,014.1	11,518.4	500.7	2,668.8	6,673.9	42.4	345.3	4,844.5	8.5	9.3	17.4
Philippines	1,353.1	7,452.5	3,102.9	1,285.9	6,496.8	3,004.4	67.2	955.7	98.5	21.1	23.0	4.7
Thailand	14.7	2,007.3	3,818.3	14.7	1,716.3	2,258.6	0.0	291.0	1,559.7	0.2	6.2	5.8
South Asia	*20.0*	*778.3*	*5,730.4*	*17.5*	*748.3*	*4,894.8*	*2.5*	*30.0*	*835.6*	*0.3*	*2.4*	*8.7*
Bangladesh	0.0	0.0	0.0	0.0	0.0	0.0	0.0	0.0	0.0	0.0	0.0	0.0
Burma	0.0	132.5	13.3	0.0	132.5	13.3	0.0	0.0	0.0	0.0	0.4	—
India	12.5	263.7	4,157.1	10.0	233.7	3,332.8	2.5	30.0	824.3	0.2	0.8	6.3
Nepal	0.0	0.0	13.0	0.0	0.0	13.0	0.0	0.0	0.0	0.0	0.0	—
Pakistan	7.5	278.8	1,176.8	7.5	278.8	1,176.8	0.0	0.0	0.0	0.1	0.9	1.8
Sri Lanka	0.0	103.3	370.2	0.0	103.3	358.9	0.0	0.0	11.3	0.0	0.3	0.6

Source: OECD, *Financial Statistics Monthly*, April 1986, August 1984.
Notes: Only the published figures are shown, but these are likely to account for a major portion of such borrowings.
A dash represents a negligible amount.

to South Asia. One study estimates that the grant element of inflows into South Asia declined from about 66 percent in the early 1970s to 56 percent in the early 1980s.[16] The hardening of terms was more pronounced for India and Sri Lanka than it was for the other South Asian countries. India's share of soft loans from the World Bank International Development Association (IDA) had to be reduced.[17] India drew on IMF resources in order to adjust its balance of payments to the external shocks of the early 1980s. The policies it followed led to increases in domestic saving and a shift in the composition of capital inflows toward private credits. India has sought to augment its access to multilateral funding by requesting ADB loans. But ADB loans are not likely to offset completely the IDA reduction.

Despite these changes, average terms on outstanding debt in South Asia have remained favorable. South Asian countries will continue to rely on ODA, much of it concessional, for their financing needs through the remainder of the century.

The Asian countries' share of total flows from OECD, OPEC, and multilateral sources (public and private) declined from about 20 percent in 1973–75 to less than 15 percent in 1976–78 (table 4.3). But the Asian countries' share in total flows to developing countries from those sources has since risen to 17 percent. There was also a sharp increase in Asia's share in private flows from 7 percent in 1976–78·to 13 percent in 1979–82 and 17 percent in 1983–85.

This increased reliance on private inflows is most pronounced for the NICs, but was also important in ASEAN-4 countries. The trend is especially pronounced for Hong Kong and Singapore, but holds also for Malaysia. The inflows of private funds to Korea, the Philippines, Thailand, Malaysia, and Indonesia were associated with the accumulation of general obligation-type external debt, since private flows were mainly in the form of commercial bank lending rather than direct foreign investment. The rapid increase in private flows during the late 1970s and early 1980s was in part stimulated by government guarantees of the loans.

The spectacular growth during the late 1970s of commercial bank lending to developing countries, including some in Asia, was reversed after 1982. The size of new bank commitments to most Asian developing countries by private lenders fell after 1981, and fell sharply in 1983 and 1984. In the ASEAN-4 the share of official sources in total net flows increased to over 50 percent in 1983–84. The reluctance of private creditors to extend new credits (particularly to the Philippines) and the difficulties developing countries face in servicing commercial debt explain their shift back to greater reliance on official sources.

Flows by Country of Origin

Table 4.5 breaks down bilateral flows by major country of origin. First, Japan contributes relatively more to Asian developing countries than it

Table 4.5. Bilateral Financial Flows from DAC and OPEC Countries by Major Country/Group of Origin (annual averages, US$ millions)

Recipient Group	Period	Total Bilateral Receipts					Official Bilateral Receipts					Private Bilateral Receipts[a]			
		Total	Japan	U.S.	Other DAC	OPEC	Subtotal	Japan	U.S.	Other DAC	OPEC	Subtotal	Japan	U.S.	Other DAC
All LDCs	1977–78	56,607	6,742	11,267	32,736	5,863	20,280	1,737	4,184	8,497	5,863	36,327	5,005	7,083	24,238
	1979–82	75,485	6,964	18,899	42,183	7,438	29,408	2,575	5,518	13,877	7,438	46,077	4,389	13,382	28,306
	1983–85	53,972	8,169	13,773	28,301	3,727	28,104	2,933	7,221	14,223	3,727	25,868	5,237	6,553	14,078
14 Asian LDCs	1976–78	6,612	1,977	1,013	2,831	791	3,985	641	1,030	1,524	791	2,626	1,337	−17	1,307
	1979–82	10,701	3,427	2,482	4,576	216	4,876	1,403	1,012	2,246	216	5,825	2,024	1,471	2,330
	1983–85	8,533	3,671	1,281	3,652	−71	4,319	1,372	844	2,176	−71	4,214	2,299	437	1,477
NICs	1976–78	1,676	527	288	814	47	533	50	331	106	47	1,143	477	−42	708
	1979–82	3,552	983	1,174	1,378	17	714	109	446	143	17	2,838	874	728	1,236
	1983–85	1,730	1,146	−15	603	−4	77	−2	26	56	−4	1,654	1,147	−41	548
ASEAN-4	1976–78	2,582	1,206	410	907	59	1,122	357	354	351	59	1,460	849	56	556
	1979–82	4,127	1,862	876	1,347	42	1,516	727	160	586	42	2,611	1,135	716	760
	1983–85	4,229	1,938	823	1,449	19	2,034	893	369	754	19	2,195	1,045	454	696
South Asia	1976–78	2,353	244	314	1,110	685	2,330	234	345	1,067	685	23	11	−31	43
	1979–82	3,022	582	432	1,852	156	2,646	567	405	1,517	156	376	15	27	335
	1983–85	2,573	587	473	1,599	−87	2,209	481	449	1,366	−87	365	107	25	233

Source: OECD, *Geographical Distribution of Financial Flows to Developing Countries*, various issues.
[a] DAC only; no private flows received from OPEC.

does to all developing countries. On the other hand, the share of other Development Assistance Committee (DAC) countries in Asia is considerably lower than it is in all developing countries, U.S. shares being somewhat smaller in Asia than they are for developing countries as a whole. Thus in Asia, Japan and the United States account for over half of all flows.

This dominance is particularly strong in East and Southeast Asia. In the NICs and ASEAN-4 the combined share of Japan and the United States has generally been well over 60 percent. In the NICs the United States contributes a disproportionately large share of official flows (over 60 percent in 1976–82), while Japan and the other DAC countries account for relatively large shares of private flows. For the ASEAN countries, Japan has clearly been the most important source of funds, with a share of 45 percent. The other DAC countries combined account for about one-third of total flows. The U.S. share in total bilateral flows has been about one-fifth (1979–85).

The South Asian picture is quite different, other DAC countries contributing over 60 percent of total and official flows (1979–85) and over 80 percent of private flows (1976–82). Japan's share of all flows, about 17 percent, is about the same as the U.S. share of official flows (16 percent). OPEC countries provided a large share of official flows in 1976–78 (30 percent), but this contribution dwindled thereafter. Private flows have been at a very low level, and the United States actually received more private capital from these countries than it disbursed to them in 1976–78. Thus, while Japan and the United States are the major sources of financial flows for Asian developing countries, the other DAC countries are also very important sources, especially in South Asia and, to a lesser extent, in the ASEAN-4. Finally, it should be noted that if military aid and multilateral contributions were included in the figures, the U.S. shares would be much larger.

The Role of Foreign Aid

The explosive growth of private capital inflows that occurred in the late 1970s would not have been thought possible at the beginning of that decade. The rationale for ODA in economic development theory was for a long time the view that private capital would not be available in amounts needed to make meaningful progress. Debate hinged on whether or not aid itself contributes to development.

Myrdal, after noting how little foreign private capital was forthcoming for development in Asia, complained bitterly that bilateral economic assistance was misallocated by political considerations.[18] Multilateral lending under the guidance of international agencies was then argued to be a more appropriate mechanism for channeling external assistance. This view has also been challenged from both the political right and left.[19] The right has focused on the alleged wastefulness of foreign aid, and the left has claimed that aid is not in the interest of the poor and leads to excessive external control over national policymaking. Serious empirical studies of the relationship between foreign aid, savings, investment efficiency, and economic growth have had mixed results.[20] But there is strong evidence in Asia that foreign aid has been highly efficient in stimulating growth when it has been accompanied by appropriate economic policies in the countries concerned. Asian countries have made greater use of IMF facilities in the 1970s than have the Latin American nations. A major reason is that the Asian LDCs' macroeconomic policies were basically in conformity with IMF recommendations.[21] Hence, loss of sovereignty never became as big a political issue in Asia as it did in Latin America.

Foreign economic assistance includes those external capital inflows that are offered on concessional terms. Interest rates are below those charged on commercial loans, and longer grace and amortization periods are the rule. Pure foreign assistance could be envisioned as a grant that transfers resources without any obligation (repayment or otherwise). In reality, most foreign assistance creates an external debt that the recipient country will have to pay off. The grant element is the difference between the present value of the assistance and that of a commercial loan of the same amount. The real value of foreign assistance is often lowered by the attachment of conditions such as the tying of development loans to purchases of specific products from donor countries (even though prices may be lower elsewhere).

Even when it is readily admitted that the real value and the face value of foreign assistance loans diverge, that often foreign aid projects do not fully meet their objectives, and that some leakages of aid into wasteful activities are unavoidable, one is still impressed with the achievements aid has made possible in Asia.

Aid played a prominent role in the successful development of Taiwan and Korea. In the 1950s, American aid to Korea and Taiwan was substantial (reaching about 15 percent of GNP on average in Korea). Foreign assistance helped these newly independent nations to stabilize their economies, rebuild or add to physical and social infrastructure, and import inputs vital to getting their economies moving forward. Foreign aid was essential to the initiation of a process of noninflationary economic growth and an atmosphere conducive to the adoption of appropriate policies. Despite the low initial income levels in both countries, human resource development was stressed even in the early 1950s. By the 1960s these countries were able to redirect their economies from the export of primary goods to the export of labor-intensive manufactured goods. Though aid declined as a fraction of total investment in both countries, it still contributed by overcoming bottlenecks in manpower, infrastructure, technology, and foreign exchange availability. Foreign aid was also a positive force in helping to motivate domestic efforts to improve organizational and policymaking capabilities.

Taiwan had less dependence on foreign capital than Korea had during the 1970s because of its stronger domestic saving performance (see pp. 73–76). In sharp contrast to Taiwan, Korea's drive to industrialize in the 1970s was financed to a substantial extent by foreign borrowings. By the early 1970s, Taiwan was able to finance its imports and capital formation entirely out of exports and domestic savings. By the 1980s it had repaid the bulk of its external debt and became a capital exporter itself. Korea followed a different path than did Taiwan in the 1970s in terms of reliance on foreign capital. But by the mid-1980s, Korea was on its way to producing a surplus of exports over imports and gradually reducing the size of its external debt.

The outward-looking development strategies were turned to during the transition the NICs had to make from reliance on foreign aid to growth sustained by domestic savings. Export promotion policies were adopted in order to overcome foreign exchange scarcities and to ensure their ability to service debts. The phenomenal success of export promotion in labor-intensive manufacturing led to full employment, an egalitarian distribution of income, and higher domestic saving. Foreign aid played a catalytic role in pushing policies in the right direction and contributing a number of valuable resources to the development effort.[22]

The NICs in Asia are in the process of graduating from the ranks of the LDCs. The speed with which they changed from low-income preindustrial economies dependent on foreign capital to high-income modern economies with a capital surplus is unprecedented.

The NICs' successful economic development, their attainment of high growth and equitable income distribution, was facilitated in part by foreign aid. Internal efforts and policies were more successful than otherwise. The NICs, like Japan, have made the transition from capital deficit to capital surplus. Aid more than fulfilled expectations in these countries. In others there have been some disappointments, but also much success. Foreign aid has had a significant role in accelerating the development of the middle-income ASEAN-4 countries and the low-income nations of South Asia. In these countries, foreign aid is likely to be of continued importance until the next century.

In the countries of South and Southeast Asia, growth is limited by the inability to mobilize sufficient domestic resources for essential expenditures and new investments. A country can supplement its own resources by borrowing abroad, within the limits of its international creditworthiness. Efficient use of foreign borrowing can accelerate GNP growth if increased production exceeds interest plus amortizations. The capacity of low-income countries to efficiently absorb large increments of external resources is limited; but the capacity expands as experience is gained and administration improves.

Asia's strong growth is consistent with the view that financial resource inflows have been used relatively effectively. The emergence of "aid fatigue" is cause for concern, especially among the low-saving countries of South Asia. For much of the rest of Asia, the rising cost and diminished availability of commercial credit from the world's capital markets are hindrances to growth. The existence of a huge outstanding external debt clouds the prospects of some Asian countries for future development.

External Debt and Asia's Development

In 1986, the total external liabilities of the LDCs exceeded the staggering figure of $1000 billion. In many LDCs, the cost of servicing their accumulated external debts exceed new commitments to them. The ten largest borrowers among the LDCs in 1986 had over half of all outstanding public and publicly guaranteed debts. Though the bulk of the external debt is concentrated in relatively few countries, the problem of debt servicing burdens a large group in all regions: Latin America, Africa, and Asia. Between 1981 and 1986, 63 countries had to reschedule debt service payments. In 1982, a year of world recession, the near defaults by megadebtors Mexico, Brazil, and Argentina sent shock waves through world capital markets. The debt crisis began to abate in 1983–84 as there was some recovery in world production. But the amounts rescheduled rose to a record high of $93 billion in 1985 when the world economy again slowed.

In 1983, the Philippines asked for a rescheduling of a major portion of its estimated $25 billion of public or publicly guaranteed external debt, in the midst of a domestic economic and political crisis. But the Philippines is not the largest debtor in Asia: Korea holds that distinction. Though Korea has had no difficulty servicing its debt, other Asian countries including Indonesia, Malaysia, and Thailand that have also resorted heavily to foreign borrowings have experienced problems. In 1984, Korea, Indonesia, Malaysia, and Thailand ranked fourth, seventh, eleventh, and fourteenth in terms of the size of outstanding public and publicly guaranteed external debt. The ability of the ASEAN nations to meet their external payment obligations without sacrificing the pace of their development has been weakened by unfavorable external conditions, particularly falling commodity prices and protectionism in the more developed countries.

Increasing External Debt

The heavy buildup of debt following the first oil price shock is understandable if one examines the choices facing policymakers. Following the oil shock and recession of 1974–75, commercial banks were extremely liquid, economic growth and trade expansion were moderate, and the cost of

Table 4.6. Developing Regions: External Debt and Debt Service Ratio[a] (values in US$ billions; ratios in percentages)

	1979	1980	1981	1982	1983	1984	1985	1986	1987[b]	1988[b]
Total developing countries										
Total debt	533.4	633.9	745.5	849.6	898.4	946.8	1,009.1	1,094.9	1,183.8	1,222.9
Debt service ratio	14.1	12.9	16.2	19.5	18.9	20.1	20.5	22.4	20.7	20.0
Africa										
Total debt	84.8	97.0	107.0	122.2	130.8	133.2	140.0	156.3	169.8	175.3
Debt service ratio	15.3	15.2	18.0	22.1	24.3	26.8	28.7	30.2	27.0	29.9
Asia										
Total debt	114.4	137.8	157.6	184.2	204.2	216.7	243.6	272.3	300.1	313.9
Debt service ratio	9.4	8.7	10.0	11.9	11.4	12.1	12.9	13.0	11.2	10.6
Europe										
Total debt	81.0	93.6	102.0	106.8	107.4	112.0	127.1	138.2	146.3	149.3
Debt service ratio	18.2	20.0	24.0	25.2	23.6	25.0	27.2	26.7	24.7	24.2
Western Hemisphere										
Total debt	188.0	231.3	288.4	333.5	342.8	361.9	368.0	383.2	408.9	417.9
Debt service ratio	39.6	33.4	41.9	51.0	43.9	41.7	38.7	45.6	44.9	40.9

Source: IMF, *World Economic Outlook*, April 1987, pp. 180–81.
[a]Excludes debt owed to the IMF.
[b]Estimates.

funds appeared to be low: expected inflation rates were often higher than interest rates. Borrowing allowed many developing countries to maintain or accelerate investment programs despite the burdens imposed by higher oil prices.

A number of Asian countries, including those heavily dependent on imported oil, had benefited from the commodity boom of the early 1970s and were able to ride out the first oil shock and recession with little difficulty. Thailand and the Philippines had current account surpluses in 1974 despite the higher oil prices. These countries and Korea had a domestic investment boom in the middle-to-late 1970s until the early 1980s. During this period, Asia's external debt rose rapidly (table 4.6).

Following the first oil shock and recession in the mid-1970s, the external public and publicly guaranteed medium- and long-term debt of LDCs continued growing at a fast rate, especially from 1976 to 1979. Fairly healthy growth in world trade during these years (averaging about 6.5 percent per annum) helped allay fears of debt problems, though structural changes like reduced reliance on energy imports, increased exports of nontraditional products, and improvements in industrial competitiveness remained incomplete.

The second oil shock of 1979–80 upset the adjustment process. It quickly forced the more prosperous but unemployment-, deficit-, and inflation-ridden OECD nations toward austerity measures. The resulting recession, unlike that after the first oil shock, was prolonged and painful. Disinflationary monetary and incomes policies seemed necessary in many high-income countries. One result was difficult financial conditions in world capital markets: nominal interest rates rose to high levels and persisted despite gradual declines in the rate of inflation. There were unprecedently high real interest rates, and alarming rises in the debt-servicing burdens of oil-importing LDCs. Some of the larger oil-exporting LDCs (Mexico, Nigeria, Venezuela, and Indonesia) continued to expand borrowing for ambitious development programs, expecting continued increases in oil revenues.

Simultaneously, protectionist pressures in high-income countries increased as a result of severe unemployment and widespread business failures. World trade growth slowed in 1980 and virtually collapsed in 1981–82. The recession plus harsh financial conditions forced declines in export receipts and slower growth in LDCs. The severe recession and energy saving in OECD nations led to declining oil prices. Oil importers were helped, but large oil exporters, Mexico in particular, had serious adjustment problems. Many Latin American and African countries suffered declines in real GDP and exports promptly after the second oil price shock; Asian LDCs continued to grow. But in 1982, Asia was hard hit by recession: real GDP growth rates fell to half the average of 1973 to 1981.

Like the recession, the external debt crisis appeared in Asia after a time lag.

By 1982, debt problems had forced reschedulings for large debtor nations in Latin America and Eastern Europe. Commercial banks then tightened lending policies. The international financial institutions found their resources stretched; high-income donor countries were unwilling to increase support to them. Asia had its first real brush with the debt crisis through the Philippines. Compared with the other regions, Asia has fared better in terms of servicing its debts. The debt service ratio (debt service payments to exports) of Asian LDCs (11 percent) during the period 1979–86 was only about two-thirds of the average ratio of 18 percent for all LDCs (table 4.6). Latin American and Caribbean countries have the highest average debt service ratio (42 percent).

The continued debt buildup by Malaysia, the Philippines, Indonesia, and Thailand during the severe recession of the early 1980s was poorly timed. The Philippines crisis has heightened the awareness of the need to make efficient use of externally borrowed funds.

There are two sides to the debt crisis in the LDCs. On one side is the unexpected deterioration in external conditions: declines in external demand, sharp drops in commodity export prices, and tightening of lending terms and conditions. On the other side are delays in adjustment measures and inappropriate domestic economic policies in some countries.

The Philippine crisis resulted from both external and internal causes. The World Bank argues that external conditions created a difficult situation but that inappropriate government domestic and macroeconomic policies turned difficulty into crisis.[23] After a decade of rapid growth, the Philippines faced problems of long-term structural adjustment and short-term stabilization. The long-term problem was to shift the economy to a more open, outward-looking stance.

The old import substitution industrialization strategy could no longer be paid for by taxing exports of primary products. The Philippines needed to promote exports of labor-intensive manufactured goods to achieve sustained economic development. This in turn required liberalization of foreign trade, including relaxation of trade restrictions and lessening of tariff rates and their dispersion. A structural adjustment program funded by the World Bank was adopted, and policy reforms were begun in earnest in 1980 (and continued until 1982).

However, before structural changes could take place, the external environment became worse. The Philippine government in the late 1970s relied more and more on capital market borrowings to cover the savings and foreign exchange gaps. The fiscal deficits mounted, and the current account deficit rose in the late 1970s. Rather than cutting expenditures and so sacrificing some growth, to stabilize the economy, the government in the early 1980s gambled that export growth would pick up as occurred in the 1970s.

Between 1980 and 1982 the budget deficit went from 1.3 percent of GDP to

4.2 percent. The current account deficit rose at the same time from 5.8 percent of GDP to 8.0 percent. Expansionary fiscal policies were financed by external borrowing. The Philippine peso appreciated against the currencies of its major trading partners; this lessened the competitiveness of exports and increased the incentives to import. The government increased investment in poorly managed state enterprises. In the meantime, capital flight reached alarming proportions. Domestic savings were discouraged by low real interest rates and the overvalued peso. The external economic environment did not help; the terms of trade deteriorated for the Philippines. This made adjustment more difficult, but was secondary to the inappropriate macroeconomic policies in bringing about the crisis.

In response to the worsening external and internal deficits, the Philippine government reversed trade liberalization policies and restricted imports rather than abandon its inappropriate spending and exchange rate policies. Subsequently, with exports falling, and access to additional external finance dwindling, the government was forced to seek a rescheduling of its huge external debt in 1983.

Real GNP declined by over 5 percent in 1984 and by 3 percent in 1985. The growth rate of the Philippine economy declined steadily after 1978, despite the government's efforts to prop it up. The growth that was attained under the mismanaged macroeconomic policies proved to be short-lived and expensive. Living conditions for much of the population were worse in the mid-1980s than in the mid-1970s. Though the Philippines experienced positive growth in 1986 and 1987, per capita incomes were still below the 1980 level. The huge foreign debt burden will make it extremely difficult for the Philippines to restore high growth and improve the living conditions of the majority.

Debt-Servicing Capacity

Debt-servicing difficulties of the heavily indebted middle-income LDCs are a serious constraint on their growth. The problem varies from country to country, and there is a short-run problem of balance-of-payments adjustment and a long-run problem of structural adjustment. In Asia, most of the foreign debt incurred financed reasonably sound investments in develpment projects. But there could have been greater efficiency in resource allocation and more reliance on domestic resource mobilization.

Information on short-term and private nonguaranteed debt is scanty; thus most of the following discussion focuses on long-term public or publicly guaranteed private debt.

As was noted above, since 1970 the external debt of the Asian LDCs increased less rapidly than that for all LDCs, the growth of which averaged about 16 percent yearly from 1970 to 1984. The terms of new loans to Asian LDCs became harder though and differed sharply among countries and subgroups. The average real interest rates on new borrowings by the Asian NICs and ASEAN-4 countries in the 1980s were twice as high in 1981 as they were in 1970; the average grace and maturity periods decreased greatly. The number of fixed interest rate loans were fewer than the number of variable rate borrowings. The proportion of concessional loans in outstanding public debt fell to only 15 percent for the NICs and to 33 percent in the ASEAN-4; but remained close to 90 percent in South Asia.[24] The worsening of conditions for borrowers caused an increase in debt-servicing payments much faster than the increase in total external public debt in the NICs and Southeast Asian countries.

"Aid fatigue" in donor nations caused further difficulties. As was mentioned above, India has been especially burdened by this contraction and will have to seek commercial sources of loans as its soft loans from the World Bank are reduced. The collapse of export growth in the 1980s, increasing protection against manufacturing exports from Asia, and doubt about the sustainability of economic recovery have caused commercial lenders to be much more cautious about extending new credit or rolling over short-term trade credits.

Though accurate data on the exact size and composition of external debt are difficult to obtain, estimates of the total foreign debt, including short-term borrowings, are available and are used in the debt indicators presented in tables 4.7 and 4.8. Ratio analysis is widely used to compare the debt situation across countries and over time. The debt-service-to-export ratio does not constitute a comprehensive measure of a country's long-term capacity to service its debts, nor does it reflect whether that capacity is strengthening or weakening. A country may increase its GNP growth and, by switching its expenditures away from imports and tradable goods, raise export growth by even more. The debt-to-GNP ratio provides a more comprehensive measure of a country's solvency, but is not an adequate measure of debt-servicing capacity at any particular time. Measures like the ratio of debt service to exports and that of debt service to GNP have not been particularly reliable for predicting which countries will have to reschedule their debts or when they will do so. The ratios are best regarded as rough indicators of the comparative severity of the debt problem. Table 4.7 presents debt-service-to-export ratios for 1982–84.

The heavily indebted Latin American countries have very high debt-service-to-export ratios, usually well over 20 percent. These ratios indicate that the burden of debt servicing is heavier in Latin America than it is in most Asian LDCs.

In Asia, only Burma, the Philippines, and Thailand have comparably high debt service ratios. Among the other Asian countries, interest payments ratios are generally well below 20 percent of exports. Interest rate declines in world capital markets in the mid-1980s have reduced debt service burdens in these

Table 4.7. Major LDC Borrowers: Total External Debt and Debt Service Ratios[a]

	Total External Debt ($ US billions)			Debt Service Ratios (percentages)		
	1982	1983	1984	1982	1983	1984
Asia						
Burma	2.3	2.6	2.7	37.4	43.1	43.9
China	7.7	9.6	12.4	8.2	8.0	6.9
India	23.2	24.0	26.6	12.9	13.0	13.2
Indonesia	27.5	30.6	32.7	17.1	18.8	19.3
Korea	39.2	42.8	47.6	20.3	20.8	21.7
Malaysia	12.2	16.5	16.5	8.5	8.9	10.6
Philippines	22.2	22.2	23.0	42.3	34.8	30.1
Thailand	12.0	14.5	15.9	21.6	25.6	26.4
Latin America						
Argentina	38.7	41.0	44.3	56.2	57.4	46.7
Brazil	94.8	98.3	105.4	79.2	49.7	53.5
Chile	17.9	17.5	20.6	72.4	59.0	62.1
Colombia	10.9	11.7	12.0	29.3	36.4	30.7
Costa Rica	3.1	3.8	3.4	18.3	31.6	28.5
Ecuador	7.0	7.4	7.5	43.9	26.2	36.6
Mexico	90.8	93.2	94.7	51.9	52.0	43.8
Peru	12.0	12.9	13.5	44.5	31.6	28.5
Uruguay	2.7	2.9	3.1	20.1	27.4	33.4
Venezuela	32.1	31.1	28.7	30.0	29.8	23.4
Africa						
Algeria	19.4	17.9	18.4	33.7	38.1	37.5
Cameroon	2.8	3.0	3.2	22.6	21.5	23.0
Morocco	10.9	11.4	12.5	49.9	46.2	47.9
Nigeria	13.3	15.9	14.1	19.2	22.6	28.4
Sudan	5.8	6.3	6.0	26.0	25.0	26.8
Tunisia	4.6	1.9	5.3	21.2	26.2	31.6

Sources: IMF, *International Financial Statistics*, Yearbooks 1986 and May 1987; OECD, *Financing and External Debt of Developing Countries, 1985 Survey*, 1986.
[a]Includes short-term debt, but excludes IMF credit.

countries to the extent they have been able to restructure their debt. Loans carrying variable interest rates have also become less burdensome.

The ratios of external debt to GNP and debt service to GNP rose sharply from 1970 to 1984 among major borrowers in Latin America and Africa (table 4.8). In Asia, the debt-to-GNP ratio worsened in some countries (Malaysia, the Philippines, Korea, Thailand, Sri Lanka, Burma, Nepal, and Bangladesh),

Table 4.8 Developing Countries: Ratios of External Debt Outstanding and Debt Service to GNP
(period averages in percentages)

	External Debt Outstanding to GNP[a]			Debt Service to GNP		
	1970–72	1980–82	1983–85	1970–72	1980–82	1983–85
NICs						
Hong Kong	0.0	1.2	0.8	0.0	0.4	0.2
Korea	24.2	28.3	31.7	3.4	5.1	5.7
Singapore	9.2	10.7	9.7	0.9	1.9	2.7
Taiwan	10.6	12.0	10.0	2.6	2.9	3.5
ASEAN-4						
Indonesia	34.1	19.4	29.3	1.1	2.4	4.0
Malaysia	12.2	23.6	41.3	1.3	2.2	7.3
Philippines	9.3	20.5	36.2	1.5	2.2	3.7
Thailand	5.0	14.8	21.0	0.6	1.8	3.2
South Asia						
Bangladesh	1.2	29.7	38.9	NA	0.8	1.3
Burma	6.2	29.0	38.3	1.0	2.1	2.6
India	15.5	11.1	12.8	1.0	0.6	0.8
Nepal	0.8	10.5	18.1	0.1	0.2	0.4
Pakistan	35.2	30.9	30.8	1.7	1.9	3.1
Sri Lanka	19.3	37.6	44.6	2.2	2.4	3.5
Africa						
Algeria	21.4	37.3	25.8	1.6	9.7	9.0
Ivory Coast	22.0	59.9	88.1	3.1	12.1	11.3
Morocco	18.7	50.3	84.9	1.8	7.9	7.8
Nigeria	4.8	8.5	17.0	0.5	1.2	4.2
Sudan	15.8	57.2	73.3	2.0	1.5	1.4
Western Hemisphere						
Argentina	9.1	22.6	46.0	1.9	4.0	4.9
Brazil	8.8	17.4	33.5	1.0	3.5	3.7
Chile	23.1	18.7	63.3	2.1	5.0	6.9
Mexico	9.0	23.6	45.7	1.9	4.7	7.4
Venezuela	8.5	18.0	30.3	1.1	4.6	4.6

Sources: ADB, *Key Indicators of Developing Member Countries of ADB*, April 1983 and July 1986; World Bank, *World Debt Tables*, 1984–85, 1986–87.

Notes: NA = Not available.

[a] External debt outstanding refers to long and medium external public debt outstanding and disbursed.

but the ratio fell or remained stable in most of the NICs, India, Indonesia, and Pakistan. The debt-service-to-GNP ratio increased in all the Asian countries except India, but it remained below 3 percent except in Korea. The low debt-service-to-GNP ratios in Bangladesh, India, and Nepal reflect the large proportion of concessional loans in the total debt. Latin American and African borrowers must pay far larger parts of current GNP to service their debt than Asian countries do in the 1980s.

Much of Asia's borrowing has been highly productive since it mainly financed investments in domestic energy, agriculture, and industrialization. But throughout East and Southeast Asia, too large a share of the external borrowings from the mid-1970s on were used to finance construction and property developments in urban areas.[25] Construction activities were useful in absorbing labor and expanding local service industries, but property investment became excessively speculative. Rates of return on office buildings, hotels and luxury housing fell sharply with recession in the 1980s. Collapsing property prices and low earnings from building investments in the 1980s led to defaults on loan repayments that contributed to the collapse of financial institutions in the Philippines as well as to numerous banking and business failures in Hong Kong, Singapore, and Malaysia.

The unexpected deterioration in the price and volumes of commodity exports in the 1980s has compounded the difficulties of the ASEAN-4 in servicing their debts. Korea, however, has benefited. By boosting exports faster than imports, Korea achieved a current account surplus in the mid-1980s. Its capacity to service its debts was strengthened as well by a sharp fall in the cost of oil imports.

Capital flight on a large scale was another problem that contributed to debt crises in heavily indebted Latin American countries and the Philippines.[26] Borrowings from commercial banks were often not invested in the country guaranteeing repayment, but were transferred to private accounts elsewhere, used to purchase property or other assets in a more politically stable location. Exchange rate distortions (the overvaluing of the borrowing country's currency), hyperinflation (three digits), and lax government institutions motivated and contributed to capital flight as well. In the Philippines, capital flight occurred on a large scale at the same time that there was a buildup of guaranteed commercial bank debt. Public officials abused the system to circumvent exchange controls there. The business community progressively lost confidence in the economy, and large amounts of money were sent overseas in the early 1980s. Expectations of devaluation of the currency, increasing inflation, and uncertainty regarding the stability of the government all contributed to the loss of confidence. External borrowing was increasingly used to shore up loss-making enterprises; some of these were in the public sector and some were owned by businessmen friendly to the Marcos regime, the so-called "crony capitalists." This steadily eroded the efficiency of investment and contributed to economic decline. Elsewhere, for example in Korea, government-guaranteed borrowings were profitably invested, in most instances, and capital flight was prevented by strong government institutions and regulations. There was less motivation to send capital out of Asian countries where inflation was low, foreign exchange was realistically valued, and the domestic investment climate was favorable.

The rise in external debt and the increased burden of debt servicing have become important domestic political issues in Korea and Thailand before the onset of a true debt crisis. The strong public concern with external debt in Korea and Thailand is likely to force a slowdown in external borrowing, at least by the governments, during the late 1980s—even at the cost of somewhat slower economic growth. Governments in much of Asia responded to the increased burden of debt servicing by reducing domestic and government spending and raising taxes and encouraging domestic saving.

Domestic Policies and External Shocks

Debt-servicing problems arise when export earnings stagnate during recessions; but crisis situations arise mostly from inappropriate domestic policies. In Asia, most countries undertook domestic policy adjustments before crises appeared. Fiscal and monetary restraints, plus relaxation of trade restrictions, flexibility in wage setting, and realistic pricing of energy, food, and foreign exchange, have been hallmarks of the majority of Asian countries' macroeconomic policies.

The differential success Asian countries had in responding to the external shocks of the 1970s illustrates the importance of appropriate policies. World inflation, the two oil price hikes, and the two recessions in high-income countries were the external shocks between 1973 and 1982. Balance-of-payments effects for oil-importing Asian LDCs can be divided into two categories. In the first category are losses from terms-of-trade deterioration. These include higher import bills from higher oil prices and downward price inflexibility of foreign-manufactured and capital goods. In contrast, prices for Asian primary-commodity exports had downward flexibility. As chapter 2 indicates, these exports were especially significant for South Asian and ASEAN-4 countries. In the second category are losses because of world recession, mainly from falling export volume, as aggregate demand and incomes fell in the high-income nations. Interest rates rose to high levels in the early 1980s in the international capital markets. The developing countries that borrowed heavily from commercial banks with variable interest rate loans were hit by an "interest rate shock" that sent debt-servicing payments up at precisely the time that external trade accounts were deteriorating. We have not factored in the interest rate shock, but certainly it would show a large negative impact on most Asian countries that had substantial commercial borrowing in the early 1980s.

We have estimated the size of the external shocks in current dollars and as a proportion of GNP (table 4.9).[27] The net oil importers had an adverse shift in balance of payments averaging 17.5 percent of GNP from 1974 to 1982. The percentage effects are greater for the small, more open countries—Singapore, Hong Kong, and Sri Lanka—and less for larger or relatively closed economies—India and Burma. The positive effects for the two oil exporters are conspicuous, especially for Indonesia, which is more dependent on oil revenues than Malaysia.

The terms-of-trade effect on the balance of payments was generally larger than the export volume effect was, except for Taiwan, Hong Kong, and Pakistan (table 4.10); that is, oil price hikes had more severe consequences than did the world recessions for the balance of payments[28] of most of these countries. Since the two effects add up to 100 percent of the balance-of-payments impact of

Table 4.9. Size of External Shocks and the Ratio of External Shocks to GNP, Average of 1974–82

	External Shocks (US$ million)	Ratio of External Shocks to GNP (percentages)
NICs	*− 2,833.7*	*− 24.8*
Hong Kong	− 2,800.1	− 26.7
Korea	− 3,668.2	− 13.3
Singapore	− 2,506.1	− 46.3
Taiwan	− 2,360.4	− 12.7
ASEAN–4	*− 2,462.9*	*− 14.9*
Indonesia	7,740.9	23.6
Malaysia	696.9	6.4
Philippines	− 2,531.8	− 14.5
Thailand	− 2,394.0	− 15.2
South Asia	*− 1,885.2*	*− 14.2*
Burma	− 50.8	− 1.8
India	− 3,808.7	− 4.6
Pakistan	− 3,152.9	− 26.8
Sri Lanka	− 528.5	− 23.5

Sources: IMF, *International Financial Statistics*, various issues; IMF, *Balance of Payments Statistics Yearbook*, various issues; United Nations, *Yearbook of International Trade Statistics*, various issues; ADB, *Key Indicators of Developing Member Countries of ADB*, various issues.

Note: For ASEAN–4 the average shown is for the Philippines and Thailand only.

external shocks, roughly three-fourths to four-fifths of the effects are from terms-of-trade losses, and the rest are from export volume declines.

Adjustment to External Shocks

Table 4.10 sets out four types of economic adjustment to external shocks (see columns 4 through 8).[29] One possible adjustment response is for a country to export more to pay for its higher import bill—and to do this, it is necessary to increase its share of world export markets by successfully competing against other producers in established markets or by expanding new exports and finding new trade partners. It is significant that an increase in export market shares was the predominant form of adjustment response by Taiwan and Korea (see column 4 of table 4.10). They were so successful in expanding exports that the additional export earnings outweighed the external shocks (additional earnings exceeded 100 percent)! Hong Kong and Singapore were also successful in boosting export market shares, but they were unable to offset the external shocks completely.

Export market shares of the two oil-importing ASEAN countries, Thailand and the Philippines, increased by a smaller proportion. Thailand's export market share went up by more than did that of the Philippines. Export shares of South Asian countries (and competitiveness) actually declined, save for India's modest increase.

Import substitution, a second type of response to external shocks, was generally smaller than export promotion (column 5, table 4.10). Taiwan and Korea were able to replace imports with domestic production even as they were expanding exports. In Hong Kong and Singapore, import substitution was negative. In Thailand and the Philippines, import substitution was minor. In South Asia, the countries most associated with import substitution industrialization policies (Burma, India, Pakistan) registered fairly low or even negative values. In Sri Lanka, import substitution was a substantial response.[30]

The comparatively low values for import substitution may indicate that by the mid-1970s the scope for further cutting imports by substituting domestic production was limited. Remaining imports were mainly essential supplies and equipment not available domestically. The financial constraints caused by external shocks may also have hindered import substitution by limiting investment in capital goods and other import-competing industries.

A third means of adjustment to external shocks was to slow growth in real GNP by lowering aggregate demand. With any given income elasticity of import demand, a fall in aggregate demand implies a fall in import expenditure. This belt-tightening type of adjustment could not be entirely avoided by most oil-importing countries, or even by the oil exporters during recession years. The moderation of average real GNP growth below trend values was a signif-

Table 4.10. External Shocks and Adjustments (percentages)

	Effect on Balance of Payments			Direct Adjustment				
	Terms of Trade	Export Volume	Total External Shocks	Export Market Penetration	Import Substitution	Import Reduction through Lower GNP Growth	Total[a]	Net External Finance
NICs								
Hong Kong	-35.6	-64.4	100.0	85.2	-2.2	13.6	96.6	3.4
Korea	-83.2	-16.8	100.0	104.5	17.1	4.6	126.2	-26.2
Singapore	-98.1	-1.9	100.0	67.0	-41.8	17.5	42.7	57.2
Taiwan	-43.8	-56.2	100.0	132.9	16.3	13.5	162.7	-62.7
ASEAN-4								
Indonesia	83.6	16.4	100.0	2.3	-1.1	0.5	1.7	-101.7
Malaysia	71.6	28.4	100.0	39.9	-25.4	4.3	18.8	-118.8
Philippines	-75.1	-24.9	100.0	17.5	2.3	-2.6	17.2	82.9
Thailand	-90.1	-9.9	100.0	25.5	8.6	2.6	36.7	63.4
South Asia								
Burma	-158.5	58.5	100.0	-153.9	-0.8	111.4	-43.3	143.3
India	-72.8	-27.2	100.0	8.3	-2.3	2.2	8.2	91.9
Pakistan	-46.7	-53.3	100.0	-8.1	0.8	-5.6	-12.9	112.9
Sri Lanka	-76.5	-23.5	100.0	-8.6	14.8	-17.5	-11.3	111.3

Sources: IMF, *International Financial Statistics*, various issues; IMF, *Balance of Payments Statistics Yearbook*, various issues; United Nations, *Yearbook of International Trade Statistics*, various issues; ADB, *Key Indicators of Developing Member Countries of ADB*, various issues.

Notes: Figures are averages of 1974–82.

[a]Direct adjustment total = export market penetration + import substitution + import reduction through lower GNP growth.

icant form of adjustment in three of the NICs (Hong Kong, Singapore, and Taiwan), though it was less so for Korea as well as Thailand and India. The Philippines adopted overly expansionary policies, as is indicated by the negative coefficient in column 6 of the table.

In Sri Lanka, higher growth occurred despite balance-of-payments deficits. For other countries the change was small. Burma cut imports by reducing growth by more than enough to offset the shocks—but the size of shocks there was small (table 4.9).

The extent of these adjustments—a combination of increased export market shares, import substitution, import savings through lower growth—indicates the extent to which each country resorted to borrowing. Net external financing (column 8 in table 4.10) is the difference between the external shocks and the direct adjustments to the shocks. The resource gap between imports and exports created by the external shocks and not offset by direct adjustments must be filled by additional net financial inflows.

Korea and Taiwan (like Malaysia and Indonesia) were net creditors in the residual resource gap measure.[31] All the other countries, save Hong Kong, relied in significant degree on added net external finance.

The last type of response among oil importers was smallest for the NICs, ranging from high negative values for Taiwan (-63 percent) to a fairly high positive value ($+57$ percent) for Singapore. Additional net external finance was important for the Philippines and Thailand, being substantially larger in the Philippines (83 versus 63 percent). In South Asia, net financial inflow actually exceeded 100 percent of the external shocks in three of the four countries and was by far the predominant mode of adjustment.

Although the NICs were most vulnerable to external shocks, they adjusted more readily and outperformed all other countries. The Asian NICs are more dependent on imported oil and have much higher reliance on international trade than most other developing countries. However, the outward-looking development strategies they had adopted in the 1960s prepared these countries to meet the 1970s external shocks by increasing their exports. They grew faster than inward-looking countries more insulated from the shocks, like those in South Asia.

Oil Exporters' Adjustment

For the net oil exporters, Indonesia and Malaysia, the challenge posed by external shocks was quite different from that confronting oil-importing countries. They did not face trade-offs as harsh as those facing the oil importers, but still had to make difficult decisions.

Malaysia and Indonesia were helped by better (oil dominated) terms of trade and injured by (recession induced) export volume declines. The first influence dominated: there was an improvement and often a surplus in the net balance-of-trade accounts of these two countries (see tables 4.9 and 4.10, column 8). Both countries still expanded external borrowing to support larger current government outlays and to finance more imports, and larger infrastructure and other investment programs. The external debt of Indonesia and Malaysia expanded, especially after the second oil shock of 1979. As the oil boom increased the earning power of the two oil-exporters, their international credit standing improved. But better international credit standing is not a panacea. Unless external funds are used efficiently, the long-run effect of higher oil earnings is not favorable. The impact of oil exports on the production of nonoil tradables, through appreciation of the real exchange rate (the "Dutch disease"), can cause problems even before the resource bonanza comes to an end.[32] Income distribution can turn against smallholders in agriculture unless countermeasures are taken; domestic prices may be forced up as oil revenues are spent; and countries are tempted to spend the windfalls in ill-advised subsidies.

Declining oil prices in the mid-1980s (the third oil shock) adversely affected Indonesia and Malaysia. Malaysia was less vulnerable because oil exports account for a smaller share of total exports than they do in Indonesia. The adversity of declining oil earnings has forced both countries to cut expenditures, imports, and growth as they attempt to diversify their exports and government revenue sources.

Policy Initiatives for Adjustment

It is important to both debtor and creditor nations that the debt crisis be resolved in a manner that permits continued economic growth in the LDCs. With the increased economic interdependence of the developed and developing countries, growth in one group is in the interest of the other. Appropriate policies need to be in place in both debtor and creditor nations. Debtor nations have a responsibility to undertake all reasonable fiscal measures to prevent lapses in debt service payments and to quickly correct them when they occur. Macroeconomic and trade policies of creditor nations that permit indebted countries to increase exports are equally desirable.

The long-term debt repayment capacity of the NICs, and Korea in particular, appears to be adequate. But the ASEAN-4 countries face considerable difficulties in debt servicing and will continue to need inflows of ODA to maintain their growth momentum, though the longer-term trend toward an increasing share of private capital inflows will likely continue. The South Asian countries will continue to rely overwhelmingly on ODA, but most of them will also look more to private sources for external finance.

The short-run task for Asian countries with problems in debt servicing is to reduce import demand and improve foreign exchange earnings so as to achieve a sustainable balance-of-payments position. Government budget deficits must be pared and inflation controlled as part of the process of stabilization.

Austerity programs are unpopular and require social stability to be implemented successfully. Care must be taken to ensure that low-income households do not bear a disproportionate share of the burden. Short-run stabilization measures should be accompanied by longer-term policies that promote structural change. Initiatives to liberalize trade and financial markets, and reduce price distortions, would encourage savings, and increase investment efficiency. Expenditure policies aimed at cutting down public sector waste, and upgrading the skills, health, and education of the labor forces are also essential for long-term economic development. The growth of new jobs in manufacturing, services, and other industrial activities can be accelerated by adopting appropriate policies.

A world economic environment conducive to renewed economic growth would ease the adjustment process of heavily indebted LDCs. Problems are the "new protectionism" in the MDCs, volatile foreign exchange and interest rate changes, and reduced private capital flows. Both protectionism and protectionist threats of the OECD nations discourage LDCs from a more outward-looking orientation.

Falling oil prices have been beneficial to most Asian LDCs—exceptions are Indonesia and Malaysia. The sharp declines in oil prices of the mid-1980s will reduce import costs and stimulate growth in the NICs, nonoil ASEAN countries, and South Asia. Indonesia and Malaysia will have to reduce reliance on oil as a source of foreign exchange and government revenues.

The state of financial flows is alarming. At a time when commercial banks are more cautious, aid fatigue has slowed the growth of ODA, and the ODA available is less concessional. Most countries are seeking alternatives to financial flows that create general obligation debts. New initiatives to encourage direct foreign investment and to increase equity participation by outside investors are being explored. These are likely to remain fairly small, however, as a proportion of total external financial inflows.

Flaws in the international system to some extent are responsible for the outbreak of debt crises in the developing countries.[33] The bulk of external financial flows into the developing countries since 1973 have been in the form of publicly guaranteed borrowings from commercial banks, financial markets, and international development agencies. Repayment of a publicly guaranteed foreign loan depends not on the economics of the specific project or program financed, but on the overall creditworthiness of the borrowing country. Though disbursement of funds may be tied to a specific project, repayment is a general nonspecific obligation of the borrowing country government.

One effect of the increased reliance on publicly guaranteed borrowings from commercial banks and international agencies was to weaken the incentives of lenders to evaluate the projects or programs they were financing. In contrast to equity inflows, where foreign investors have a strong interest in the success of the project, there is no such incentive under general obligation credits.[34] It doesn't matter to the commercial lenders whether funds are used to invest in irrigation projects or to provide the directors of public enterprises with Mercedes Benz automobiles. Whether or not the specific loan has a high rate of return matters little as long as debt servicing continues in a timely manner. The risks of success or failure of development programs financed in this manner are borne by the guarantor. Risk sharing between borrowers and investors is minimal under general obligation bank credits. The only mechanism to shift risks inherent in financing development projects in this manner is nonperformance at the country level. The system concentrates risks on LDC borrowers instead of spreading them to investors with a comparative advantage in risk bearing.[35] The problem is most severe for low-income LDCs like those in sub-Saharan Africa with few exports and weak government institutions. Also, in countries with large and autonomous public enterprises (as in the Philippines) abuses of the system tend to become rife.

The increased reliance on bank credits carrying variable interest rates increased the likelihood that debt crisis would break out in the LDCs. There is a perverse negative correlation between the burden of servicing these bank credits and an LDC's ability to pay.[36] The attractive feature of bank credits to the LDCs was that they appeared to minimize the level of direct foreign involvement in and control over their own economies. For the banks, government guarantees made it easy to push out loans (and earn substantial fees) without carefully assessing individual projects and in many cases overall development strategies.[37]

The wave of debt reschedulings that swept across Latin America and Africa in the first half of the 1980s imposed heavy deadweight losses on borrowers and creditors alike. The ability of the Asian countries, except the Philippines, to avoid the debt crisis is closely related to sound macroeconomic management, the promotion of exports, and the strengthening of government institutions. In Korea, there was substantial reliance on guaranteed external borrowings from commercial banks. The government has been able to direct the borrowed funds through the banking system to efficient investment projects. Debt servicing has not been a problem because exports have grown by more than enough to meet repayment obligations.

Still, the Asian countries that have large outstanding foreign debts, particularly publicly guaranteed debts with variable interest rates, will have to control spending, maintain incentives to increase exports, and raise the saving rate. These countries are attempting to shift their reliance from foreign loans to foreign private investments. The international agencies and banks will also need to consider means of increasing the flexibility of debt-servicing requirements in future lending. The scope for general obligation lending has dwindled. "Debt fatigue" is endemic among both borrowers and lenders. There is a strong aversion in the Asian developing countries to incurring more external debt, and greater attention is being given to possibilities for an expanded role for private equity capital in the form of foreign direct investment.

Direct Foreign Investment

Direct foreign investment, though relatively small in relation to total capital inflows in Asia, has been an important element in outward-looking development strategies. Like foreign aid, private foreign direct investment can be important in helping fill the savings gap and foreign exchange gap. The real effects of private foreign investment may also be substantial in providing more productive capital, technology, management, the training of labor, and linkages elsewhere in the host economy.

Direct foreign investment (DFI) did not increase as much as other types of capital inflows, although there was a surge in the early 1970s (table 4.11). However, DFI was an important catalyst to domestic activity and, with a few exceptions, appears to have complemented the outward-looking development strategies of the NICs and ASEAN-4. This role was particularly important in resource extraction, certain manufacturing activities (especially textiles and electronics), and the service sector. The growing importance of service sector DFI is especially conspicuous.

Becoming competitive in new areas so as to facilitate the restructuring of trade has required some difficult transitions in Asian developing countries. Limited capital, technological, and managerial resources continue to be important factors policymakers need to take into account. One way in which these constraints have been loosened is through the encouragement of direct foreign investment. Although the capital transfer involved is usually minimal, the technology and managerial skills transferred through DFI have often been of far greater importance than the size of the capital flow. Furthermore, foreign firms are often very export oriented and promote the integration of the domestic and world economies. Finally, with the decline of other foreign capital flows, official development assistance, and commercial bank lending, DFI can be expected to increase in importance as a source of capital and other resources.

Unfortunately, analysis of the role of DFI is hampered by a severe data problem; there is no internationally accepted way of compiling data, and sometimes the result is large differences between different sources and a lack of relevant data for some countries. This fact mandates caution in interpreting the informa-

Table 4.11. Average Annual Net Direct Foreign Investment (DFI) and Its Share of Total Investment

Host Region/ Economy	Period	Total DFI[a] DFI (US$ millions)	Percentage of Total Investment[c]	DFI from DAC[b] DFI (US$ millions)	Percentage of Total Investment[c]
Hong Kong	1966–76	NA	NA	NA	NA
	1977–85	NA	NA	476.7	6.55
Korea	1966–76	50.0	1.55	NA	NA
	1977–85	89.8	0.45	71.1	0.40
Singapore	1966–76	274.5[d]	22.53[d]	NA	NA
	1977–85	982.6	17.34	401.8	7.91
Taiwan	1966–76	46.1	1.82	NA	NA
	1977–85	155.8	1.41	88.7	0.84
Indonesia	1966–76	108.4	4.23	NA	NA
	1977–85	227.8	1.30	540.2	3.49
Malaysia	1966–76	193.5[d]	13.94[d]	NA	NA
	1977–85	868.9	10.93	80.9	1.12
Philippines	1966–76	20.7	0.83	NA	NA
	1977–85	55.8	0.65	119.2	1.39
Thailand	1966–76	63.6	2.19	NA	NA
	1977–85	201.2	1.69	136.0	1.24
India	1966–76	− 7.0	− 0.06	NA	NA
	1977–85	0.0[e]	0.00[e]	32.5	0.09
Pakistan	1977–85	61.7	1.43	9.6	0.24
Sri Lanka	1966–76	− 0.5	− 0.12	NA	NA
	1977–85	33.8	2.90	11.3	1.05

Sources: ADB, *Key Indicators of Developing Member Countries of ADB*, July 1986; Hong Kong, Census and Statistics Department (CSD), *Estimates of Gross Domestic Product 1966–1983*, 1983; Hong Kong, CSD, *Hong Kong Monthly Digest of Statistics*, February 1986; IMF, *Balance of Payments Statistics Yearbook*, various issues; IMF, *International Financial Statistics*, yearbooks 1979 and 1986, January 1987, various issues; OECD, *Geographical Distribution of Financial Flows in Developing Countries*, various issues; Republic of China, Central Bank of China (CBC), *Balance of Payments, Taiwan District, Republic of China*, 1958–1982 summary, September 1986, various issues; Republic of China, CBC, *Financial Statistics, Taiwan District, Republic of China*, January 1981–September 1986, various issues.

Note: NA = Not available.

[a]Sum of net DFI flows to the host economy as reported in balance-of-payments data. Ideally, this figure includes equity capital, reinvested earnings, and other capital movements, both long- and short-term; however, one or more of these items often go unreported.

[b]Sum of net DFI disbursements by DAC countries as reported by the OECD; components of these flows are not given. Data refer to the period 1976–84.

[c]Total investment refers to gross domestic capital formation including changes in stocks.

[d]Excludes 1966.

[e]Excludes 1984–85.

tion presented in this section, although it is possible to isolate some important characteristics of DFI in Asia.

First, as was mentioned above, direct foreign investment flows have generally been rather small and accounted for small shares of total investment. Table 4.11 illustrates this. According to IMF data, the only countries in which total DFI exceeded 10 percent of gross domestic capital formation for 1965–84 were Malaysia and Singapore. OECD data show that DFI from the DAC countries exceeded 5 percent of gross domestic capital formation in Hong Kong and Singapore alone. Of particular note are the small shares observed in Korea and Taiwan; it is often asserted that these two countries have benefited greatly from DFI;[38] yet, shares were under 2 percent for 1966–85 in both these countries. There are small shares of DFI in all South Asian countries except Sri Lanka.

Second, Japan and the United States have been the major sources of DFI in East and Southeast Asia. Given the small amount of DFI in South Asia, this makes these two countries the major investors in the Asian region. With the exception of Indonesian, Malaysian, and Thai approval based figures, which exclude investment in oil and other key sectors, host country data show that Japanese and U.S. investment together have accounted for more than one-half of the total DFI in the NICs and the ASEAN-4. However, this combined share is much smaller in the South Asian countries for which information is available.

In addition, the United States appears to be the largest single investor in all NICs and all ASEAN-4 countries except Korea and possibly Malaysia. In this respect, investing country data are consistent with available host country figures except in Indonesia and Malaysia. U.S. investment in Malaysia is shown to be larger than Japanese investment; this contradiction is probably a result of accounting for investments in oil and other sectors not subject to approval. The discrepancy in the Indonesian case is more difficult to explain. Here, Japanese investment is shown to be larger than U.S. investment, a finding contradicting estimates based on Indonesian data including oil.

Third, the industrial pattern of direct investment has differed between the United States and Japan. The U.S. investors have been more involved in service activities and petroleum than in manufacturing. Available data (table 4.12) indicate that the major share of U.S. investment in Southeast Asia has been in petroleum, while in the NICs, service activities, especially banking, finance, and commerce have predominated. In South Asia, U.S. investment was mainly in manufacturing, with smaller shares in services and petroleum.

Japanese direct investment has, in contrast, been more focused on manufacturing; it accounted for 40 percent of Japanese direct investment in 1984. Mining (including petroleum) is the second largest area for overall Japanese investment. Between 1976 and 1984, the share of Japanese service investments rose in the NICS and the share of manufacturing fell. In Southeast Asia over the same period, the manufacturing share of Japanese investment rose somewhat. Japanese investment in South Asia has been concentrated in manufacturing and mining, as it has in Southeast Asia.

However, these patterns, especially the Japanese one, have been changing. A study comparing U.S. and Japanese direct investment in Korea between 1962 and 1972 found that Japanese investment was slightly more concentrated in labor-intensive, low-technology industries than was U.S. direct investment.[39] Patterns changed during 1973–78; both U.S. and Japanese direct investment became concentrated in skill-intensive, high-technology industries. The United States put greater emphasis on capital-intensive industries than Japan did. The changing pattern of Japanese investment found in the study reflects a structural change in Japan's economy from labor-intensive, low-technology industries to skill-intensive, high-technology industries. Structural differences between the U.S. and Japanese economies have lessened, and one can expect differences in foreign investment patterns to subside as well.

The increasing service and technology orientation of both the U.S. and Japanese economies is likely to be reflected in future direct foreign investment patterns in Asia. Less developed Asian countries should try to take advantage of these changes, particularly in view of their efforts to liberalize financial and trade policies in order to boost foreign exchange earnings. These shifting patterns of trade and investment reflect structural changes. As the NICs have become labor-scarce economies, labor-intensive and low-technology industries have tended to relocate to labor-abundant Southeast and South Asian nations and to China.

Fourth, it is important to note that foreign firms have been directly involved in host country trade to a large extent. Though data are unavailable for many countries, surveys show that foreign firms accounted for substantial portions of foreign trade in some countries. In 1974–78 they accounted for 27.9 to 33.7 percent of annual Korean imports and 22.3 to 25.4 percent of annual Korean exports.[40] In Taiwan they accounted for 12.5 to 18.0 percent of annual imports and 18.2 to 29.4 percent of annual exports for 1974–83.[41] In Singapore, foreign-majority-owned manufacturing firms accounted for over 80 percent of direct manufacturing exports in 1975–84.[42] Nayyar shows that foreign firms accounted for "nearly 70 percent" of Singaporean manufactured exports in 1970.[43] He also gives foreign firm shares of manufactured exports for other countries: Hong Kong, 1972, 10 percent; Korea, 1971, at least 15 percent; Taiwan, 1971, at least 20 percent; and India, 1970, approximately 5 percent.

Thus, foreign firms account for shares of trade much greater than those of gross domestic capital formation in several countries. While one would expect the difference between foreign firm trade/total trade and direct foreign investment/gross domestic capital formation ratios to be the highest in the NICs men-

Table 4.12. Japanese and U.S. Direct Foreign Investment (DFI) in Asian LDCs and the World by Sector (US$ millions and percentages)

	Japan[a]						United States[b]					
	All Industries		Manufacturing		Mining		All Industries		Manufacturing		Petroleum	
	1976	1984	1976	1984	1976	1984	1976	1984	1976	1984	1976	1984
World	14,661	71,431	6,035	22,048	4,859	11,158	133,335	212,994	57,651	85,253	26,636	59,189
% of World	100%	100%	41%	31%	33%	16%	100%	100%	43%	40%	20%	28%
Asia[c]	5,464	18,027	2,218	7,057	2,152	5,883	5,346	15,119	1,440	3,396	2,352	6,389
% of Asia	100%	100%	41%	39%	39%	33%	100%	100%	27%	22%	44%	42%
NICs	1,670	6,924	1,017	3,065	3	13	2,172	6,659	627	1,956	424 + D	775 + D
% of NICs	100%	100%	61%	44%	0%	0%	100%	100%	29%	29%	20% + D	12% + D
Hong Kong	448	2,799	100	233	0	5	1,166	3,249	195	364	260	372
South Korea	690	1,548	485	908	2	3	359	731	149	190	D	D
Singapore	305	1,930	221	1,352	—	3	402	1,943	109	911	148	403
Taiwan	227	647	211	572	1	2	245	736	174	491	16	D

ASEAN-4	3,641	10,604	1,151	3,847	2,059	5,764	2,649	7,514	500	1,077	1,638	5,244
% of ASEAN-4	100%	100%	32%	36%	57%	54%	100%	100%	19%	14%	62%	70%
Indonesia	2,703	8,015	682	2,270	1,755	5,261	1,298	3,987	103	92	1,029	3,618
Malaysia	356	1,046	205	759	102	120	419	1,175	76	395	278	630
Philippines	354	832	92	311	197	378	698	1,264	274	427	215	202
Thailand	228	711	172	507	5	5	234	1,088	47	163	116	794
South Asia[d]	32	168	29	89	0	12	330	403	262	296	22	D
% of South Asia	100%	100%	91%	53%	0%	7%	100%	100%	79%	73%	7%	D
India	32	79	29	60	0	12	330	403	262	296	22	D
Sri Lanka	NA	89	NA	29	NA	0	NA	NA	NA	NA	NA	NA

Sources: Japanese Ministry of Finance, *Zaisei Kinyu Tokei Geppo* (Monthly statistical review of public finance and money), nos. 305 and 404, September 1977 and December 1985; U.S. Department of Commerce, *U.S. Direct Investment Abroad 1977*, 1981; U.S. Department of Commerce, *Survey of Current Business* 66, no. 8 (August 1986).

Notes: NA = Not available; D = Not disclosed.

[a]These data refer to total DFI approved by the Ministry of Finance as of fiscal year end (March 31 of the following calendar year). Note that these approval-based figures apparently overstate the true amount of investment; for 1965–84, total net DFI abroad as reported in balance-of-payments statistics was US$37,974 million, only 54% of the approved total (US$70,100 million) for the same period. Note also that petroleum is not listed as a separate category.

[b]These data refer to the U.S. direct investment position abroad as of calendar year end. Mining sector figures are very small or not reported. The 1976 data are based on the 1977 benchmark survey, and the 1984 data on the 1982 benchmark survey.

[c]For the U.S. this category includes other less developed countries in Oceania, although DFI in these countries is minimal.

[d]Data for other South Asian countries were unavailable.

Table 4.13. Export/Sales Ratios for Japanese and U.S. Affiliates in Asian LDCs and the World by Sector (percentages)

	Japan[a]						United States[b]					
	All Industries		Manufacturing		Mining		All Industries		Manufacturing		Petroleum	
	1975	1981	1975	1981	1975	1981	1977	1982	1977	1982	1977	1982
World	36.8	50.1	35.4	25.9	63.0	77.2	38.2	34.5	30.8	33.9	49.5	35.4
Asia[c]	44.7	58.8	42.6	34.5	31.7	73.4	60.9	58.7	57.0	D	67.5	63.7
NICs												
Hong Kong	45.5	NA	35.0	NA	NA	NA	77.5	59.5	80.5	77.4	D	55.6
Korea	65.4	NA	65.3	NA	45.0	NA	58.5	44.0	68.5	D	NA	D
Singapore	40.9	NA	40.2	NA	NA	NA	67.4	82.0	93.2	91.8	30.4	82.9
Taiwan	49.5	NA	50.3	NA	0.0	NA	58.9	49.9	71.4	59.4	D	D
ASEAN–4												
Indonesia	27.8	NA	9.6	NA	NA	NA	80.9	66.1	40.8	D	D	73.2
Malaysia	48.4	NA	48.2	NA	50.0	NA	44.3	47.4	76.2	81.5	19.0	29.3

Philippines	41.8	NA	36.0	NA	90.0	NA	17.2	15.7	25.7	26.5	0.0	D
Thailand	19.9	NA	13.7	NA	0.0	NA	11.4	17.5	D	D	D	D
South Asia[d]												
India	NA	NA	NA	NA	NA	NA	D	7.8	3.6	D	0.0	D

Sources: Japan, Ministry of International Trade and Industry, *Wagakuni Kigyo no Kaigai Jigyo Katsudo* (Overseas activities of domestic firms), 7th (covering fiscal 1975) and 12th–13th (covering 1981–82) surveys, 1977 and 1984; U.S. Department of Commerce, *U.S. Direct Investment Abroad 1977*, 1981; U.S. Department of Commerce, *U.S. Direct Investment Abroad, 1982 Benchmark Survey Data*, 1981.

Notes: Ratios (in percentages) are calculated as (1 – (local sales/total sales)). NA = Not available or not applicable. D = not disclosed.

[a]These data come from annual Ministry of International Trade and Industry surveys and refer to the corresponding fiscal year ending March 31 of the following calendar year. Petroleum is not listed as a separate category, and country breakdowns have not been published since 1975. Original data are given in percentages.

[b]These data come from the U.S. Department of Commerce benchmark surveys and refer to calendar years. Mining sales are small or not reported. Original data are given in U.S. dollars.

[c]For the United States, this category includes other LDCs in Oceania.

[d]Data for other South Asian countries were unavailable.

tioned above, a substantial gap is to be expected in the ASEAN-4 and is suggested in India as well. Another perspective on this is provided in table 4.13. There, it is shown that a large portion of Japanese and U.S. affiliate sales are exported. These export/sales ratios are especially high in the NICs and in Malaysia's manufacturing sector. Notably low ratios are only observed in India (United States), Indonesia (Japan), the Philippines (United States), and Thailand (Japan and the United States).

Finally, intrafirm trade is an important element of this trade and should be highlighted. This type of trade is less threatened by trade restrictions and has the advantage of raising productivity in both less developed and more developed nations through specialization in production. Intrafirm trade of transnational corporations with divisions in Asia has made Asian countries' foreign exchange earnings more susceptible to business conditions in MDCs. As an example, direct foreign investment and intrafirm trade have had a major impact on the export of electrical machinery from Southeast Asian nations. In 1970, exports of electrical components hardly existed in Southeast Asia. The growth of these exports from 2 percent to almost 30 percent of manufactured exports between 1970 and 1983 was almost entirely derived from sales to the United States and the NICs.[44] The change indicates that in Southeast Asian countries, electronic components are mainly manufactured in subsidiaries of U.S. firms, and increasingly, also in subsidiaries of parent companies from the NICs that have shifted labor-intensive parts of the production process to Southeast Asia. Export growth of electrical machinery in Southeast Asia is dependent on the business prospects facing parent companies in their home markets.

The preceding discussion indicates the importance of direct foreign investment as a source of industrial competitiveness and especially as a source of new technology. This role appears to have been limited in South Asia (except Sri Lanka) where arm's-length licensing arrangements have been the major source of foreign technology. However, direct foreign investment has been a much more important source of U.S. technology than such agreements in Southeast Asia.[45] Furthermore, the supplies of Japanese and U.S. technology are both becoming more sophisticated, and the NICs are becoming the main suppliers of standardized technology in Southeast Asia.[46]

Foreign capital and technology have been especially important in the development of natural resources in Southeast and South Asia and are likely to become even more significant. The slower growth of official development assistance and the high costs of external commercial loans make direct foreign investment an attractive source of such capital and technology. Because of large capital and technology requirements, the costs of resource extraction and development of related industries are often too great for internal financing in these countries. Specifically, direct foreign investment could be helpful in development of Thailand's offshore natural gas, India's offshore oil, Burma's gas and oil, Nepal's minerals and hydropower resources, and Indonesia's mineral, geothermal, and hydropower potentials.

To attract direct foreign investment, various incentive schemes have been adopted. However, the proliferation of incentives has had less effect in bringing in new investment than the overall business climate and each country's political stability, economic growth, and the consistency of its regulations. Competitive incentive schemes introduced by several countries simultaneously can be costly and have the effect of reducing the net benefits of direct foreign investment to the host country that "wins" the competition. Strong economic growth and favorable business climates in Asian countries do the most to make these countries attractive to foreign investors. Thus, special schemes which may distort investment allocation are not necessary.

Table 4.A1. Total Net Capital Flows and Net Investment Income by Recipient Country and Type (annual averages, US$ millions)

Period	Net Capital Flows							Net Investment Income	
	Total Net Flow[a]	Private Unrequited Transfers	Official Unrequited Transfers	Direct Investment	Portfolio Investment	Other Long-Term Capital[b]	Other Short-Term Capital	Direct Investment Income	Other Investment Income
NICs									
Korea									
1970–72	783	106	65	52	NA	477	165	−4	−84
1973–75	1,614	156	57	84	0	912	608	−22	−250
1976–78	808	266	81	70	62	1,483	181	−46	−546
1979–82	4,664	417	55	−2	31	2,594	2,379	−33	−2,316
1983–85	1,859	546	25	72	501	1,793	1	−56	−3,031
Singapore									
1970–72	591	−15	10	133	NA	55	97	NA	20
1973–75	681	−31	4	532	0	75	−6	NA	−65
1976–78	395	−41	−3	575	50	43	154	NA	−50
1979–82	1,141	−57	−9	1,063	10	356	336	NA	−363
1983–85	412	−174	−14	1,087	100	−93	674	NA	−58
Taiwan									
1970–72	−216	13	1	46	NA	−90	−18	−25	−10
1973–75	385	10	−4	59	0	311	150	−67	14
1976–78	−948	3	−4	74	7	327	−1,141	−68	−79
1979–82	−645	−131	−5	102	76	1,034	460	−133	30
1983–85	−7,015	−152	−2	174	−18	−511	−1,803	−185	801

ASEAN-4

Indonesia									
1970–72	393	0	54	143	NA	246	72	−214	−4
1973–75	373	0	44	147	0	538	−586	−1,060	16
1976–78	808	0	18	286	34	1,369	−179	−1,566	−20
1979–82	629	0	117	192	117	2,372	−260	−3,077	161
1983–85	3,440	41	109	262	96	3,035	370	−3,320	−408
Malaysia									
1970–72	63	−63	10	103	NA	113	4	−168	45
1973–75	265	−59	13	364	89	87	64	−373	44
1976–78	−413	−54	15	429	65	156	101	−630	65
1979–82	1,337	−47	23	1,042	780	210	−32	−1,104	183
1983–85	1,915	−49	23	914	916	1,064	58	−1,512	−600
Philippines									
1970–72	162	48	99	−19	NA	97	177	−26	−94
1973–75	494	127	148	52	−2	243	427	−61	−37
1976–78	1,266	164	118	146	7	825	347	−170	−160
1979–82	2,614	294	140	22	5	1,187	1,063	−179	−888
1983–85	1,749	176	237	33	3	1,460	−1,272	−130	−1,831
Thailand									
1970–72	210	13	37	50	NA	65	36	−15	17
1973–75	408	135	26	117	9	115	197	−15	10
1976–78	938	68	23	78	25	361	518	−16	−100
1979–82	2,089	56	102	179	97	1,400	272	−19	−743
1983–85	2,379	86	119	303	386	878	443	−31	−1,217

(table continues on following page)

133

Table 4.A1. Total Net Capital Flows and Net Investment Income by Recipient Country and Type (annual averages, US$ millions) (continued)

		Net Capital Flows							Net Investment Income	
	Period	Total Net Flow[a]	Private Unrequited Transfers	Official Unrequited Transfers	Direct Investment	Portfolio Investment	Other Long-Term Capital[b]	Other Short-Term Capital	Direct Investment Income	Other Investment Income
South Asia										
Bangladesh	1973–75	782	27	315	0	0	381	−7	0	3
	1976–78	724	85	323	0	0	338	−11	0	−28
	1979–82	1,721	316	778	0	0	431	7	0	−44
	1983–85	1,621	524	716	−0	−1	495	−23	0	−70
Burma	1970–72	69	1	18	0	NA	6	−1	NA	−6
	1973–75	65	1	15	0	0	48	6	NA	−9
	1976–78	135	2	16	0	0	94	−1	NA	−16
	1979–82	452	7	65	0	0	359	5	NA	−44
	1983–85	332	7	70	0	0	180	16	NA	−45
India	1970–72	656	97	148	3	NA	532	5	NA	−302
	1973–75	890	259	802	−10	0	157	12	NA	−269
	1976–78	−140	902	413	−3	0	792	−64	NA	−112
	1979–82	4,565	2,262	563	0	0	728	−161	NA	308
	1983–84	5,065	2,464	468	0	0	2,150	397	NA	−155
Nepal	1976–78	54	19	33	0	0	17	−8	0	6
	1979–82	153	33	82	0	0	48	−3	0	12
	1983–85	53	37	86	0	0	75	1	0	2

Pakistan	1973–75	956	200	79	8	0	346	55	−1	−94
	1976–78	1,767	912	110	17	0	502	91	−2	−168
	1979–82	3,413	2,196	279	74	0	460	105	−8	−296
	1983–85	4,004	2,915	330	77	43	366	201	−33	−456
Sri Lanka	1970–72	55	−3	16	0	NA	49	1	−5	−16
	1973–75	135	1	44	1	3	67	8	−2	−15
	1976–78	49	13	59	0	0	87	−48	−2	−15
	1979–82	782	163	150	51	0	265	32	−9	−48
	1983–85	784	273	172	33	0	335	15	−11	−121

Sources: IMF, *International Financial Statistics*, Yearbooks 1979 and 1986, various monthlies; IMF, *Balance of Payments Statistics Yearbook*, various issues; Republic of China, CBC, *Balance of Payments, Taiwan District, Republic of China*, 1958–82 summary, various monthlies.

Note: NA = Not available.

[a]The total net flow is defined as minus the balance of trade (merchandise and other goods, services, and income) and equal to the sum of the components listed plus the following: net errors and omissions, counterpart items, exceptional financing, liabilities constituting foreign authorities' reserves, and total change in reserves.

[b]For 1970–72, direct investment only.

Table 4.A2. Financial Flows from OECD, OPEC, and Multilateral Institutions (US$ millions)

Period	Total Flows	Official Flows			Private Flows[a]			
		Subtotal	Bilateral	Multilateral	Subtotal	Direct Investment	Portfolio Investment	Export Credits
NICs								
Hong Kong								
1970–72	273	70	70	0	203	NA	NA	NA
1973–75	192[b]	73	67	6	119	NA	NA	NA
1976–78	286	3	3	0	284	184	−3	103
1979–82	1,227	31	16	15	1,198	614	91	493
1983–85	302	−1	−3	2	303	356	−254	201
Korea								
1970–72	510	414	361	53	96	NA	NA	NA
1973–75	813	537	340	197	276	NA	NA	NA
1976–78	1,445	780	414	367	665	98	21	546
1979–82	1,360	848	417	431	513	40	248	225
1983–85	1,629	562	198	364	1,067	117	1,136	−186
Singapore								
1970–72	114	53	34	19	61	NA	NA	NA
1973–75	176	67	46	22	108	NA	NA	NA
1976–78	250	49	25	23	202	100	104	−3
1979–82	895	43	42	1	852	566	112	173
1983–85	360	0	9	−8	360	459	−54	−45
Taiwan								
1970–72	190	84	28	56	106	NA	NA	NA
1973–75	311	128	90	38	183	NA	NA	NA
1976–78	66	73	92	−19	−7	22	−44	16
1979–82	494	220	239	−20	275	101	69	105
1983–85	−220	−144	−126	−18	−76	139	−104	−111

ASEAN-4

Indonesia	1970–72	745	523	483	40	222	NA	NA	NA
	1973–75	1,712[b]	746	585	161	966	NA	NA	NA
	1976–78	1,684	954	674	280	730	366	143	221
	1979–82	2,407	1,261	768	493	1,146	760	191	195
	1983–85	2,742	1,560	743	817	1,182	144	372	666
Malaysia	1970–72	124	70	46	24	54	NA	NA	NA
	1973–75	267[b]	118	68	51	149	NA	NA	NA
	1976–78	250	171	81	90	80	87	–17	9
	1979–82	808	238	115	123	570	35	217	317
	1983–85	1,070	397	319	79	673	137	430	106
Philippines	1970–72	222	159	136	22	64	NA	NA	NA
	1973–75	354[b]	265	178	87	88	NA	NA	NA
	1976–78	954	384	216	169	570	138	218	214
	1979–82	1,079	655	260	395	424	174	95	155
	1983–85	1,017	982	522	459	35	–107	115	27
Thailand	1970–72	102	86	61	25	16	NA	NA	NA
	1973–75	179	108	54	54	71	NA	NA	NA
	1976–78	378	297	151	146	81	33	36	12
	1979–82	1,215	743	373	371	472	151	119	202
	1983–85	1,207	902	450	452	305	149	219	–63

(table continues on following page)

Table 4.A2. Financial Flows from OECD, OPEC, and Multilateral Institutions (US$ millions) (continued)

Period	Official Flows				Private Flows[a]			
	Total Flows	Subtotal	Bilateral	Multilateral	Subtotal	Direct Investment	Portfolio Investment	Export Credits
South Asia								
Bangladesh								
1970–72	NA	NA	NA	NA	NA	NA	NA	NA
1973–75	678	674	484	190	4	NA	NA	NA
1976–78	770	763	525	238	7	6	0	–0
1979–82	1,252	1,246	871	374	6	3	2	1
1983–85	1,157	1,147	671	475	10	0	–15	25
Burma								
1970–72	43	38	38	1	5	NA	NA	NA
1973–75	66	62	51	11	4	NA	NA	NA
1976–78	179	149	83	66	30	0	0	30
1979–82	417	321	227	93	96	0	5	91
1983–85	327	312	207	105	14	0	–1	16
India								
1970–72	824	803	671	132	22	NA	NA	NA
1973–75	1,240[b]	1,227	731	496	13	NA	NA	NA
1976–78	1,398	1,427	860	567	–29	11	–18	–21
1979–82	2,045	1,916	663	1,254	129	73	9	33
1983–85	2,215	1,881	571	1,310	334	13	230	91
Nepal								
1970–72	26	26	21	5	0	NA	NA	NA
1973–75	39	38	25	13	0	NA	NA	NA
1976–78	70	70	38	32	0	0	0	0
1980–82	170	170	96	74	1	0	0	0
1983–85	215	214	110	104	1	0	–0	1

Pakistan								
1970–72	NA	NA	NA	NA	NA	NA	NA	NA
1973–75	598	643	553	90	−45	NA	NA	NA
1976–78	905	881	669	213	24	9	2	13
1979–82	992	880	504	376	112	15	28	69
1983–85	728	803	294	509	−75	0	−11	−63
Sri Lanka								
1970–72	60	59	48	10	2	NA	NA	NA
1973–75	106[b]	126	93	33	−21	NA	NA	NA
1976–78	215	225	156	69	−9	−4	−1	−5
1979–82	413	380	284	96	33	10	−3	26
1983–85	584	504	355	149	80	27	12	42

Sources: OECD, *Geographical Distribution of Financial Flows to Developing Countries*, 1976–82 through 1982–85 issues; ADB, *Key Indicators of Developing Member Countries of ADB*, April 1984, April 1985, and July 1986.

Note: NA = Not available.

[a]DAC countries only; no private flows recorded from other countries or agencies.

[b]Sum of components; does not add up to total given in source (1975 only).

5 Asian Agriculture in Transition

Introduction

A number of theories of economic development saw agriculture as peripheral to the main task of industrialization.[1] The rural sector was thought to abound with surplus labor that could be transferred at little or no cost to the industrial sector. Agricultural producers could be taxed to provide resources for industrial development, receiving little or nothing in return from government.

By the early 1960s, economists began to recognize a more positive role for agriculture in economic development as they became familiar with the experiences of Japan and Taiwan. However, hardly any thought was given to the idea that overall development would be difficult or impossible in Asia unless the agricultural sector was itself developed.

Agriculture and rural development were neglected in part because of some misconceptions about peasant behavior. Peasant farmers were often regarded in development circles as tradition-bound and unresponsive to market incentives.[2] The path-breaking work of Nobel Laureate Theodore Schultz did much to change this view.[3] The "rational peasant" was poor but efficient, operating at minimum cost within the limits of existing technology.[4] Moreover, peasants would respond substantially to price changes. The problem was one of opening up new opportunities in agriculture through research and technological advances. At the same time, education was needed to increase the capacity of farmers to skillfully adopt innovations. Economic incentives would speed up the process by making increased production more profitable, and offsetting the higher risks associated with new methods of farming.

Economists and policymakers began to recognize that the sluggish growth of agriculture in the 1950s and early 1960s was related to the failure to invest in rural development and from a lack of incentives. The experiences of two Southeast Asian neighbors makes for an interesting comparison. Burma and Thailand traditionally have been major rice-exporting nations. In the early

1960s, Burma accounted for about a quarter of total world rice exports and Thailand a fifth. Burma had some initial advantages over Thailand. Educational levels were higher, rice land was richer, and rainfall was more abundant. Both countries taxed rice exports in order to maintain low and stable domestic prices and also to acquire government revenue. The major difference between the two was in economic policy. Thailand invested in improving agricultural infrastructure, especially irrigation and roads, often with funds from external donors. It adopted an outward-looking policy stance and, except for the rice premium, allowed market forces to operate rather freely. Burma, on the other hand, became extremely inward looking, and socialistic government controls over economic activity became pervasive. Investment in rural improvements declined as Burma cut itself off from the external world.

Agricultural growth accelerated in Thailand during the 1960s when farmers took advantage of expanding domestic markets and world trade. Despite the rice export tax, Thailand managed to keep a constant share of the world rice market, even as it began to diversify its agricultural exports. In contrast, Burma's share of world rice exports declined by over two-thirds. With no government support for diversification and little incentive to generate marketable surpluses, agricultural growth barely kept pace with Burma's population in the 1960s.

The Asian countries that neglected agriculture in the pursuit of industrialization through import substitution in the 1950s experienced an overall slowdown in economic growth in the 1960s.[5] India and the Philippines both adopted import substitution industrialization strategies heavily biased against agriculture in the 1950s. The annual average real rate of economic growth in India was 3.6 percent during the First Five-Year Plan (1951–55) and 4.0 percent during the Second Plan (1956–60). Subsequently, real growth fell during the Third Plan period (1961–65) to an average annual rate of only 2.2 percent. In the Philippines the decline was from 8 percent in the first half of the 1950s to less than 5 percent from 1956 to 1970. In contrast, Taiwan emphasized agriculture in the 1950s and experienced an acceleration of growth from 7.6 percent in the 1950s to nearly 10 percent in the 1960s.[6]

Agricultural Conditions in Monsoon Asia

Asian agriculture has some distinctive features that pose major challenges to development. The monsoon rainfall pattern that covers most of Asia has profound effects on the rhythm of economic activity. The seasonality of demand for rural labor is extremely pronounced in monsoon Asia.

Wet rice cultivation is the most labor-intensive type of agriculture in the world. In Asia, population densities by the late 1940s were already much higher than anywhere else in the world.[7] The monsoon belt extends from Japan and Korea in the north through China and Southeast Asia across the Indian Ocean to southern India and Pakistan. During the rainy season (about four to five months a year) much of the rural work force is engaged in an intensive effort to produce sufficient food for rapidly expanding numbers under severe resource constraints.

Over the centuries, irrigation systems were built up to provide greater control over the environment and to support more intensive cultivation. Many parts of Asia have long faced an acute scarcity of agricultural land. By the 1960s, most Asian countries had reached the end of their land frontiers. Population pressures and hunger for land have since resulted in serious environmental problems (discussed on pp. 157–158).

The average size of farm holdings in Asia is less than one-tenth the world average. The prevalence of extremely small farms in Asia and the dependence of most on monsoon rains meant that scientific farming technologies developed under western conditions were inapplicable. The technology of the "green revolution" had to be developed and adapted to the particular conditions of monsoon Asia.

By the 1960s, high rates of population growth and increasing urbanization were creating strong growth in demand for food. Many governments, in the interests of political expediency, kept food prices artificially low, substantially benefiting urban consumers at the expense of farmers. Outside of some of the traditional food surplus countries (Thailand and Taiwan), most of the Asian countries were having difficulties in expanding domestic food supplies adequately, despite technological advances that promised higher cereal yields.

Asian governments in the mid-1960s began to give greater attention to agriculture. In doing so, they sought to resolve the complex problem of maximizing the contributions of agriculture to total development (outlined in chapter 1 and on p. 159) in a manner consistent with the improvement of the well-being of the rural population. The establishment of priorities and the identification of trade-offs and of conflicts in objectives are essential to designing an appropriate agricultural development strategy.

Most difficult is the conflict between the objective of fostering structural transformation by achieving a net flow of resources from agriculture and the objective of improving the living conditions of the rural population. Once governments recognized that agriculture could not make a sustained contribution to overall development unless it was itself developed, governments sought a strategy that takes full advantage of positive interactions between agriculture and other sectors.[8]

In reviewing agricultural contributions to industrial growth, Reynolds observed:

> It is incorrect, however, to suppose that an expanding industrial sector can be fueled for more than a short time by resource transfers from a static

agricultural sector. The economic potential of agriculture must be mobilized before it can be used. The requirements for such mobilization lie at the core of development theory and policy.[9]

The production of food grains, rice and wheat in particular, was a logical focus of government efforts. The food grains sector encompassed almost 70 percent of Asian farm lands and, because of its labor intensity, an even higher share of total agricultural employment. Governments, supported by external donors, made major efforts to encourage the rapid spread of new seed varieties, to promote the use of chemical fertilizers, and to expand irrigation works so that two or three crops could be raised annually on the same parcel instead of only one.

Despite all these efforts, in the mid-1970s, food self-sufficiency appeared to be even further out of reach in most of Asia than it had been in the mid-1960s. Droughts, pest infestations, and inadequate agricultural support services led to widespread harvest failures between 1972 and 1975. Per capita food supplies were not much larger than they had been in the 1960s (figure 5.1), and in some cases, for example, in India, they were lower. Cereal imports reached record levels, and food grain prices skyrocketed.

The Second Asian Agricultural Survey of the Asian Development Bank[10] presented a grim picture. Outside of the NICs and possibly Malaysia, rural poverty was spreading, landlessness was on the rise, and agricultural real wages were falling. Because larger farmers were apparently the main beneficiaries of

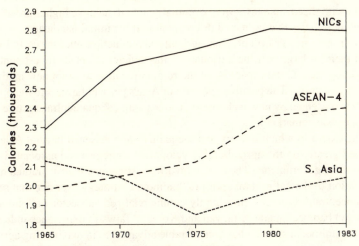

Figure 5.1   Daily Per Capita Calorie Supply, 1965–83
Sources: ABD, *Key Indicators of Developing Member Countries of ADB*, 1986 and earlier years.

government programs in the areas of credit, extension, and infrastructure, rural income distribution seemed to be worsening.[11] There were fears that increasingly rural populations were being polarized into haves and have-nots, landed and landless.

If internal conditions were unfavorable, external events gave little cause for optimism. Sudden upsurges in fuel and fertilizer prices in 1973–74 made it more difficult to promote crop intensification. The 1970s closed with a second oil shock that again increased farm input prices, followed by a long period of reduced demand for agricultural exports and increased agricultural protectionism in the more developed countries. Yet in spite of all the internal and external difficulties, by the mid-1980s Asia was producing a large surplus of food grains. Though it was uneven, undeniable progress had been made in improving living conditions in many rural areas.

At the beginning of the 1970s, the conditions for agricultural growth—land availablity, the concentration of land holdings, irrigation and infrastructural development, the commercialization of agriculture, and most importantly, the level of skill, education, and health of the rural work force— differed between countries and subgroups.[12] The relationship between these initial physical and social conditions and subsequent agricultural development are complex. The countries—like Thailand and Malaysia—that had the most favorable starting conditions, indicated by higher income levels, more land per capita, a low concentration of landholdings, a high ratio of exports to total agricultural output, better infrastructure, and higher literacy rates, tended to grow faster than the others. But some Asian countries—like Indonesia, India, and Pakistan that began with disadvantages—were eventually able to achieve higher growth by adopting policies that corrected or compensated for initial handicaps.

The impressive growth of Asian agricultural production since the early 1970s must then, in large part, be attributed to the policies adopted. Investments in technology and in the capability of the rural population to adapt new methods paid high returns. The positive response of Asia's peasant farmers to the opportunities presented by new technology in areas with adequate infrastructure and services was remarkable.

The extent to which poverty and inequality were lessened in rural Asia depended greatly on the agricultural development strategies and associated policies of the governments. The choice favoring a strategy aimed at gradual modernization of the entire rural sector (a "unimodal" strategy over one that seeks to concentrate resources on a highly commercialized subsector (a "bimodal" strategy) had been made in Taiwan and Korea.[13] Taiwan's experience indicates that the unimodal strategy has considerable advantages in maximizing agriculture's contribution to overall development and simultaneously raising rural living standards.[14]

Recent Agricultural Growth Performance

In the 1970s (1971–81), agricultural GDP including crops, livestock, forest products, and fisheries increased in the Asian LDCs at an average annual rate of 3.6 percent. Asian countries' average agricultural GDP growth exceeded that of Latin American and African countries (figure 5.2). In the first half of the 1980s, Asian agricultural GDP growth fell to only about 3 percent. Food and cereals production continued to grow rapidly in the 1980s. Most of the decline in growth was in the export crops and forest products, both of which suffered from depressed external markets.

Agricultural production growth also exceeded population growth in most of Asia. ASEAN-4 and South Asian countries moved toward greater food self-sufficiency as much of sub-Saharan Africa became more dependent on food imports.

Rates of agricultural growth varied widely in Asia. Korea and the ASEAN-4 countries enjoyed generally higher rates of growth of agricultural production (including food production) than the countries of South Asia (table 5.1).

During the 1970s, structural change—measured as the change in the share of agriculture in GDP and total employment of the labor force—was pro-

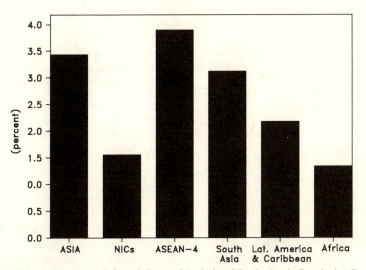

Figure 5.2. Average Annual Growth Rates of Agricultural Production in Developing Regions, 1973–84

Sources: World Bank, *World Development Report*, 1986; ADB, *Key Indicators of Developing Member Countries of ADB*, July 1986.

Note: Regional figures are simple averages of countries listed in table 5.A1 with the exception of South Asia, which excludes Burma.

Table 5.1. Agricultural Production and Labor Force Growth Rates, 1970–85 (in percentages)

	Share of Agriculture					Real Growth of Agriculture	
	GDP			Employment		Output	Output per Agricultural Worker
	1960	1970	1985	1970	1985	1970–85	1970–85
NICs							
Korea	37	27	14	50	25	3.1	5.0
Taiwan	29	16	6	35	17	1.4	2.9
ASEAN-4							
Indonesia	54	47	25	62[a]	55[b]	3.8[c]	2.3[d]
Malaysia	36	31	20	48[e]	36	4.7[f]	4.0[f]
Philippines	26	28	27	54	49	3.9	0.9
Thailand	40	28	17	72[g]	69	4.5[h]	0.8[i]
South Asia							
Bangladesh	58	55	48	74[j]	64	3.1[k]	1.7[k]
Burma	33	38	48	60	66	4.6	2.3
India	47	43	30	74	69[l]	2.1[m]	0.6[n]
Nepal	NA	68	53	94	93[o]	1.6[p]	NA
Pakistan	44	33	25	57	53	2.5	0.1
Sri Lanka	32	28	24	51[a]	44[q]	4.8[r]	NA

Sources: World Bank, *World Development Report*, 1986; World Bank, *World Tables*, 1983, 1980; ADB, *Key Indicators of Developing Member Countries of ADB*, April 1986, 1985, 1984; International Labor Office, *Yearbook of Labor Statistics*, 1985, 1980.

Note: NA = Not available.

[a]1976.
[b]1982.
[c]1971–82.
[d]1976–82.
[e]1971.
[f]1971–85.
[g]1972.
[h]1972–85.
[i]1972–83.
[j]1973.
[k]1973–85.
[l]1980.
[m]1971–84.
[n]1970–80.
[o]1981.
[p]1975–85.
[q]1983.
[r]1975–83.

nounced throughout Asia. The rate of change in the importance of agriculture's GDP and employment shares varied a great deal among countries and subgroups. The South Asian countries, save Burma, all experienced declines in the share of agriculture in GDP. Agricultural employment fell as a share of total employment, but still accounted for a large share of total employment in these countries (table 5.1). The rate of structural change from agriculture to industry and services varied with industrial sector performance. Agriculture's employment share in South Asia declined more slowly, in general, because of the capital-intensive pattern of industrial development. Though the service sector absorbed a greater part of the labor force than previously, the increase was often in low-productivity informal occupations.

In contrast, in Taiwan and Korea, the strong shift of resources out of agriculture was associated with continued rapid industrialization during the 1970s.

Among the ASEAN-4, Indonesia and Malaysia had sharp drops in agriculture's GDP share during the 1970s. In Indonesia the rapid fall in agriculture's GDP share was not matched by a decline in agriculture's share of total employment as it was in Malaysia. Malaysia had greater success in creating new jobs in industry and services than the other ASEAN-4 countries had.

However, South Asian countries, except Nepal, generally attained cereal production growth rates almost as high as those of the Southeast Asian countries. Food production in these countries (except Nepal) outpaced population growth because of strong performance in cereal production. However, output per agricultural worker stagnated or declined in Pakistan and Nepal and showed only modest gains elsewhere in South Asia.

India was able to all but eliminate reliance on food grain imports by the mid-1980s. In years of adverse weather there was need to import some grain, and after prolonged drought in the early 1980s there was concern that India would lose the race for self-sufficiency. With normal weather, however, India has surpluses of wheat and rice. The impressive achievement of meeting effective domestic demand entirely from domestic supply does not mean that the food problem has been solved. Malnutrition is still widespread because the poor in both rural and urban areas have low incomes and lack purchasing power.

Burma, Sri Lanka, Pakistan, and Bangladesh had fairly high rates of food and cereals production growth. Since 1970, Burma has had one of the highest rates of agricultural growth in Asia, close to 5 percent per annum. Burma's high growth in agricultural production since 1970 reflects a recovery from its abysmal performance in the 1960s. In the first half of the 1970s, Burma's rice exports shrank to about one-tenth of the volume attained in the early 1960s. To reverse this trend, beginning in the mid-1970s, Burmese policymakers improved incentives to rice farmers through the introduction of subsidized inputs, new high-yielding rice seeds, better infrastructure, and expanded irrigation works. This resulted in the rapid spread of high-yielding varieties (HYVs), and associated inputs and greatly improved rice yields. Rice exports recovered as annual growth in rice production in the latter half of the 1970s averaged over 10 percent.

Indonesia, the largest Asian LDC aside from China and India, has made substantial progress in domestic production of cereals and other food products. Between the late 1960s, when high-yielding rice varieties were introduced, and 1984, production more than doubled, and rice self-sufficiency was achieved (figure 5.3). Over a period of 15 years, rice output increased at an average rate of 5 percent a year—by any standard a remarkable achievement. The strength of agriculture helped Indonesia to adjust to falling oil prices in the 1980s, particularly by reducing the expense of food imports and providing an alternative source of foreign exchange earnings.

In the Philippines, Malaysia, and Thailand, agricultural growth was also exceptional. The Philippines during the 1970s became self-sufficient in rice and was a large net exporter of a variety of tropical agricultural commodities. However, increased government intervention in pricing, marketing, processing, and trading hampered growth in the late 1970s.

The Philippine government established the National Food Authority (NFA) and gave it a monopoly in its export and import trade in rice. The NFA was supposed to set support prices that would provide farmers with adequate incentives and was also supposed to control retail prices so as to protect consumer interests. The NFA was to accomplish these objectives by means of a buffer stock scheme making use of domestic paddy procured from farmers at the sup-

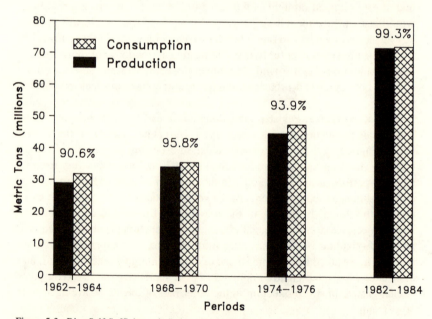

Figure 5.3. Rice Self-Sufficiency in Indonesia, 1962–84

Sources: USDA, *Foreign Agricultural Circular: Grains*, September 1982; FAO, *FAO Production Yearbook*, 1984 and earlier years; FAO, *FAO Trade Yearbook*, 1984 and earlier years; FAO, *Monthly Bulletin of Statistics*, March 1986.

Note: Figures are totals for three-year periods, not annual averages.

port price, supplemented if necessary by imports. In practice, the NFA had inadequate budgetary resources to procure more than 10 percent of domestic rice production and also had limited warehouse facilities for storage. In years of surplus production, the NFA was powerless to prevent domestic paddy prices from falling below the support price. During lean years, limited foreign exchange and inadequate buffer stocks prevented NFA from stabilizing retail prices. By driving private rice traders out of the business, the government policies aggravated retail price fluctuations. Both rice farmers and consumers were worse off than they had been under free trade conditions.[15]

The improvements in agricultural technology and irrigation and strong external demand for Philippine exports helped growth in the 1970s. After 1980, the growth rate of agriculture in the Philippines fell sharply. During the 1970s, incomes of smallholders and rural landless grew much more slowly than those of large farmers, plantation owners, and forest concessionaires. In the 1980s, smallholders experienced deterioration in incomes. The pervasive government controls over marketing and external trade coupled with price disincentives, an overvalued peso, and deteriorating rural wages worsened income distribution.[16]

There was also a failure to generate off-farm employment opportunities in the Philippines: average productivity per worker in agriculture rose only by 0.9 percent per year between 1970 and 1985 (table 5.1). Rural real wages and incomes deteriorated in the 1980s and landlessness increased.

In Malaysia and Thailand, unprecedented growth in the production of a wide variety of agricultural exports helped sustain high rates of overall economic growth. Labor productivity in agriculture, on average, rose by 4 percent per year in Malaysia. Though Malaysia is a net importer of rice, it was able to achieve high agricultural growth by investing in a number of other crops, especially palm oil and rubber. It also greatly expanded exports of forestry products. Thailand was even more successful in diversifying its agricultural export base, and it remained a major food grains and rice exporter.

In the NICs, structural change led to transfers (at an increasing rate) of labor and other resources out of agriculture and into manufacturing and services. The agricultural labor force began declining absolutely in Taiwan by the late 1960s and in Korea by the mid-1970s; but agricultural output continued to rise. In Korea, modernization and mechanization of agriculture are shown in the 5 percent annual average gain in agricultural labor productivity during the 1970s. Korea and Taiwan sustained output growth by diversifying into higher value crops, and into fishery- and livestock-related products.

The increase in farm household income in the NICs has provided strong growth in demand for domestic manufactured goods, including agricultural machinery. Much of the total household income of farm families in Taiwan is derived from nonagricultural employment.[17] There are some pressing problems in the NICs' agricultural sector. Even the NICs have found it difficult to balance adequate returns to rice farmers against cheap prices to consumers.

In Korea, large rice deficits have made imports necessary, and the attainment of full rice self-sufficiency would be costly, given the goal of low consumer rice prices. Taiwan has protected its rice sector and has a chronic problem of high-cost surplus rice production. Continued protection of rice production poses a major policy dilemma in both countries. In Taiwan and Korea, efforts to consolidate farm holdings into larger, more economical units have been set back by resistance among part-time farmers and owners of small parcels of paddy land. Protection of the rice sector since 1973 has artificially increased the market value of farmland as well. This has now become a serious impediment to further structural change and increased specialization in agriculture.

The sources of growth in agriculture have shifted perceptibly in land-scarce monsoon Asia since the 1960s. The need to make technological progress in noncereal crops, animal husbandry, and other subsectors and the changing patterns of resource availablity and trade have placed new challenges before the developing countries of Asia in their design of agricultural development policies.

Agricultural Intensification and Cereals Production

Agricultural land, as was noted above, is a relatively scarce factor of agricultural production in most of Asia. Agricultural land per capita averaged under one-fifth of a hectare in 1980. Population density in rural areas of Asia is more than twice as great as it is in Africa, and over three times as great as it is in Latin America.[18]

Between 1966 and 1982, the agricultural land area increased by less than 4 percent in South Asia, while the agricultural labor force grew more than 21 percent. In Southeast Asia, the area of arable land expanded by 25 percent, while the agricultural working population increased by 21 percent. If Thailand is excluded, the agricultural labor growth of 16 percent outpaced the arable land area growth of 12 percent. The expansion of the agricultural frontier in Thailand came to a virtual halt in the early 1980s. The pattern of growth is shifting to the intensive margin in Thailand as elsewhere in Asia. In the future, only eastern Malaysia and the outer islands of Indonesia offer much potential for clearing new land for agricultural settlement. In Korea and Taiwan, where farm area per capita is only one-twentieth of a hectare, the decline in the agricultural labor force was more than offset by conversion of agricultural land to other uses.

The scarcity of land relative to agricultural labor has induced a pattern of more intensive use of scarce farm land in Asia. Asian farmers have strived for production growth through the adoption of land-saving technology and use of inputs complementary to labor. Crop yields per unit of land have become the focus of growth. Yield increases have involved irrigation investment, the practice of multiple cropping, greater use of fertilizer and chemicals, improved seeds, selective adoption of mechanical equipment and tools for weeding, improved farm management, a variety of agricultural services, and continuous research to improve technology.

Rice is by far the most important crop in Asia, in terms of land area, production value, and impact on employment, incomes, and nutrition. Of the total cereals area harvested in 1983 in Asian LDCs (178 million hectares), over half was accounted for by rice, about a fifth by wheat, and one-tenth by maize. Gains have been rapid in the production of rice and other cereals in Asia since the introduction of modern seed varieties. Most of the gains in rice production since the late 1960s (about three-quarters) have been due to increases in land productivity rather than the extension of the land area. Though the shares of gains in wheat and maize production due to yield increases are lower, those shares are rapidly rising as land becomes still scarcer.

Three major interrelated factors contributed to the upsurge in food grains production in Asia. Among the most important has been the rapid dissemination of modern seed varieties. The rates at which farmers in Asia have adopted high-yielding seeds have been exceptional—even exceeding the rates achieved by more developed nations.[19] Since their introduction in the mid-1960s, modern rice varieties expanded by the late 1970s to cover over 70 percent of the rice area in the Philippines and Sri Lanka, and over 50 percent of that in Pakistan and Indonesia. Within seven years of the introduction of modern wheat varieties in India, they covered over two-thirds of the total area planted to wheat.

A second major factor was a greater use of chemical fertilizers. Total fertilizer consumption increased by more than fourfold in South Asia and sixfold in Southeast Asia between 1966 and 1982. South Asian farmers used 36 kilograms per hectare in 1982 and only 7 in 1966; in Southeast Asia, the increase was from under 9 kilograms to over 47. The availability of fertilizer-responsive seed varieties and irrigation lifted the profitability of fertilizer use substantially; and so consumption increased in spite of higher fertilizer costs caused by the two oil price hikes.

Irrigation investment was the third major component of Asia's cereal revolution. The proportion of farmland under irrigation was about 20 percent in the mid-1960s; by 1982 it was over 28 percent. More than 22 million hectares were added to the irrigated area between 1966 and 1982. The expansion of the irrigated area was accompanied by large-scale rehabilitation and the improvement of existing irrigation systems. The improved quality of irrigation also contributed to production growth.

The total amount of rice produced in less-developed Asian countries rose from 140 million tons per year in the early 1970s to 190 million tons in the early 1980s. Rice imports into South and Southeast Asia fell from almost 9 million tons per year in the mid-1970s to less than 1 million tons in the early 1980s. By the mid-1980s, production exceeded 210 million tons, and Asia had a substantial surplus of rice.

Wheat, the second most important cereal crop in Asia, showed even more impressive growth than rice. Wheat production was up by almost 110 percent in the five major producing countries (South Asia, excluding Sri Lanka) between 1973 and 1984, a growth rate in excess of 7 percent a year. Net imports of wheat in normal crop years in wheat-growing South Asia declined significantly in the mid-1980s from net imports in the mid-1970s.

The production of maize, Asia's third largest cereal crop, expanded by over 30 percent in the 1970s. Indonesia, the Philippines, and Thailand had high rates of growth due to both area and yield increases. Thailand emerged in the late 1970s as a substantial net exporter of feed corn. Maize production expanded at a slow rate during 1970–84 in parts of South Asia, except in Burma (where rapid percentage increases came from a small base), Sri Lanka, and Pakistan. Millet, sorghum, and barley are grown in dry areas of Asia. Most of the past production increases in these grains have been from area expansion (mainly in Burma, Thailand, and India). Newly developed drought and disease-resistant strains of millet, sorghum, and other coarse grains should lead to growth in per hectare yields and overall production.

Cereal yields have increased at an annual rate of about 3 percent in South and Southeast Asia on average since the introduction of HYVs in the mid-1960s. The average yield of cereal crops still is less than 2 metric tons per hectare in South Asia, while it is 2.5 tons in ASEAN-4 and over 4 tons in Korea and Taiwan (figure 5.4).

Large variations in yields exist between countries in South Asia and ASEAN-4. In Burma and Sri Lanka, cereal yields were approaching 3 metric tons, but were only half that in Pakistan and India. Indonesian yields were about 3.5 tons, twice that of the Philippines. The large disparities in yields reflect differences in levels of development, but also indicate that good scope exists for further improvements in a number of countries.

(The policy interventions that various governments have made to promote higher productivity, in the food grains sector, and future policy issues, are assessed on pp. 158–169.)

Farm Income and Linkages to Other Sectors

The rapid increases in cereals production in the period since the introduction of new varieties had strong positive effects on farm incomes and

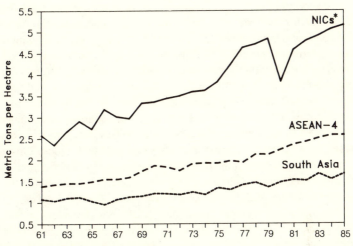

Figure 5.4. Cereal Yields in Asia, 1961–85
Sources: FAO, *FAO Production Yearbook*, 1985 and earlier years; FAO, *Monthly Bulletin of Statistics*, March 1986.
Note: NICs in this instance include only Taiwan and Korea.

expenditures. These, in turn, through linkages with the other sectors of the economy, have fostered structural changes and overall economic growth. The share of farm output that is sold commercially increased dramatically in areas where the new technology has been widely adopted. In Java, Indonesia, for example, in the early 1960s, only about 20 percent of rice production was marketed; by the late 1970s the marketable surplus was equivalent to almost half the total production.[20]

Gains in production and commercial sales lead to increases in farmers' cash incomes. Expenditures for agricultural inputs (chemicals, fertilizer, seed), tools, and machinery (ploughs, irrigation pumps) go up. Farm households also tend to purchase more simple consumer goods (clothing, cosmetics, furniture) and to consume more food products (including processed food) with higher income elasticities of demand. The growth in farm incomes stimulates domestic industrial production and services, particularly trade, transport, and marketing.

In Taiwan, productivity growth in agriculture and particularly in cereals was rapid enough to allow farm incomes to rise even though a significant net transfer of resources was made to other sectors.[21] Farmers purchased more inputs and consumer goods, thus increasing the market for domestic manufacturers and service establishments. These tended to be very labor intensive, and their growth led to increased off-farm employment opportunities. The rising demand for rural labor reduced poverty incidence sharply.

Village surveys in West Java, Indonesia, show that since the mid-1970s, the rapid gains in rice and food production have led to increased positive interaction between agriculture and other sectors. Rapid growth in off-farm employment and higher farm incomes have contributed to a significant improvement in living standards in the villages surveyed. Poverty incidence fell from about half to only one-third of the population between the mid-1970s and mid-1980s.[22]

One aspect of Taiwan's experience that deserves emphasis was the role agricultural exports played in releasing the constraint on farm cash earnings from domestic sales alone, especially during the initial period of rural development. By taking advantage of external markets for agricultural goods, Taiwan was able to achieve structural transformation much more quickly than otherwise. Exports of agricultural goods (including processed items) accounted for over half the total cash sales in the 1950s and early 1960s. Though most cereal sales were for domestic use, a large share of noncereal crops, livestock, and forestry and fishery products were exported, often in processed form.

Agricultural Exports and Growth

Most Asian countries in the 1970s were successful in rapidly expanding the value of agricultural product exports, despite sharp fluctuations in commodity prices. Table 5.2 shows that between 1970–72 (a period of booming commodity demand) and 1983–85 (a period of depressed demand), real agricultural product exports increased sharply in the ASEAN-4 countries except the Philippines. Agricultural exports were growing fastest in the countries with the highest rates of agricultural growth (Thailand and Malaysia). Burma, as was explained above, is an exception. Much of its incremental agricultural production was to meet rapidly growing domestic food demand.

Per capita exports of agricultural products (also in table 5.2) were very low in South Asia (except Sri Lanka) in comparison with those in the NICs and ASEAN-4 countries. The high levels of agricultural exports per capita reported by Singapore and Hong Kong in table 5.2 are really re-exports from neighboring countries. The higher growth rates of agricultural GDP in ASEAN-4 compared to those in the South Asian countries are related to the differences in agricultural export performance. Macroeconomic and trade policies in ASEAN-4 were fairly conducive to the expansion of agricultural exports. This was often not the case in the South Asian countries. By expanding agricultural exports, the ASEAN-4 countries realized greater foreign exchange earnings and improved the linkages between agriculture and other sectors, especially processing and related service industries. The contribution of agricultural exports in easing the constraint on farm earnings was much greater in the ASEAN economies than it was in South Asia.

There are some inherent difficulties in relying on agricultural exports for increasing rural incomes and foreign exchange earnings in larger countries and

Table 5.2. Agricultural Exports[a]

	Real Average Agricultural Exports (US$ millions)[b]		Real Average Agricultural Exports per Capita (US$)[b]		Real Average Agricultural Exports as a Percentage of Merchandise Exports (percentages)	
	1970–72	1983–85	1970–72	1983–85	1970–72	1983–85
NICs						
Hong Kong	588.7	1,837.9	145	342	6	6
Korea	738.0	1,533.1	22	38	25	5
Singapore	NA	2,780.7	NA	1,100	19	11
Taiwan	509.6	629.7	34	33	7	2
ASEAN-4						
Indonesia	2,422.8	4,262.0	20	27	50	19
Malaysia	4,926.1	7,910.1	460	521	62	42
Philippines	2,041.5	2,064.1	54	39	76	36
Thailand	1,967.5	5,012.7	52	101	72	59
South Asia						
Bangladesh	276.3[c]	327.5	4[c]	4	45[c]	32
Burma	338.4	410.6	12	11	89	85
India	2,850.1	3,090.8	5	4	38	27[d]
Nepal	244.9	47.6	23	3	[e]	35
Pakistan	671.0[c]	924.3	10[c]	10	38[c]	30
Sri Lanka	836.8	923.5	66	60	96	60

Sources: United Nations, Food and Agricultural Organization (FAO), *FAO Trade Yearbook*, 1985 and earlier years; ADB, *Key Indicators of Developing Member Countries of ADB*, April 1983, and July 1986; IMF, *International Financial Statistics*, Yearbook 1986, vol. 40, no. 5 (May 1987); *Taiwan Statistical Data Book*, 1986.

[a]Agricultural exports include forestry and fishery products.

[b]Deflated by export unit values of each country except for Bangladesh, India, Nepal, Indonesia, Malaysia, Hong Kong, Singapore, and Taiwan, where export unit values of total Asia were used (1980 = 100).

[c]1973–75.

[d]1983–84.

[e]Data are not consistent for 1970–72.

even in small ones that rely on one or a few primary commodities. World supply tends to outstrip demand of farm products. Though the early 1970s saw periods of booming prices for primary goods, there has been a persistent fall in the terms of trade for primary product exporters in the 1980s. Thailand's experience indicates that by exporting an array of agricultural goods, some buoyant external markets can usually be found. Thailand also was able to increase exports by increasing farm productivity and competitiveness in external markets, despite terms of trade losses. The diversity of Thai agricultural exports contrasts sharply with the situation in Burma, where rice and teak continued to account for over two-thirds of merchandise exports in the 1980s. Throughout developing Asia the share of agricultural exports in total merchandise exports fell, in most cases sharply, during the 1970s and 1980s (table 5.2). In some South Asian countries and Burma the high share of agricultural exports reflected the poor performance of manufactured exports rather than the exceptional growth of agricultural exports.

The agricultural export performance of Asian countries was closely related to their success in expanding supplies of noncereal crops, livestock, and fishery and forestry products.

Noncereal Crops

The noncereal crops range from pulses and root crops often produced for subsistence purposes by low-income limited resource farmers in rainfed plots to a variety of tree crops, fibers, and horticultural products sometimes produced by highly commercialized, agribusiness firms or modern plantations. A number of cash crops are simultaneously raised by smallholders and on modern estates (rubber, cocoa, coconut, sugar, tobacco, cotton, jute). Usually, the estates generate higher yields and better quality, though they are not necessarily more efficient than smallholders when economic costs and returns are considered.[23]

The share of noncereal crops in agricultural GDP varies among countries, but acounts for 20 to 30 percent of total agricultural output in South and Southeast Asia. The noncereal crops account for a considerably larger share of agricultural exports than do cereals. In Taiwan and Korea the noncereal crop sector is smaller, and accounts for a lower share of agricultural exports than it does in South Asia or the ASEAN-4 countries.

The ASEAN-4 countries had a higher growth in the production of noncereal crops and particularly major export crops (palm oil, rubber, coconut, coffee, sugar) than did South Asia. The stronger growth of agricultural production and exports in the ASEAN-4 countries during the 1970s is largely because of the faster growth of noncereal crops. The ASEAN-4 countries had more abundant land resources than did South Asia or the NICs for the expansion of noncereal crops. These countries also did more to promote noncereal crop production, and their policies left agricultural product and factor markets relatively undistorted. This allowed a degree of diversification to occur in response to market incentives.

Livestock, Fisheries, and Forestry

Livestock are an integral component of smallholder agriculture throughout Asia. The larger animals (buffalo and cattle) are valued more as a source of draft power, manure, and transport than they are as a food source in low-income rural areas. In most of Asia, cattle and dairy production are constrained by the scarcity of land for grazing purposes. Technical services are less developed, and diseases adversely affect the size and quantity of larger ruminants.

On the demand side, the consumption of meat, milk, and eggs is very low, though income growth has increased the demand for these income-elastic products, particularly in the NICs and more prosperous parts of South and Southeast Asia. Meat and dairy production has been expanding most rapidly in Korea and Taiwan—an increase reflected in the large importation of animal feed by these countries.

The production of poultry and pork has increased rapidly in South and Southeast Asia, but overall, the livestock sector has been lagging, and its share of agricultural GDP has been stagnant or declining.

In contrast to livestock, fishery production has been one of the most dynamic aspects of Asian agriculture since the 1970s. The total fish production of the Asian developing countries doubled between 1965 and 1982. Its share in total world production increased from 12 percent in 1965 to 20 percent in 1982.[24] The rapid growth of fishery production increases protein supplies to consumers, provides employment opportunities, and brings in foreign exchange. Fish products provide the main source of animal protein consumed in most Asian countries. Fish product exports increased much faster than overall agricultural exports in all three subregions of Asia. Taiwan and Korea showed the largest increases in fish product exports—but gains were also made by South and Southeast Asian countries. Marine production accounted for four-fifths of the total. The extension of exclusive economic zones to a distance 200 miles from the coasts has changed the distribution of marine resources, expanding opportunities for some countries and reducing them for others. Overfishing and pollution in many coastal areas near population centers have had a negative impact on small, village-based fishermen. Freshwater capture fisheries have been adversely affected as well by population pressures, and production has stagnated. Aquaculture technologies for developing high-yielding fishponds present new opportunities for expanding production in Asia.

The forestry sector's contribution to agricultural growth and foreign exchange earnings in Asia rose sharply in the second half of the 1970s, but declined in the recessionary conditions of the 1980s. The size and importance of forestry as an economic activity vary enormously within the Asian LDCs, a reflection of the uneven distribution of forest resources.

At the beginning of the 1980s, about one-third of the land area in the Asian developing countries—over 300 million hectares—was formally classified as forest land. The aggregate figure greatly overstates the actual area covered by forests. Few stands remain of primary tropical rain forest in Asia, outside of

Burma, eastern Malaysia, and some of Indonesia's large outer islands. The distribution of forest land is very uneven within the region. The ASEAN-4 countries and Burma account for most of the region's forest resources. They have approximtely two-thirds of a hectare of forest per capita. In contrast, South Asian countries have under one-tenth of a hectare of forest per person; Taiwan and Korea have around four-tenths of a hectare per capita.

Forest product exports accounted for about one-fourth of total agricultural exports in ASEAN-4 and Korea in the 1970s, but were less than 5 percent of agricultural exports in South Asia. The share of forest product exports in total agricultural exports fell from one-fifth in the late 1970s to one-seventh in the 1980s. This decline was not only because of depressed prices in overseas markets. Rapid depletion of forests was another reason. In the mid-1980s, annual deforestation in Asia was estimated at over 10 million hectares—a rate in excess of 3 percent![25] In Southeast Asia the destruction of tropical forests has reached alarming proportions. Thailand used to be a major exporter of hardwood logs, but it must now import a major part of its lumber. Rapid expansion of agricultural land for farming has all but eliminated the rain forests of Thailand. The Philippines is expected to also become a net importer of wood by the early 1990s if not before. Even Malaysia and Indonesia are encountering difficulties in supplying wood-processing industries with raw materials.

The rate of forest exploitation has exceeded the natural capacity of forests to regenerate. Hunger for land, demand for fuel wood, carelessness, and the pursuit of quick short-term profits have all contributed to the degradation of Asia's forests. Vast areas of South and Southeast Asia are now covered by worthless but tenacious alang-alang grass—mainly the result of logging followed by shifting cultivation. In South Asia, roughly two-thirds of rural energy consumption is met by fuel wood. Forests are critically depleted, and fuel wood is becoming increasingly scarce. The environmental effects of deforestation on other agricultural activities are severe. The destruction of forests in watershed areas leads to soil erosion, flooding, and siltation of irrigation reservoirs and canals. The high costs of wanton deforestation include reduced overall agricultural production in the long term.

Assessment of Agricultural Policies

The improvement of agricultural production in Asia between the mid-1960s and the mid-1980s is in large part because of the type of policies adopted by governments. Policy changes have been instrumental in improving both the incentives to produce and the capacity of the sector to respond. Advances in technology, large investments in infrastructure, institutional reforms, and increased human capital formation have all contributed to Asia's agricultural performance. The macroeconomic environment has also played a strong role in agricultural development.

Government policies affecting agriculture can be conceptually separated into those that influence the pattern of incentives (price interventions) and those that operate on the underlying ability and capacity of rural households to produce (nonprice interventions). In practice, a neat separation between the two is difficult. Interactions of incentives and capacities to produce are fundamental to the process of agricultural growth. Before sector policies are examined in detail, the broader macroeconomic environment is considered. In a number of Asian case studies, sound macroeconomic policies were found to be essential for the success of more specific agricultural policies.[26]

Macroeconomic Policies and Prices

The fundamental importance of agriculture to economic development was first elaborated by Johnston and Mellor.[27] They enumerated five vital functions or contributions: (1) meeting the demand for food of a growing population to the extent consistent with comparative advantage; (2) providing a source of foreign exchange earnings or savings; (3) providing a source of savings for investment in development of other sectors; (4) providing manpower and raw materials for other sectors; (5) providing internal demand for domestic industry and services sectors.

Each of these functions is sensitive to macroeconomic policy. But macroeconomic policy was hardly ever made with the importance of agriculture in mind. The view that agricultural production was price inelastic, the fallacy of the irrational peasant, and the somewhat narrow sector orientation of agricultural policy specialists contributed to the neglect of the effects of macroeconomic policies on agriculture.

Too often policymakers and economists concerned with agriculture have tended to neglect broader policy issues in their preoccupation with micro-level and sector-based concerns. In the late 1960s and much of the 1970s, research on agricultural development eschewed macroeconomics in favor of village studies in which researchers sought to gain a "view from the paddy." Valuable as these studies were for understanding peasant behavior and specific problems of adapting new technology and institutional change, they sometimes led researchers astray in deriving policy implications.[28]

Awareness of the importance of macroeconomic policy for agricultural development was revealed in only a few studies of the development process. Little, Scitovsky, and Scott (1971), McKinnon (1973), and Johnston and Kilby (1975) argued that in a number of developing countries, agricultural development was adversely affected by high rates of inflation, tariff and trade protection that was biased in favor of capital-intensive import substitution industries, overvalued domestic currencies, and government interventions that set interest rates too low and wage rates too high.[29]

Pakistan and India, countries that both adopted import substitution industrialization strategies in the 1950s, restricted imports by means of high tariffs, exchange controls, and a system of import licensing. Protected industrial firms were encouraged to adopt capital-intensive techniques by government policies that underpriced capital and raised the cost of unskilled labor. Artificially low interest rates and underpricing of foreign exchange enabled privileged firms (often public enterprises) to avail of cheap government credits and to import capital equipment "inexpensively." Of course, unprivileged firms and producers in other sectors were unable to get credit except from moneylenders at much higher interest rates. Exports and savings were discouraged. Investment was inefficient and consumers faced limited choices—to buy low-quality domestic goods at high prices or do without. Farmers had little incentive to increase marketable supplies of food or primary exports. Agricultural production growth in Pakistan was under 2 percent in the 1950s. Domestic markets for manufactured goods produced by protected firms failed to expand. Growth slowed and underemployment increased. Slow structural transformation resulted.

In Taiwan, macroeconomic policies kept the exchange rate at a realistic level, raised interest rates to encourage savings, prevented high inflation, and gradually improved the intersectoral terms of trade for agriculture. Agriculture grew at an annual real rate of between 4 and 5 percent during the 1950s and 1960s in Taiwan.[30]

The trauma of world inflation, recession, and the demise of the system of fixed exchange rates in the 1970s underscored the importance of macroeconomic policy for agriculture. Peter Timmer and his colleagues focused attention on the interactions of "macro prices"—exchange rates, interest rates, wage rates, inflation rates, and the intersectoral terms of trade—and agricultural performance.[31] The experience of Timmer and others advising the Indonesian government convinced them of the significance of macroeconomics for agriculture.

Until the late 1960s, Indonesian farmers labored under the weight of high inflation, an overvalued rupiah, acute shortages of credit, and deteriorating internal terms of trade (caused by the setting of artificially low food prices in urban markets). Between 1958 and 1966, agricultural exports fell by a third, and an agricultural production growth rate of 1.6 percent failed to keep pace with population growth.[32]

The complete turnaround in agricultural performance in the post-Sukarno era, when the growth rate more than doubled from less than 2 to almost 4 percent, was in large part because of the improved macroeconomic environment. The intersectoral terms of trade were reasonably stable, inflation was kept under control, a liberal exchange rate policy was adopted, interest rates were raised to economic levels encouraging an increase in the supply of funds, wage rates were left to market forces, taxation was moderate, and the pattern of protection, though far from ideal, allowed producers to respond to international market opportunities.[33]

Macroeconomic policies in other Asian countries that experienced strong records of agricultural development—Thailand and Malaysia—provided an environment broadly supportive of agricultural development. Policies kept inflation rates under control, permitted international markets to stimulate domestic producers, gave incentives to save and invest, kept taxation of agriculture moderate, and did not turn internal terms of trade against farmers. Specific agricultural sector policies and programs work far more effectively than otherwise when introduced under favorable macroeconomic conditions. In Korea, agricultural prices rose in relation to nonagricultural prices. The protectionist Korean agricultural policy increased the growth rate of agriculture, but did so at the cost of reducing growth in other sectors.[34]

When macroprices are freed from excessive distortion, more efficient resource allocation is one result. But market-priced foreign exchange and interest rates also expand the total supply of foreign exchange and savings available. More investment and employment become possible. With a reduction in trade protection and a lower relative cost of labor, more producers have access to more and cheaper inputs. Income distribution improves, and this tends to lead to a pattern of consumer demand that favors producers of food and labor-intensive commodities. The positive linkages between agriculture and industry are stimulated.

Bottlenecks may still appear in agriculture and constrain the growth process. Agricultural policies are necessary to overcome these. Price and nonprice policy interventions were made by Asian governments to help overcome constraints on agricultural production.

Agricultural Pricing

The pricing of agricultural products and staple foods in particular is a sensitive political issue in most Asian countries. Governments must balance the objectives of providing food to consumers at affordable prices and adequate incentives to farmers. In Asia, rice and edible oils make up a large share of consumer expenditures. Unstable prices for these major items can have large effects on overall price stability and on real incomes. It is not an exaggeration to say that price instability for rice can lead to political instability for Asian governments.[35]

During the 1950s and 1960s, farm incentives were often sacrificed in favor of low consumer prices. The belief that peasant farmers were unresponsive to price incentives was a convenient rationale. Also, with limited double cropping and low yields, most farm households were only in the market as sellers once a year. During the long months between harvests, more and more farm households became buyers of rice. Therefore, governments wished to attain a seasonal balance in staple food prices—slightly higher during harvests and lower in the lean period preceding harvests. Meeting this objective obliged governments in deficit countries to encroach more and more on food grain markets, reducing the scope for merchants and private operators of storage and marketing facilities or driving them out altogether. Government food agencies were not particularly successful in stabilizing the prices of rice and other staples in deficit countries because import prices themselves could be quite volatile. Indonesia's Bureau of Logistics, for example, was unable to prevent retail rice prices from more than doubling from 1972 to 1973, when a domestic shortfall in the rice harvest made it necessary to import over 1 million tons of rice on an emergency basis. Large-scale harvest failures in the Soviet Union and China that year had driven up international rice prices by almost 400 percent. Similar difficulties were experienced in other Asian rice importing countries.

The early-to-middle 1970s were difficult years for price stability of any kind in Asian countries. The booming commodity markets of 1972–74 enabled some countries with exportable crops (Thailand and the Philippines) to accumulate surpluses that helped them overcome the effects of the oil shock and subsequent world recession. Domestic political and economic stability were threatened by sharp jumps in food prices. The green revolution appeared to be losing momentum or petering out completely in some countries—Pakistan, Indonesia, and India. To counter the problem of a slowdown in cereals production, most Asian governments acted to increase farm incentives.

Probably the most important individual prices to the majority of farmers in Asia are those of rice and fertilizer at the farm gate. Variation in yields and production levels of rice can be largely accounted for by differences in fertilizer application.[36] The intensity of fertilizer use, in turn, is positively correlated with the farm gate ratio of rice-to-fertilizer prices (table 5.3).

After the mid-1970s, the paddy-fertilizer price ratio was increased or at least maintained in every Asian country except Taiwan. In Taiwan, the ratio was still rather high in 1981, and the country continued to produce a rice surplus. The price incentives were improved most in Sri Lanka, Indonesia, and Korea. Sri Lanka increased domestic rice production to over 90 percent of consumption needs (figure 5.5). The price ratios remained low in the Philippines, Thailand, Pakistan, and India.

The use of subsidies to promote fertilizer use was extensive in Burma, Bangladesh, Sri Lanka, Pakistan, Malaysia, Indonesia, and Thailand. In some cases fertilizer subsidies were used to offset low domestic paddy prices (Burma, Pakistan, Sri Lanka, Thailand, Indonesia). Budget deficits ballooned after fertilizer costs moved sharply upward in 1979 to 1981, and domestic rice prices fell below the cost of imported rice. Governments tried to avoid the problem of fluctuations in import prices by building up stocks. But storage costs proved to be excessively high. Governments learned that overreliance on price manipulation and buffer stock arrangements to attain rice self-sufficiency could be very costly indeed. Other factors, particularly irrigation, agricultural research and extension, farmer education, transportation, marketing, and communica-

Table 5.3. Paddy Yields, Ratio of Paddy Price to Fertilizer Price, and Fertilizer Applied per Hectare of Rice

	Farm Gate Price Ratio of Paddy and Fertilizer			Fertilizer Applied per Hectare of Planted Rice (kg/ha)		Paddy Yields (kg/ha)	
	1976	1981	Location	1976[a]	1981[b]	1976	1981
NICs							
Korea	0.65	0.84	Hwaseong-gun	311	351	5,966	5,841
Taiwan	1.25	0.75	Taichung	205	287	4,539[c]	4,953[c]
ASEAN-4							
Indonesia	0.40	0.62	Central Java[d]	57	74	2,784	3,493
Malaysia	0.49	0.56	Selangor[e]	97[f]	92	2,733	3,225
Philippines	0.28	0.27	Central Luzon	29	32	1,821	2,362
Thailand	0.24	0.30	Suphan Buri[g]	11	18	1,780	1,952
South Asia							
Bangladesh	0.51	0.57	Joydebpur	11	44	1,784	1,955
Burma	0.55	0.55	Rangoon	9	17	1,799	2,942
India	0.17	0.37	Coimbatore	32	34	1,637	1,962
Nepal	0.33	0.45	Kathmandu[h]	8	9	1,891	2,000
Pakistan	0.27	0.28	Punjab[i]	46	53	2,347	2,604
Sri Lanka	0.60	0.93	Kurunegala[d]	65	77	1,971	2,646

Sources: FAO, *FAO Production Yearbook*, 1983, 1979; FAO, *FAO Fertilizer Yearbook*, 1984; *Taiwan Statistical Data Book*, 1985; Adelita C. Palacpac, *World Rice Statistics*, 1982; R. Barker, R. W. Herdt, with B. Rose, *The Rice Economy of Asia*; B. Rose, *Appendix to the Rice Economy of Asia*, March 1985.

[a]This column is obtained by extrapolating total fertilizer used per hectare of rice from 1971 to 1975.

[b]Total fertilizer consumed per hectare of arable land and permanent crops. Fertilizer statistics are not widely collected in Asia; the figures provided here must be viewed as estimates of total use. And since rice is the major crop planted and grown in Asia, the figures are approximations for fertilizer used in rice.

[c]According to Beth Rose (1985), rice production in Taiwan is reported in metric tons of brown (husked) rice, and the conversion factor is 1 kg of paddy equal to 0.76 kg of brown rice, as used in this table.

[d]1976 and 1978–80.   [g]1976 and 1977.
[e]1976 and 1982.   [h]1977 and 1978.
[f]West Malaysia.   [i]1977 and 1979.

tion infrastructure, and improved institutions are more important in determining long-run supply.[37] Investments in these complementary factors were stepped up during the 1970s. Across developing Asia, traditional importers of rice moved closer to self-sufficiency. Government promotion of rice self-sufficiency has become excessive in some cases, especially in Japan, Korea, and

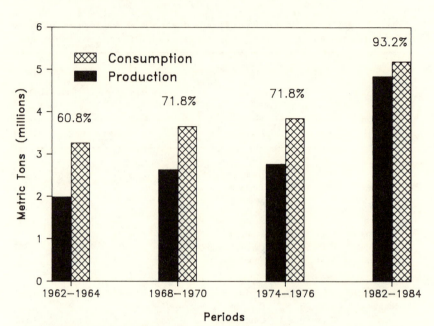

Periods

Figure 5.5. Rice Self-Sufficiency in Sri Lanka, 1962–84
Sources: USDA, *Foreign Agricultural Circular: Grains*, September 1982; FAO, *FAO Production Yearbook*, 1984 and earlier years; FAO, *FAO Trade Yearbook*, 1984 and earlier years; FAO, *Monthly Bulletin of Statistics*, March 1986.
Note: Figures are totals for three-year periods, not annual averages.

Taiwan. In Sri Lanka it has also been found that the cost of additional domestic rice production is several times as high as that in nearby rice-exporting countries like Pakistan, Burma, and Thailand.[38]

Technology, Infrastructure, and Institutions

Montague Yudelman described the investment in yield-improving cereal varieties and the investments in irrigation, rural credit, fertilizer distribution, and related infrastructure as the largest transfer of technology in modern history, affecting millions of farmers in Asia.[39] Agricultural technology continued to advance at an exceptional rate in the years after the initial development of high-yielding grain varieties.

Asian developing countries increased budgets for agricultural research and developed closer links between national centers and the international crop research institutions.[40] In the 1970s, new seed varieties that outperformed the initial HYVs were developed. The new strains were more disease resistant, faster to mature, more capable of withstanding weather and rainfall variations, and more palatable.

Massive investments in improving rural infrastructure—irrigation, roads, communications, electrification, and health and educational facilities—were undertaken during the 1970s across rural Asia. These infrastructural investments paralleled the green revolution. Irrigation works facilitated the rapid acceptance of new varieties, encouraged higher levels of input use, and allowed multiple cropping to spread. About 50 to 60 percent of the increase in food production in the developing world since the mid-1960s came from new or rehabilitated irrigated lands—mainly in Asia.[41] The annual investments in irrigation and related infrastructure works run to almost $10 billion in Asia. A parallel "transport revolution" in rural Asia reduced the costs of marketing and improved the returns earned by farmers, particularly where competition increased among grain merchants and farm input suppliers.

Other support facilities were also built up. Improved storage, handling, and distribution facilities have helped control losses from spoilage and pests. Efficient development of additional capacity for postharvest operations requires a clear demarcation of the roles of the private and government sectors. Expansion of government facilities has sometimes displaced the private sector. Also government agencies often have higher rates of grain spoilage and are not very quick in responding to changes in the market for grains.

Government intervention in grain marketing and other agricultural trading activities is common in less developed countries where food prices and supplies are so politicized. Asian countries have not permitted government marketing boards to completely monopolize trading as they do in parts of Africa. The private sector continues to play the major role in marketing, and nongovernment organizations like cooperatives have been organized to provide farmers with better access to inputs and credit and to reduce marketing costs.

The institutional changes associated with new technology can have a significant impact on employment and income distribution. The technology of the green revolution was itself "scale neutral." That is, it could provide roughly the same gains in productivity per hectare to small or large farms. The problem was that successfully adapting the technology required larger cash inputs and greater risks than using traditional varieties did. The technology could not be neatly separated from the institutional and policy environment into which it was introduced. Large farmers have easier access to credit and can more easily accept the risks associated with a new technology.

Mechanizing agriculture in countries with an abundance of rural labor is undesirable if machines displace laborers. Government distortion of prices sometimes induced premature mechanization; well-to-do farmers were encouraged to purchase tractors and other machines through concessional credits, duty-free importation, and overvalued domestic currencies. Large landholders may favor mechanization since it reduces the need to hire and monitor numerous laborers. There was some evidence in the 1970s of labor displacement in parts of Indonesia, Pakistan, and the Philippines, but it is not a universal problem.

Government research and extension agencies, and administrators of credit programs, are themselves influenced by the prevailing rural power structure. Loan and extension agents could be expected to spend more time with the politically powerful, prosperous, and educated rural elite than they did with the rural poor. Large and prosperous farmers tended, therefore, to more quickly adapt the new technologies. If they benefited disproportionately from credit programs and other public services, income equalities would be increased. The neutrality claim of the green revolution could be invalidated by the real world institutional setting.[42]

To offset the potential for a worsening income distribution, governments introduced reforms to provide greater access to credit and greater security of tenure.

Rural financial institutions were expanded and provided a larger share of farm credit. In Korea and Taiwan, banking institutions provided two-thirds of farm credits by the late 1970s. In Thailand the share of farm credit from institutional sources rose from 7 percent in the mid-1970s to almost two-thirds by 1981. The share of institutional finance was lower in South Asia, but was gradually rising during the 1970s.[43] In making rural credit available to small farmers, a number of problems were encountered. Loan programs had to be tailored to the needs of small farmers, who often lacked collateral. Costs of administering many small loans were high, and many new institutions lacked experience. Undue emphasis was given to pushing out loans to meet lending targets. Lax enforcement of repayments led to high default rates and caused severe difficulties for the rural banks.

In the countries of South and Southeast Asia, rural financial institutions have considerably improved their performance as they have built up expertise in lending. As was discussed in chapter 3, these institutions are now placing greater emphasis on attracting savings deposits.

Land reform legislation in Asia has been aimed at preventing the concentration of land ownership and at protecting the rights and security of tenant farmers. Land reform was notably successful in Taiwan and Korea in establishing an even distribution of income in rural areas, but has been less successful in South and Southeast Asia. In the latter countries, estimates of idle or surplus land were sometimes exaggerated. In none (outside Korea and Taiwan) was as much as 5 percent of the land transferred to the landless. Land reform laws may have, at best, helped slow the trend toward increasing the concentration of land holdings in parts of South and Southeast Asia.

Factors other than institutional reform have been more important in reducing rural poverty in Asia. The spread of educational facilities, improvements in health and nutrition, and development of skills through vocational training (see chapter 6) are some of these. The development of nonagricultural activites in rural areas and the growth of off-farm employment have transformed many rural communities.

The experience of rural development in densely populated Java indicates that a broader view than that from the paddy is required to understand the process of change. Java, containing over 60 percent of Indonesia's population on only 7 percent of the land area, provides an important test case for the new rice technology. By the mid-1970s, traditional "poverty-sharing" institutions such as rice-harvesting arrangements were being rapidly displaced. Under the traditional system, all villagers, using small knives, had a right to participate in rice harvesting. The harvesting of rice was a major source of employment and income for the rural poor and landless. The introduction of modern rice varieties made it possible for farmers to earn substantially higher returns by restricting harvesting to a team of hired laborers using sickles. This, coupled with the introduction of mechanical rice milling in place of hand pounding, was thought to have severely negative effects on income distribution and the rural poor. Initially, fears were expressed by scholars that rural Java would be "polarized" into haves and have-nots on the basis of unequal access to land and capital. Village surveys later showed the fears of polarization were somewhat exaggerated.

In fact, new rice varieties, by allowing up to three harvests per year, did not displace labor. And as employment in nonagricultural occupations rose sharply, rural real wages actually started to increase. The incomes of the lowest 40 percent have grown faster between 1977 and 1983 than the incomes of other groups, and this growth has reduced both poverty and inequality.[44]

In principle and practice, better income distribution through institutional reform need not be at the cost of worsened resource allocation and slower growth of agricultural production. Reforms that improve the operation of markets can contribute to growth with equity. A successful transformation requires the political and economic reorganization of rural society (the "software" of agricultural development) to accompany greater investment in technology and infrastructure (the "hardware").

Future Problems and Prospects

Agricultural production achievements in the 1980s were spectacular in most of Asia. By the mid-1980s a huge surplus of rice led to falling real food prices. A number of countries that had serious deficits in cereal production during the mid-1970s—Indonesia, India, Sri Lanka—were in the mid-1980s attempting to cope with the problem of disposing of surplus production. The countries that traditionally have exported rice—Burma, Thailand, and Pakistan—will have to deal with shrinking markets.

The improved cereal production means that Asian countries will have to establish new priorities for agricultural development. Diversifying agriculture, however, requires a technological and infrastructural base that is more complex than that needed for producing food grains alone. Of the ASEAN-4 countries, Thailand and Malaysia have successfully established the underpinnings for a diversified agriculture. Thailand and Malaysia have adapted to changing international markets and shown an ability to export a wide range of processed and semiprocessed agricultural goods in addition to staples. But other ASEAN and South Asian countries have to reorient agricultural policies (and macroprices) to provide suitable incentives for shifting resources from cereals to other crops. The technological requirements of developing a diversified agriculture are challenging. But some initial steps have already been taken.

Genetic research has been extended to crops other than wheat, rice, and maize. Better varieties of root crops, legumes, and other food crops are being developed. These foods can substitute for cereals in diets and are important to farm households in areas outside the prospering irrigated rice floodplains of Asia.

Research money has also been devoted to improving quality and yields of a number of commercial and industrial crops like palm oil, sugarcane, coconut, rubber, and various natural fibers.

The success with rice and wheat has stimulated policymakers to advocate expanding the green revolution to unirrigated and upland farms. But because cropping patterns and environmental conditions are far more varied and complex outside of the rice plains, it will be more difficult to repeat past success. A "package" approach to technology and inputs worked for rice, but this is not likely to be feasible for limited resource farmers in rain-fed and upland areas of rural Asia. More location-specific research and even greater reliance on market signals will be necessary to succeed in developing the uplands. Reforestation and soil protection programs that allow upland farms to prosper require innovative research and creative implementation.

Upland farmers can supply Asian urban centers with a variety of products—vegetables, fruit, dairy and livestock products, tree crops—that have higher income elasticities of demand than do cereals or other staples. The markets for these goods have improved and will continue to grow in the future.

The diversification of agriculture offers one means of coping with rural poverty, but must overcome a number of internal and external constraints. The capital requirements for further agricultural development are projected to be very large.[45] FAO projected that the capital requirements to sustain an agricultural growth of 3–4 percent a year will be above $20 billion (1982 prices) in 1990 for South Asia and over $7 billion for the ASEAN-4.[46] These estimates may be excessive, given the rapid improvements being made in technology and the gradual replacement of old equipment by more efficient machinery (fuel efficient irrigation pumps, multipurpose small tractors, etc.). Nevertheless, the amounts required are not small and point out the need for vigorous efforts to mobilize domestic savings in rural Asia.

Even if the internal constraints can be overcome, the world trade environment for agricultural commodities is harsh. A number of Asian countries have experienced severe terms-of-trade losses in the 1980s. World markets for primary commodities were depressed by sluggish demand growth in the OECD countries coupled with supply gluts for most major primary goods. Real prices for food and agricultural raw materials fell by nearly 20 percent in 1981–82, after recovering by about 8 percent in 1983–84, then dropped by over 12 percent in 1985.[47]

Trade conflicts emerged between Asian exporters and the developed countries. Protection of domestic agriculture and subsidies to exporters have been combined by a number of European countries. Japan's market for many agricultural goods is highly protected. The United States has adopted export subsidies in order to compete with European exporters, but in doing so has harmed Asian primary exporters. The reversal of protectionism would greatly facilitate agricultural diversification in Asia. Asian countries could benefit from inexpensive imports of temperate zone products and expand exports of a variety of processed and semiprocessed tropical goods.

In making rural development a success, human resources will be a fundamental determinant. The ability to cope with disequilibrium, as Schultz observed, is directly related to the development of human skills and knowledge.[48] The transformation of rural Asia gained momentum in the 1970s and 1980s. The achievement of production growth far outstripped expectations. Though vast problems remain—poverty, diminishing forest resources, erosion, income inequalities, ethnic tensions—prospects are excellent for continued progress, provided good policies are made and international cooperation advances.

Table 5.A1. Listing of Countries in Regional and Subregional Groups

Region	Country
NICs	Korea, Taiwan
ASEAN-4	Indonesia, Malaysia, Philippines, Thailand
South Asia	Bangladesh, Burma, India, Nepal, Pakistan, Sri Lanka
Latin America and Caribbean	Argentina, Bolivia, Brazil, Chile, Colombia, Costa Rica, Dominican Republic, Ecuador, Guatemala, Haiti, Honduras, Jamaica, Mexico, Nicaragua, Panama, Paraguay, Peru, Trinidad and Tobago, Uruguay, Venezuela
Africa	Burundi, Cameroon, Central African Republic, Chad, Congo, Ethiopia, Ghana, Ivory Coast, Kenya, Lesotho, Liberia, Madagascar, Malawi, Mali, Mauritania, Niger, Nigeria, Senegal, Sierra Leone, Sudan, Tanzania, Togo, Uganda, Upper Volta, Zaire, Zambia, Zimbabwe

6 Human Resource Development

Introduction

Human resource economics scarcely existed in the early 1950s. Tinbergen observes that only "gradually was the importance of human skills for the development process discovered."[1] Despite the neglect of human as opposed to physical capital in early economic development theory, by the late 1950s, many government leaders were convinced that investment in education deserved priority.[2] The experience of Asian countries with human resource development strongly supports the view that human resource development is essential to increasing the wealth of nations. The NICs accomplished their remarkable social and economic performance through the development of skills, the knowledge and talent of the labor force, and the fullest use of its energies and capacities.

Numbers of people and their rate of increase drew increased attention in the 1960s when it was realized that population growth was higher than expected and seemed to be accelerating most in the poorest countries. The demographic patterns of today's less developed Asian nations are unlike historical patterns of the present higher income nations. Population growth in much of Asia is far in excess of that ever experienced in the more developed nations. Net emigration as a percentage of population in most Asian countries is far smaller than that from Europe to the new world colonies a century and more ago. Declines in mortality and birth rates are much steeper in less developed Asian countries than those experienced among the higher income countries during their demographic transition. But the excess of birth over death rates remains: rapid population growth burdens the Asian LDCs.

In the Asian LDCs, where populations depend mainly on agriculture for their income and employment, the increments in rural population add greater pressure to the limited agricultural land and water resources. Rapid population growth is occurring at a time when social and economic institutions, and physical infrastructure, are still underdeveloped. The most rapid population growth occurs among impoverished people who suffer most from its effects. There is a gap between the social effects and private perceptions of gain from having many children. The gap is particularly acute among the poorest.

The effects of the rapid past growth of population for employment are apparent in South Asia and ASEAN-4 countries. The population is young. Age pyramids (figures 6.1 and 6.2) for the Philippines (1983) and Pakistan (1981), countries without vigorous population policies in the past, show that 44.5 and 41.0 percent of their population were under 15 years of age. Countries at comparable income levels to the Philippines (Thailand) and Pakistan (Sri Lanka) with strong family planning programs have a smaller percentage of population under 15. In 1984, Thailand had 37.2 percent of its population in the youngest age groups (figure 6.3); Sri Lanka had only 33.5 percent (figure 6.4). Korea (1984), at a higher income level and with strong family planning policies, had 31.6 percent of its population under 15 (figure 6.5). Singapore (1984) had less than one-fourth of its population under 15 years of age (figure 6.6).

Births to fertile young adults will cause continued labor force explosion until the early twenty-first century. Unless dramatic declines in fertility can be brought about, job creation will be an imposing challenge well into the next century. With limited land resources, the rapid growth of the rural population implies that nonagricultural employment growth must be more rapid. Employment growth will occur mainly in existing or new urban centers and will produce an explosion of rapid urbanization. Bombay, Jakarta, Madras, Karachi, Seoul, Manila, Bangkok, and Delhi could all have populations of over 10 million by the turn of the century. Dislocation and change can have negative effects because they threaten traditional lifestyles. Urbanization will lead to the proximity of culturally, religiously, and socially heterogeneous groups in large urban centers. There is potential for conflict, especially in multiracial societies with wide disparities in income and opportunity.

Assessment of the consequences of population growth has a long tradition in economics, though only in recent decades has population dynamics been developed as a separate field of study.

The classiscal economists differ in their views of the consequences of population growth and of the need for government policies or other social measures. Adam Smith saw population growth in the "progressive state" as a lagged response to an increasing demand for labor and rising real wages. At a time when the New World colonies were offering abundant land and the industrial revolution was dawning, population growth seemed to Smith only an indicator of prosperity. For Malthus, the possibility that population would outstrip the growth of capital and the means of subsistence was a very real worry. His early writing stressed that famine, disease, and war would check population growth. Later, Malthus became more optimistic and saw delayed marriage and moral restraints before marriage acting as possible checks on population growth.

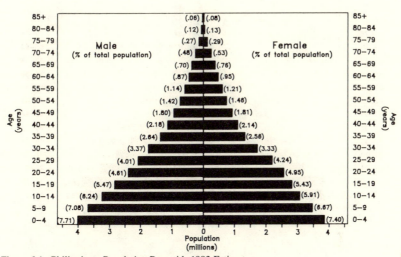

Figure 6.1. Philippines: Population Pyramid, 1983 Estimates

Source: United Nations, *1984 Demographic Yearbook*, 1986.

Explanatory note to figures 6.1 to 6.6: Numbers in parentheses represent percentages of total population in each age bracket for each sex.

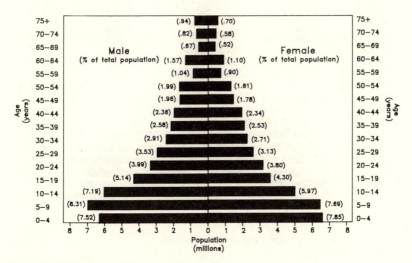

Figure 6.2. Pakistan: Population Pyramid, 1981 Census

Source: United Nations, *1984 Demographic Yearbook*, 1986.

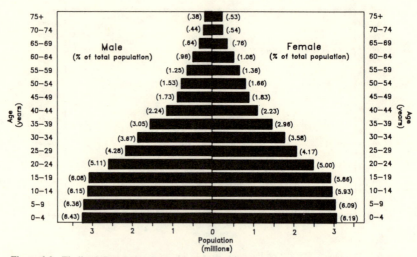

Figure 6.3. Thailand: Population Pyramid, 1984 Estimates
Source: United Nations, *1984 Demographic Yearbook*, 1986.

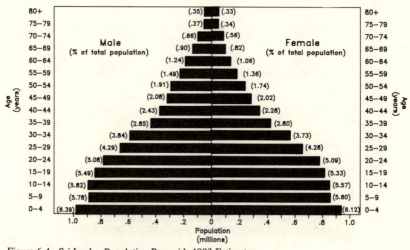

Figure 6.4. Sri Lanka: Population Pyramid, 1983 Estimates
Source: United Nations, *1984 Demographic Yearbook*, 1986.

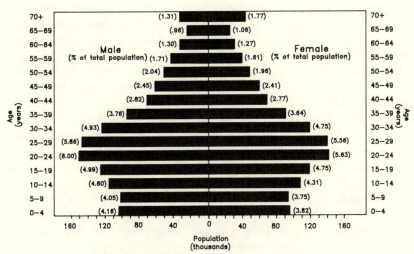

Figure 6.5. Korea: Population Pyramid, 1984 Estimates
Source: United Nations, *1984 Demographic Yearbook*, 1986.

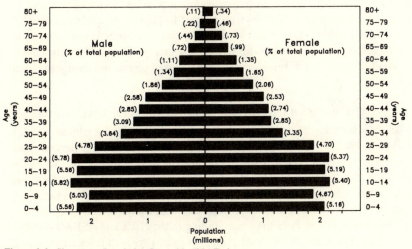

Figure 6.6. Singapore: Population Pyramid, 1984 Estimates
Source: United Nations, *1984 Demographic Yearbook*, 1986.

Ricardo carried the classical analysis further. Population growth would eventually stop in a stationary state where profits would fall to zero, as land rents would absorb any surplus, and wages would equal subsistence. Capital accumulation is the prime mover in Ricardo's system. But capital stops growing once the land constraint is sharp enough, and returns to new investments are near zero. Subsistence wages bring birth rates into line with death rates. Population no longer increases.

More recent writers see technology and institutions changing under the pressures of rapid population growth. Contraception, delayed marriage, and the rise of the small family ideal serve to replace the fearsome Malthusian checks. Innovations in agriculture and accelerating growth in nonagriculture prevent the onset of Ricardo's stationary state. The adoption of high-yielding varieties of cereal grains, intensification of land use in densely populated areas, and institutional changes—supplementing employment—accommodate the growing labor supply. These are, in part, "induced innovations"—economic, technological, and institutional responses to rapid population growth.[3]

The extension of economic analysis to the household and its decisions regarding fertility is of relatively recent origin. The "new household economics" approach applies the maximization postulate of microeconomic theory to the family.[4] Understanding the interaction of economics and demographics is crucial to framing appropriate policies with respect to population quality and size.[5] The limited current state of knowledge in economics is one cause for caution in suggesting policy remedies for human resource problems. With this caveat in mind, we examine the problems and prospects of population change in Asian countries.

Population Growth and Its Implications for Development

The population of the developing Asian countries (excluding China) was 1.3 billion in 1982, or one-fourth of the world total. The six South Asian countries alone had one-fifth of world population and one-fourth that of all LDCs. By the year 2000, the World Bank projects the population of the Asian LDCs at nearly 1.9 billion. India will have almost 1 billion people by the year 2000, and will shortly thereafter be more populous than China.

Population growth rates have been falling in the NICs and ASEAN-4 (table 6.1). In South Asia, although the picture is mixed, growth rates are expected to start declining before the end of this century. Sinking death rates have in the past century and more been the main cause of high population growth. In recent years, declining birth rates have been responsible for the reduction of population growth rates in Asia.

In South Asia birth rate declines have been largely offset by the lessening of mortality rates. Pakistan and Bangladesh have crude birth rates of over 40 per

1000: these rates have changed little since 1965. Pakistan has had a population growth of around 3 percent a year since 1965. At this rate, population doubles in 24 years. In Nepal, population growth has accelerated because of declines in infant mortality and overall mortality, combined with continued high fertility. India's population growth has held steady at an average of about 2.3 percent a year since the 1960s. The birth rate has dropped sharply in some states, but has decreased hardly at all in others: the average birth rate was about 33 per 1000 in 1984. Sri Lanka is the only country in South Asia that has reduced its population growth rate below 2 percent. It has done so by cutting its birth rate to under 30 per 1000. Sri Lanka's death rate at 6 per 1000 is one of the world's lowest.

In the NICs and ASEAN-4, vigorous family planning and population control

Table 6.1. Population Growth Rates (percentages)

	Population (millions)		Average Annual Growth Rate of Population (percentages)		
	1984	2000[a]	1965–1973	1973–1984	1980–2000[a]
NICs					
Hong Kong	5	6	2.0	2.4	1.2
Korea	40	49	2.2	1.5	1.4
Singapore	3	3	1.8	1.3	1.0
Taiwan	19	NA	2.7	1.9	1.4
ASEAN-4					
Indonesia	162	212	2.1	2.3	1.9
Malaysia	15	21	2.6	2.4	2.1
Philippines	53	76	2.9	2.7	2.2
Thailand	51	66	2.9	2.2	1.7
South Asia					
Bangladesh	96	141	2.6	2.5	2.4
Burma	37	49	2.3	2.0	2.1
India	738	994	2.3	2.3	1.9
Nepal	15	24	2.0	2.6	2.6
Pakistan	93	138	3.1	2.9	2.6
Sri Lanka	16	21	2.0	1.8	1.8

Sources: World Bank, *World Development Report*, 1986; ADB, *Key Indicators of Developing Member Countries of ADB*, supplement October 1985, April 1985; *Taiwan Statistical Data Book*, 1985; Population Reference Bureau, *1985 World Population Data Sheet*, April 1985.

Note: NA =Not available.

[a]Projected.

programs were adopted early (though India has been the pioneer). Since 1965, birth rates have decreased in Hong Kong, Taiwan, Korea, Singapore, and Thailand by more than 30 percent. Crude birth rates were under 30 per 1000 in all of the NICs, and 14 and 17 per 1000 in Hong Kong and Singapore, respectively, by 1984. In ASEAN-4 they remained above 30 for Indonesia and the Philippines, but were 30 and below in Thailand and Malaysia in 1984. The decline in mortality between 1965 and 1984 was also significant. The reduction in birth rates has cut the rate of population growth from about 2.4 percent in 1965 to 2.0 percent in 1984. Population growth rates are substantially lower in the NICs than they are in the ASEAN-4.

The NICs have achieved population growth rates that are among the lowest in the less developed countries of the world, though in the mid-1960s they had rates averaging 2.5 percent per annum. Their success in checking population growth accompanied the full employment of labor and near-eradication of the worst forms of poverty. The decrease in population growth rates was mainly due to the declining rates of fertility induced by more educational and employment opportunities for women, later marriages, more equitable distribution of income gains, more birth control and family planning services, and rapid rural development. The growing prosperity of the NICs and their social stability have helped to reduce the desire for large numbers of children by low-income families in the farming sector and elsewhere. The size of the farm population has even begun to decline absolutely as labor resources are absorbed in fast-growing manufacturing, construction, and services sectors.

In contrast to the declining numbers in the NICs, the numbers of rural people and poor people continue to rise in South and Southeast Asia. At currently projected population growth rates, given the large share of rural households in the total and the slow growth of nonfarm employment, not until the next century will rural populations cease expanding in most of South and Southeast Asia.

Private Gains and Social Costs of Population Growth

Higher fertility is usually found in poorer countries and poorer social groups. There are several reasons why poor people perceive gains from having many children.[6] One reason is the high infant and child mortality rates; and families want to have some surviving children. Parents expect children to provide old-age security in societies where financial saving opportunities are limited and social security programs do not exist. A second reason is the more immediate economic contribution children can make in rural households. When women's wages are low, the opportunity cost of childbearing is also low. The income lost for the period the mother is unable to work can be recouped by the child several years after birth, as the child collects firewood, tends livestock, and helps in farm tasks. With limited educational opportunities, as children grow older their capacity to work and earn increases and peaks quickly. Finally, there may be cultural pressures to have a large family. Even if birth control is socially acceptable, accurate information on family planning and birth control may be hard to obtain, and birth control devices or pills may be costly.

Poor parents may gain from large families. The children themselves are likely to lose. When food is not abundant, children in larger families may not receive enough. Even in high-income countries, children of low-income parents with many siblings tend to be smaller. Children gain when family budget allocations rise for health and education. Larger families must spend proportionately more on food and still may not escape malnutrition. Even when government spends more on health and education and tries to make services equally accessible to all families, the poor child from a large family benefits less than the well-off child from a small family.

Children in poor large families usually suffer from poor nutrition, poor health care, and substandard education. When they are adults they also will tend to have large numbers of children. An intergenerational vicious poverty cycle results: low investment per child causes future low skills and low income.

The social and private costs and returns from having many children differ because of the higher social overhead expenditures and greater pressures on resources like fuel wood, land, and water. Resources can be rapidly exhausted, and so future income growth will be restricted. Here is one justification for government intervention to lower fertility. Another is the possibility that people may want to have fewer births. If so, information about and access to effective fertility control is a service to them and so an addition to their current real income.

Before the scope for government policy and the experience of Asian developing countries with population policies are presented, some of the implications of alternative population growth paths for economic development will be considered.

Between 1973 and 1984, population growth rates ranged from a low of 1.3 percent in Singapore and 1.5 percent in Korea to 2.9 percent in Pakistan, 2.7 percent in the Philippines and 2.6 percent in Nepal. Population growth rates are projected to fall to 1.0 percent in Singapore and to 1.4 percent in Korea between now and the turn of the century.[7] In Pakistan the expected rate is an average of 2.6 percent, and for the Philippines 2.2 percent. In Nepal, no decline is foreseen as likely over the same period.

These cases lie at the extremes of past experience and future population growth projections for Asian LDCs. Continued rapid population growth in the South and Southeast Asian countries has dire implications for the development of both natural and human resources.[8] In the NICs, natural resources are very limited. However, educational levels are already fairly high, investment in physical infrastructure is quite advanced, and political and economic institutions are fairly resilient.

The South Asian and ASEAN-4 countries (with the possible exceptions of Thailand and Malaysia) cannot claim to have attained the administrative capacity—much less the human skill level—of the NICs. The ASEAN-4 countries and Burma have some natural resources in abundance: but they are not assured of rapid progress. The NICs demonstrate that a strong natural resource base is not necessary for development. In South Asia, the acute scarcity of undeveloped agricultural land or untapped natural resources (with the possible exceptions of hydropower in Nepal and oil in Pakistan and India) makes rapid population growth an unfavorable factor for development. Thus far, technological change in agriculture has kept food production ahead of population increase. Agricultural growth has required sizable investments. Meanwhile, income inequalities have remained great or worsened, and the numbers in poverty have increased.

Adverse Effects of Rapid Population Growth

One significant effect of rapid population growth is the subsequent explosion in the labor force. Moderate population growth means a moderate number of new entrants to the work force, who are likely to possess a higher skill level and more education than those they replace. Rapid population growth creates problems: higher unemployment and difficult decisions for governments with limited resources as to what should be priorities for development spending. Capital-widening expenditures on the health, education, and infrastructural needs of an expanding population can all but eliminate prospects for governments to invest in substantially upgrading the skills of the work force. In low-income countries, even the low quality standards of existing programs in education and health may be difficult to maintain. This problem is apparent in Nepal, Pakistan, and Bangladesh and in some states of India.

Deterioration of social services from existing low standards is a major problem in South Asia. To the extent that poorer regions and groups (usually with more rapid population growth) suffer the sharpest cuts in quantity and quality of public services, social tensions are likely to increase. The governments have found it difficult to reduce regional and ethnic income disparities precisely because population growth amongst the poor has outstripped the government's capacity to provide services.

In much of Asia, work force growth will exceed the population growth rate for many years to come. In Pakistan, Nepal, Malaysia, and the Philippines, labor force growth will equal or exceed 2.6 percent per year. Such rapid growth of the work force is less of a problem for a resource-rich country like Malaysia, but in the low-income agrarian setting of Pakistan and Bangladesh, there could be an explosive social situation if sufficient employment is not created.

Table 6.2 Labor Force Growth Rates (percentages)

	Average Annual Growth Rate of Labor Force		
	1965–1973	1973–1984	1980–2000[a]
NICs			
Hong Kong	3.5	3.7	1.1
Korea	2.9	2.7	1.9
Singapore	3.4	2.2	1.1
Taiwan	4.2	3.0	2.3[b]
ASEAN-4			
Indonesia	1.9	2.3	2.1
Malaysia	2.9	3.2	2.9
Philippines	2.1	3.1	2.6
Thailand	2.4	3.0	1.9
South Asia			
Bangladesh	2.3	2.6	2.4
Burma	1.3	1.3	2.0
India	1.8	2.1	2.1
Nepal	1.6	2.3	2.6
Pakistan	2.3	3.3	2.9
Sri Lanka	2.0	2.1	2.2

Sources: World Bank, *World Development Report*, 1986; ADB *Key Indicators of Developing Member Countries of ADB*, supplement October 1985, April 1983; *Taiwan Statistical Data Book*, 1985.
[a]Projected.
[b]1980–85.

In the Philippines the labor force is growing much more rapidly than it did in the past (table 6.2). In the 1960s, the work force increased at only a little more than 2 percent per year because of the impact of World War II. By the 1970s, the rate of growth had accelerated to 3.0 percent and will continue to increase by 2.6 percent up to the year 2000. Accelerated growth of the work force in Nepal will place greater strain on that impoverished nation's agricultural land, water, and forest resources.

Barring unforeseen change, Burma will also face rapid and accelerating labor force growth. There will be serious employment problems unless new agricultural land can be cheaply and effectively brought into use, and unless a clear change in policy that allows scope for private investment stimulates more dynamic and market-oriented industry.

India's labor force will grow about 2.1 percent a year until the turn of the century. The annual amount of new employment required is staggering: in 1982 the work force exceeded 400 million, and grew in that year by 8.5 million.

Regionally, work force growth within India is uneven, the burden tending to fall more heavily on poorer states. Sri Lanka, though it has had success in lowering birth rates, will have steady labor force growth at about 2 percent until the turn of the century. The growth of the labor force will be much higher in Pakistan, Bangladesh, and Nepal. In South Asia, policies and strategies that provide for rapid employment growth will have to be favored over alternatives that create the same amount of output but require fewer hands.

In the ASEAN-4 countries and the NICs, labor force growth rates are falling owing to past successes in population control. The most dramatic changes are found in Hong Kong and Singapore, where labor force expansion averaged 3.7 and 2.2 percent during 1973–84, but will average only 1.1 percent until the end of the century. The change is due to a reduced inflow of workers from nations on their borders, and lessening population growth. These nations, and Taiwan and Korea, are shifting their development strategies toward more skill-intensive products requiring greater investment per worker and more scientific manpower.

Thailand especially will benefit from lower population growth. During the 1980s and 1990s, labor force expansion will average 1.9 percent (down from 3.0 percent). Indonesia will continue to experience a high labor force growth of 2.3 percent.The absolute numbers of new entrants will be very high; also, Indonesia has the added problem that over 60 percent of her people are concentrated in Java, on about 7 percent of total land. Both Malaysia and the Philippines are confronting the effects of past high population growth rates, but Malaysia is in a much better position to equip its new entrants with skills, capital, and other resources than is the Philippines.

Throughout Southeast Asia, labor force absorption in manufacturing and modern service industries is essential to more equitable development. The more rapid the expansion of the labor force in countries highly dependent on traditional agriculture, the more likely it is that income inequality and poverty will rise. Education can to some extent offset other disadvantages facing new entrants to the work force. But many of the young workers entering the labor force in South and Southeast Asia have low levels of education and technical training; hence the productivity and wages of those finding jobs are also low. The continued high growth of unskilled labor will put downward pressure on wage rates, and with rapid labor force growth, the proportion will grow of underemployed in occupations requiring little capital and producing only low incomes (hawkers, handicrafts, vendors of personal services).

The debilitating effects of rapid population growth include the slowing of change in the composition of the work force from agriculture to industry and services and the deterioration of the environment. The redistribution of the work force from traditional agriculture (or other traditional activities) to manufacturing and modern service industries was envisioned as a smooth process in labor surplus models. In reality, uneven structural changes in countries with rapid population growth have created new problems of excessive rural-urban migration, urban unemployment, and poverty.

If land and other agricultural resources are limited, high growth rates in agricultural labor will depress the wage-rent ratio and increase the numbers of landless labor. Income inequality will be greater and the incidence of poverty will be higher, as is the case in Bangladesh and Nepal.[9] In Bangladesh and the Philippines, labor force growth accelerated in the 1970s. Real agricultural wages declined. Technological change that is land saving (chapter 5) can help offset these trends. So can the rapid growth of off-farm employment, as it did in Taiwan and Korea, where real wages have risen steadily since the mid-1960s. But industrial employment growth has been inadequate in the countries of South Asia and ASEAN-4, except Malaysia (chapter 2). Technological change and investment in irrigation have kept food production growing in advance of population in most of Asia (the exception is Nepal, where per capita total food production has been falling since the early 1970s). The acceleration in Nepal's population growth rate is a major factor in its change from being a net grain exporter to an importer.

Even if food and agricultural output expand more or less in line with the number of mouths to feed, overly-rapid population growth can lead to ecological deterioration. Farming populations push into steeply sloped areas, cutting down forest stands, and clearing away vegetation that best serves to protect soils, absorb rainfall, and regulate water flows. The resulting problems of deforestation, soil erosion, silting of irrigation and hydropower facilities, and periodic flood and drought are evident in many parts of Asia. These disasters will be exacerbated by continued high population growth.

Between 1960 and 1980, throughout Asia, the share of total population in urban areas rose sharply. The number of cities with populations over one-half million increased from 25 to 73. In Bangladesh, Pakistan, Indonesia, Thailand, and Korea, over half of the total urban population was concentrated in the largest cities. Rapid population growth and high rates of rural-urban migration will make urban centers hard pressed to meet needs for water, sanitation, housing, health, education, utilities, and public security. Lower fertility rates generally found in urban areas have been thought to be due to higher child-rearing costs, but the evidence is not conclusive. In some urban areas of Pakistan, Thailand, and Indonesia, there is higher fertility than there is in rural areas.

Rapid population growth has been thought to have lowered the private saving rate and overall domestic resource mobilization (chapter 3). Econometric studies have tested the linkage between the population dependency ratio and the rate of domestic saving: the inverse relationship has generally not been strong. But in the Asian LDCs there is a negative and significant relationship between population growth and saving rates. In the life-cycle model of savings, high rates of population growth can, through increases in the dependency ratio, reverse the positive effect of increased economic growth on the saving rate.[10] There is less saving at any income level; and since the timing of saving is delayed in private households with more children, increases in per capita income can lead to a lower rate of saving. Conversely, reducing the population growth rate while accelerating real income growth can lead countries into a virtuous cycle: more income growth causes a higher domestic saving rate, which causes investment, which causes further increases in economic growth.

Most Asian governments are convinced that population policies are of the utmost importance for long-term economic development. Government policies can be critical in checking population growth, and in promoting investment in human resources.

Population Policy

The view that market forces alone can bring population growth down to a tolerable level in the LDCs has little basis in experience. The position that governments and other organizations have a responsible role to play in bringing fertility down to manageable levels, in contrast, has considerable validity because theory and experience both show that policies can effectively slow population growth and thereby expedite the attainment of development objectives.

Countries like the NICs that have attained higher living standards and more equitable income distribution and have reduced poverty are now experiencing sharp declines in population growth. The relationship is not coincidental.

Programs for preventing unwanted pregnancies can succeed when economic and other incentives are accompanied by safe, effective, and practical family planning programs. Attention to making information on preventive devices pervasive, backed up by the effective organization of the supply of devices, will help make programs more successful.

The experience of Asian LDCs with population programs and related social programs that influence fertility offers useful insights. Table 6.3 gives data on family planning policies in the Asian LDCs. (The only nation in Asia that has no governmental support for family planning is Burma.) Policies have varied in the length of time programs have been in place, degree of commitment, and recent changes in effectiveness.

India was the first LDC to implement a national family planning policy (in the 1950s). The Indian government's Family Welfare Program has been in every Five-Year Plan and has expanded since the Second Plan (1956–61). Spending for family planning has risen greatly between the Second Plan and the Sixth Plan (1978–83).[11] The percentage of couples using modern birth control mea-

Table 6.3. Family Planning Policies

	Year Official Program Initiated	Family Planning Index	
		1972	1982
NICs			
Hong Kong	1973	B	B
Korea	1961	A	A
Singapore	1965	A	A
Taiwan	1968	A	A
ASEAN-4			
Indonesia	1968	C	B
Malaysia	1966	C	B
Philippines	1970	C	C
Thailand	1970	D	C
South Asia			
Bangladesh	1971	E	C
Burma	NA	E	E
India	1952	B	B
Nepal	1966	D	D
Pakistan	1960	D	C
Sri Lanka	1965	C	B

Source: World Bank, *World Development Report*, 1984, pp. 200–201; see also pp. 188–89 for an explanation of how the family planning index was constructed.

Note: NA = Not available. A = very strong, B = strong, C = moderate, D = weak, E = very weak or none.

sures rose from 0.2 percent during the Second Plan to 22.5 percent by the end of the Fifth Plan in 1978. Progress slowed so that by 1982, 23.7 percent of all couples were thought to be using birth control. The 1971–81 census indicated a recent population growth of 2.28 percent a year, rather higher than the expected 2.20. Since 1983, the government has renewed its efforts and raised the percentage of couples with effective coverage to 32 percent in 1985.

India's program relies heavily on outreach efforts in remote rural areas. The success of the Family Planning Program is partly due to the long-term commitment of the government programs, and the close association of family planning with overall health care and government to raise agricultural productivity. The program has also benefited from the fact that over 80 percent of India's population is Hindu, a religion that has no aversion to voluntary family planning.

In many rural areas of low-income states, however, the program has not been successful. One reason is its reliance on underpaid and undertrained health workers, who may lack commitment to what they are doing. Another is the failure to communicate accurate information on birth control methods and their effects. Low literacy rates among recipients is no help. The low status of women in some areas has compounded the problem; so has overexuberance in the past in promoting sterilization over other means of birth control.

There are signs of change. India has made progress in raising both overall and female literacy rates, though they are still quite low: 40.8 and 25.7 percent, respectively. Male primary and secondary school enrollment rates were still in 1981 nearly twice those of females. The rate of population growth was 1.8 percent (1971–81) in Kerala state where female literacy rates were 59 percent in 1971 and 71 percent in 1981. In Rajasthan, population growth was 2.9 percent and female literacy was 9 percent in 1971 and only 12 percent in 1981. The family planning program is experimenting with new methods focusing on local conditions and making use of a multi-media approach. The numbers of public health centers have been expanded; one now exists for every ten villages. The government's persistent efforts are likely to lead to further declines in fertility.

Other South Asian countries have followed India's lead. Sri Lanka has made the strongest effort. Its relatively low rate of population growth attests to its success. Bangladesh has failed to arrest population growth and reduce fertility rates, but is considering new incentive schemes aimed at limiting family size for both rural and urban areas.

In Southeast Asia, the adoption of family planning policies has been slower than it was in South Asia, perhaps because of the apparent abundance of natural resources and agricultural land. In Indonesia, where government efforts have been continuous, there has been more success than in Malaysia and the Philippines, where government commitments have waxed and waned.

Thailand is accorded a fairly low score for its family planning policies in table 6.3. The rating is based on a very limited survey. Though Thailand has not spent large amounts to subsidize contraceptive use, it has achieved by far the highest degree of coverage of married women (15–49 years of age) among the 32 lower- to middle-income countries included in the World Bank survey.

The NICs had all created strong family planning programs by the mid-1960s. Taiwan had a population growth rate of 3.6 percent in the 1950s, 2.8 percent in the 1960s, and 1.9 percent in the early 1980s. Much of the credit goes to family planning efforts there. In its early recognition of the problem and strength of government efforts, Korea has been unsurpassed. Singapore has been a leading experimenter with economic incentives. Income tax deductions were limited to three children; after two children, maternity benefits were restricted and child-delivery costs raised; children from small families have had priority in school admission; and state housing has been allocated regardless of family size. Fertility has declined sharply since these disincentives to large families were implemented in the late 1960s and early 1970s.

There is excess demand for family planning services in much of Asia. In South Asia, in 1980, total fertility rates averaged 5.22; only 20 percent of the couples were thought to use contraceptives. The fertility surveys and contraceptive prevalence surveys of the World Bank indicate that the unmet need for contraceptives equaled about 18 percent. If the unmet need had been fulfilled, total fertility would have been only 4.15.[12]

The costs of family planning services have varied widely. They are often more costly in the early years (table 6.4). In Nepal, in 1980, the cost per contraceptive user was nearly seven times as great as it was in India. The NICs and ASEAN-4 countries have generally been able to deliver family planning services to a high proportion of the population at a low unit cost. In South Asia, India and Sri Lanka have achieved coverage of a significant proportion of couples at lower unit costs than elsewhere. Lower unit costs of contraception indicate the wider coverage and greater institutional development of family planning programs. Unmet demand for contraceptive devices is smaller where programs are well developed.[13]

Table 6.4. Public Expenditure on Population Programs, 1980

	Total Public Expenditure (US$ millions)	Expenditure per Contraceptive User (US$)
NICs		
Hong Kong	2.0	3
Korea	27.1	9
Singapore	1.8	7
Taiwan	NA	NA
ASEAN-4		
Indonesia	86.2	11
Malaysia	16.4	19
Philippines	37.6	11
Thailand	28.1	7
South Asia		
Bangladesh	45.1	26
India	226.9	10
Nepal	10.6	69
Pakistan	24.5	33
Sri Lanka	6.2	7

Source: World Bank, *World Development Report*, 1984, p. 149.
Note: NA = Not available.

Private expenditure on contraceptive devices, and private sector supply of them, varies directly with income levels. In low-income countries, poor households would be hard pressed to meet the full cost of modern contraceptive methods. A year's supply of oral contraceptives would cost the equivalent of nearly a fifth of income per capita in Bangladesh.

In the NICs, private suppliers are predominant. In Korea, for example, about 54 percent of the married women using oral contraceptives had private suppliers. In Thailand, government programs supplied about 80 percent of the married women using oral contraceptives.

The expansion of family planning programs requires additional financial resources, and trained people are needed for them. Financing the programs is a burden to government, but there is every reason to believe that added spending would result in substantial future savings for other items. In South Asia, spending on family planning has been highly effective and economical, despite low per capita incomes ($100 to $400 per annum), literacy rates averaging 40 percent, high infant mortality, poor transport and communications facilities, inadequate health facilities, and lack of trained people. Cost-effectiveness is likely to continue to improve, making investments in family planning more and more rewarding. Progress in related social development areas also needs to be sustained. Fertility declines will be facilitated by improvements in the status of women, and in overall social development.

Infant mortality has an important influence on fertility. When infant mortality rates are high, parents want more offspring to ensure sufficient survivors. Because breast-feeding delays regular ovulation, child death shortens the interval between pregnancies. Where infant mortality declines rapidly, there is a short-run effect of higher population. But parents devote more attention to each of fewer children, and investment in child health and education tends to rise. These changes reinforce a desire for smaller families. Public health policies, including those that improve the nutrition and health of expectant and nursing mothers, contribute to lessened infant mortality and thus to reduced fertility. So do public health measures that provide immunizations to infants, and prevent or cure intestinal disorders in babies and young children.

Integrating health service with family planning, as is done in India, Thailand, and Indonesia, is particularly effective. The village-based health care plus family-planning services have done much to reduce fertility rates in these three countries.

The educational level of women is a critical factor in reducing fertility. Everywhere, women who have completed primary school have fewer children than those with no education. As women's educational levels rise, the average number of children declines further. Male education does not necessarily lead to the same result. The opportunity cost of childbearing is higher for educated women than it is for the uneducated. Educated women are also more aware of birth control measures and know how to use them effectively. Women receiving secondary and tertiary instruction delay marriage—partly because of the time it takes to complete their education. Educated women also tend to be more career oriented, and to spend more time finding a suitable husband. Where modern sector activities are open to women, fertility tends to be lower. When women have respect and authority in household affairs, they have a stronger say in the planning of their families.

There are strong reasons for Asian LDCs to attach high priority to expenditure programs for social development, particularly for education and health-related programs.

Education Policy

The improvement in the quality of human resources through education and vocational training is thought to be a key element in explaining economic growth.[14] There have been numerous studies of the social value of investment in education in the LDCs. These indicate that the social rates of return are highest for primary education, but are also quite high for secondary and tertiary training.[15]

In Asia, most societies place a strong cultural emphasis on education. This is particularly true for East Asian cultures. Throughout Asia, a strong demand for education exists. Government leaders have also placed great emphasis on schooling. Rising enrollment ratios and literacy rates of the past few decades show this emphasis. Formal education costs have also been rising. The efficiency with which basic educational skills have been imparted to the fast-growing school-age population seems to have been uneven: high dropout rates of South and Southeast Asian countries reflect the problem (discussed later).

In the low-income and middle-income countries of South and Southeast Asia there are conspicuous problems of policy: appropriately matching educational outputs with development priorities; providing the broadest possible access to educational opportunity within financial, organizational, and human resource constraints; and balancing the quality of instruction with the need to rapidly expand.

Formal education can be supplemented and applied in programs at the workplace in extension programs for farm households, and through electronic mass media. It is efficient to concentrate on areas of practical need (improved techniques of farming, family planning, nutrition, and health), and to coordinate efforts in formal and nonformal education. On-the-job training programs and preemployment vocational training deserve greater emphasis in South Asia and the ASEAN-4 countries. The incentives for participation are strong because returns are prompt.

Economic and social change is becoming more rapid: education should equip students with the capacity and skills to learn more on their own. Rural Asia is undergoing a rapid transformation from traditional agriculture to a more complex diversified economy. Young people in rural areas will face new challenges in a changing job market. Educational systems and facilities are unevenly distributed and often those in rural areas are ill-equipped to prepare young people to meet changing conditions.

Government and nongovernment organizations involved in education need to adjust educational institutions to changing demands. Poor planning has resulted in an overexpansion of secondary and higher education in some Asian countries. In some there is almost no control over the numbers of students either through entry qualifications or fees. This has contributed to the rise in unemployment among the educated.[16] It has also reduced resources available for primary education—where returns are highest. Better planning of formal education can reduce inequalities and improve the economic benefit of educational expenditures.[17]

The enhancement of the educational level is a means of relieving poverty both by raising income-earning potential and by enabling other development programs (population control, health maintenance, nutrition) to work more effectively. Poverty and lack of education are closely linked.[18] Without the attainment of a minimum level of education, a society is unprepared to cope with development challenges. But when enough of the population attains literacy, there is a leap forward in development potential. Spillover benefits from education multiply. They strengthen the functioning of social institutions and give impetus to success in various programs and projects. One study concludes:

> Unless the primary school enrollment ratio is over 80 percent, the performance of the socio-economic system seems fundamentally constrained in the long run . . . and the society seems to begin falling backwards. . . . At schooling rates over 80 percent . . . per capita income rises and population growth steadily declines.[19]

Taiwan and Korea had already placed strong emphasis on primary education in the 1950s and 1960s, as did Hong Kong. These countries entered the 1970s with a better-educated work force. Improved income distribution, lower fertility, and higher economic growth were all furthered by an emphasis on primary education. But to provide enough primary school teachers, secondary schools and colleges need to expand.

Public education is one of the largest recurrent expenditure categories in the budgets of Asian LDCs. Within Asia there are wide differences in the percentage of total resources devoted to education, the mix between public and private expenditures on education, and the composition of expenditures by level of

Table 6.5. Central Government Expenditures on Education, 1972 and 1983

	Percentage of GNP		Percentage of Central Government Expenditure	
	1972	1983	1972	1983
NICs				
Hong Kong	NA	NA	NA	NA
Korea	2.9	3.8	15.9	20.5
Singapore	2.6	5.1	15.7	21.6
Taiwan[a]	3.5	4.8	17.3	19.5
ASEAN-4				
Indonesia	1.2	2.3	7.5	9.4
Malaysia	6.5	6.5[b]	23.4	15.9
Philippines	2.2	3.0	16.3	25.6
Thailand	3.4	4.1	19.9	20.7
South Asia				
Bangladesh	1.4[c]	NA	14.9[c]	NA
Burma	3.0[c]	NA	15.0[c]	11.2
India	NA	0.3	NA	1.9
Nepal	0.6	1.7	7.2	9.9
Pakistan	0.2[c]	0.6	1.2[c]	3.1
Sri Lanka	3.3[c]	2.4	13.0[c]	7.1

Sources: World Bank, *World Development Report*, 1986, table 22, pp. 222–23; *Taiwan Statistical Data Book*, 1985, pp. 160–61.
Note: NA = Not available.
[a]Includes all levels of government.
[b]1982.
[c]1973.

education. (Where there are significant private school sectors, the emphasis given to education is understated, and quality comparisons are distorted.) The low share of expenditures on public education in low-income South Asian countries, in terms both of total central government expenditures and GNP, is striking (table 6.5).

In the ASEAN-4 the picture is different. The Indonesian and Philippine governments are increasing their share of expenditures for public education from low past levels, and there is also a large private education sector. In Malaysia, substantial outlays to public education have fallen as a share of central government spending, but have been constant as a share of GNP. In much of South and Southeast Asia, it has been difficult to maintain or improve educational quality because of the low pay of school teachers at all levels.

In the NICs the increasing emphasis on education fits in with the shift toward more skill-intensive and technologically advanced industries. The ability to acquire and apply new advances in technology and knowledge depends to a large degree on the attitudes and motivations a population gains through its educational experience. The NICs, with limited natural resources, have had to focus on developing their wealth in human resources—but then, these are the most important of all resources. The erosion of past comparative advantage in semiskilled and labor-intensive operations has led the NICs to seek niches in human-resource-intensive industries, and this has placed heavier demands on the educational system.

When one examines the achievement of Asian countries in terms of enrollment ratios, dropout rates, and literacy rates, the patterns are similar (tables 6.6, 6.7, and 6.8). Impressive gains have been made in total and female primary school enrollment ratios in South Asian countries. Only Bangladesh and Pakistan were much under the 80 percent figure for total enrollment. Female secondary enrollment continued to lag, and primary dropout rates were substantially high.

All ASEAN-4 countries have attained primary enrollment ratios much in excess of 80 percent. The primary dropout ratios are still large in the Philippines and Indonesia (above 40 percent), though much lower in Thailand (16 percent) and Malaysia (10 percent). In South Asia, dropout rates exceeded 50 percent except in Sri Lanka. The low level of expenditure per pupil is not the only reason for high dropout rates. The burden of costs on poor families is extremely heavy, even when public education is provided free of charge. In Malaysia, it was found that up to 20 percent of household income of the poorest quintile of families is required for out-of-pocket expenses related to education.[20] This accounting does not include income forgone by the household when family members attend school instead of working. The high dropout rates are not surprising. In the NICs, primary enrollment rates are high, and dropout rates are below 10 percent.

How government expenditures for public education are allocated between primary, secondary, and higher levels of schooling differs widely among countries and subgroups. In South Asia, expenditures are concentrated on upper levels of education. India actually allocates a larger share of its education budget to colleges than to primary schooling. Pakistan, Nepal, and Burma allocated the largest share of spending to the primary grades, but in not one of the three was the share much over 40 percent.[21] In the NICs and ASEAN-4, all countries gave the largest share to primary schools, the next largest share to secondary schools, and the smallest share to higher education. Such a distribution favors lower-income groups.

Table 6.6 Primary School Enrollment Ratios and Dropout Rates, 1960 and 1983

| | Number Enrolled as a Percentage of Population Aged 6-11 | | | | | | Dropout ratio (various years) |
| | Total | | Male | | Female | | |
	1960	1983	1960	1983	1960	1983	
NICs							
Hong Kong	87	106	93	107	79	104	NA
Korea	94	103	99	104	89	102	8 (1972)
Singapore	111	113	121	115	101	111	9 (1973)
Taiwan	96	100	NA	NA	NA	NA	1 (1970)
ASEAN-4							
Indonesia	71	115	86	118	58	112	53 (1971)
Malaysia	96	99	108	100	83	98	10 (1973)
Philippines	95	114	98	115	93	113	41 (1970)
Thailand	83	99	88	101	79	97	16 (1973)
South Asia							
Bangladesh	47	62	66	67	26	55	66 (1967)
Burma	56	91	61	87[a]	52	81[a]	75 (1970)
India	61	85	80	100	40	68	61 (1969)
Nepal	10	73	19	100	1	43	76 (1970)
Pakistan	30	49	46	63	13	33	54 (1975)
Sri Lanka	95	101	100	103	90	99	44 (1969)

Sources: World Bank, *World Development Report*, 1986, 1984; Republic of China, *Statistical Yearbook of the Republic of China*, 1984; S. Naya et al., *Developing Asia*, 1982.

Note: NA = Not available.

[a] 1982.

193

Table 6.7. Secondary and Higher Education Enrollment Ratios and Dropouts Rates, 1960 and 1983

	Number Enrolled in Secondary School as a Percentage of Population Aged 12–17		Dropout Ratio (various years)	Number Enrolled in Higher Education as a Percentage of Population Aged 20–24	
	1960	1983		1960	1983
NICs					
Hong Kong	20	68	NA	4	12
Korea	27	89	32 (1972)	5	24
Singapore	32	69	8 (1973)	6	12
Taiwan	30	87	NA	3[a]	11[a]
ASEAN-4					
Indonesia	6	37	25 (1970)	1	4
Malaysia	19	49	50 (1973)	1	4
Philippines	26	63	31 (1970)	13	26
Thailand	13	29	79 (1972)	2	22
South Asia					
Bangladesh	8	19	20 (1969)	1	4
Burma	10	23	NA	1	5
India	20	34	71 (1966)	3	9
Nepal	6	22	29 (1969)	1	5
Pakistan	11	16	49 (1975)	1	2
Sri Lanka	27	56	87 (1969)	1	4

Sources: See table 6.6.
Note: NA = Not available.
[a]In Taiwan, the age group is 18–24.

Table 6.8 Literacy Rates, 1960, 1970, and 1980 (percentages)

	1960	1970	1980
NICs			
Hong Kong	71	77	90
Korea	71	88	96
Singapore	50	72	84
Taiwan	54	85	90
ASEAN-4			
Indonesia	47	57	62
Malaysia	23	58	60
Philippines	72	83	75
Thailand	68	79	86
South Asia			
Bangladesh	NA	NA	26
Burma	58	70	66
India	24	34	36
Nepal	10	13	19
Pakistan	16	21	24
Sri Lanka	61	78	86

Sources: ADB, *Key Indicators of Developing Member Countries of ADB*, April 1985; World Bank, *World Development Report*, August 1978; World Bank, *World Tables*, 1976.
Note: NA = Not available.

The enrollment ratios in secondary and higher education are far higher in the NICs and ASEAN-4 countries than they are in South Asia. The gap between the average cost of secondary and higher education per student and the cost of primary education is greater in South Asia than it is in the ASEAN-4; and far greater in both of these than it is in the NICs. The short-changing of primary education in the low-income countries and in the ASEAN-4 must be reversed if the educational needs of the masses of the poor are to be adequately met. The desirability for such a reallocation is supported by studies of 30 LDCs: the social rate of return to primary education is calculated as twice that of higher education, and about two-thirds more than that for secondary schooling.[22] The progress of South Asian and ASEAN-4 countries in poverty alleviation, fertility reduction, and the improvement of the skills of the labor force depends on full primary education for the greatest possible numbers of the school-age population. This achievement requires more investment in primary schools and a reallocation of current spending toward primary schooling and other measures to reduce dropout rates. Attention to curriculum development and to adequate incentives for teachers is also needed.

In the NICs the strong primary school base and changing labor market require a different emphasis. There, a strengthening of technical and higher education is needed while the quality of primary schools is still maintained. In the ASEAN-4 and South Asian countries, rural education presents a major challenge. Indonesia's shift toward primary education in recent budgets is consonant with its overall development program. Throughout South and Southeast Asia, middle-level technical and trained management people, and some kinds of skilled labor, have been in short supply. Secondary education and vocational training programs can be appropriately changed to meet needs in these areas.

Since female education substantially reduces fertility, increasing female enrollment at all levels deserves more attention. Enhanced educational opportunities for the poor are essential if Asian countries are to have a basis for the eradication of widespread poverty and for better income distribution. The positive externalities from education on fertility, health and nutrition, entrepreneurial ability, the resilience of social institutions, and the functioning of markets provide powerful arguments for greater investment in education.

Health and Nutrition

The delivery of effective health care services and improvement of nutrition are important components of any human resource development strategy. Governments can substantially improve health and nutritional levels among low-income households, and thereby boost labor productivity, enhance the abilities of poor children for educational attainment, lower infant and child mortality, and reduce fertility.

The availability of public health services and their quality varies enormously not only among countries and subregions, but within countries as well. The number of persons per physician ranged from over 30,000 in Nepal in 1981 to slightly over 1,000 in Singapore (table 6.9). Between 1960 and 1981, large strides were made in reducing the population per health worker in South Asia and Indonesia; but health personnel and facilities are still concentrated in urban and more prosperous regions.

Parasitic and intestinal diseases remain a major cause of illness and death in South Asia and the ASEAN-4. Waterborne and insect-carried diseases are particularly frequent and cause lower labor productivity and much school absenteeism. Safe supplies of drinking water are crucial for a lower incidence of most of these diseases. Throughout Asia, the percentage of the population with access to safe water has been rising, particularly in rural areas, but generally, it is still woefully low (table 6.10).

The financing of even a minimum standard of health services for the millions of poor in rural hinterlands and sprawling urban communities is a severe problem. But training local community health workers in basic health care and family

Table 6.9. Selected Health Indicators

| | Life Expectancy at Birth (years) | | | | Infant Mortality Rate (age less than 1 year) | | Population per Medical Profesional | | | |
| | Male | | Female | | | | Physician | | Nursing Person | |
	1960	1984	1960	1984	1960	1984	1960	1981	1960	1981
NICs										
Hong Kong	61	73	69	79	37	10	3,060	1,260	2,910	800
Korea	52	65	56	72	78	28	3,540	1,440	3,240	350
Singapore	62	70	66	75	35	10	2,380	1,110	650	340
Taiwan	61	70[a]	67	75[a]	32	8[a]	1,661	1,318	1,484	13,196
ASEAN-4										
Indonesia	40	53	42	56	150	97	46,780	11,320	4,510	2,300[b]
Malaysia	52	66	56	71	72	28	7,060	3,920	1,800	1,390
Philippines	51	61	54	65	106	49	6,940	2,150	1,440	2,590
Thailand	50	62	55	66	103	44	7,900	6,770	4,830	2,140
South Asia										
Bangladesh	45	50	42	51	159	124	NA	9,010	NA	19,400
Burma	42	57	45	60	158	67	15,560	4,660	8,520	4,890
India	43	56	42	55	165	90	4,850	2,610	10,980	4,670
Nepal	39	47	38	46	195	135	73,470	30,060	NA	33,430
Pakistan	44	52	42	50	162	116	5,400	3,320	16,960	5,870
Sri Lanka	62	68	62	72	71	37	4,490	7,620	4,170	1,260

Sources: World Bank, *World Development Report*, 1986, 1984; Republic of China, *Statistical Yearbook of the Republic of China*, 1984.
Note: NA = Not available.
[a]1983.
[b]1980.

Table 6.10. Access to Safe Drinking Water and Calorie Consumption

| | Percentage of Population with Access to Safe Drinking Water | | | | Daily per Capita Calorie Consumption | | | | |
| | Urban | | Rural | | | | | | |
	1970	1980	1970	1980	1965	1970	1975	1980	1982
NICs									
Hong Kong	92.5	NA	48.8	NA	2,370	2,690	2,580	2,920	2,750
Korea	84.0	85.0	38.0	54.9	2,280	2,580	2,700	3,000	2,980
Singapore	96.0	100.0	NA	100.0	2,430	2,800	2,850	3,120	2,890
Taiwan	69.9	NA	26.7	NA	2,270	2,660	2,720	2,810	2,720
ASEAN-4									
Indonesia	10.0	41.0	1.0	18.0	1,920	1,970	2,040	2,340	2,380
Malaysia	100.0	93.0	1.0	4.9	2,310	2,530	2,540	2,660	2,680
Philippines	67.0	66.0	20.0	33.0	1,890	1,960	2,050	2,320	2,390
Thailand	60.0	49.0	10.0	12.0	2,190	2,260	2,330	2,310	2,300
South Asia									
Bangladesh	13.0	15.0	47.0	55.0	1,960	2,100	1,760	1,950	1,920
Burma	35.0	30.0	13.0	13.0	2,020	2,180	2,220	2,300	2,460
India	60.0	83.0	6.0	20.0	2,150	2,000	1,790	1,910	2,050
Nepal	53.0	81.0	NA	5.0	2,020	2,070	2,030	1,930	2,020
Pakistan	77.0	60.0	4.0	17.0	2,190	2,210	2,210	2,310	2,280
Sri Lanka	46.0	45.0	14.0	13.0	2,080	2,400	2,020	2,250	2,380

Source: ADB, *Key Indicator of Developing Member Countries of ADB*, April 1985.
Note: NA = Not available.

planning has achieved much success in part of Thailand, India, and Indonesia. Professional health workers, especially physicans, need incentives to serve in rural areas. At present the rural areas typically have 10 to 100 times the number of persons per health professional than the urban areas do. It may be necessary to assign newly trained people to several years of mandatory service in rural areas.

Private health facilities are significant in most of the Asian LDCs. Private sector health facilities can provide services to more prosperous segments of the population and so release government resources for basic preventive health care in outlying rural areas.

Government regulation needs strengthening, especially in licensing and controlling the distribution of drugs and pharmaceutical products. In most of the Asian LDCs, the distribution of substandard and overpriced drugs of dubious benefit has been a consequence of inadequate laws, information, and organization. More competition, the careful screening of drugs, and the importation and manufacture of generic drugs are measures that would improve quality and safety at minimum cost.

Health education can lower the cost of delivery of health services. Inoculations and other preventive measures are needed in greater quantity. To treat intestinal disorders, low-cost and effective rehydration therapy is available, and gaining broader use.

Government health care expenditures in some Asian countries flagrantly favor the well-to-do; for instance, state-of-the-art hospital facilities in the primary cities of Southeast Asia are specialized in modern surgical techniques and advanced medicine, but are far beyond the financial reach of low-income people. At the same time, many rural communities do not have even rudimentary health care facilities.

The prevention of many common tropical diseases is far cheaper than their treatment. Recent research on endemic diseases has emphasized finding preventive measures that are effective and low in cost. Developing vaccines for malaria would revolutionize health care in much of Asia and provide a powerful boost to productivity.

Nutrition is closely related to health issues. In much of South Asia the per capita consumption of calories and protein was static or declining between 1965 and 1975 (table 6.10). Since then it has begun to rise, except in Nepal. Calorie consumption in South Asia, on average, exceeds minimum standards only in Sri Lanka, Burma, and Pakistan. But malnutrition is widespread among the poor in rural South Asia, since the distribution of food is only slightly less skewed than that of income in societies at per capita income levels of between $100 and $400 per year. Inadequate income and poverty are the chief causes of malnutrition in Asia—not scanty supplies of food.

In ASEAN-4 countries, caloric consumption per capita has shown sharp improvement since the early 1970s and is now above minimum standards. Still, malnutrition is conspicuous in rural communities dependent on dryland farming, and in fishing communities where marine resource exploitation has been excessive and there is no alternative employment. Income reductions in times of poor crops or fish catches create great hardships.

Throughout the NICs, nutritional levels appear to be adequate, and malnutrition a fairly rare phenomenon. Per capita protein consumption in the NICs is typically twice as high as that in low-income South Asia.

Hunger in agricultural communities presents the problem of meeting the needs of the poor without destroying incentives to produce more food. Over half the population of South Asian countries is thought to suffer from inadequate diet. Adequate nutrition is vital to all other aspects of human resource development.

Nutritional improvements are essential for reducing infant mortality. Special attention needs to be given to pregnant and lactating women, and to children. Educational programs on nutrition would supplement entitlements to food. These would help accelerate reductions in fertility as family planning and health care programs expand.

Malnutrition is especially severe among children under 10 years of age in South and Southeast Asia. Village surveys in southern India revealed that 50 percent of the children between one and four years of age were malnourished and that half the child deaths were caused by malnutrition.[23] The surviving children frequently have impaired abilities because of nutritional deficiencies.

General food subsidies have not been very effective in reducing malnutrition. Often urban middle-income consumers benefit most from government food subsidies. In Sri Lanka, it was estimated that for each additional calorie consumed by those with inadequate diets, 13 calories went to people with enough to eat (or to those who resold the subsidized food at commercial prices).[24] The budgetary costs of general food subsidies often force governments to seek to keep domestic agricultural prices low. This reduces producer incentives and can, in food-deficit countries, lead to large increases in food imports. Balance-of-payments burdens then are increased.

Non government organizations (NGOs) have had highly effective, low-cost food assistance programs in Asia. Governments have learned from the experiences of NGOs that a more cost-effective approach to the problem is possible. The most important step is to target food assistance to the people most at risk from malnourishment. By aiming feeding programs at children of preschool age and expectant mothers, governments keep costs down and the incidence of malnutrition is sharply reduced.[25] India and Sri Lanka have made food entitlement programs more effective in reaching the needy and have significantly lowered program costs by targeting food assistance more carefully. This has been accompanied by an increased investment in food production so that food supplies from domestic sources have risen and reduced the need to import food.

Growth with Equity

Economic development is not measured properly if one compares only the average level and growth of GNP or even GNP per capita. Participation of the poor in economic growth is fundamental to development. The emphasis we have placed on social indicators and employment in previous chapters reflects our concern with the issue of distribution of the rewards of economic growth. If the poor are unable to participate in productive activities they will be unable to share fully in the benefits of growth. Even if the poor are employed, if they lack access to public services and are poorly paid and if their incomes are implicitly taxed by inappropriate policies, they will have less incentive and less ability to work, to save, and to invest.

There are strong interactions between production and distribution. Asian countries like the Philippines that initiated capital-intensive growth strategies shortly after they became independent concentrated resources in a few favored industries and incomes of participants in those industries rose faster than incomes of people in agriculture, services, and less-favored (labor intensive) industries. The result was a widening income inequality. The pattern of demand generated by a capital-intensive strategy will further distort production and resource allocation in a manner that worsens or perpetuates inequality. The increasing demand for income-elastic luxury imports may impose strains on the balance of payments and ultimately reduce the rate of economic growth.

In Taiwan, a strategy of labor-intensive growth improved the incomes of those in agriculture and, by stimulating the demand for labor, resulted in more egalitarian income distribution. Demand patterns favored goods that could be produced efficiently by domestic industry. Small and medium-sized enterprises developed, producing labor-intensive manufactured goods, absorbing surplus labor, and eventually expanding exports. Incentives to save and to work improved, so that the growth rate was raised even higher. The varied experience of the Asian developing countries in the area of income distribution provides useful insight into the past policies and future prospects of these countries.

Too few studies are available in most Asian LDCs to compare accurately the time trends of income distribution. The data that do exist can be used only for broadly comparative purposes.[26] The data from household income surveys reported by the World Bank are used to compute two indicators of relative income inequality in table 6.11. The first index of inequality (I1) is simply the income share of the poorest quintile (20 percent) of families divided by that of the top quintile. The higher the ratio is, the less the gap is between the income shares

Table 6.11. Income Distribution (percentages)

	Year	Q1	Q2	Q3	Q4	Q5	I1[a]	I2[b]
NICs		6.7	11.9	16.0	22.2	43.2	0.15	50.9
Taiwan	(1976)	8.9	13.6	17.5	22.7	37.3	0.24	40.0
Korea	(1976)	5.7	11.2	15.4	22.4	45.3	0.13	55.4
Hong Kong	(1980)	5.4	10.8	15.2	21.6	47.0	0.11	57.2
ASEAN-4		5.2	8.5	12.9	21.0	52.3	0.10	66.6
Malaysia	(1973)	3.5	7.7	12.4	20.3	56.1	0.06	72.8
Philippines	(1970–71)	5.2	9.0	12.8	19.0	54.0	0.10	68.0
Thailand	(1975–76)	5.6	9.6	13.9	21.1	49.8	0.11	61.8
Indonesia	(1976)	6.6	7.8	12.6	23.6	49.4	0.13	66.0
South Asia		6.3	10.0	14.1	19.9	49.7	0.13	59.4
India	(1975–76)	7.0	9.2	13.9	20.5	49.4	0.14	59.8
Sri Lanka	(1969–70)	7.5	11.7	15.7	21.7	43.4	0.17	50.2
Nepal	(1976–77)	4.6	8.0	11.7	16.5	59.2	0.08	78.4
Bangladesh	(1976–77)	6.2	10.9	15.0	21.0	46.9	0.13	55.8
U.S. and Japan		7.0	12.6	17.7	24.1	38.7	0.18	45.5
United States	(1980)	5.3	11.9	17.9	25.0	39.9	0.13	49.8
Japan	(1979)	8.7	13.2	17.5	23.1	37.5	0.23	41.2
Latin America		3.3	7.4	12.5	20.7	56.1	0.06	73.6
El Salvador	(1976–77)	5.5	10.0	14.8	22.4	47.3	0.12	59.4
Costa Rica	(1971)	3.3	8.7	13.3	19.9	54.8	0.06	69.6
Peru	(1972)	1.9	5.1	11.0	21.0	61.0	0.03	84.0
Chile	(1968)	4.4	9.0	13.8	21.4	51.4	0.09	65.6
Brazil	(1972)	2.0	5.0	9.4	17.0	66.6	0.03	93.2
Argentina	(1970)	4.4	9.7	14.1	21.5	50.3	0.09	63.6
Mexico	(1977)	2.9	7.0	12.0	20.4	57.7	0.05	76.2
Panama	(1970)	2.0	5.2	11.0	20.0	61.8	0.03	83.6
Venezuela	(1970)	3.0	7.3	12.9	22.8	54.0	0.06	73.6
Africa		5.4	9.2	13.4	18.8	53.3	0.10	66.5
Malawi	(1967–68)	10.4	11.1	13.1	14.8	50.6	0.21	61.2
Tanzania	(1969)	5.8	10.2	13.9	19.7	50.4	0.12	60.8
Sierra Leone	(1967–69)	5.6	9.5	12.8	19.6	52.5	0.11	65.0
Kenya	(1976)	2.6	6.3	11.5	19.2	60.4	0.04	80.8
Sudan	(1967–68)	4.0	8.9	16.6	20.7	49.8	0.08	61.0
Zambia	(1976)	3.4	7.4	11.2	16.9	61.1	0.06	82.8
Egypt	(1974)	5.8	10.7	14.7	20.8	48.0	0.12	57.6

Sources: World Bank, *World Development Report*, 1986; *Taiwan Statistical Data Book*, 1984.
Note: Top row in each section shows averages.
[a]I1 = (Q1/Q5), where Q1 is the poorest percentile and Q5 is the richest.
[b]I2 = Σ(Qi-20)   i = 1 . . . 5.

of the richest and the poorest. The second index of inequality (I2) is the sum of the differences in the share of income and of families in each quintile if pluses and minuses[27] are ignored. The sum would be zero if there were perfect quintile equality.

The NICs have the highest I1 ratio and the lowest I2 ratio. In Taiwan (in 1976) the distribution of income was as even as that of any of the more developed nations, including Japan. Though income distribution was less egalitarian in Korea than it was in Taiwan, by developing country standards these NICs have done well. The land reforms and agricultural development in Taiwan and Korea proved favorable to the development of labor-intensive manufacturing and service industries. Domestic demand patterns favored labor-intensive goods like processed foods, clothing, and simple durables. The achievement of full employment allowed housewives to join the labor force and earn money to further their children's education. This, in turn, reduced family size and increased the average educational attainment of youth. Falling birth rates by the late 1960s allowed new technologies to be adopted that substituted capital for labor and more skilled for less skilled workers, without creating unemployment.

Korea has a less equitable income distribution than Taiwan because of the concentration of industry in larger enterprises and conglomerates (the so-called *chaebol*).[28] Income disparities were aggravated by government industrial policies in Korea during the 1970s.[29] However, the Korean government in the mid-1980s moved to lessen the use of credit subsidies to large established firms, to reduce its emphasis on heavy and large-scale industries, and to improve social services and the quality of life. These measures should help reverse any long-term trend toward greater income inequality.

Singapore and Hong Kong had greater income inequality than Taiwan and Korea because of their large and heterogenous service sectors. Great disparities exist within services between traditional firms having little capital and employing unskilled workers and modern service firms.[30]

The ASEAN-4 countries have the highest degree of income inequality among the three groups (table 6.11). The high degree of inequality is related to the "dualism" found in agriculture between large commercial farms and plantations on the one hand and small-scale peasant farms on the other. Limited opportunities for off-farm employment in services and manufacturing and high population growth are also to blame. The uneven ownership of land (except in Thailand) and the concentrated ownership of mineral and other natural resources heighten the inequalities. In the ASEAN-4 countries, urban-rural and regional income disparities are large. The gap between the incomes of the urban elite and those of the urban poor is also very pronounced.

Malaysia's very high income inequality despite a per capita income comparable to Korea's is related to ethnic differences and to the uneven access to natural resources. In Malaysia, the relative weight of capital-intensive extractive activities and plantation agriculture in the economy is higher than it is anywhere else in Asia. Despite the New Economic Policy aimed at promoting the economic interests of the indigenous Malays (the "sons of the soil" or bumiputras), there is little indication that overall inequality has fallen much.[31] Though the mean income of the bumiputras has risen slightly in relation to that of the Chinese and Indian population, no data are available on income distribution within the various ethnic groups.

The Philippines' inequality is probably greater than is indicated by the figures. Underreporting of income by the highest quintile was probably greater there than anywhere else in Asia.[32] Thailand's relatively even income distribution is related to a policy of allowing peasants rather freely to clear and settle public land for agricultural purposes. Thailand's industrial sector is the most labor-intensive in ASEAN and has strong linkages to agriculture. Indonesia was strongly affected by the oil boom of the 1970s and early 1980s. This undoubtably contributed to the concentration of income, despite government efforts to offset unfavorable distributional effects through subsidies, devaluations, and an expanded agricultural development program. The skewed income distribution is related to the extreme dualism in Indonesia's industrial sector.[33]

The quality and availability of the data on income distribution are lowest in South Asia. The overall inequality appears to be slightly less than it is in the ASEAN-4 countries, but not as much as one would expect for these low-income agrarian societies.[34] Nepal, surprisingly, has the greatest degree of inequality in all of Asia. The extreme concentration of land ownership there may explain this relationship.[35] Inequality is only moderate in Sri Lanka, where social welfare policies have been in place since before independence. The low inequality indices may mask differences between ethnic groups and regions that create social frictions. Even the perception of unequal treatment between ethnic, religious, and regional groupings can be explosive in the heterogenous South Asian countries. Available studies indicate that despite avowed government emphasis on distributional equity even at the expense of growth, income disparities in South Asian countries have been increasing.[36] The promotion of heavy industries by the Indian, Pakistani, and Sri Lankan authorities during the 1950s, 1960s, and 1970s created an inefficient mix of capital-intensive industries that generate little employment. Policy changes introduced in the late 1970s to emphasize more outward-looking and labor-intensive industrial development have begun to result in higher growth, but not much information on very recent trends in income distribution is available.

In comparison to Latin American and African countries, Asian developing countries have a far better record of income distribution. The average I1 ratio for

Latin America in the 1970s was 0.06—less than even that of the ASEAN-4. For the African countries the I1 ratio was 0.10. The I2 index for the four Latin American countries was 74, almost twice as high as it was in Taiwan (41) and much higher than I2 indexes in other Asian countries. The African countries' I2 index value of 67 was as high as that of the ASEAN-4, though the per capita income level of the African countries (1983) was only $400, while it was $700 in the ASEAN-4. The evidence on income distribution is that high growth need not come at the expense of improved equality and the sharing of the poor in growth, provided appropriate policies are in place. The record of the Asian countries tends to substantiate the view that government resources are more effective when they are used for developing agriculture, infrastructure, and human resources, instead of subsidizing inward-looking, capital-intensive industries.

Conclusion

Rapid population growth burdens economic development efforts. A growing population absorbs much of the agricultural surplus obtainable from new technologies. Rapid population growth puts a heavy strain on the government's limited resources for providing basic health care, education, and infrastructure and leaves a smaller part of public resources for financing development programs. The large flow of new entrants to the labor force resulting from high population growth adds to the pool of the unemployed and underemployed in rural and urban areas. And population pressure leads to the deterioration of forestry and water resources.

Although low-income countries in Asia have managed to reduce their birth rates, family planning programs still deserve high priority. Services and information need to be made available to villagers, since poor rural households produce the most offspring. The success of family planning programs in some of the Asian LDCs suggests that there is widespread willingness to adopt birth control measures. Success depends on offering birth control measures that are widely available, low in cost, and simple to apply.

For Asian countries with higher per capita incomes and higher income growth rates, priority in population policy should be given to the expansion of educational and job opportunities for women and of employment to the rural poor. These changes will indirectly lead to lower birth rates.

Having a literate population has numerous advantages. The lower income Asian countries should devote a larger share of government expenditure to public education. In South Asia, primary education should be emphasized more than higher education. In the middle-income ASEAN-4 countries, vocational and technical courses are needed in secondary schools to improve job opportunities for their students. Rapidly expanding higher education without carefully evaluating priorities is a dubious policy. University graduates in a number of South Asian and ASEAN-4 countries find it hard to obtain suitable employment.

With respect to public health and nutrition policies, there is much to be done in the low- and middle-income countries of South Asia and ASEAN-4. Preventive measures are far more cost-effective than curative efforts are. It is essential that public health services reach poorer individuals and those in outlying areas. Village-based programs combining health care and family planning can be very effective.

The ability of low-income South Asian countries to accelerate their development hinges on reducing population growth through more rapid declines in fertility rates so that human "capital-deepening" can occur. The processes are mutually reinforcing when they are in operation over long periods: lower population growth allows more investment per person, which in turn causes faster per capita income growth and further reductions in fertility.

The remarkable achievements of some of the low-income countries of Asia (India, Sri Lanka) in slowing population growth give hope that the future development of these economies can be the next economic success story in Asia. Much remains to be done even in countries as advanced as those of the ASEAN region, where high population growth rates in the past have created a labor force explosion in the present. Employment-focused development programs must operate to reduce the supply of labor as well as to increase the demand for labor. The NICs illustrate this double success in conquering the employment problem.

For Asian LDCs to realize their potentials, fuller use of human resources must be made. Policies need improvement; institutional advances are essential. Governments must improve their own learning and implementation capacities, if their policy reforms and innovations are to succeed.

7 Policy Lessons and Future Prospects

Outward-Looking Development Strategies

By the early 1970s, the success of the East Asian countries that had followed a strategy of export-led development was becoming widely heralded.[1] The remarkable growth and industrialization in the 1950s and 1960s first of Japan and then of Hong Kong, Taiwan, Singapore, and Korea challenged the old orthodoxies of export pessimism and industrialization through import substitution.[2] There was some skepticism regarding the applicability of export-led growth strategies to other LDCs. The external shocks of the early 1970s seemed to confirm this skepticism.

Surprisingly, a second group of Asian developing countries—the ASEAN-4 —deliberately chose to become more export oriented in the 1970s. The economic growth of this second tier of Asian LDCs was mixed in the 1960s; Thailand and Malaysia (the more trade-oriented countries) had done relatively well, but more inward-looking Indonesia and the Philippines had slower growth.[3] All of the NICs and ASEAN-4 countries grew much faster in the 1970s than was expected, even by those economists advocating an export-led growth strategy.[4] The 1970s growth rates of most of these countries—Indonesia, Singapore, Korea, the Philippines, Malaysia, and Taiwan—equaled or exceeded those of the 1960s, the external shocks notwithstanding.

By the late 1970s, a third tier of Asian countries, including Asia's two giants—China and India—began experimenting with more open, outward-looking economic policies. The South Asian countries, which had stagnated for much of the 1960s and early 1970s, began to grow faster as they implemented measures to increase exports and liberalize imports.

The prolonged world recession in the early 1980s and the weak subsequent recovery through the mid-1980s have cast new doubt on the advisability of following an export-oriented growth strategy. The different world economic conditions of the 1980s and the internal structural changes that have transpired in the Asian countries are evaluated in the section entitled "Future Prospects." Here, it is sufficient to note that despite the disappointing events in the 1980s, the Asian countries have still been growing more rapidly than have countries in any other part of the world. There appears to be no viable alternative to an outward-looking development strategy. International trade in the 1980s may not be the engine of growth it was in previous decades. This alone does not controvert the case for an export-oriented or outward-looking strategy. Even if it is not the engine of growth, trade may be, as Kravis has said, the "handmaiden of growth."[5]

Asia's experience makes a clear case for a more open, outward-looking development strategy. Among the most important issues is what type of policies are needed to move a relatively inward-looking country like Pakistan, India, or Indonesia successfully to a more outward-looking strategy.

The Importance of Appropriate Policies

There can be no doubt that inappropriate macroeconomic and trade policies have been the bane of economic development in many developing countries. Export-oriented growth and appropriate macroeconomic policies were mutually reinforcing aspects of economic development in the NICs. A key element in the successful Asian countries, especially the NICs, is the relative absence of large price distortions created by government intervention or private monopoly. The major elements of appropriate policies are uniform exchange rates, removal or at least minimization of quantitative restrictions on imports and exchange controls, liberalization of financial markets, and non-inflationary fiscal-monetary policies.

The neoclassical policy prescription to "get prices right" by means of lowering tariff barriers, freeing exchange rates and interest rates, keeping wage costs competitive, and allowing other input and output prices for tradables to change in line with international prices is well-meaning, but avoids the critical issue of how and in what sequence to correct or reduce distortions. Should tariffs be reformed and trade restrictions lessened before, during, or after exchange controls are removed? Should capital markets be liberalized before trade reforms and exchange rate changes are implemented? Can such reforms be introduced before macroeconomic stabilization—control of inflation and reining in of fiscal deficits—is achieved?

There are no readily apparent generally applicable answers to these questions. The difficulties World Bank structural adjustment loan programs have confronted (for example in the Philippines) indicate that the issues involved in the optimal sequencing of liberalization measures and their relationship to political realities are not well understood.[6] The speed and timing of liberalization measures are also subject to disagreement. Gradualism has the benefit of easing the adjustment process, but allows adversely affected interest groups to dig in their heels and try to sabotage implementation of reform measures. Shock therapy, on the other hand, preempts hostile coalitions, but carries the risk of destabilizing the economy. The unhappy experience of Chile and other Latin American countries in the mid-1970s points out the shortcomings of sudden, but incomplete, liberalization.[7]

Trade liberalization cannot be effective in improving exports and economic growth when macroeconomic policies are inconsistent and destabilizing. Even if macroeconomic stabilization is achieved, trade reform may not be immediately effective in boosting exports. Export markets have to be developed and contested with competitors. There are risks involved in exposing domestic industry to international competition. In moving to a more export-oriented, outward-looking strategy, each government must consider, within its own institutional context, how best to proceed. The international development agencies have become increasingly attuned to the need to support policy reform with research, and technical and financial assistance. We believe that a consideration of the role of government and government policies in a comparative context may provide some initial insights that are useful to reform efforts.

The Role of Government

Government actions to reduce the uncertainty facing businesses and to provide support for innovation have been important, particularly for the NICs.[8] The role of the government in the rapid industrial growth of the NICs, with the possible exception of Hong Kong, seems to have been much greater than that allowed for by neoclassical economics. But the manner and effects of state intervention in the NICs also appear to be quite different from the frequently adversarial government-business relations found in the West. The central motive behind government intervention in the NICs has been to spur economic growth. Growth and exports are the yardsticks of success in those societies.

A number of scholars have attacked the "new" orthodox development economists (meaning the advocates of export-led growth strategy) on the grounds that they miss the point in praising the NICs for their minimal government distortions, free trade, and market-oriented policies.[9] Rather, some authors stress heavy direct government intervention particularly in "picking winners" in the industrial sector and relentlessly promoting exports as central features of economic development in Korea, Taiwan, Singapore, and also Japan.[10] Some political scientists argue that export-promotion strategies required authoritarian government and very special historical circumstances to succeed as much as they have.[11]

The criticism of neoclassical economics that it plays make-believe in explaining the success of the Asian NICs by extolling the reliance on the market while neglecting the visible hand of state industrial policies and active export promotion is only half true. Many "neoclassicals" are keenly aware that the NICs' planning agencies, like Japan's Ministry of Trade and Industry (MITI), have tried to pick the winners and support them through access to credit, duty-free imports of equipment, export subsidies, insurance, transport preferences, and so forth. They do not suggest that the governments of Japan and the NICs are uninvolved, but neither do they go to the opposite extreme and paint these governments as the sole architects of success.[12] The governments of these countries relied on markets to a large extent. As we point out later, human resource policies and the presence of entrepreneurs have also been vital institutional ingredients to successful development.

The NICs to an extent did use an interventionist approach in order to selectively promote labor-intensive manufacturing in the 1960s and early 1970s. The choice to develop exports of labor-intensive industries was practical and had beneficial side effects—it reduced unemployment and improved income distribution. The "pick-the-winner approach" may have been feasible when rather labor-intensive activities—textiles, garments, footwear, processing, light consumer goods—were involved. But selective government industrial promotion policies can be very costly when applied to capital-intensive or high-technology areas. Labor-intensive industries involve standardized technology that is readily available in the marketplace. These industries require relatively low inputs of capital, skills, and technology. In contrast, heavy and technology-intensive industries are more complex and require substantial inputs of highly skilled manpower and large capital investments. These industries present special difficulties in management and quality control. Picking the winners becomes much more difficult, and the price of establishing industries not suited to a country's factor endowment or disfavored by subsequent market and technological developments elsewhere can be very high. Countries that pursue the development of heavy industries prematurely risk losing flexibility and bearing high losses in both economic growth and employment.

Singapore and Korea excessively promoted heavy industries (e.g., shipbuilding, petrochemicals, integrated circuits) in the late 1970s and early 1980s. They both had near disasters as a result. When the NICs have moved away from outward-looking, market-oriented policies, they have had problems—slower economic growth and increasing income inequalities. Governments find it increasingly difficult to guide and direct industrial development as an economy becomes more complex. The integration of the NICs' industries into world and regional economies is essential to their long-term growth. Achieving better integration requires less direct government intervention and greater reliance on private initiative and market forces. Greater freedom would allow foreign investors and domestic entrepreneurs to establish links, adapt technologies, and develop markets.

The relatively sound macroeconomic policies and undistorted prices in the NICs' economies will permit the governments in Singapore and Korea to quickly overcome the mistakes they made in excessive promotion of inappropriate heavy industries. Loss-making (sunset) industries will not be perpetuated indefinitely through subsidies or conversion into public enterprises that drain the budget. The NICs have show the flexibility to phase out losers so that scarce resources are released for new endeavors.

The theory of industrial organization extends the neoclassical economic model to include analysis of direct government interventions and their impact on economic growth and development. In the NICs (and Japan), powerful government agencies charged with the responsibility for overseeing economic planning, trade, and industrial development have forged close relationships with the private business sector. In the NICs, government is expected to actively promote economic growth and use its resources to direct and support private industry.

The hierarchical relationship between government planning agencies and private business and the coincidence of objectives between government and business leaders facilitate the efficiency of policy implementation. Government and business, instead of behaving like adversaries, act as if they were linked in a "quasi-internal organization."[13] Government support in the context of an outward-looking strategy helps to encourage risk taking and innovation by business. The hierarchical relationship allows coordinated and timely responses to unforeseen contingencies.[14]

The commitment to outward-looking development and export promotion by government encourages efficient policies. The prices established in world markets outside the NICs are regarded by them as parameters. As such, governments cannot arbitrarily distort internal prices for long or by much to offset the consequences of inappropriate policies. Losses by private firms are treated as losses by the internal organization as a whole. If the government must cover private losses with subsidies, treasury losses are incurred. These losses require resources that could have been invested elsewhere, and they usually lead the government to quickly discard the mistaken policies.[15]

The close working relationship between government and business in the NICs and the high degree of professionalism in the ranks of the civil service are well known. These are not Myrdal's "soft-states."[16] One need only compare the record of land reform implementation in Taiwan, Korea, and Japan with that of the Philippines and India to appreciate the differences in governmental efficiency. The prevalence of corruption and inefficiency in the civil service of most ASEAN-4 and South Asian countries has increasingly been the target of outspoken criticism from reform-minded political leaders.[17] The honesty and efficiency of government and the likelihood that government will be able to correct market failures and to intervene in a manner that improves the well-being of society are closely related.[18]

The high cost of government failure has given impetus to moves toward greater reliance on market forces and the private sector in most South Asian and Southeast Asian countries, as well as in China. These moves are accompanied by efforts to improve government institutions and the skills and abilities of government employees. Technocratic and economic measures of success are adopted only slowly in countries where patronage and nepotism are the prevailing standards.

The issue of whether authoritarianism is the price to be paid for efficient government is somewhat misplaced, however. A strong government does not ensure efficiency. Some authors usefully distinguish between "hard" and "soft" states or strong and weak authoritarian governments.[19] Many authoritarian rulers in South and Southeast Asia, as well as Africa and Latin America, have been notoriously corrupt and inefficient. Governmental efficiency in economic management in each of the NICs has been facilitated by a policymaking process in which economic policy could be set independently of political pressures from various interest groups. Top political-military leadership provides backing to decisions of economic technocrats, thus undercutting the political strength of groups prone to oppose market-based economic policies (labor unions, "sunset industries," landlords). Policymakers have been able to sustain economic reforms so that long-term benefits can be reaped. Some potential "rent-seeking" groups have been effectively controlled or eliminated (e.g., rural landlords). Moreover, by the 1980s, the process of political liberalization was clearly gaining momentum in Taiwan, Korea, and Singapore.[20]

Government efficiency can also be measured in more mundane terms—the ability to provide local public goods and services—potable water, sewage systems, roads, public health facilities, public schools. In the NICs, governments have proven successful in mobilizing resources and allocating them effectively for public purposes at the local level. These governments have done well in providing the basics—law and order, public goods, and defense. Sadly, in much of South Asia, limited government resources have all too often been squandered on capital-intensive public enterprises at the cost of neglecting basic services, infrastructure, and public security.[21] The result of governmental failure in South Asia has been weak human resource development because of inadequate resources. At the same time, government policies have adversely affected incentives to work, to innovate, and to raise productivity. Functions normally left to entrepreneurs have been taken over by bureaucrats. The excessively protectionist policies have created public and private monopoly and have suppressed and discriminated against efficient entrepreneurs in business, trade, and small-scale industry.

The quality of human resources is central to the success of the NICs (and Japan). Theodore Schultz argues that investment in human capital and education, in particular, is crucial to people's ability to reallocate resources in response to disturbances. Schultz emphasizes the relationship between human resource development and the emergence of innovators and entrepreneurs. Schultz states: "The mainspring of development consists of the 'creative and innovative responses' of the entrepreneur."[22]In Schultz's view, investment in education and training can increase the efficiency with which people undertake equilibrating activities, in response to internal or external disturbances. Greater investment in human resources, therefore, enhances the efficiency of markets.

Jagdish Bhagwati regards the willingness to take risks as a vital component of building entrepreneurial and technological abilities.[23]

> Perhaps the chief lesson of the success story of the EP (export-promotion)–strategy countries is not in the demonstration of the success of this strategy per se. Rather, it may be in the demonstration that economic success comes from taking risks, from recognizing and seizing opportunities. The risk-averse export pessimists saw the postwar trade opportunities pass them by; the Schumpeterian risk-takers of the Far Eastern four . . . seized the opportunities and prospered.

The slower growing economies in Asia have been those where returns on the expenditure of energy and time are, on average, higher in rent-seeking and redistributional activities than in the creative responses to disequilibrium stressed by human capital theorists. Nowhere is this more apparent than in countries' abilities to take advantage of changing international trade opportunities. The size, growth, and diversity of exports is far greater in the countries with efficient government, relatively undistorted markets, and increasing human capital. As Hla Myint has said, export-oriented policies can only succeed when supported by corresponding "open" domestic policies.[24] These enable an economy to flexibly adjust to external changes through internal factor mobility and innovation.

The International Economy and Export Prospects

With the slow growth of world trade in the 1980s there is truly cause for concern regarding the prospects for development of the trade-dependent Asian countries. Export-GNP ratios are close to 40 percent or more in Korea, Malaysia, Taiwan, Hong Kong, and Singapore and over 20 percent in the other ASEAN countries and Sri Lanka. We must now ask: To what extent can export-oriented industrial development continue?

External Demand and New Export Pessimism

Despite the success of the NICs and ASEAN-4 countries in the 1960s and 1970s, a new export pessimism is being expressed and appears to be gaining currency in some quarters. The pessimists contend that the experience of the NICs constitutes a unique historical episode not to be repeated, that slow growth in the MDCs and protectionism will limit the exports from LDCs, and that over the longer run the importance of international trade will diminish.

Growing demand for imports in the U.S. and Japanese markets is especially important for the Asian LDCs. The relatively open American market has been the major source of growth in demand for the NICs' exports in the 1980s. Half of Taiwan's exports and more than a third of Korea's and Hong Kong's went to the United States in the mid-1980s. About one-fifth of ASEAN-4 and Singapore's exports went to the United States as these nations increasingly diversified into manufactured exports. But access to the U.S. market will become more difficult. Increases in the already huge U.S. trade deficit are untenable. Political pressures to reduce the budget deficit and protect declining industries indicate that the United States is no longer willing to serve as a locomotive to world trade.

Shinohara argues that although Japan has contributed to Asian growth by supplying capital goods, it has failed to provide much support for Asian growth from the demand side.[25] He stresses that Japan's regional role would be much enhanced if Japan would more rapidly increase its imports from the Asian developing countries.

Japan's market is potentially huge for labor-intensive and simpler capital- and skill-intensive manufactured products in which Asian LDCs can be competitive. Import liberalization and adoption of expansionary demand policies by Japan would benefit other Asian economies—ASEAN-4 countries in particular.

China is a major new export market that is growing rapidly. The Asian LDCs will find China's open-door policy a mixed blessing because China may compete with them for external markets in some primary goods (rice, feed, oil) and labor-intensive manufactures as well.

If demand slackens in the United States and Japan, or if Asian developing countries are denied market access, an export-led growth strategy will be more difficult to maintain. But this fear can be overdrawn. Contradicting the commonly held belief that LDC export growth depends on income growth in the MDCs, a study by Riedel emphasizes supply conditions in the LDCs rather than external demand as the principal cause of LDC manufactured export performance.[26] Competitive LDC manufactured exports can substitute for domestic production in MDCs. Several country studies convincingly show that domestic policy is much more important than overseas market constraints in explaining export performance.[27] Further, the emphasis on protection can be overdone. Despite lower economic growth rates and more protectionism, manufactured exports of the LDCs rose more rapidly during the 1970s then they did in the 1960s; and LDCs' share in the markets of the MDCs also rose. Asian LDCs did particularly well in capturing larger export market shares, substantially outperforming the Latin American countries.[28]

Haggard, in a study of three major East Asian industrial sectors (textiles and apparel, automobiles, and semiconductors), concludes:

> Protectionist trends coexist with the quest for expanded trade and investment opportunities, creating new forms of regional interdependence. Crosscutting pressures, both from export-oriented industries and from the growing multinationality within industries such as autos and semiconductors, limit the demand for protection. . . . Contemporary protection in the form of quotas actually encourages this multinationalization, also providing incentives for market and product diversification.[29]

The textile agreement concluded between the European Economic Community (EEC) and ASEAN in 1986 (and running to 1991) is less restrictive than the previous agreement was. This helps offset the more restrictive U.S. posture. The EEC rewarded Singapore with a higher annual growth in its quota in recognition of that country's free market policies. The EEC's moves to liberalize the Multi-Fibre Arrangement came despite virulent demands for increased protection by EEC textile producers. The defeat of the protectionist Jenkin's bill in the United States also was a major victory for the freer trade forces. Even with quantitative restrictions, there is scope for export product improvement, since the various quota and other "voluntary restraint" agreements tend to specify a maximum growth rate in quantity, but not in value. The exporting countries may then shift toward higher value-added exports. If the MDCs attain higher rates of growth, there should be less protectionism.

It should be remembered that the Asian LDCs themselves constitute a huge market for the exports of the MDCs. For example, the Asian LDCs have surpassed Latin America as the largest LDC market for U.S. exports. They are also the largest LDC market for Japan. Between 1983 and 1985, nonoil imports of developing Asian countries increased at an average annual rate of over 7 percent, while import compression (negative growth) occurred in other developing regions.[30] Rapid growth and relatively strong external payments positions of Asian LDCs will lead to further expansion of their demand for imports from the MDCs in future.

The Multiple Catching-up Process in Asia

Asking whether others can follow the Asian NICs in export-led industrialization, some authors have raised the fear of market saturation.[31] But one should not view the future simply by dividing up a fixed amount of exports.

It is characteristic of the export of manufactures that they become ever more diversified. Asian LDCs like Thailand and Malaysia have also succeeded at diversifying and expanding exports of primary goods. Empirical studies have shown that intra-industry trade through horizontal specialization has increased and that the extent of intra-industry trade of MDCs has grown much more rapidly with LDCs than with other MDCs.[32]

The experience of the ASEAN-4 countries indicates that newcomers may follow a path of export growth similar to that of the NICs earlier.[33] Beginning with some exports of resource-based manufactures and modest amounts of the classical "trio" of clothing, textiles, and miscellaneous manufactures, these countries can subsequently expand exports of the labor-intensive trio and then make a modest start in exporting more sophisticated consumer goods. There is some concern that computerization and robotics may erode comparative advantage based on low labor costs in traditional labor-intensive manufacturing sectors.[34] The rapid growth of these labor-intensive exports from South Asian countries during the 1980s indicated that this effect has possibly been exaggerated.

The NICs have been able to capitalize on dynamic forces that create changes in comparative advantage and that lead to a "multiple catching-up process."[35] The ever changing structure of comparative costs allows a given country to proceed up the ladder of comparative advantage from specialization in primary products to unskilled labor-intensive exports, to skilled labor-intensive exports, to capital-intensive exports, and to knowledge-intensive exports. And as one country moves up the ladder, another country below is able to climb another rung: as Japan has risen on the ladder toward knowledge-intensive exports, the Asian NICs have replaced the Japanese as exporters of skill-intensive manufactures and services and some heavy industrial goods.

Similarly, as the NICs proceed through the various stages of comparative advantage, there is room for other countries to replace them in the markets for the more labor-intensive manufactures and resource-based goods. The middle-income ASEAN countries like Thailand, Malaysia, and the Philippines (and, in South Asia, Sri Lanka) have begun to gain a stronger presence in world markets for manufactures of resource-based goods, the classical trio, and consumer electronic items. It should also be noted that India, Pakistan, and other South Asian countries have low export proportions and, as a consequence, have a much greater margin to increase their supply of labor-intensive manufactured exports. Because their participation remains small and their trade orientation is modest, these countries plus Indonesia are still able to increase manufactured exports rapidly.[36]

As factor endowments shift with capital accumulation in the high-income MDCs, and as the NICs shift their industrial structures toward the more skill-intensive and capital-intensive production activities, other Asian LDCs will more easily be able to enter into labor-intensive manufacturing for export. The multiple catching-up process has not been an easy or smooth transition—numerous challenges must be surmounted by the NICs in making a transition to more sophisticated exports. There have been failures as well as successes.

The ASEAN-4 countries have been called quasi-NICs, but have had more difficulties in transforming their industrial structures away from heavily protected import substitution industries to a more competitive export-orientation. The labor-abundant economies of South Asia have only recently started to promote manufactured exports. Encumbered by inefficient industrial structures as they are, the South Asian countries are likely to make only slow progress.

Policy liberalization—lesser quantitative restrictions and reduced bureaucratic controls, lower tariffs, more liberal investment terms, and foreign exchange regulations—all are under consideration in South and Southeast Asian countries as well as in Korea and Taiwan. Many of the Asian developing countries are in the process of liberalizing and reforming trade and other economic policies under terms of agreements made with the International Monetary Fund and World Bank. We believe it would be to the advantage of these countries to adopt trade liberalization measures under the General Agreement on Tariffs and Trade (GATT) auspices. In the GATT, the Asian countries could exchange their own tariff cuts for concessions from the MDCs.

General Agreement on Tariffs and Trade

The negotiations in preparation of the Punta del Este (Uruguay) round of the GATT present the opportunity for the developing Asian countries to further the cause of the maintenance of a liberal and open system of international trade. The inclusion of a number of new issues in the talks could substantially benefit the Asian nations and help reduce trade frictions between them and their major trading partners—the United States, Japan, and the EEC. Among the new issues of significance are agriculture, trade in services, the preservation of intellectual property, and foreign investment- and trade-related issues like local content and export performance requirements.

The ASEAN-4 and South Asian countries stand to benefit most from the liberalization of agricultural trade. For progress to be made in this area, these countries will themselves have to make concessions in opening their markets. Trade in services was estimated to account for about one-fourth of the total world trade in 1985. It is of particular importance to the EEC, Japan, and the United States as net exporters of services. As the NICs have undergone continued structural change, service exports have also begun to grow more rapidly. Though it is to be expected that GATT negotiations will not be rapidly concluded, the type of trade environment that evolves in the 1990s will depend in good measure on the success of the GATT in resolving these issues. The favorable resolution of the talks would allow Asian developing countries to capture dynamic gains from trade and accelerate growth and structural change. The complementarity of resource endowments and levels of industrial development in the Asian region could be better used with greater openness in agriculture, services, and investment areas. Recognizing and protecting intellectual property would stimulate technological advances and encourage the rapid diffusion of innovations.

The talks also present the Asian developing countries with a forum to highlight the moves they are making to reform trade and investment policies, and to negotiate for halting and dismantling protectionist devices erected in key manufacturing sectors like textiles and clothing. Developing countries' past practice of protesting against restrictions of their exports and ignoring their own protectionist policies would be counterproductive.

Intra-regional Trade

There is increasing scope for trade among the Asian LDCs themselves. In 1970, Asian NICs exported only about 10 percent of their total exports to the ASEAN-4 countries, about 0.5 percent to South Asia, and 7 percent to other NICs. The ASEAN countries' trade with other Asian LDCs was equal to less than one-fourth of the total. South Asian LDCs' exports to other Asian

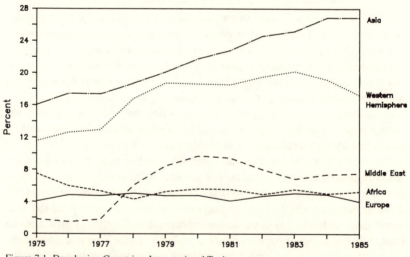

Figure 7.1. Developing Countries: Intra-regional Trade
Source: IMF, Direction of Trade Statistics, yearbook 1986, and May 1987.
Note: Regional groupings according to IMF and includes all Asian and Pacific countries.

LDCs were less than 9 percent of all exports. Intraregional trade increased in the 1970s as shown in figure 7.1, a reflection of the increased heterogeneity among the countries and subgroups. This increase demonstrates the considerable potential for trade expansion among countries at various levels of income and different resource endowments. Trade expansion might be enhanced if the various Asian countries would together reduce import protection and adopt more outward-oriented policies. The higher the rate of economic growth achieved by the Asian LDCs, the greater will be intra-LDC trade and the less the Asian LDCs will depend on the growth of the United States and Japan. Of course, trade between LDCs need not be confined to the Asia-Pacific region. If other LDCs in Africa, the Middle East, Latin America, and Southern Europe relax trade restrictions, more trade is possible with Asian LDCs.

Future Prospects: Renewed Growth or Stagnation?

In the 1980s, economic growth and trade expansion have fallen short of expectations in most of the NICs and ASEAN-4 countries. For these, rapid growth seemed almost automatic during the 1960s and 1970s. Yet in the mid-1980s, zero or negative economic growth rates were experienced by the Philippines, Singapore, Hong Kong, and Malaysia. Growth rates were down significantly in the others as well.

In contrast to the countries to their east, South Asian developing countries were able to sustain economic growth in the 1980s at rates comparable to or even better than those of previous decades. It is tempting to conclude from this that adverse changes in external conditions explain the different, and noticeably poorer, growth performances of the ASEAN-4 and NICs in the 1980s compared to those in the 1970s. And it is tempting to add that if outward-looking development strategies appeared superior in the buoyant decades of world trade in the sixties and seventies, then inward-looking strategies seemed better suited to the stagnant eighties.

There is truth to the view that deteriorating external conditions—falling commodity prices, slower growth in the developed countries, protectionism, unstable financial conditions, and exchange rate changes—are the cause of overall slower growth in the 1980s. But the substantial differences in growth rates across countries cannot be explained simply by the worsening external conditions.

The difficulties Asian countries experienced in the 1980s are mainly the result of inadequate domestic policy responses to changing world economic conditions and the failure of some countries to make necessary structural changes in the 1970s. The lesson to be learned from the slower growth in the 1980s is not that outward-looking development strategies are outmoded.

The more open, outward-looking countries will continue to perform better than inward-looking ones. Those countries that have taken steps to become more open and market oriented in the 1980s, like some of the South Asian countries (and China), have improved their growth rates.

The slowdown in world economic activity in the 1980s exposed a number of structural weaknesses in the ASEAN economies. And although the South Asian countries performed creditably in terms of economic growth, they also have glaring structural problems.

The major deficiencies are those described in previous chapters. The ASEAN-4 countries relied excessively on external borrowing to propel growth in the late 1970s and early 1980s. Their failure to translate enough of these publicly guaranteed borrowings into viable investments that generate foreign exchange earnings and savings has forced them to reduce expenditures and cut imports. Positive adjustment policies are needed to promote export-oriented and labor-intensive activities, to encourage greater savings, better revenue collection, and more efficient investment and expenditure programs. Given their heavy debt burden, it is unlikely they will be able to restore growth without meaningful policy change.[37]

The South Asian countries have extremely large trade deficits and budget deficits, and their reliance on foreign funds for domestic investment has increased. In these countries, employment and poverty problems are even more severe than they are in the ASEAN-4. Yet, since they began experimenting in the late 1970s with policy reforms to make it less costly to trade, the South Asian countries have achieved higher growth rates. They have turned the corner in solving the problem of enough agricultural production and are able to diversify rural activities as the ASEAN-4 began to do in the 1970s.

The NICs are undergoing a process of change in several important directions. Structurally, the NICs are becoming more like advanced industrial-service economies. Agriculture's share of income and employment is very small except in Korea, where it is falling rapidly. The intersectoral change is being accompanied by rapid modernization within sectors as well. Manufacturing activities are becoming more sophisticated and skill intensive, and the composition of exports will reflect this transition. The export of heavy industrial products and differentiated consumer durables, including automobiles and personal computers, finds the NICs emerging as competitors of Japan in some areas.[38]

At the macroeconomic level, led by Taiwan, the NICs are becoming net capital exporters. Trade surpluses and an excess of domestic saving over investment are expected to continue and grow. Korea will have the means to reduce the growth and then the size of its external debt. The other countries will have increased funds for foreign direct and portfolio investment. There are too few domestic investment opportunities in the smaller NICs. They will have to devise investment strategies to take advantage of their transition. The relocation of more labor-intensive industries to other parts of Asia will be an important part of the NICs' reorientation from being export or trade-oriented to becoming investment-oriented economies. Japan has already begun to become investment oriented with the internationalization of Tokyo's financial market. Increased financial and investment links will accelerate the process of industrial restructuring throughout Asia.

Projections

A number of short- and medium-term forecasts of economic growth are available for the ASEAN-4 and NICs. Projections for Pakistan and India are included in forecasts prepared by Project Link. The one projection for growth for 1988 to 1992 is presented in table 7.1. Even when the favorable effects of lower oil prices and a higher yen are taken into account, the projected growth rates are substantially lower than the forecasts prepared before 1985 growth figures became available.[39] Projected growth rates are between about 3 to 7 percent for most countries to 1992, and, Korea, the Philippines, Hong Kong, and Taiwan are among the growth leaders.

The average growth projected for the NICs and ASEAN-4 is low by their previous performance standards, but is higher than can be expected in any other region. The increases in per capita incomes in the NICs are such that they would continue to close the gap between themselves and the more developed countries including Japan. The relatively low growth projected in Indonesia will result in little gain in per capita incomes. However, the other ASEAN-4 countries are projected to have reasonable growth, with the annual growth of Thailand and the Philippines at about 6 percent between 1988 and 1992. Pakistan, if it overcomes structural problems, can be expected to have large enough increases in per capita income to rise to lower-middle-income status. To do so, Pakistan will have to sustain a growth of 6 to 7 percent through 1990. India would also have per capita income gains of better than 2 percent per year if it attains the projected growth rates.

The projections for a resurgence of Asian economic growth in the 1990s are valid only to the extent that the explicit (and some implicit) assumptions are valid. These include an assumed growth of real GNP in the MDCs in the range of 3 percent per annum. Another critical assumption is that agricultural production is sustained and not damaged by the failure of the monsoon. A number of internal factors could prevent the resumption of growth in Asian developing countries even if external conditions improve.

New Challenges to Asian Development

A common challenge facing numerous Asian countries is that of making a smooth transition from old to new political leaderships. This challenge threatens political stability from Korea and Taiwan in East Asia to Pakistan in West Asia. Managing political change goes beyond the issue of replacing

Table 7.1. Real GDP Growth Forecasts

	Estimates		Forecasts				Compounded growth,
	1987	1988	1989	1990	1991	1992	1988–92 (percentage)
NICs							
Hong Kong	12.8	7.3	6.2	6.0	6.0	6.4	6.1
Korea[a]	12.2	8.1	7.3	6.5	6.5	6.8	6.8
Singapore	8.5[b]	5.5	5.5	5.0	5.8	NA	5.5[c]
Taiwan[a]	10.6	7.2	6.4	5.5	5.8	6.2	6.0
ASEAN-4							
Indonesia[a]	3.2	3.4	2.5	2.5	3.0	3.3	2.8
Malaysia	3.5[b]	4.5	4.2	4.0	4.0	NA	4.1[c]
Philippines[a]	5.1	5.5	5.8	6.1	6.6	6.8	6.3
Thailand	6.2[b]	5.9	5.7	5.9	6.1	NA	5.9
South Asia							
India	5.0[b]	1.6	4.6	5.9	NA	NA	5.2[d]
Pakistan	7.0	6.7	6.0	6.1	5.4	5.3	5.7

Source: J.M. Dowling, Jr. and J. P. A. Verbiest, "Short-Term and Medium-Term Prospective for Selected Asian-Pacific Economies," March 1988.
Note: NA = Not available.
[a]GNP.
[b]Forecasted value, not an estimate.
[c]1988–91.
[d]1988–90.

aging leaders with new younger ones. The process of selecting political leaders itself is the focus of debate.

In some countries, no generally accepted institutional mechanism is in place for political succession. There is the danger of conflict in several countries as a result of the failure to legitimize the process in the eyes of the citizenry. Ethnic, regional, and religious conflicts add to the political tensions, particularly in South and Southeast Asian countries. Unless these issues are successfully handled, a serious disruption of economic development is likely. Politically induced economic crises have already occurred in the Philippines and Sri Lanka and have threatened Pakistan, India, Bangladesh, Indonesia, and Malaysia.

The other major internal issue is that of managing structural change in a positive manner. This issue is closely related to that of political stability. In several Asian developing countries, governments have initiated effective programs to liberalize imports, investment regulations, and financial markets and to reduce budgetary deficits. Structural adjustments at both the macro and micro levels are necessary to restore sustainable growth in Asian countries with large external debts or with excessive current deficits. At the macro level, exchange rates must be adjusted and then maintained at appropriate levels to encourage exports; investment must also be given proper emphasis; and monetary-fiscal policies must be balanced to keep inflation low to moderate. At the micro level, it is necessary that trade restrictions be reduced, the price system be allowed to operate more freely, financial systems be developed, and public enterprises be made more efficient, in some cases by selling them to private investors.

Positive adjustment entails the achievement of a sustainable balance-of-payments position with export, employment, and income growth. Economic growth should also be accompanied by social and human resource development.

For structural adjustment to succeed, the Asian developing countries must continue to have access to the markets of the more developed countries. Improved international relations require concessions on the part of more and less developed countries. The increasing interdependence in the Asia-Pacific region and the world economy is widely recognized. The severe recession and international debt crisis of the 1980s have led the United States and Japan to present complementary plans to assist the indebted developing countries in renewing economic growth. At the same time that expanded programs of financial assistance are enacted through the World Bank, IMF and other international agencies, it will be essential that the basic framework for an open system of international trade and investment be strengthened. The financial packages will be unsuccessful unless trade expansion is forthcoming.

Regional groupings like ASEAN and the newly formed SAARC (South

Asian Association for Regional Cooperation) can be more effective in promoting developing countries' interests in a stronger system of open trade than in a closed and protectionist system. These regional groupings could begin by doing more to liberalize member countries' own trading and investment practices so that they more closely conform to international rules and standards. This would do much to revitalize cooperative efforts and would accelerate trade and other ties between member countries.

There is vast potential for increased beneficial investment and trade linkages among the developing countries in the region and also between developed and developing countries. The United States and Japan and also Canada, Australia and New Zealand, can provide new technology, capital, and supply sources for new products, as well as energy and other resources. They can also provide large markets for tropical-resource-based products and manufactured exports of the developing Asian countries.

The appreciation of the Japanese yen against the dollar and most currencies of the other Asian countries since late 1985 has made the manufactured exports of the NICs, ASEAN-4, and South Asian countries more competitive. Even prior to the higher yen, the NICs and ASEAN-4 were gaining competitive strength relative to Japan in a number of manufacturing sectors[40]. The yen's appreciation, if sustained, will lead to a substantially greater sourcing of inputs and components by Japanese industry in other Asian countries. Intra-industry trade is likely to expand particularly rapidly in machinery industries. Machinery accounts for a large share of the imports of MDCs and LDCs alike. The enormous number and diversity of machinery products present great opportunities for the development of intra-industrial linkages among Japan, the NICs, and ASEAN-4 countries as well as the United States.

The higher yen should significantly reduce the bilateral problems in United States–Japanese trade, provided the United States is able to reduce its budgetary deficits. The NICs, like Japan, will have to implement policy changes that allow the United States and other countries to compete in their domestic markets.

The yen appreciation is not all favorable for the NICs, ASEAN-4, and South Asian countries. A large share of their imports are capital goods, consumer durables, and other producer goods from Japan. They will continue over the medium term to require spare parts and other imports from Japan, and these will be more costly. Those that have borrowed in yen-denominated instruments will face higher debt-servicing costs. But the realignment of the yen will also make U.S. machinery and equipment more competitive, and this should help ease trade frictions between Asian developing countries and the United States as well.

The NICs are emerging as new sources of finance and standard technologies useful to ASEAN and South Asian countries. They, like Japan, are large net importers of resources and resource-based products. Their complementary relationship with ASEAN and South Asia can be further developed. There is also scope for expanding ties among South Asian countries and between South Asia and the ASEAN region.

The emergence of China after decades of self-imposed isolation is in no small way related to the rapid economic development occurring in neighboring countries. China's open-door policy introduces a new element of dynamism, and also provides a new source of competition, particularly for countries promoting labor-intensive manufactured exports. China's rapid economic growth following the adoption of policies to provide incentives to farmers and to encourage profit making and exports again demonstrates the lessons of Asian development.

China's modernization policies and the new initiatives in South Asia for economic reform and regional cooperation are very encouraging. Whether or not the changes are successful depends critically on the adoption of good policy in each country. Regional cooperation can enhance the environment for policy change—it is no panacea.

The analysis of this volume indicates that fundamental policy changes are needed in order to reduce the gap between potential and actual development performance in most of the South Asian and ASEAN-4 countries.

Ultimately, the future of Asian development will depend on narrowing the gap between good policy analysis and good policymaking. But if appropriate policies (as advocated in this volume) are to be realized, economists will have to give more attention to improving the process of development policymaking.

Broadly speaking, government policies have been adjusted in the proper direction: to encourage exports, to liberalize imports, to enhance domestic savings, and to rely more on private business and markets to allocate resources.

In appraising the future prospects of the Asian developing countries, economists should give due weight to the internal policy adjustments that these countries are making. In the past, economists have underestimated the ability of the Asian countries to adapt to changing conditions. We do not wish to gloss over the difficulties the Asian developing countries face in sustaining satisfactory growth rates. The development progress of countries like Thailand, Korea, Taiwan, Hong Kong, Singapore, Indonesia, and Malaysia has regularly exceeded the expectations of policymakers and economists. South Asian countries formerly regarded by smug western politicians as basket cases have shown great resilience. The Philippines' remarkable democratic revolution has at least increased the chances for an economic recovery and renewed growth with more equity.

In assessing the external conditions for Asian development, it is important to recognize the negative features of the 1980s—sporadic world economic growth, protectionism, debt-servicing problems, aid and debt fatigue, uncertainties with regard to exchange and interest rate changes, and mounting international tensions. Counterbalancing positive developments should not be overlooked. Low world inflation, declining interest rates in the world financial markets, inexpensive and abundant supplies of raw materials and energy, and increasingly rapid technological progress are favorable for growth. Asia's attainment of food self-sufficiency, the improvement of transport and communication, and rising standards of health, education, and nutrition are significant developments beyond mere growth statistics.

The major policy challenge for the remainder of this century if for the Asian countries to restore growth and simultaneously to raise the quality of economic growth. For South and Southeast Asian countries, economic growth that is intensive in employment creation and balanced among regions and rural and urban communities is to be desired. Throughout the region, improved environmental conditions and increased investment in human resources can raise the quality of life. There is also a need for development efforts to rely on domestic savings more than they do on foreign borrowing. External resources will still be necessary; direct foreign investment and other forms of equity finance are likely to increase in importance.

Throughout, we have stressed the importance of domestic policies for development. Yet, it is undeniable that the basis of Asian success in economic development has been the growth of international economic relations. This very growth has magnified the economic interdependence of all countries in the region. Therefore, the prospects for further progress in the economic development of the region depend, in large part, on a conducive international environment. The national development efforts of the developing Asian countries have turned increasingly in the direction of greater openness and increased freedom for markets. We believe that the policy direction of developing Asia is likely to have favorable long-term effects. It is in the interests of the more developed countries to nurture this process by every means at their disposal. The benefits of international cooperation and policy reform are likely to be substantial. Policies that favor the growth of international economic relations will allow the greatest improvement in living standards throughout the region.

Notes

Bibliography

Index

Notes

1. Development Performance: An Overview

1 We excluded China and Indochina (consisting of Vietnam, Kampuchea, and Laos), as well as Afghanistan, Mongolia, North Korea, and Brunei.
2 Brunei is not included because it is considered a high-income country. It derives a major portion of its income from oil exports.
3 W. A. Lewis, "Economic Development with Unlimited Supplies of Labor," *The Manchester School*, May 1954, pp. 139–91.
4 H. B. Chenery and A. M. Strout, "Foreign Assistance and Economic Development," *American Economic Review* 56 (September 1966): 679–733. See also R. Findlay, "Growth and Development in Trade Models," in *Handbook of International Economics*, vol. 1, edited by R. W. Jones and P. B. Kennen (Amsterdam: North-Holland, 1984), pp. 215–18.
5 A. Marshall, *Principles of Economics*, 8th ed. (London: Macmillan for the Royal Economic Society, 1930), p. 461. Also see G. M. Meier, *Emerging from Poverty: The Economics That Really Matters* (New York: Oxford University Press, 1984), pp. 179–80.
6 Meier, *Emerging from Poverty*, pp. 179–180.
7 T. W. Schultz, *Investing in People* (Berkeley: University of California Press, 1981); T. W. Schultz, "Nobel Lecture: The Economics of Being Poor," *Journal of Political Economy* 88, no. 4 (August 1980): 639–50.
8 H. B. Chenery, M. S. Ahluwalia, C. L. G. Bell, J. H. Duloy, and R. Jolly, *Redistribution with Growth* (London: Oxford University Press, 1974).
9 P. Streeten et al., *First Things First* (New York: Oxford University Press, 1981).
10 Lewis, "Development with Unlimited Supplies of Labor," pp. 139–91; J. C. H. Fei and G. Ranis, *Development of the Labor Surplus Economy* (Homewood, Ill.: Richard P. Irwin, 1964); G. Ranis, "The Dual Economy Framework: Its Relevance to Asian Development," Asian Development Review 2, no. 1 (1984): 39–51.

11 H. B. Chenery and M. Syrquin, *Patterns of Development, 1950–1970* (London: Oxford University Press, 1975); H. Chenery, "Growth and Structural Change," *Finance and Development* 8, no. 3 (1971): 21–25.

12 H. B. Chenery, "Interaction between Theory and Observation in Development," *World Development* 11, no. 10 (October 1983): 853–62.

13 See D. Nayyar, "International Relocation of Production and Industrialization in LDCs," *Economic and Political Weekly* (July 1983): 13–26. W. R. Cline, "Can the East Asian Model of Development Be Generalized?" *World Development* 10 (February 1982): 81–99. In the case of Japan, A. C. Kelley and J. Williamson challenge the view that Japan can provide a "model" for contemporary LDCs to follow. See A. C. Kelley and J. Williamson, *Lessons from Japanese Development: An Analytical Economic History,* (Chicago: University of Chicago Press, 1974). However, Okhawa and Rosovsky argue that there is much in Japan's experience that can be transferred to today's LDCs—particularly those in Southeast Asia; See K. Okhawa, *Dualistic Development and Phases: Possible Relevance of the Japanese Experience to Contemporary Less Developed Countries* (Laxenburg, Austria: International Institute for Applied Systems Analysis, 1980). K. Okhawa and H. Rosovsky, *Japanese Economic Growth: Trend Acceleration in the Twentieth Century* (Stanford, Calif.: Stanford University Press, 1973).

14 G. Ranis, "The Dual Economy Framework: Its Relevance to Asian Development," *Asian Development Review* 2, no. 1 (1984): 39–51.

15 W. A. Corden and J. P. Neary, "Booming Sector and De-Industrialization in a Small Open Economy," *Economic Record* (December 1982): 825–48. R. G. Gregory, "Some Implications of the Growth of the Mineral Sector," *Australian Journal of Agricultural Economics*, (August 1976): 71–91. A. C. Harberger, "The Dutch Disease: How Much Sickness, How Much Boon? *Resources and Energy 5* (1983): 1–20.

16 H. Oshima, "Manpower Quality in the Differential Growth between East and Southeast Asia," *Philippine Economic Journal*, nos. 3 and 4 (1980).

17 For example, the work of G. Papenek, *Pakistan's Development: Social Goals and Private Incentives* (Cambridge, Mass.: Harvard University Press, 1967), shows that Pakistan's industrial entrepreneurs came from groups not culturally predisposed to industrial development.

18 Compare T. Killick, "Development Planning in Africa: Experiences, Weaknesses and Prescriptions," *Development Policy Review* 1 (1983): 47–76. Although he refers to Africa, Killick's critique of the sources of weak planning and implementation may also be applied to Asian countries; namely, deficiencies in the plan documents, inadequate planning resources, institutional and bureaucratic weaknesses, exogenous shocks, and political factors.

19 C. P. Timmer, "Choice of Technique in Rice Milling in Java," *Bulletin of Indonesian Economic Studies* 9, no. 2, (1973): 76.

20 World Bank, *World Development Report* (New York: Oxford University Press, 1983), p. 62. Also see World Bank, *World Development Report*, 1985, p. 54. Agarwala, *Price Distortions and Growth in Developing Countries*, World Bank Staff Working Paper no. 575 (Washington, D.C., 1983).

21 Asian Development Bank Economics Office, *Domestic Resource Mobilization through Financial Development*, 2 vols. (Manila, February 1984).
22 J. Lee and E. Banaria, *Meeting Basic Human Needs in Asian Developing Countries*, Asian Development Bank Economic Staff Paper no. 32 (Manila, March 1985).

2. Industrialization and Trade Policies

1 S. Kuznets, "Quantitative Aspects of the Economic Growth of Nations, 1, Levels and Variability of Rates of Growth," *Economic Development and Cultural Change*, (October 1956): 5–94; S. Kuznets, "Quantitative Aspects of the Economic Growth of Nations, 10, Level and Structure of Foreign Trade: Long-Term Trends." *Economic Development and Cultural Change* (January 1967): 1–140; H. B. Chenery and L. Taylor, "Development Patterns: Among Countries and Over Time," *Review of Economics and Statistics* (November 1968): 39–416. See also H. B. Chenery and M. Syrquin, *Patterns of Development, 1950–1970* (London: Oxford University Press, 1975).

2 See, for example, A. O. Hirschman, *The Strategy of Economic Development* (New Haven, Conn.: Yale University Press, 1958); R. Prebisch, "Commercial Policy in the Underdeveloped Countries," *American Economic Review* (May 1959): 251–91; K. N. Raj and A. K. Sen, "Alternative Patterns of Growth under Conditions of Stagnant Export Earnings," *Oxford Economic Papers* (February 1961): 43–52; I. M. D. Little, T. Scitovsky, and M. Scott, *Industry and Trade in Some Developing Countries: A Comparative Study* (New York: Oxford University Press, 1971); R. Nurkse, *Problems of Capital Formation in Underdeveloped Countries*, 2d ed. (New York: Oxford University Press, 1967); P. N. Rosenstein-Rodan, "Problems of Industrialization of Eastern and Southeastern Europe," *The Economic Journal* (June–September 1943), reprinted in *The Economics of Underdevelopment*, edited by A. N. Agarwala and S. P. Singh (New York: Oxford University Press, 1963), pp. 245–55.

3 J. Bhagwati, "Development Economics: What Have We Learned?" *Asian Development Review* 2, no. 1 (1984): 23–38, discusses the old export pessimism.

4 For background reading, see J. B. Donges, "A Comparative Survey of Industrialization Policies in Fifteen Semi-Industrial Countries," *Weltwirtschaftliches Archiv* 112 (1976): 626–59; B. Balassa, *Policy Reform in Developing Countries* (New York: Oxford University Press, 1977); A. O. Krueger, *Foreign Trade Regimes and Economic Development: Liberalization Attempts and Consequences* (Cambridge, Mass.: Ballinger Press and National Bureau of Economic Research, 1978); and A. O. Krueger, "Comparative Advantage and Development Policy Twenty Years Later," in *Economic Structure and Performance: Essays in Honor of Hollis B. Chenery*, edited by M. Syrquin, L. Taylor, and L. Westphal (New York: Academic Press, 1984); pp. 135–56.

5 L. Westphal, "The Republic of Korea's Experience with Export-Led Industrial Development," *World Development* 6, no. 3 (1978): 364.

6 For a period in the 1970s, Korea in a few cases was promoting exports excessively

in the sense that for selected industries, exports were granted higher net subsidies than was production for domestic markets. Ibid., p. 356. The practice of subsidizing exports in selected industries is becoming more common in South Asian countries, expecially Pakistan and India. See, for example, S. Naqvi and A. R. Kemal, *The Structure of Protection in Pakistan, 1980–81*, 2 vols. (Islamabad: Pakistan Institute of Development Economics, 1983); Subroto Roy, *Pricing, Planning and Politics: A Study of Economic Distortions in India*, Institute of Economic Affairs Occasional Paper no. 69 (London, 1984).

7   Developing countries are usually considered to be small countries in terms of world trade and thus price takers. Export prices are exogenously determined (especially for agricultural goods), and therefore export taxes must be borne by domestic producers. They cannot be shifted to foreigners. Export taxes and the higher domestic currency make exporting less attractive.

8   The seminal articles on effective protection are those of B. Balassa, "Tariff Protection in Industrial Countries: An Evaluation," *Journal of Political Economy* 73 (1965): 573-94; W. M. Corden, "The Structure of a Tariff System and the Effective Protection Rate," *Journal of Political Economy* 74 (1966): 221–37; H. G. Johnson, "The Theory of Tariff Structure with Special Reference to World Trade and Development," *Trade and Development* (Geneva: Institut Universitaire de Hautes Études Internationales, 1965).

9   See, for example, J. N. Bhagwati and T. N. Srinivasan, "The General Equilibrium Theory of Effective Protection and Resource Allocation," *Journal of International Economics* 3 (1973): 259–81; W. M. Corden, "The Substitution Problem in the Theory of Effective Protection," *Journal of International Economics* 1 (1971): 37–57.

10   Small- and medium-scale industrial firms are defined as enterprises employing between 5 and 99 workers. For background on the role of small-scale industry, see D. Anderson, *Small Industry in Developing Countries: Some Issues*, World Bank Staff Working Paper no. 518 (Washington, D.C., 1982); E. Staley and R. Morse, *Modern Small Industry for Developing Countries* (New York: McGraw-Hill, 1965). For general experiences of Asian developing countries, see R. Clapham, *Small and Medium Entrepreneurs in Southeast Asia*, Institute of Southeast Asian Studies, ASEAN Economic Research Unit, Research Notes and Discussion Papers no. 49 (Singapore, 1985); M. Bruch and U. Hiemenz, "Small- and Medium-Scale Manufacturing Establishments in ASEAN Countries: Perspectives and Policy Issues," Asian Development Bank Economics Staff Paper no. 14 (Manila, March 1983); S. Naya, "The Role of Small-Scale Industries in Employment and Exports of Asian Developing Countries," *Hitosubashi Journal of Economics* (December 1985): 147–63.

11   This has fallen over time to be less than 15 percent of the total value in 1981 as the industrial structure of Japan shifted toward heavy and chemical industries. S. Sugitani, "Japan's Exports and Small-Scale Industry," *Kwansei Gakuin University Annual Studies* 31 (December 1982); S. Sugitani "International Strategy of Small and Medium-Sized Enterprises," *Kwansei Gakuin University Annual Studies* 32 (December 1983).

12   R. H. Myers, "The Economic Development of the Republic of China in Taiwan, 1965–81," in *Models of Development: A Comparative Study of Economic Growth in South Korea and Taiwan*, edited by L. J. Lau (San Francisco: Institute for Contemporary Studies, 1986).

13   Bruch and Hiemenz, "Small- and Medium-Scale Manufacturing," pp. 35–66.

14   See United Nations, Economic and Social Commission for Asia and the Pacific (ESCAP), *Economic and Social Survey of Asia and the Pacific 1985* (Bangkok, 1986, pp. 116–21, for a brief survey of such studies. It should also be noted that other studies have not found direct causality from exports to GDP. See, for example, M. W. Hsiao, "Tests of Causality and Exogeneity between Exports and Economic Growth: The Case of Asian NICs." Paper presented at the North American Annual Meeting of the Econometric Society (Dallas, Tex., December 1984).

15   See, for example, A. O. Krueger, "Import Substitution versus Export Promotion," *Finance and Development* 22, no. 2 (June 1985): 20–23.

16   A. Young, "Increasing Returns and Economic Progress," *Economic Journal* (December 1928): 527–42.

17   See table 1.5, chapter 1. As chapter 5 indicates, agricultural growth itself has been an important stimulus to industrial growth in South and Southeast Asian countries. For additional discussion, see H. T. Oshima, *Comparative Economic Growth of Monsoon Asia* (Tokyo: Tokyo University Press, 1988).

18   For an overview, see U. Heimenz, "Industrial Growth and Employment in Developing Asian Countries: Issues and Perspectives for the Coming Decade," Asian Development Bank Economic Staff Paper no. 7, (Manila, March 1982); see also the following country studies: (1) For Korea, Westphal, "Republic of Korea's Experience," pp. 347–82; D. C. Rao, "Economic Growth and Equity in the Republic of Korea," *World Development* 6, no. 3 (1978): 383–96; Balassa, *Policy Reform in Developing Countries*, chapters 8 and 9; (2) for Taiwan, S. W. Y. Kuo, *The Taiwan Success Story* (Boulder, Colo.: Westview Press, 1981); W. Galenson, ed. *Economic Growth and Structural Change in Taiwan—The Postwar Experience of the Republic of China* (Ithaca, N. Y.: Cornell University Press, 1979); G. Ranis, J. Fei, and S. W. Y. Kuo, *Growth with Equity: The Case of Taiwan* (New York: Oxford University Press, 1979); (3) for Singapore, S. Y. Chia, "The Role of Foreign Trade and Investment in the Development of Singapore," in *Foreign Trade and Investment: Economic Growth in the Newly Industrializing Asian Countries*, edited by W. Galenson (Madison: University of Wisconsin Press, 1985), pp. 259–97; A. H. H. Tan and O. C. Hock, "Singapore," in *Development Strategies in Semi-Industrial Economies*, edited by B. Balassa et al. (Washington, D. C.: World Bank, 1982) pp. 280–309; (4) for Hong Kong, T. Liu and Y. Ho, *Export-Oriented Growth and Industrial Diversification in Hong Kong*, Economic Research Center, Chinese University of Hong Kong Series Occasional Paper no. 7 (1980); T. B. Lin and V. Mok, "Trade, Foreign Investment and Development in Hong Kong," in *Foreign Trade and Investment: Economic Growth in the Newly Industrializing Asian Countries*, edited by W. Galenson (Madison: University of Wisconsin Press, 1985), pp. 219–56.

19   For example, Korea and Taiwan had carried out major land reforms before entering the stage of rapid industrial development. See I. M. D. Little, "An Economic Re-

naissance," in *Foreign Trade and Investment*, edited by W. Galenson, pp. 448–507. Also see S. W. Y. Kuo, *Taiwan Success Story*, 1981.

20 See R. Findlay, "Trade and Development: Theory and the Asian Experience," *Asian Development Review* 2, no. 2 (1984): 23–42.

21 See, for example, W. W. Lockwood, *The Economic Development of Japan* (Princeton, N.J.: Princeton University Press, 1963).

22 B. Balassa et al., eds., *Development Strategies in Semi-Industrial Economies* (Washington, D.C.: World Bank, 1982), table 2.3.

23 Foreign exchange controls prevented capital flight from occurring. T. Scitovsky, "Economic Development in Taiwan and South Korea, 1965–81," *Food Research Institute Studies*, 19, no. 3 (1985): 1–26.

24 S. Y. Kwack, "The Economic Development of the Republic of Korea, 1965–1981," in *Models of Development*, edited by L. J. Lau (San Francisco: Institute for Contemporary Studies, 1986) pp. 65–134.

25 Real wages in manufactures began to increase rapidly after 1968 in Taiwan, growing at about 4 percent annually from 1953 to 1968, but at more than 10 percent from 1968 to 1978. S. W. Y. Kuo, *The Taiwan Economy in Transition* (Boulder, Colo.: Westview Press, 1983), pp. 68–70. In Korea, annual growth of real wages in manufacturing ranged from about 6 to -6 percent in the mid-1960s (average 3.8 percent, 1960–66), but averaged more than 10 percent through the mid-1970s (1967–77). International Labour Office, *Yearbook of Labour Statistics*, various issues, Geneva. International Monetary Fund (IMF), *International Financial Statistics Yearbook* (Washington, D.C., 1985).

26 S. P. S. Ho, *Small-Scale Enterprises in Korea and Taiwan*, World Bank Staff Working Paper no. 384 (Washington, D.C., 1980).

27 Scitovsky, "Economic Development in Taiwan and Korea."

28 Bruch and Hiemenz, "Small- and Medium-Scale Manufacturing," p. 9, table II-1.

29 Ibid., p. 34.

30 Ho, *Small-Scale Enterprises*, p. 48.

31 I. Yamazawa and T. Watanabe, "Industrial Restructuring and Technology Transfer," in *Development Strategy and Productivity Issues in Asia*, edited by S. Ichimura (Tokyo: Asian Productivity Organization, 1988), chap. 5.

32 Balassa, *Policy Reform in Developing Countries*, pp. 131, 133, 145ff.

33 A. H. H. Tan, "Singapore's Economy: Growth and Structural Change," paper presented at Conference on Singapore and the United States into the 1990s, Tufts University, Fletcher School, Asia Society, and Institute of Southeast Asian Studies (Cambridge, Mass., 1985).

34 P. Bowring, "Hong Kong's Problems Masked by Prosperity," *Far Eastern Economic Review*, September 26, 1985, pp. 102–103.

35 United Nations, *Statistical Yearbook* (New York, 1978, 1981). IMF, *International Financial Statistics Yearbook*, 1986.

36 For overviews, see the following country studies: (1) For Indonesia, P. McCawley, *Industrialization in Indonesia: Developments and Prospects*, Development Studies Center Occasional Paper no. 13 (Canberra: Australian National Unversity, 1979); J. B. Donges, B. Stecher, and F. Wolter, "Industrialization in Indonesia," in *The*

Indonesian Economy, edited by G. Papenek (New York: Praeger Publishers, 1980), pp. 357–405; (2) for Malaysia; K. Young, W. Bussink, and P. Hasan, *Malaysia: Growth with Equity in a Multiracial Society* (Baltimore: Johns Hopkins University Press, 1980); L. Hoffman and S. E. Tan, *Industrial Growth, Employment and Foreign Investment in Peninsular Malaysia* (New York: Oxford University Press, 1980; (3) for the Philippines, R. M. Bautista, J. Power, and associates, *Industrial Promotion Policies in the Philippines* (Manila: Philippine Institute for Development Studies, 1979); B. de Vries, *Transition toward More Rapid and Labor-Intensive Development: The Case of the Philippines*, World Bank Staff Working Paper no. 424, (Washington, D.C., 1980); (4) for Thailand, N. Akrasanee, "The Manufacturing Sector in Thailand; A Study of Growth, Import-Substitution and Effective Protection During 1960–1969," Ph.D. dissertation, Johns Hopkins University, Baltimore, 1973; World Bank, *Industrial Development Strategy in Thailand*, World Bank Country Study (Washington, D.C., 1980). For an overview of the ASEAN countries, see M. Ariff and H. Hill, *Export-Oriented Industrialization: The ASEAN Experience* (Sydney: Allen and Unwin, 1985).

37   See Ariff and Hill, *Export-Oriented Industrialization*, and also H. Y. Rhee, *Protection Structures of the Developing Countries in South and East Asia* (Seoul: Pacific Cooperative Task Force Workshop on Trade in Manufactured Goods, 1983).

38   These results are from a private communication to the authors. See also Ariff and Hill, *Export-Oriented Industrialization*.

39   L. Hoffman and S. E. Tan, *Industrial Growth, Employment, and Foreign Investment in Peninsula Malaysia* (New York: Oxford University Press for the Institut für Weltwirtschaft, 1980). Ethnic issues have been less of a problem in Thailand and the Philippines, although some concern exists. Chinese dominance of industry in Thailand was a factor for the adoption of low tariffs during the 1950s. Ariff and Hill, *Export-Oriented Industrialization*, p. 125.

40   This point has been emphasized by E. S. Shaw, *Financial Deepening in Economic Development* (New York: Oxford University Press, 1973), and by R. I. McKinnon, *Money and Capital in Economic Development* (Washington, D.C.: Brookings Institution, 1973). Also see Asian Development Bank, Economics Office, *Domestic Resource Mobilization through Financial Development*, vol. 1 (Manila, February 1984).

41   See Bautista, Power, and associates, *Industrial Promotion in Philippines*, p. 32.

42   Bautista et al. (ibid.) found that the legal minimum industrial wage in the Philippines was roughly 20 percent higher than the shadow wage rate in 1977. But the minimum wage law is not enforced with equal vigor across economic sectors and geographic regions. This unequal enforcement acts to deepen dualism between both the modern and informal, and urban and rural activities. The incentive to migrate from rural to urban areas is intensified. Excessive migration from rural areas adds substantially to urban infrastructure costs and harms economic growth and development. See P. M. Hauser, D. B. Suits, and N. Ogawa, eds., *Urbanization and Migration in ASEAN Development* (Tokyo: National Institute for Research Advancement, 1985).

43   M. Santikarn, *Regionalization of Industrial Growth*, Thai University Research As-

sociation Report no. 6 (Bangkok, 1980), p. 18, shows that the real minimum wage in Thailand doubled between 1972 and 1979 and contributed to the sluggish growth of labor demand in manufacturing.

44   In the Philippines, value added in capital-intensive industries grew much faster than it did in labor-intensive industries from 1960 to 1974. A similar pattern prevailed in other Southeast Asian countries. See de Vries, *Transition toward a More Rapid Development*, p. 25.

45   See Ariff and Hill, *Export-Oriented Industrialization*; Bruch and Hiemenz, "Small- and Medium-Scale Manufacturing"; Naya, "Role of Small-Scale Industries in Employment and Exports of Asian Developing Countries"; and D. Anderson and F. Khambata, *Small Enterprise and Development Policy in the Philippines: A Case Study*, World Bank Staff Working Paper no. 468 (Washington, D.C., 1981); Institute for Small-Scale Industries, *Entrepreneurship and Small Enterprises Development: The Philippine Experience* (Quezon City: University of the Philippines, 1979); C. P. Lim, "Small Enterprises in ASEAN: Need for Regional Cooperation," *ASEAN Economic Bulletin*, November 1984, pp. 89–114; S. Lumbantobing, "Small and Medium Industries in Indonesia," paper presented at Conference on Management Development of Small and Medium Enterprises in Asia (Tokyo, March 5–7, 1984); S. Sanguanruang, "Small and Medium Manufacturing Enterprises in Thailand," paper presented at the Conference of Management Development of Small and Medium Enterprises in Asia, Tokyo, March 5–7, 1984; M. A. Santiano, "Small and Medium Enterprises in the Philippines," paper presented at Conference on Management Development of Small and Medium Enterprises in Asia (Tokyo, March 5–7, 1984).

46   Bruch and Hiemenz, "Small- and Medium-Scale Manufacturing," p. 24.

47   Bautista, Power, and associates, pp. 29–30, 79. P. Rana, *The Impact of the Current Exchange Rate System on Trade and Inflation of Selected Developing Member Countries*, ADB Economic Staff Paper no. 18 (Manila, September 1983). In his study, Rana found that real effective exchange rates appreciated in the Philippines, Thailand, and Indonesia between 1967 and 1979, an indication of deterioration in international competitiveness.

48   H. W. Arndt and R. M. Sundrum, "Devaluation and Inflation: The 1978 Experience," *Bulletin of Indonesian Economic Studies* 10, no. 1 (April 1984): 83–97.

49   For a good summary, see U. S. Agency for International Development, *Free Zones in Developing Countries: Expanding Opportunities for the Private Sector*, A.I.D. Program Evaluation Discussion Paper no. 18 (Washington, D.C.: Sabre Foundation, November 1983).

50   G. Ranis, "Prospective Southeast Asian Strategies in a Changing International Environment," in *New Directions in Asia's Development Strategies* (Tokyo: Institute of Developing Economies, 1980), pp. 1–29.

51   Bank of Indonesia data; also cited by the World Bank in restricted reports on Indonesia.

52   For overviews, see the following studies: (1) General, M. Ahmad, *Strategy for Industrialization and Equity: An Approach for South Asian Countries* (Bangkok: ESCAP, 1979); (2) for India, I. J. Ahluwalia, *Industrial Growth in India: Stagna-*

tion since the Mid-1960's (New York: Oxford University Press, 1985); A. Vaidyanathan, *Indian Economic Performance and Prospects*, ESCAP Development Planning Division Discussion Paper no. 2 (Bangkok, 1981); V. R. Panchamukhi and K. M. Raipuria, "Productivity and Development Strategy in India: Major Dimensions, Issues, and Trends, 1965/66 to 1982/83," in *Development Strategies and Productivity Issues in Asia*, edited by S. Ichimura (Tokyo: Asian Productivity Organization, 1988) chapter 12; (3) for Pakistan, ADB, *Strategies for Economic Growth and Development: The Bank's Role in Pakistan* (Manila, 1985); R. H. Syed, *Development Strategies and Productivity Issues in Asia: A Country Paper on Pakistan*, (Tokyo: Asian Productivity Organization, March 1985); M. Baquai, *Pakistan's Development Patterns and Prospects*, ESCAP Development Planning Division Discussion Paper no. 4, (Bangkok, 1981); (4) for Sri Lanka, B. Hewaritharana, *New Patterns and Strategies of Development: The Case of Sri Lanka*, ESCAP Development Planning Division Discussion Paper no. 3 (Bangkok, 1981). For additional reading, see D. Lal, "Nationalism, Socialism, and Planning: Influential Ideas in the South," *World Development* 13, no. 6 (1985): 749–59. Also, ESCAP, *Policies, Programmes, and Perspectives for the Development of the ESCAP Region: Regional Development Strategy for the 1980s* (Bangkok, January 1980).

53 G. Papenek, *Pakistan's Development: Social Goals and Private Incentives* (Cambridge, Mass.: Harvard University Press, 1967).

54 J. Adams and S. Iqbal, *Exports, Politics and Economic Development: Pakistan 1970–1982* (Boulder, Colo.: Westview Press, 1983).

55 Industries range from banking, insurance, railways, airlines, cement, steel, chemicals, fertilizers, and shipbuilding to wristwatches. S. Roy, *Pricing, Planning and Politics: A Study of Economic Distortions in India*, Institute of Economic Affairs Occasional Paper no. 69 (London, 1984), p. 37.

56 From 1966 to 1970, the black market exchange rate was 48 percent lower than the official exchange rate of Rs 7.50 per US$1. The rupee was devalued in 1971, but remained 24 percent above the black market rate. Ibid., p. 43. See also J. Bhagwati and T. N. Srinivasan, *Foreign Trade Regimes and Economic Development: India* (New York: National Bureau of Economic Research, 1975).

57 Ahluwalia, *Industrial Growth in India*.

58 For example, in India, the inefficiency of public sector industries can be seen by the fact that they accounted for 62 percent of total capital and 27 percent of total employment, but less than 30 percent of total value added in 1978–79. P. K. Bardhan, *The Political Economy of Development in India* (London: Basil Blackworth, 1984), p. 65.

59 G. Papenek, *Development Strategy, Growth, Equity and the Political Process in Southern Asia* (Washington, D.C.: U.S. Agency for International Development, 1985).

60 K. O. Junginger-Dittel and H. Reisen, "Import Instability and LDC's Response: The Destabilization of the Inflow of Capital and Intermediate Goods," *Weltwirtschaftliches Archiv* 115, (1979): 653ff. They show that foreign exchange shortages tend to reduce the import volume of capital goods and industrial intermediate inputs—the levels of raw material and food imports are maintained.

61   United Nations Conference on Trade and Development (UNCTAD), *Handbook of International Trade and Development Statistics* (New York, 1985).
62   K. Akamatsu, "A Historical Pattern of Economic Growth in Developing Countries," *The Developing Economies*, preliminary issue no. 1 (March–August 1962): 3–25; also, cf, I. Yamazawa and A. Hirata, "Industrialization and External Relations: Comparative Analysis of Japan's Historical Experience and Contemporary Developing Countries Performance," *Hitotsubashi Journal of Economics* 18, no. 2 (February 1978): 33–61.
63   W. E. James, "Energy Conservation in Rapid-Growth Economies of Asia," *Natural Resources Forum* 9, no. 3 (August 1985): 197–204.

3. Domestic Savings and Financial Development

1   For discussion see G. M. Meier, *Emerging from Poverty: The Economics That Really Matters* (New York: Oxford University Press, 1984), pp. 137-56. Also, W. A. Lewis, "Development with Unlimited Supplies of Labor," *The Manchester School*, May 1954, pp. 139–91, especially p. 155, where he sets forth the saving and investment rate criteria for development.
2   J. M. Keynes, *The General Theory of Employment, Interest and Money* (New York: Harcourt, Brace and World, 1936), pp. 31, 219–20, refers to differences in saving rates between rich and poor nations. J. Power, "The Economics of Keynes," in *Economics and Human Welfare: Essays in Honor of Tibor Scitovsky*, edited by M. Boskin (New York: Academic Press, 1980), pp. 321–60, provides a formal treatment of the macroeconomic growth problems of MDCs and LDCs.
3   R. I. McKinnon, *Money and Capital in Economic Development* (Washington, D.C.: Brookings Institution, 1973), p. 8. See also Meier, *Emerging from Poverty*, p. 150.
4   G. M. Meier, *Leading Issues in Economic Development* (New York: Oxford University Press, 1976), pp. 267–70. T. Morgan, "Investment vs. Economic Growth," *Economic Development and Cultural Change* 17, no. 3 (April 1969): 392–414.
5   J. G. Gurley and E. S. Shaw, *Money in a Theory of Finance* (Washington, D.C.: Brookings Institution, 1960).
6   D. C. Cole and H. T. Patrick, "Financial Development in the Pacific Basin Market Economies," in *Pacific Growth and Financial Interdependence*, edited by A. H. H. Tan and B. Kapur (Sydney: Allen and Unwin, 1986), p. 43. Also see R. I. McKinnon, "Issues and Perspectives: An Overview of Banking Regulation and Monetary Control," pp. 320–25, in the same volume.
7   J. G. Gurley and E. S. Shaw, "Financial Development and Economic Development," *Economic Development and Cultural Change* 15, no. 3 (April 1967): 257–78.
8   In 1984 Sri Lanka's domestic saving rate rose to 20 percent on the strength of large increases in government revenues from tea exports. Fluctuations in tea prices and export volumes strongly influence the government's current revenues. On average the rate of domestic saving reached about 15 percent in the first half of the 1980s.
9   The NICs' dearth of natural resources appears to be a disadvantage in mobilizing

tax revenues. The presence or absence of natural resource wealth is possibly important in explaining the different financial development strategies found in the ASEAN-4 countries and the NICs. ASEAN-4 countries could rely on taxing natural resources for a large part of their savings. There was less pressure on them to encourage financial development.

10 G. Papenek, *Development Strategy, Growth, Equity and the Political Process in Southern Asia* (Washington, D.C.: U.S. Agency for International Development, 1985), p. 36. For a discussion of these countries' inheritance of effective tax machinery from the British, see G. Myrdal, *Asian Drama: An Inquiry into the Poverty of Nations*, vol. 1 (New York: Random House, 1968), pp. 257–360.

11 See I. J. Ahluwalia, *Industrial Growth in India: Stagnation since the Mid-Sixties* (New York: Oxford University Press, 1985), pp. 140–44.

12 See Asian Productivity Organization, *Farm Credit Situation in Asia* (Tokyo, 1984), pp. 22–24, for comparison on interest rates charged by formal and informal lenders in the Philippines, Nepal, Korea, Indonesia, and Thailand. Also see T. Mujaiton, "Factors Affecting Variation in Interest Rates: A Case Study of Rural Thailand," Ph.D. dissertation, University of Hawaii, 1985. Noninstitutional lending rates were as high as 193 percent in some villages surveyed. Bank rates for agricultural loans ranged from 10 to 18 percent during the same period. D. C. Cole and Y. C. Park, *Financial Development in Korea, 1945–1978* (Cambridge, Mass.: Harvard University Council on East Asian Studies, 1983), assess the conditions under which interest rates will converge or diverge between formal and informal markets for credit.

13 H. Myint, "Organizational Dualism and Economic Development," *Asian Development Review* 3, no. 1 (1985), p. 25.

14 H. W. Arndt, "Two Kinds of Credit Rationing," *Banca Nazionale Del Lavoro Quarterly Review*, December 1982, pp. 417–26. W. E. James, *Credit Rationing, Rural Savings and Financial Policy in Developing Countries*, Asian Development Bank Economic Staff Paper no. 13, (Manila, September 1982).

15 Cole and Patrick, "Financial Development in Pacific Basin," pp. 56–60. Also see J. D. Von Pischke et al., *Rural Financial Markets in Developing Countries* (Baltimore: Johns Hopkins University Press, 1983).

16 Gurley and Shaw, "Financial Development," pp. 257–78. Cole and Patrick, "Financial Development in Pacific Basin," pp. 51–53, demonstrates the positive relationship between real economic growth and real financial growth in Asia using inflation-adjusted M2/GNP ratios.

17 See R. Agarwala, *Price Distortions and Growth in the 1970s*, World Bank Staff Working Paper no. 575 (Washington, D.C., 1983). Agarwala's study indicates that Asia had less distortion of interest rates, on average, than Latin America or Africa. Also see H. W. Arndt, "Survey of Recent Developments," *Bulletin of Indonesian Economic Studies* 19, no. 2 (1983): 1–26. Indonesia's financial policy reforms enacted since 1984 have reversed the situation reported in table 3.3 so that real deposit and lending rates are positive.

18 E. S. Shaw, *Financial Deepening in Economic Development* (New York: Oxford University Press, 1983), pp. 12–13.

19   Ibid., pp. 13–14.
20   T. Scitovsky, "Economic Development in Taiwan and South Korea: 1965–1981," *Food Research Institute Studies* 19, no. 3 (1985): 225–26. Also See R. I. McKinnon, "Issues and Perspectives: An Overview of Banking Regulations and Monetary Control," in *Pacific Growth and Financial Interdependence*, edited by A. H. H. Tan and B. Kapur (Sydney: Allen and Unwin, 1986), p. 327.
21   Scitovsky, "Economic Development," p. 246.
22   Ibid., p. 247.
23   G. Myrdal, *Asian Drama: An Inquiry into the Poverty of Nations*, abridged by S. S. King (New York: Random House, 1971), pp. 163–64, Cole and Patrick, "Financial Development in Pacific Basin," pp. 56–57, point out that funds from the Chinese business communities are a major factor in the rise of Hong Kong and Singapore as financial centers serving all of Southeast Asia.
24   The prevalence of rent seeking and redistributive interventions by the state in the ASEAN-4 countries and their relative absence in the NICs is possibly linked to the differing natural resource endowments of the two sets of countries. The dearth of natural wealth in the NICs made growth-oriented policy interventions imperative. Control over natural resources gave politicians and bureaucrats in ASEAN-4 countries a means to enrich themselves and to benefit select groups.
25   Asian Development Bank Economics Office, *Improving Domestic Resource Mobilization through Financial Development* (Manila, September 1985), p. 20.
26   Ibid., p. 38.
27   W. S. Kim, *Financial Development and Household Savings: Issues in Domestic Resource Mobilization in Asian Developing Countries*, ADB Economic Staff Paper no. 10 (Manila, July 1982), p. 25.
28   V. V. Bhatt and J. Meerman, "Resource Mobilization in Developing Countries: Financial Institutions and Policies," *World Development*, 6, no. 1 (January 1978): 50.

4. External Financial Flows and External Debt

1   See H. J. Bruton, "Egypt's Development in the Seventies," *Economic Development and Cultural Change* 31, no. 4 (July 1983): 679–704. Bruton's article concludes: "What foreign exchange-rich countries are now learning is that foreign exchange is really not the heart of the development matter. The heart must be the indigenous resources and their commitment to the nation's development." One could also contrast the development experience of oil-exporting developing countries like Indonesia that adopted appropriate internal development policies with those like Nigeria that failed to.
2   B. O. Campbell, *Petrodollar Recycling 1973-1980*, 1, *Regional Adjustments and the World Economy*, Asian Development Bank Economic Staff Working Paper no. 8 (Manila, April 1982).
3   J. Sachs, "The Current Account and Macroeconomic Adjustment in the 1970s," *Brookings Papers on Economic Activity* 1 (1981): 201–82.

4   T. Morgan, "Investment versus Economic Growth," *Economic Development and Cultural Change* 17, no. 3 (April 1969): 392–414. G. M. Meier, *Emerging from Poverty: The Economics That Really Matters* (New York: Oxford University Press, 1984).

5   See P. C. Lohani, "Nepal's Economy in Retrospect and Its Prospects for the 1980s," *Economic Bulletin for Asia and the Pacific* (1982): 63–93. Also see Meier, *Emerging from Poverty*, pp. 184–87. I. M. D. Little, *Economic Development: Theory, Policy, and International Relations* (New York: Basic Books, 1982), pp. 29–76, makes a scathing assessment of Indian economic planning.

6   R. F. Mikesell and J. E. Zinser, "The Nature of the Savings Function in Developing Countries: A Survey of the Theoretical and Empirical Literature," *Journal of Economic Literature*, March 1973, pp. 1–26. T. Weisskopf, "The Impact of Foreign Capital Inflows on Domestic Savings in Underdeveloped Countries," *Journal of International Economics* 2 (1972): 25–38. For an assessment of the relationship in Asian developing countries, see J. M. Dowling and U. Hiemenz, "Aid, Saving, and Growth in the Asian Region," *The Developing Economies*, March 1983: 3–13.

7   E. Go and J. S. Lee, "Foreign Capital, Balance of Payments and External Debt in Developing Asia," in *Development Strategies and Productivity Issues in Asia* edited by S. Ichimura (Tokyo: Asian Productivity Organization, 1988), chap. 6.

8   Foreign savings is defined as net imports minus net factor income from abroad. Transfer payments from abroad should be included as part of foreign savings to the extent that capital transfers are involved, since these finance investment. The balance-of-payments statistics do not distinguish between current and capital transfers. A. O. Krueger, *The Developmental Role of the Foreign Sector and Aid* (Cambridge, Mass.: Harvard University Press, 1979), includes foreign transfers in foreign savings.

9   K. Areskoug, "Foreign Direct Investment and Capital Formation in Developing Countries," *Economic Development and Cultural Change* 24, no. 3 (April 1976): 539–47. G. Papenek, "Aid, Foreign Private Investment, Savings and Growth in Less Developed Countries," *Journal of Political Economy* 81, no. 1 (January/February 1973): 120–30. D. R. Lessard, *International Financing for Developing Countries: The Unfulfilled Promise*, World Bank Staff Working Paper no. 783 (Washington, D. C., 1986).

10 E. Go, *Patterns of External Financing of Developing Member Countries*, Asian Development Bank Economic Staff Paper no. 26 (Manila, May 1985).

11 World Bank, *World Development Report 1986* (New York: Oxford University Press, 1986).

12 India was able to issue bonds on the Eurocurrency market as early as 1971. See Go and Lee, "Foreign Capital," chap. 6.

13 J. S. Lee, "External Debt Servicing Capacity of Asian Developing Countries," *Asian Development Review* 1, no. 2 (1983): 68–71.

14 World Bank, *World Development Report 1986*, statistical appendix.

15 Ibid.

16 Go and Lee, "Foreign Capital," chap. 6, discount the value of ODA flows by 10

percent to take into account the negative effects of tying aid. Meier, *Emerging from Poverty*, p. 46, points out that the real value of tied aid may be only 50–70 percent of the face value.

17 The entry of China into the World Bank has placed considerable new demands on the Bank's "soft" loan (IDA) funds. China will also become a member of ADB, and though the ADB had initiated lending operations in India, the amounts involved are not large and are probably available only on less concessional terms.

18 G. Myrdal, *Asian Drama: An Inquiry into the Poverty of Nations*, abridged by S. S. King (New York: Random House, 1971), pp. 118–21. In recent years, multilateral lending has also come in for criticism as being politically motivated. IMF conditionality is an anathema to economic nationalists; see Meier, Emerging from Poverty, pp. 35–37.

19 For a view from the right, see P. T. Bauer, *Dissent on Development* (London: Weidenfield and Nicholson, 1971), pp. 95–135. For a leftist critique, see F. M. Lappe, J. Collins, and D. Kinley, *Aid as Obstacle* (San Francisco: Institute for Food and Development Policy, 1980).

20 For a review see J. Bhagwati and R. S. Ekaus, eds., *Foreign Aid* (London: Penguin, 1970). For more recent treatment of Asian countries see E. K. Y. Chan, *Hyper-Growth in Asian Economies: A Comparative Study of Hong Kong, Japan, Korea, Singapore and Taiwan* (New York: Holmes and Meier, 1979). Also see Dowling and Hiemenz, "Aid, Saving and Growth." pp. 3–13.

21 C. Y. Lin, *Developing Countries in a Turbulent World Economy: Patterns of Adjustment since the Oil Crisis* (New York: Praeger Publishers, 1981).

22 See Meier, *Emerging from Poverty*, pp. 149–51, 230–41.

23 World Bank, *World Development Report 1986*, pp. 30–31.

24 J. S. Lee, "External Debt Servicing Capacity," p. 69.

25 H. Oshima, *Comparative Economic Growth in Monsoon Asia* (Tokyo: University of Tokyo Press, 1988).

26 World Bank, *World Development Report 1985* (New York: Oxford University Press, 1985), pp. 63–65. The World Bank reports that between 1979 and 1982, capital flight as a percentage of gross capital inflows averaged over 50 percent in six Latin American countries, but less than 5 percent in South Korea.

27 This section is based on the work of S. Naya and W. E. James, "External Shocks, Policy Responses and External Debt of Asian Developing Countries," in *Pacific Growth and Financial Interdependence*, edited by H. H. Tan and B. Kapur, (Sydney: Allen and Unwin, 1986), pp. 292–316. Also see S. Naya, D. H. Kim, and W. E. James, "External Shocks and Policy Responses: The Asian Experience," *Asian Development Review* 2, no. 1 (1984): 1–22. The methodology is similar to that applied originally by B. Balassa, *The Newly-Industrializing Countries after the Oil Crisis*, World Bank Staff Working Paper no. 437, (Washington, D.C., October 1980).

28 This result is similar to Balassa's (see the previous note).

29 In table 4.10, the positive numbers in columns 1 and 2 for the oil-exporting countries correspond to the favorable balance-of-payments effects of the rise in oil prices (as they do in table 4.9 also).

30 Sri Lanka initiated a far-reaching program of trade liberalization in 1977. The positive contribution of import substitution partly reflects the decreased need to import rice; see chapter 5, figure 5.5.

31 The statistic reported here results from the fact that the actual resource gap (imports minus exports) was smaller than the trend gap (without external shocks) predicted.

32 See H. W. Arndt, "Survey of Recent Developments," *Bulletin of Indonesian Economic Studies* 19, no. 2 (August 1983): 1–26.

33 Lessard, "International Financing," presents analysis of these flaws.

34 Ibid. The World Bank, ADB, and bilateral aid agencies conduct detailed project feasibility studies. The ADB and World Bank both conduct extensive postevaluation studies. These show that the great majority of the projects are economic successes. See also Meier, *Emerging from Poverty*, pp. 30–33.

35 J. Eaton and M. Gersovitz, "Debt with Potential Repudiation: Theoretical and Empirical Analysis," *Review of Economic Studies* 48 (1981): 289–309.

36 Lessard, "International Financing," p. 37. There is a strong negative correlation between debt service payments as a proportion of total debt outstanding and the terms of trade of developing nations (1973–83).

37 The World Bank's structural adjustment loan (SAL) programs are an attempt to overcome this flaw. The SAL programs are commented on in chapter 7.

38 W. Galenson, ed., *Foreign Trade and Investment: Economic Growth in the Newly Industrializing Countries* (Madison: University of Wisconsin Press, 1985).

39 See C. H. Lee, "On Japanese Macroeconomic Theories of Direct Foreign Investment," *Economic Development and Cultural Change* 32, no. 4 (July 1984): 713–24.

40 B. Y. Koo, "The Role of Foreign Direct Investment in Korea's Economic Growth," in *Foreign Trade and Investment*, edited by W. Galenson, pp. 176–216. Republic of Korea Economic Planning Board, *Major Statistics of Korean Economy*, 1982–84 issues.

41 Republic of China (ROC), Council for Economic Planning and Development, *Taiwan Statistical Data Book*, 1975 and 1984 issues, Taipei. ROC, Ministry of Economic Affairs, Investment Commission, *A Survey of Overseas Chinese and Foreign Firms and Their Effects on National Economic Development*, 1980–1984 issues, Taipei (in Chinese).

42 Republic of Singapore, Department of Statistics, *Report on the Census of Industrial Production* (Singapore, 1975–82).

43 D. Nayyar, "Transnational Corporations and Manufactured Exports from Poor Countries," *The Economic Journal* 88, no. 349 (March 1978): 59–84.

44 Refer to chapter 2, table 2.6.

45 See S. Naya, *Resources, Trade, Technology and Investment: Southeast Asia in the Pacific Cooperative System*, Resource Systems Institute Working Paper 85–5 (Honolulu: East-West Center, 1985). Also see a condensed version published as a Pacific Forum Report Supplement, March 1986.

46 Ibid.

5. Asian Agriculture in Transition

1   For a discussion of the changing views on agriculture in economic development, see I. M. D. Little, *Economic Development: Theory, Policy and International Relations* (New York: Basic Books, 1982), chap. 10.

2   This assumption underlies some development theories based on "disguised unemployment"; e.g., P. Rosenstein-Rodan, *The Theory of Economic Growth* (London: Allen and Unwin, 1955).

3   T. W. Schultz, *Transforming Traditional Agriculture* (New Haven, Conn.: Yale University Press, 1964). For related empirical studies, see J. Roumasset, *Rice and Risk: Decision-Making Among Low-Income Farmers* (Amsterdam: North-Holland Publishing Co., 1976).

4   Schultz, *Transforming Traditional Agriculture*. We borrow the phrase *rational peasant* from S. L. Popkin, *The Rational Peasant: The Political Economy of Rural Society in Vietnam* (Berkeley: University of California Press, 1979).

5   B. Johnston and J. Mellor, "The Role of Agriculture in Economic Development," *American Economic Review* (September 1961): 566–93, first helped focus attention on the importance of agricultural development for overall development. India neglected agriculture and suffered slow growth. See I. J. Ahluwalia, *Industrial Growth in India: Stagnation since the Mid-1960s* (New York: Oxford University Press, 1985), especially chapters 2 and 3; S. Roy, *Pricing, Planning and Politics: A Study of Economic Distortions in India*, Institute of Economic Affairs Occasional Paper no. 69 (London, 1984); W. E. James, "Asian Agriculture and Economic Development," ADB Economic Staff Paper no. 5 (Manila, March 1982).

6   See B. Johnston and P. Kilby, *Agriculture and Structural Transformation* (New York: Oxford University Press, 1975), especially chap. 7; also, H. Oshima, *Comparative Economic Growth of Monsoon Asia* (Tokyo: Tokyo University Press, 1988); Y. Hayami, V. Ruttan, and H. Southworth, *Agricultural Growth in Taiwan, Korea and the Philippines* (Baltimore: Johns Hopkins University Press, 1979); S. P. S. Ho, "Decentralized Industrialization and Rural Development: Evidence from Taiwan," *Economic Development and Cultural Change* 28 (1979): 77–96; S. W. Y. Kuo, *The Taiwan Success Story* (Boulder, Colo.: Westview Press, 1981); G. Ranis, J. C. H. Fei, and S. W. Y. Kuo, *Growth with Equity: The Case of Taiwan* (New York: Oxford University Press, 1979); W. E. James, "Asian Agriculture in Transition: Key Policy Issues," ADB Economic Staff Paper no. 19 (Manila, September 1983).

7   See Oshima, *Comparative Economic Growth*.

8   See Johnston and Kilby, *Agricultural and Structural Transformation*, chap. 2.

9   L. G. Reynolds, *Image and Reality in Economic Development* (New Haven, Conn.: Yale University Press, 1977), p. 121.

10 Asian Development Bank, *Rural Asia: Challenge and Opportunity* (New York: Praeger Publishers, 1978).

11 Y. Hayami and M. Kikuchi, *Asian Village Economy at the Crossroads: An Economic Approach to Institutional Change* (Baltimore: Johns Hopkins University Press, 1981). Also Y. Hayami and V. Ruttan, *Agricultural Development: An Inter-*

national Perspective, 2d ed. (Baltimore: Johns Hopkins University Press, 1985).

12 V. S. Vyas, "Asian Agriculture: Achievements and Challenges," *Asian Development Review* 1, no. 2 (1983): 27–44.

13 Compared with Taiwan, Korea was late in seeking to develop its agricultural sector. Both, however, had egalitarian land reforms after World War II. For a discussion of differences, see Oshima, *Comparative Economic Growth*.

14 Johnston and Kilby, *Agricultural and Structural Transformation*, chapters 4 and 7.

15 L. Unnevehr and A. Balisacan, *Changing Comparative Advantage in Philippine Rice Production*, Philippine Institute of Development Studies Staff Working Paper (Makati, Philippines, 1983).

16 R. Clarete and J. Roumasset, "Anatomy of Stagnation: Economic Policy and Agricultural Development in the Philippines," in *U.S. Agricultural Exports and Third World Development: The Critical Linkage*, edited by R. Purcell and E. Morrison (Boulder, Colo.: Lynn and Rienner Publishers, 1987), pp. 115–39. R. M. Bautista, *Domestic Price Distortions and Agricultural Incomes in Developing Countries*, (Washington, D.C.: International Food Policy Research Institute, 1986).

17 H. Oshima, *The Significance of Off-Farm Employment and Incomes in Post-War East Asian Economic Growth*, Asian Development Bank Economic Staff Paper no. 21 (Manila, January 1984).

18 See Food and Agriculture Organization, *Production Yearbook* (Rome: United Nations, 1972).

19 See Vyas, "Asian Agriculture," p. 33.

20 L. Mears, *The New Rice Economy of Indonesia* (Yogyakarta: Gadjah Mada University Press, 1981).

21 See T. H. Lee, *Intersectoral Capital Flows in the Economic Development of Taiwan, 1895–1960* (New York: Cornell University Press, 1971).

22 Data are based on analyses of rural labor market surveys of 1977 and 1984 by C. Manning and cited in World Bank, *Indonesia's Policies for Growth and Employment*, part 1 (Washington, D.C., April 23, 1985,) pp. 131–40, appendix 1. Since the sharp decline in oil prices in 1985–86, Indonesia's economic growth has slowed down dramatically. The effects of reduced growth on off-farm employment could be serious.

23 See, for example, C. Barlowe and Muharminto, "The Rubber Smallholder Economy," *Bulletin of Indonesian Economic Studies* 18, no. 2 (July 1982): 86–119.

24 Asian Development Bank, *Agriculture in Asia: Its Performance and Prospects*, ADB Staff Working Paper (Manila, September 1984), pp. 63–67. Also see Food and Agriculture Organization, *Yearbook of Fisheries Statistics* 54 (Rome, 1982).

25 Estimates of the rate of deforestation vary significantly. This estimate is cited in "Southeast Asia's Forests: Lost for the Trees," *Far Eastern Economic Review*, April 10, 1986, p. 64.

26 See, for example, B. Glassburner, "Macroeconomics and the Agricultural Sector," *Bulletin of Indonesian Economic Studies* 21, no. 2 (August 1985): 51–73; C. P. Timmer, W. P. Falcon, and S. R. Pearson, *Food Policy Analysis* (Baltimore: Johns Hopkins University Press, 1983); C. C. David, "Economic Policies and Agricultural Incentives," *Philippine Economic Journal* 22, no. 2 (1983): 154–82.

27 Johnston and Mellor, "Role of Agriculture," pp. 566–73. See also Glassburner, "Macroeconomics and the Agricultural Sector," pp. 51–73.

28 For example, in Java, researchers initially thought that the demise of traditional harvesting arrangements and mechanization of rice milling were likely to substantially increase rural unemployment and reduce rural wages. See, for example, W. Utami and J. Ihalaw, "Some Consequences of Small Farm Size," *Bulletin of Indonesian Economic Studies* 19, no. 2 (July 1973): 46–56. Some advocated breaking linkages between agriculture and modern sector activities in order to prevent "adverse" institutional changes. See, for example, J. Nugent and P. Yotopoulos, "What Has Orthodox Development Economics Learned from Recent Experience?" *World Development* (1979): 541–54. The rapid expansion of employment in nonfarm occupations and the positive impact macroeconomic policy changes were having on nonfarm incomes were neglected. These changes made all the difference. See, for example, W. Collier et al., "The Acceleration of Rural Development in Java," *Bulletin of Indonesian Economic Studies* 18, no. 3 (1982): 84–101.

29 I. M. D. Little, T. Scitovsky, and M. Scott, *Industry and Trade in Some Developing Countries* (New York: Oxford University Press, 1971); R. I. McKinnon, *Money and Capital in Economic Development* (New York: Brookings Institution, 1973); and Johnston and Kilby, *Agriculture and Structural Transformation*, p. 317.

30 Johnston and Kilby, *Agriculture and Structural Transformation*, p. 317; and Oshima, *Significance of Off-Farm Employment*, pp. 42–58.

31 C. P. Timmer, "Energy and Structural Change in the Asia-Pacific Region: The Agricultural Sector," in *Energy and Structural Change in the Asia-Pacific Region*, Proceedings of the 13th Pacific Trade and Development Conference, edited by S. Naya and R. M. Bautista (Manila: Philippine Institute of Development Studies and Asian Development Bank, 1984), pp. 51–78. Also, see Timmer, Falcon, and Pearson, *Food Policy Analysis*. This thesis is also supported by T. Killick, "Economic Environment and Agricultural Development—The Importance of Macroeconomic Policy," *Food Policy* 10, no. 1 (February 1985): 29–40. Killick contends that the choice of effective macroeconomic policies is to be viewed as a necessary condition for the promotion of agricultural growth.

32 I. Ahmad, Indonesian Agricultural Productivity Growth and Its Relationship to Development Strategy: A Value-Added Approach, Ph.D. dissertation, University of Florida, Gainesville, 1982.

33 Glassburner, "Macroeconomics and Agricultural Sector," pp. 51–73.

34 World Bank, *World Development Report 1986*, pp. 62–65.

35 See R. Barker, R. W. Herdt, and B. Rose, *The Rice Economy of Asia* (Washington, D.C.: Resources for the Future, 1985).

36 C. P. Timmer and W. P. Falcon, "The Political Economy of Rice Production and Trade in Asia," in *Agriculture in Economic Development*, edited by L. G. Reynolds (New Haven, Conn.: Yale University Press, 1975), pp. 373–410. Also see W. E. James and T. R. Ramirez, "New Evidence on Yields, Fertilizer Application and Prices in Asian Rice Production," *Asian Development Bank Economic Office Report Series no. 20* (Manila, July 1983).

37   This is emphasized by Y. Hayami, E. Bennagen, and R. Barker, "Price Incentives versus Irrigation Investment To Achieve Food Self-Sufficiency in the Philippines," *American Journal of Agricultural Economics* 59, no. 4 (November 1977): 717–21. Also see Johnston and Kilby, *Agricultural and Structural Transformation,* pp. 256–57, in reviewing the improved rice production in Taiwan that occurred in spite of a "negative subsidy" under the rice-fertilizer barter scheme. James and Ramirez, "New Evidence on Yields," also support this finding.

38   T. Bertrand, *Agricultural Incentives in Sri Lanka: An Analysis of Agricultural Tax, Subsidy, and Pricing Policies* (Washington, D.C.: Country Policy Department, World Bank, 1985).

39   M. Yudelman, *The World Bank and Agricultural Development: An Insider's View,* World Resources Institute Paper no. 1 (Washington, D.C., 1985).

40   Ibid., pp. 4–5, 13.

41   Ibid., p. 21.

42   B. Koppel and E. Oasa, "Induced Innovation Theory and Asia's Green Revolution: A Case Study of an Ideology of Neutrality," *Development and Change* 18 (1987): 29–68.

43   See Vyas, "Asian Agriculture," pp. 27–44. Also see W. E. James and V. S. Vyas, "Agricultural Development in Asia: Performance, Issues and Policy Options," in *Development Strategies and Productivity Issues in Asia,* edited by S. Ichimura (Tokyo: Asian Productivity Organization, 1988), chap. 7.

44   These are the findings reported in the World Bank report cited in note 22.

45   Food and Agriculture Organization, *Agriculture Towards 2000: Regional Implications with Special Reference to the Third Development Decade* (Rome, 1979).

46   Ibid.

47   International Monetary Fund, *World Economic Outlook* (Washington, D.C., April 1986).

48   T. W. Schultz, "The Value of the Ability to Deal with Disequilibria," *Journal of Economic Literature* 13 (September 1975): 827–46.

6. Human Resource Development

1   J. Tinbergen, "Development Cooperation as a Learning Process," in *Pioneers in Development,* vol. 1, edited by G. M. Meier and D. Seers (New York: Oxford University Press, 1984), pp. 326–27. Tinbergen credits J. Mincer with the first use of the phrase "investment in human capital." T. W. Schultz helped pioneer the application of human capital theory to economic development and was among the first to focus on the role of education in development.

2   I. M. D. Little, *Economic Development: Theory, Policy and International Relations* (New York: Basic Books, 1982), pp. 189–93.

3   Y. Hayami and V. Ruttan, *Agricultural Development: An International Perspective* (Baltimore: Johns Hopkins University, 1971); V. Ruttan, "Induced Institutional Change," in *Induced Innovation: Technology, Institutions and Development,* edited by H. P. Binswanger and V. Ruttan (Baltimore: Johns Hopkins University, 1978).

Also see J. Roumasset and J. Smith, "Population, Technological Change and Land-less Workers," *Population and Development Review* 7, no. 3 (September 1981): 401–20.

4   See G. Becker, "An Economic Analysis of Fertility," in *Demographic and Economic Changes in Developed Countries*, edited by C. Dwyer (Princeton, N.J.: Princeton University Press for National Bureau of Economic Research, 1960), pp. 209–31. Also see Y. Ben-Porath, ed., "Income Distribution and the Family," *Population and Development Review* 8, supplement (1982).

5   See H. Leibenstein, "Economic Decision Theory and Fertility Behavior," *Population and Development Review* 7, no. 3 (September 1981): 381–400.

6   World Bank, *World Development Report 1984* (New York: Oxford University Press, 1984), pp. 51–53.

7   Projections are from World Bank, *World Development Report 1986*, table 25, pp. 228–29.

8   P. M. Hauser, D. B. Suits, and N. Ogawa, eds., *Urbanization and Migration in ASEAN Development* (Tokyo: National Institute for Research Advancement, 1985).

9   H. Oshima, "Income Distribution in Selected Asian Countries," in *Development Strategies and Productivity Issues in Asia*, edited by S. Ichimura (Tokyo: Asian Productivity Organization, 1988).

10   M. J. Fry and A. Mason, "The Variable Rate-of-Growth Effect in the Life-Cycle Saving Model: Children, Capital Inflows, Interest and Growth in a New Specification of the Life-Cycle Model Applied to Seven Asian Developing Countries," *Economic Inquiry* 20, no. 3 (July 1982): 426–42. Also see M. J. Fry, "Saving, Financial Intermediation and Economic Growth in Asia," *Asian Development Review* 2, no. 1 (1984) 82–91.

11   World Bank, *World Development Report 1984*, pp. 148–54; also F. B. Hobbs, *Demographic Estimates, Projections and Selected Social Characteristics of the Population of India*, Center for International Research Staff Paper no. 21 (Washington, D.C.: U.S. Bureau of the Census, May, 1988), p. 14.

12   World Bank, *World Development Report 1984*, table 7.6, p. 153.

13   Ibid.

14   Little, *Economic Development*, p. 189, points out that investment in human capital explains the large size of technical change or "residual" coefficients in growth accounting exercises.

15   See World Bank, *World Development Report 1980*, chap. 5, pp. 46–68.

16   M. Blaug, *Education and the Employment Problem in Developing Countries* (Geneva: International Labour Office, 1973). Also see P. M. Hauser, ed., *World Population and Development: Challenges and Prospects* (Syracuse, N.Y.: Syracuse University Press, 1979).

17   F. Harbison, *Human Resources as the Wealth of Nations* (New York: McGraw-Hill, 1973); S. Anand, "Aspects of Poverty in Malaysia," *Review of Income and Wealth* (March 1977) 1–16; S. W. Y. Kuo, "Income Distribution by Size in Taiwan: Changes and Causes," in *Income Distribution, Employment and Economic Development in Southeast and East Asia*, papers and proceedings of the seminar sponsored by Japan Economic Research Centers (JERC) and the Council for Asian Manpower Studies

(CAMS) (Tokyo, July 1975) (hereafter JERC-CAMS); O. A. Meesook, "Income Inequality in Thailand, 1962/63 and 1968/69," in JERC-CAMS; P. K. Bardhan, "The Pattern of Income Distribution in India: A Review," in *Poverty and Income Distribution in India*, edited by T. N. Srinivasan and P. K. Bardhan (Calcutta: Statistical Publishing Society, 1974); G. Papenek, "The Poor of Jakarta," *Economic Development and Cultural Change* (October 1975) 120-30; J. M. Dowling, Jr., "Education as a Human Capital Basic Needs Strategy for Asian LDCs," *Southeast Asian Journal of Social Science* 10, no. 2 (1982): 13–31.

18 G. S. Fields, "Education and Income Distribution in Developing Nations: A Review of the Literature," part 5, in *Education and Income*, edited by T. King, World Bank Staff Working Paper no. 402 (Washington, D.C., July 1980), p. 238, states: "If you sought to determine an individual's income and could ask only one question, you would do best to ascertain how much education the individual in question had received."

19 M. J. Bowman, "Education and Economic Growth: An Overview," part 1 in *Education and Income*, edited by T. King, World Bank Staff Working Paper no. 402 (Washington, D.C., July 1980), pp. 37–38, quoting D. Wheeler, *Human Resource Development and Economic Growth in Developing Countries: A Simultaneous Model*, World Bank Staff Working Paper no. 407 (Washington, D.C., July 1980), pp. 90–91. R. A. Easterlin, "Why Isn't the Whole World Developed?" *Journal of Economic History* (March 1984): 1–17, argues that the establishment of an effective primary education system that enrolls the great bulk of the school age population is the most important single factor in explaining the spread of modern economic growth.

20 J. Meerman, *Public Expenditure in Malaysia, Who Benefits and Why* (New York: Oxford University Press, 1979). Also see Dowling, "Education as Human Capital," pp. 13–31.

21 UNESCO, *Statistical Yearbook 1975* (New York, 1975); see also S. Naya et al., *Developing Asia: The Importance of Domestic Policies*, Asian Development Bank Economic Staff Paper no. 9 (Manila, May 1982), chap. 7; and Dowling, "Education as Human Capital," pp. 13–31.

22 World Bank, *World Development Report 1980*, table 5.4, p. 49.

23 World Bank, *World Development Report 1986*, pp. 94–95.

24 Ibid., p. 93.

25 Ibid., pp. 94–95. Also see A. K. Sen, *Poverty and Famines: An Essay on Entitlement and Deprivation* (Oxford: Clarendon Press, 1981).

26 Household income and expenditure surveys are not conducted with sufficient frequency in most Asian countries to permit comparative assessment of time trends in income distribution. The survey data usually suffer from underreporting of income that is more pronounced among the highest and lowest income groups. Therefore, only large differences between countries can be accepted as broadly indicative of actual conditions.

27 These simple measures of income inequality are preferable to using a Lorenz curve, given the imprecision in the data and the difficulties in interpreting the cumulative income shares of cumulated households. See H. Oshima, "Income Dis-

tribution is Asia: A Brief Comparative Review," in *Development Strategies and Productivity Issues in Asia*, edited by S. Ichimura (Tokyo: Asian Productivity Organization, 1988), chap. 8.

28 This point is stressed by T. Scitovsky, "Economic Development in Taiwan and South Korea, 1965-1981," *Food Research Institute Studies* 19, no. 2 (1985): 1–26.

29 See H. Koo, "The Political Economy of Income Distribution in South Korea: The Impact of the State's Industrialization Policies," *World Development* 12, no. 10 (October 1983): 1029–38.

30 It is likely that the income disparities within the service sector exceed even those in agriculture and industry. H. Oshima, *Economic Growth of Monsoon Asia: A Comparative Survey* (Tokyo: University of Tokyo Press, 1988), chap. 10.

31 The *Fourth Malaysian Five Year Plan, 1981–1985* published by the Government of Malaysia (Kuala Lumpur, 1981), chap. 9, indicated there was a reduction in poverty incidence, but little change in relative inequality during the 1970s. The bumiputras include some non-Muslim indigenous groups as well. The mean income of bumiputras improved from about 52 percent of Chinese mean incomes to 57 percent during the Fourth Plan period.

32 Capital was systematically sent outside the Philippines by the wealthy, especially by high government officials, to secretly acquire assets in the United States, Europe, and other locations during the 1970s and early 1980s. The new Philippine government is attempting to reclaim at least part of the fortune that the Marcoses and their cronies spirited out of the country.

33 See M. Bruch and U. Hiemenz, *Small- and Medium-Scale Manufacturing Establishments in ASEAN Countries: Perspectives and Policy Issues*, Asian Development Bank Economic Staff Paper no. 14, (Manila, March 1983).

34 This finding contradicts the Kuznets curve argument—that inequality is low at low per capita income levels. See Oshima "Income Distribution in Asia." Also, J. M. Dowling, Jr., and D. Soo, *Income Distribution and Economic Growth in Developing Asian Countries*, Asian Development Bank Economic Staff Paper no. 15 (Manila, March 1983).

35 See Oshima, "Income Distribution in Asia," chap. 8. Also, National Planning Commission, *A Survey of Employment, Income Distribution and Consumption Patterns in Nepal*, (Kathmandu, 1983).

36 See J. M. Dowling, Jr., *Income Distribution and Poverty in Selected Asian Countries*, Asian Development Bank Economic Staff Paper no. 22 (Manila, November 1984), for Bangladesh. Also see Oshima, "Income Distribution in Asia"; Oshima, *Economic Growth of Monsoon Asia*. Worsening inequality stems mainly from the poor performance of South Asian countries in generating off-farm employment, particularly in manufacturing industries.

7. Policy Lessons and Future Prospects

1 See the Asian Development Bank funded survey by H. Myint, *Southeast Asia's Economy: Development Policies in the 1970s* (New York: Praeger Publishers, 1972).

2   J. Bhagwati, "Development Economics: What Have We Learned?" *Asian Development Review* 2, no. 1 (1984): 23–78.

3   The Indonesian economy was in crisis for much of the 1960s as the Sukarno regime crumbled. It required a few years for President Suharto to restore stability to an economy racked by hyperinflation, capital flight, and poor rice harvests. See G. Papenek, ed., *The Indonesian Economy* (New York: Praeger Publishers, 1980). The Philippines' growth rate declined sharply in the 1960s as the easy phase of import substitution came to an end, and the agricultural land frontier was reached. See J. Power and G. Sicat, *The Philippines: Industrialization and Trade Policies* (New York and London: OECD Development Center, 1971).

4   K. Kojima and T. Nakauchi, "Economic Conditions of Asian Development," in *Development Strategies and Productivity Issues in Asia* edited by S. Ichimura (Tokyo: Asian Productivity Organization, 1988), chap. 4.

5   I. B. Kravis, "Trade as a Handmaiden of Growth: Similarities between the Nineteenth and Twentieth Centuries," *Economic Journal* (December 1970): 850–72.

6   See, for example, S. Fischer, "Issues in Medium-Term Macroeconomic Adjustment," *World Bank Research Observer* 1, no. 2 (July 1986): 163–82.

7   See V. Corbo, "International Prices, Wages and Inflation in an Open Economy: A Chilean Model," *Review of Economics and Statistics* 67, no. 4 (November 1985): 564–73.

8   R. Wade, *The Role of Government in Overcoming Market Failure: Taiwan, South Korea and Japan*, (Washington, D.C.: World Bank, December 1985). Also C. R. Frank, Jr., K. S. Kim, and L. W. Westphal, *Foreign Trade Regimes and Economic Development: South Korea* (New York: National Bureau for Economic Research, Columbia University Press, 1975). L. P. Jones and I. Sakong, *Government, Business and Entrepreneurship in Economic Development: The Korean Case* (Cambridge, Mass.: Harvard University Press, 1980).

9   R. Wade, *The Role of Government*; and R. Wade, *The Organization and Effects of the Developmental State in East Asia*, (La Jolla: Center for U.S.-Mexican Studies, University of California, May 1986).

10   R. Wade, *The Role of Government*. See also R. Hofheinz, Jr., and K. E. Calders, *The East Asia Edge* (New York: Basic Books, 1982). C. Johnson, *MITI and the Japanese Miracle: The Growth of Industrial Policy, 1925–1975* (Stanford, Calif.: Stanford University Press, 1982).

11   See S. Haggard, "The Newly Industrializing Countries in the International System," *World Politics* (January 1986): 343–70.

12   I. M. D. Little, *Economic Development: Theory, Policy and International Relations* (New York: Basic Books, 1982). On p. 24, Little says that the NICs fit the neoclassical growth model very closely, and on p. 11, he points out that Taiwan set up China Steel for political reasons and that economic efficiency was harmed.

13   C. H. Lee and S. Naya, "Trade in East Asian Development with Comparative Reference to Southeast Asian Experience," paper presented at Conference on East Asia, Vanderbilt University, Nashville, Tenn., October 1986. Also O. Williamson, *Markets and Hierarchies: Analysis and Anti-Trust Implications* (New York: The Free Press, 1975).

14 Lee and Naya, *Trade in East Asian Development*, p. 34.
15 Haggard, "Newly Industrializing Countries"; Lee and Naya, *Trade in East Asian Development*, pp. 29–35.
16 G. Myrdal, *Asian Drama: An Inquiry into the Poverty of Nations*, vol. 1 (New York: Random House, 1968).
17 The loss of confidence in the Marcos regime in the Philippines was in large part related to the corruption issue. Opposition movements in many countries served to focus attention on government irregularities and graft. Indonesia initiated some sweeping reforms in the mid-1980s, including the complete overhaul and replacement of the notorious customs service.
18 H. W. Arndt, "Asian Epic," manuscript (Canberra: Research School for Pacific Studies, The Australian National University, 1986).
19 S. Haggard, "Politics of Stabilization: Lessons from the IMF's Extended Fund Facility," *International Organization* (Summer 1985): 473–534.
20 Opposition groups began to make stronger gains in local elections than ever before in the 1980s. Ruling parties showed increased flexibility in accomodating popular sentiments and a more vocal and powerful democratic opposition. See East-West Center, *Asia-Pacific Report: Trends, Issues, Challenges* (Honolulu, 1986), pp. 3–15.
21 S. Roy, *Pricing, Planning and Politics: A Study of Economic Distortions in India* (London: Institute of Economic Affairs, 1984), pp. 56–59.
22 T. W. Schultz, "The Value of the Ability To Deal with Disequilibria," *Journal of Economic Literature* 13 (September 1975): 827–46.
23 Bhagwati, "Development Economics," p. 30.
24 H. Myint, "Inward and Outward-Looking Countries Revisited: The Case of Indonesia," *Bulletin of Indonesian Economic Studies* 20, no. 2 (August 1984): 41–42.
25 M. Shinohara, *The Japanese Economy and Southeast Asia: In the New International Context*, IDE Occasiona Papers Series no. 15 (Tokyo: Institute of Developing Economies, 1977). See also T. Watanabe, "Pacific Manufactured Trade and Japan's Contributions," Japan Association of International Affairs, 30th Conference Proceedings, Yokohama, September 1986. On p. 17 Watanabe acknowledges: "To be sure, the limited propensity to import manufactures is one of the serious structural problems the Japanese economy is encumbered with." Also, T. Watanabe and H. Kajiwara, "Pacific Manufactured Trade and Japan's Options," *The Developing Economies* 31 (December 1983): 313–39.
26 See J. Riedel, "Trade as an Engine of Growth in Developing Countries Revisited," *Economic Journal* 94 (March 1984): 56–73.
27 In the South Asian countries, often problems of reliably supplying goods of sufficient quality at competitive prices are more constraining on exports than external demand problems. J. Adams and S. Iqbal, *Exports, Politics and Economic Development: Pakistan 1970–1982* (Boulder, Colo.: Westview Press, 1983), pp. 56–64; M. Wolf, *India's Exports* (New York: Oxford University Press, 1982).
28 J. G. Lopez, "The Post-War Latin American Economies: The End of the Long Boom," *Banca Nazionale Del Lavoro Quarterly Review*, no. 154 (September 1985): 233–60.

29   S. Haggard, "The International Politics of East Asian Industrialization," *Pacific Focus: Inha Journal of International Studies* 1, no. 1 (Spring 1986), p. 123.

30   E. Brau, K. B. Dillon, C. Puckahitkom, and M. Xafa, *Export Credits: Developments and Prospects*, International Monetary Fund, World Economic and Financial Surveys (Washington, D.C., July 1986), p. 27.

31   See G. M. Meier, "New Export Pessimism," in *Economic Policy and Development: New Perspectives, Essays in Honor of Saburo Okita*, edited by T. Shishido and R. Sato (London: Auburn House Publishing Co., 1985) pp. 221–37, for an overview of these issues. W. R. Cline, "Can the East Asian Model of Development Be Generalized?" *World Development* 10 (February 1982): 81–99; D. Nayyar, "International Relocation of Production and Industrialization in LDCs," *Economic and Political Weekly* (July 1983): 13–26.

32   G. Ranis, "Equity with Growth in Taiwan: How 'Special' is the 'Special Case'?" *World Development* 6 (1978): 392–409.

33   O. Havrylshyn and I. Alikhani, "Is There Cause for Export Optimism? An Enquiry into the Existence of a Second Generation of Successful Exporters," *Weltwirtschaftliches Archiv* 118, no. 4 (1982): 651–63.

34   This argument is made by W. Leontief, "Technological Advance, Economic Growth, and Income Distribution," *Population and Development Review* 9, no. 3 (September 1983): 403–10.

35   I. Yamazawa, K. Taniguchi, and A. Hirata, "Trade and Industrial Adjustment in Pacific Asian Countries," *The Developing Economies* 21, no. 4 (December 1983): 282-312. T. Watanabe, "An Analysis of Economic Interdependence among the Asian NICs, the ASEAN Nations and Japan," *The Developing Economies* 28, no. 4 (October 1980): 393–411. Also, I. Yamazawa and T. Watanabe, "Industrial Restructuring and Technology Transfer," in *Developing Strategies and Productivity Issues in Asia*, edited by S. Ichimura (Tokyo: Asian Productivity Organization, 1988), chap. 5.

36   B. Balassa, "Comments," in *Trade Policy in the 1980s*, edited by W. R. Cline (Cambridge, Mass.: MIT Press, 1983), pp. 713–14. H. W. Arndt and R. M. Sundrum, "Devaluation and Inflation: The 1978 Experience," *Bulletin of Indonesian Economic Studies* 10, no. 1 (April 1984): 83–97, report that manufactured exports (particularly of labor-intensive goods like garments) grew rapidly soon after the devaluation, with little prompting.

37   Fischer, "Issues in Medium-Term Macroeconomic Adjustment," p. 165.

38   S. Naya, "Trade and Trade Policies," in *Development Strategies and Productivity Issues*, edited by S. Ichimura, chap. 3, stresses that competition coexists with complementarity in trade relations between the NICs, ASEAN, and Japan.

39   Government of Japan, Economic Planning Agency, *Perspectives of the Pacific Era* (Tokyo, July 1985).

40   Watanabe, "Pacific Manufactured Trade."

Bibliography

Adams, J., and S. Iqbal. *Exports, Politics, and Economic Development: Pakistan 1970–1982*. Boulder, Colo.: Westview Press, 1983.

Agarwala, R. *Price Distortions and Growth in Developing Countries*. World Bank Staff Working Paper no. 575. Washington, D.C., 1983.

Ahluwalia, I. J. *Industrial Growth in India: Stagnation since the Mid-1960s*. New York: Oxford University Press, 1985.

Ahmad, I. "Indonesian Agricultural Productivity Growth and Its Relationship to Development Strategy: A Value-Added Approach." Ph.D. dissertation, University of Florida, Gainesville, 1982.

Ahmad, M. *Strategy for Industrialization and Equity: An Approach for South Asian Countries*. Bangkok: United Nations Economic and Social Commission for Asia and the Pacific, 1979.

Akamatsu, K. "A Historical Pattern of Economic Growth in Developing Countries." *The Developing Economies*, preliminary issue no. 1 (March-August 1962): 3–25.

Akrasanee, N. "The Manufacturing Sector in Thailand: A Study of Growth, Import-Substitution, and Effective Protection during 1960–1969." Ph.D. dissertation, Johns Hopkins University, Baltimore, 1973.

Anand, S. "Aspects of Poverty in Malaysia." *Review of Income and Wealth* 23, no. 1 (March 1977): 1–16.

Anderson, D. *Small Industry in Developing Countries: Some Issues*. World Bank Staff Working Paper no. 518. Washington, D.C., 1982.

Anderson, D., and F. Khambata. *Small Enterprises and Development Policy in the Philippines: A Case Study*. World Bank Staff Working Paper no. 468. Washington, D.C., 1981.

Areskoug, K. "Foreign Direct Investment and Capital Formation in Developing Countries." *Economic Development and Cultural Change* 24, no. 3 (April 1976): 539–47.

Ariff, M., and H. Hill. *Export-Oriented Industrialization: The ASEAN Experience*. Sydney: Allen and Unwin, 1985.

Arndt, H. W. "Asian Epic." Mimeographed. Research School for Pacific Studies, Australian National University, Canberra, 1986.

Arndt, H. W. "Survey of Recent Developments." *Bulletin of Indonesian Economic Studies*, 19, no. 2 (August 1983): 1–26.

Arndt, H. W. "Two Kinds of Credit Rationing." *Banca Nazionale del Lavoro Quarterly Review* 35, no. 143 (December 1982): 417–26.

Arndt, H. W., and R. M. Sundrum. "Devaluation and Inflation: The 1978 Experience." *Bulletin of Indonesian Economic Studies* 10, no. 1 (April 1984): 83–97.

Asian Development Bank, Economics Office. *Asian Development Bank Annual Report 1986*. Manila, 1987.

Asian Development Bank, Economics Office. *Domestic Resource Mobilization through Financial Development*. 2 vols. Manila, February 1984.

Asian Development Bank, Economics Office. *Improving Domestic Resource Mobilization through Financial Development*. Manila, September 1985.

Asian Development Bank. *Key Indicators of Developing Member Countries of ADB*. Manila, various years.

Asian Development Bank. *Rural Asia: Challenge and Opportunity*. New York: Praeger Publishers, 1978.

Asian Development Bank. *Strategies for Economic Growth and Development: The Bank's Role in Pakistan*. Manila, 1985.

Asian Productivity Organization. *Farm Credit Situation in Asia*. Tokyo, 1984.

Balassa, B. "Comments." In *Trade Policy in 1980s*, edited by W. R. Cline, pp. 711–22. Cambridge, Mass.: MIT Press, 1983.

Balassa, B. *Policy Reform in Developing Countries*. New York: Oxford University Press, 1977

Balassa, B. "Tarriff Protection in Industrial Countries: An Evaluation." *Journal of Political Economy 73*, no. 4 (December 1965): 573–94.

Balassa, B. *The Newly-Industrializing Countries after the Oil Crisis*. World Bank Staff Working Paper no. 437. Washington, D.C., October 1980.

Balassa, B., et al. *Development Strategies in Semi-Industrial Economies*. Baltimore and London: Johns Hopkins University Press, 1982.

Bandyopadhyay, A. K. *Economics of Agricultural Credit: With Special Reference to Small Farmers in West Bengal*. New Delhi: Agricole Publishing Academy, 1984.

Baquai, M. *Pakistan's Development Patterns and Prospects*. UN-ESCAP Development Planning Division Discussion Paper no. 4. Bangkok, 1981.

Bardhan, P. K. "The Pattern of Income Distribution in India: A Review." In *Poverty and Income Distribution in India*, edited by T. N. Srinivasan and P. K. Bardhan. Calcutta: Statistical Publishing Society, 1974.

Bardhan, P. K. *The Political Economy of Development in India*. London: Basil Blackworth, 1984.

Barker, R., R. W. Herdt, and B. Rose. *The Rice Economy of Asia*. Washington, D.C.: Resources for the Future, 1985.

Barlowe, C., and Muharminto. "The Rubber Smallholder Economy." *Bulletin of Indonesia Economic Studies* 18, no. 2 (July 1982): 86–119.

Bauer, P. T. *Dissent on Development*. London: Weidenfield and Nicholson, 1971.

Bautista, R. M. *Domestic Price Distortions and Agricultural Incomes in Developing Countries*. Washington, D.C.: International Food Policy Research Institute, 1986.

Bautista, R. M., J. Power, and Associates. *Industrial Promotion Policies in the Philippines*. Manila: Philippine Institute for Development Studies, 1979.

Bautista, R. M., and S. Naya, eds. *Economic and Structural Change in the Asia-Pacific Region*. Proceedings of the 13th Pacific Trade and Development Conference. Manila: Philippine Institute for Development Studies and Asian Development Bank, 1984.

Becker, G. "An Economic Analysis of Fertility," in *Demographic and Economic Changes in Developed Countries*. National Bureau of Economic Research no. 11, edited by C. Dwyer, pp. 209–240. Princeton: Princeton University Press, 1960.

Ben-Porath, Y., ed. "Income Distribution and the Family." *Population, and Development Review* 8, supplement (1982).

Bertrand, T. *Agricultural Incentives in Sri Lanka: An Analysis of Agricultural Tax, Subsidy, and Pricing Policies*. Washington, D.C.: World Bank Country Policy Department, 1985.

Bhagwati, J. "Development Economics: What Have We Learned?" *Asian Development Review* 2, no. 1 (1984): 23–38.

Bhagwati, J., and R. S. Ekaus, eds. *Foreign Aid*. London: Penguin, 1970.

Bhagwati, J., and T. N. Srinivasan. *Foreign Trade Regimes and Economic Development: India*. New York: National Bureau of Economic Research, 1975.

Bhagwati, J., and T. N. Srinivasan. "The General Equilibrium Theory of Effective Protection and Resource Allocation." *Journal of International Economics* 3, no. 3 (August 1973): 259–81.

Bhatt, V. V., and J. Meerman. "Resource Mobilization in Developing Countries: Financial Institutions and Policies." *World Development* 6, no. 1 (January 1978): 45–59.

Blaug, M. *Education and the Employment Problem in Developing Countries*. Geneva: International Labour Office, 1973.

Bowman, M. J. "Education and Economic Growth: An Overview." In *Education and Income*, edited by T. King, pt. 1, pp. 1-71. World Bank Working Paper no. 402. Washington, D.C., July 1980.

Bowring, P. "Hong Kong's Problems Masked by Prosperity." *Far Eastern Economic Review*. September 26, 1985, pp. 102–03.

Brau, E., K. B. Dillon, C. Puckahitkom, and M. Xafa. *Export Credits: Development and Prospects*, pp. 1–34. World Economic Surveys. Washington, D.C.: International Monetary Fund, July 1986.

Bruch, M., and U. Hiemenz. *Small- and Medium-Scale Manufacturing Establishments in ASEAN Countries: Perspectives and Policy Issues*. Asian Development Bank Economic Staff Paper no. 14. Manila, March 1983.

Bruton, H. J. "Egypt's Development in the Seventies." *Economic Development and Cultural Change* 31, no. 4 (July 1983): 679–704.

Campbell, B. *Petrodollar Recycling 1973–1980*, 1, *Regional Adjustments and the World Economy*. Asian Development Bank Economic Staff Working Paper no. 8. Manila, April 1982.

Chen, E. K. Y. *Hyper-Growth in Asian Economies: A Comparative Study of Hong Kong, Japan, Korea, Singapore, and Taiwan*. New York: Holmes and Meier, 1979.

Chenery, H. B. "Growth and Structural Change." *Finance and Development* 8, no. 3 (September 1971): 21–25.

Chenery, H. B. "Interaction between Theory and Observation in Development." *World Development* 11, no. 10 (October 1983): 853–62.

Chenery, H. B., and A. M. Strout. "Foreign Assistance and Economic Development." *American Economic Review* 56, no. 3 (September 1966): 679–733.

Chenery, H. B., and M. Syrquin. *Patterns of Development, 1950–1970.* London: Oxford University Press, 1975.

Chenery, H. B., and L. Taylor. "Development Patterns: Among Countries Over Time." *Review of Economics and Statistics* 50, no. 4 (November 1968): 391–416.

Chenery, H. B., M. S. Ahluwalia, C. L. G. Bell, J. H. Duloy, and R. Jolly. *Redistribution with Growth.* London: Oxford University Press, 1974.

Chia, S. Y. "The Role of Foreign Trade and Investment in the Development of Singapore." *Foreign Trade and Investment: Economic Growth in the Newly Industrializing Asian Countries*, edited by W. Galenson, pp. 259–97. Madison: University of Wisconsin Press, 1985.

Clapham, R. *Small and Medium Entrepreneurs in Southeast Asia.* Research Notes and Discussion Papers no. 49. Singapore: Institute of Southeast Asian Studies, ASEAN Economic Research Unit, 1985.

Clarete, R., and J. Roumasset. "Anatomy of Stagnation: Economic Policy and Agricultural Development in the Philippines." *U.S. Agricultural Exports and Third World Development: The Critical Linkage*, edited by R. Purcell and E. Morrison, pp. 115–39. Boulder, Colo.: Lynn & Rienner Publishers, 1987.

Cline, W. R. "Can the East Asian Model of Development Be Generalized?" *World Development* 10, no. 2 (February 1982): 81–99.

Cole, D. C., and Y. C. Park. *Financial Development in Korea, 1945–1978.* Cambridge, Mass.: Harvard University Council on East Asian Studies, 1983.

Cole, D. C., and H. T. Patrick. "Financial Development in the Pacific Basin Market Economies." In *Pacific Growth and Financial Interdependence*, edited by A. H. H. Tan and B. Kapur, pp. 39–67. Sydney: Allen and Unwin, 1986.

Collier, W., et al. "The Acceleration of Rural Development in Java." *Bulletin of Indonesian Economic Studies* 18, no. 3 (November 1982): 84–101.

Corbo, V. "International Prices, Wages, and Inflation in an Open Economy: A Chilean Model." *Review of Economic and Statistics* 67, no. 4 (November 1985): 564–73.

Corden, W. M. "The Structure of a Tariff System and the Effective Protection Rate." *Journal of Political Economy* 74, no. 2 (June 1966): 221–37.

Corden, W. M. "The Substitution Problem in the Theory of Effective Protection." *Journal of International Economics* 1, no. 1 (February 1971): 37–57.

Corden, W. M., and J. P. Neary. "Booming Sector and De-industrialization in a Small Open Economy." *Economic Journal* 92, no. 368 (December 1982): 825–48.

David, C. C. "Economic Policies and Agricultural Incentives." *Philippine Economic Journal* 22, no. 2 (1983): 154–82.

de Vries, B. *"Transition toward More Rapid and Labor-Intensive Development: The Case of the Philippines."* World Bank Staff Working Paper no. 424. Washington, D.C., 1980.

Donges, J. B. "A Comparative Survey of Industrialization Policies in Fifteen Semi-Industrialized Countries." *Weltwirtschaftliches Archiv* 112, no. 4 (1976): 626–59.

Donges, J. B., B. Stecher, and F. Wolter. "Industrialization in Indonesia." In *The Indonesian Economy*, edited by G. Papenek, pp. 357–405. New York: Praeger Publishers, 1980.

Dowling, J. M., Jr. "Education as a Human Capital—Basic Needs Strategy for Asian LDCs." *Southeast Asian Journal of Social Science* 10, no. 2 (1982): 13–31.

Dowling, J. M., Jr. *Income Distribution and Poverty in Selected Asian Countries*, Asian Development Bank Economic Staff Paper no. 22. Manila, November 1984.

Dowling, J. M., Jr., and U. Hiemenz. "Aid, Saving, and Growth in the Asian Region." *The Developing Economies* 21, no. 1 (March 1983): 3–13.

Dowling, J. M., Jr., and D. Soo. *Income Distribution and Economic Growth in Developing Asian Countries*. Asian Development Bank Economic Staff Paper no. 15. Manila, March 1983.

Dowling, J. M., Jr., J. P. A. Verbiest, C. N. Castillo, and S. Montreevat. "Short-Term Economic Prospects for Selected Developing Economies in the Asian-Pacific Region." Paper presented at the Project LINK Meeting, United Nations, New York, March 9–11, 1987.

East-West Center. *Asia-Pacific Report: Trends, Issues, Challenges.* Honolulu, 1986.

Easterlin, R. A. "Why Isn't the Whole World Developed?" *Journal of Economic History* 44, no. 1 (March 1984): 1–17.

Eaton, J., and M. Gersovitz. "Debt with Potential Repudiation: Theoretical and Empirical Analysis." *Review of Economic Studies* 48, no. 2 (April 1981): 289–309.

Far Eastern Economic Review. *Asia 1986 Yearbook.* Hong Kong, 1986.

Fei, J. C. H., and G. Ranis. *Development of the Labor Surplus Economy.* Homewood, Ill.: Richard D. Erwin, 1964.

Fields, G. S. "Education and Income Distribution in Developing Nations: A Review of the Literature." In *Education and Income*, edited by T. King, pp. 231–315. World Bank Staff Working Paper no. 402. Washington, D.C., July 1980.

Findlay, R. "Growth and Development in Trade Models." *Handbook of International Economics*, vol. 1, edited by R. W. Jones and P. B. Kennen, pp. 215–18. Amsterdam: North-Holland, 1984.

Findlay, R. "Trade and Development: Theory and the Asian Experience." *Asian Development Review* 2, no. 2 (1984): 23–42.

Fischer, S. "Issues in Medium-Term Macroeconomic Adjustment." *World Bank Research Observer* 1, no. 2 (July 1986): 163–82.

Floro, S. L. "Credit Relations and Market Interlinkage in Philippine Agriculture." Ph.D. dissertation, Stanford University, 1987.

Frank, C. R., Jr., K. S. Kim, and L. W. Westphal. *Foreign Trade Regimes and Economic Development: South Korea.* New York: National Bureau for Economic Research and Columbia University Press, 1975.

Fry, M. J. "Saving, Financial Intermediation, and Economic Growth in Asia." *Asian Development Review* 2, no. 1 (1984): 82–91.

Fry, M. J., and A. Mason. "The Variable Rate-of-Growth Effect in the Life-Cycle Saving Model: Children, Capital Inflows, Interest, and Growth in a New Specification of the Life-Cycle Model Applied to Seven Asian Developing Countries." *Economic Inquiry* 20, no. 3 (July 1982): 426–42.

Galenson, W., ed. *Economic Growth and Structural Change in Taiwan—The Postwar Experience of the Republic of China*. Ithaca and London: Cornell University Press, 1979.

Galenson, W., ed. *Foreign Trade and Investment: Economic Growth in the Newly Industrializing Countries*. Madison: University of Wisconsin Press, 1985.

Glassburner, B. "Macroeconomics and the Agricultural Sector." *Bulletin of Indonesian Economic Studies* 21, no. 2 (August 1985): 51–73.

Go, E. *Patterns of External Financing of Developing Member Countries*. Asian Development Bank Economic Staff Paper no. 26. Manila, May 1985.

Go, E., and J. S. Lee. "Foreign Capital, Balance of Payments, and External Debt in Developing Asia." In *Challenge of Asian Developing Countries: Issues and Analyses*, edited by S. Ichimura, chap. 6. Tokyo: Asian Productivity Organization, 1988.

Gregory, R. G. "Some Implications of the Growth of the Mineral Sector." *Australian Journal of Agricultural Economics* 20, no. 2 (August 1976): 71–91.

Gurley, J. G., and E. S. Shaw. "Financial Development and Economic Development." *Economic Development and Cultural Change* 15, no. 3 (April 1967): 257–78.

Gurley, J. G., and E. S. Shaw. *Money in a Theory of Finance*. Washington, D.C.: The Brookings Institution, 1960.

Haggard, S. "Politics of Stabilization: Lessons from the IMF's Extended Fund Facility." *International Organization*, summer 1985, pp. 473–534.

Haggard, S. "The International Politics of East Asian Industrialization." *Pacific Focus: Inha Journal of International Studies* 1, no. 1 (Spring 1986): 97–124.

Haggard, S. "The Newly Industrializing Countries in the International System." *World Politics* (January 1986): 343–70.

Harberger, A. C. "The Dutch Disease: How Much Sickness, How Much Boon?" *Resources and Energy*, no. 5 (1983): 1–20.

Harbison, F. *Human Resources as the Wealth of Nations*. New York: McGraw-Hill, 1973.

Hauser, P. M., ed. *World Population and Development: Challenges and Prospects*. Syracuse, N. Y.: Syracuse University Press, 1979.

Hauser, P. M., D. B. Suits, and N. Ogawa, eds. *Urbanization and Migration in ASEAN Development*. Tokyo: National Institute for Research Advancement, 1985.

Havrylyshyn, O., and I. Alikhani. "Is There Cause for Export Optimism? An Enquiry Into the Existence of a Second Generation of Successful Exporters." *Weltwirtschaftliches Archiv* 118, no. 4 (1982): 651–63.

Hayami, Y., and M. Kikuchi. *Asian Village Economy at the Crossroads: An Economic Approach to Institutional Change*. Tokyo: Tokyo University Press and Baltimore, Md.: Johns Hopkins University Press, 1981.

Hayami, Y., and V. Ruttan. *Agricultural Development: An International Perspective*, 2d ed. Baltimore, Md.: Johns Hopkins University Press, 1985.

Hayami, Y., E. Bennagen, and R. Barker. "Price Incentives versus Irrigation Investment to Achieve Food Self-Sufficiency in the Philippines," *American Journal of Agricultural Economics* 59, no. 4 (November 1977): 717–21.

Hayami, Y., V. Ruttan, and H. Southworth. *Agricultural Growth in Taiwan, Korea, and the Philippines*.Baltimore, Md.: Johns Hopkins University Press, 1979.

Hiemenz, U. "Industrial Growth and Employment in Developing Asian Countries: Issues and Perspectives for the Coming Decade." Asian Development Bank Economic Staff Paper no. 7. Manila, March 1982.

Hewaritharana, B. *New Patterns and Strategies of Development: The Case of Sri Lanka*. UN-ESCAP Development Planning Division Discussion Paper no. 3. Bangkok, 1981.

Hirschman, A. O. *The Strategy of Economic Development*. New Haven, Conn.: Yale University Press, 1958.

Ho, S. P. S. "Decentralized Industrialization and Rural Development: Evidence from Taiwan." *Economic Development and Cultural Change* 28, no. 1 (October 1979): 77–96.

Ho, S. P. S. *Small-Scale Enterprises in Korea and Taiwan*. World Bank Staff Working Paper no. 384. Washington, D.C., 1980.

Hobbs, F. B. *Demographic Estimates, Projections, and Selected Social Characteristics of the Population of India*. Center for International Research, U. S. Bureau of the Census, Staff Paper no. 21. Washington, D.C., May 1986.

Hoffman, L., and S. E. Tan. *Industrial Growth, Employment, and Foreign Investment in Peninsular Malaysia*. New York: Oxford University Press, 1980.

Hofheinz, R., Jr., and K. E. Calders. *The East Asia Edge*. New York: Basic Books, 1982.

Hong Kong, Census and Statistics Department. *Estimates of Gross Domestic Product 1966–1983*. Hong Kong, 1984.

Hong Kong, Census and Statistics Department. *Hong Kong Monthly Digest of Statistics*. February 1986.

Hsiao, M. C. "Tests of Causality and Exogeneity between Exports and Economic Growth: The Case of Asian NICs." Paper presented at the North American Annual Meeting of the Econometric Society, Dallas, Tex., December 1984.

Institute for Small-Scale Industries. *Entrepreneurship and Small Enterprises Development: The Philippine Experience*. Quezon City: University of the Philippines, 1979.

International Labour Office. *Group-based Savings and Credit for the Rural Poor*. Geneva, 1983.

International Labour Office. *Yearbook of Labour Statistics*. Geneva, various years.

International Monetary Fund. *Balance of Payments Statistics Yearbook*. Various issues. Washington, D.C., various years.

International Monetary Fund. *Government Finance Statistics Yearbook*. Washington, D.C., 1980.

International Monetary Fund. *International Financial Statistics*. Yearbook. Washington, D.C., 1985.

International Monetary Fund. *World Economic Outlook*. Washington, D.C., April 1986, April 1987.

James, W. E. "Asian Agriculture and Economic Development." Asian Development Bank Economic Staff Paper no. 5. Manila, March 1982.

James, W. E. "Asian Agriculture in Transition: Key Policy Issues." Asian Development Bank Economic Staff Paper no. 19. Manila, September 1983.

James, W. E. *Credit Rationing, Rural Savings, and Financial Policy in Developing Coun-*

tries. Asian Development Bank Economic Staff Paper no. 13. Manila, September 1982.

James W. E. "Energy Conservation in Rapid-Growth Exonomies of Asia." *Natural Resources Forum* 9, no. 3 (August 1985): 197–204.

James, W. E., and T. R. Ramirez. *New Evidence on Yields, Fertilizer Application, and Prices in Asian Rice Production.* Asian Development Bank Economic Office Report Series no. 20. Manila, July 1983.

Japan, Economic Planning Agency. *Perspectives of the Pacific Era.* Tokyo, July 1985.

Japan, Ministry of Finance. *Zaisei Kinyu Tokei Geppo (Monthly Statistical Review of Public Finance and Money).* nos. 305 and 404. In Japanese. Tokyo, September 1977, December 1985.

Japan, Ministry of International Trade and Industry. *Wagakuni Kigyo no Kaigai Jigyo Katsudo (Overseas Activities of Domestic Firms).* Seventh, twelfth, and thirteenth surveys. In Japanese. Tokyo: Ministry of Finance Printing Office, 1977, and Toyo Hoki, 1984.

Johnson, C. *MITI and the Japanese Miracle: The Growth of Industrial Policy, 1925–1975.* Stanford, Calif.: Stanford University Press, 1982.

Johnson, H. G. "The Theory of Tariff Structure with Special Reference to World Trade and Development." In *Trade and Development.* Geneva: Institut Universitaire de Hautes Études Internationales, 1965.

Johnston, B., and P. Kilby. *Agriculture and Structural Transformation.* London and Toronto: Oxford University Press, 1975.

Johnston, B., and J. Mellor. "The Role of Agriculture in Economic Development." *American Economic Review* 51, no. 4 (September 1961): 566–93.

Jones, L. P., and I. Sakong. *Government, Business, and Entrepreneurship in Economic Development: The Korean Case.* Cambridge, Mass.: Harvard University Press, 1980.

Junginger-Dittel, K. O., and H. Reisen. "Import Instability and LDC's Response: The Destabilization of the Inflow of Capital and Intermediate Goods." *Weltwirtschaftliches Archiv* 115, no. 4: 653–59.

Kelley, A. C., and J. Williamson. *Lessons from Japanese Development: An Analytical Economic History.* Chicago: University of Chicago Press, 1974.

Kendrick, J. W. *Productivity Trends in the United States.* Princeton, N.J.: Princeton University Press, 1961.

Keynes, J. M. *The General Theory of Employment, Interest, and Money.* New York: Harcourt, Brace, and World, 1936.

Killick, T. "Development Planning in Africa: Experiences, Weaknesses, and Prescriptions." *Development Policy Review,* 1 no. 1 (1983): 47–76.

Killick, T. "Economic Environment and Agricultural Development—The Importance of Macroeconomic Policy." *Food Policy* 10, no. 1 (February 1985): 29–40.

Kim, W. S. "Financial Development and Household Savings: Issues in Domestic Resource Mobilization in Asian Developing Countries." ADB Economic Staff Paper no. 10. Manila, July 1982.

Kojima, K., and T. Nakauchi. "Economic Conditions of Asian Development." In *Challenge of Asian Developing Countries: Issues and Analyses,* edited by S. Ichimura, chap. 4. Tokyo: Asian Productivity Organization, 1988.

Koo, B. Y. "The Role of Foreign Direct Investment in Korea's Economic Growth." In *Foreign Trade and Investment: Economic Growth in the Newly Industrializing Countries*, edited by W. Galenson, pp. 176–216. Madison: University of Wisconsin Press, 1985.

Koo, H. "The Political Economy of Income Distribution in South Korea: The Impact of the State's Industrialization Policies." *World Development* 12, no. 10 (October 1983): 1029–38.

Koppel, B., and E. Oasa. "Induced Innovation Theory and Asia's Green Revolution: A Case Study of an Ideology of Neutrality." *Development and Change* 18, no. 1 (1987): 29–68.

Krause, L. B. "Introduction." In *Foreign Trade and Investment: Economic Growth in the Newly Industrializing Asian Countries*, edited by W. Galenson, pp. 3–41. Madison: University of Wisconsin Press, 1985.

Kravis, I. B. "Trade as a Handmaiden of Growth: Similarities between the Nineteenth and Twentieth Centuries." *Economic Journal* 80, no. 320 (December 1970): 850–72.

Kreuger, A. O. "Comparative Advantage and Development Policy Twenty Years Later." *Economic Structure and Performance: Essays in Honor of Hollis B. Chenery*, edited by M. Syrquin, L. Taylor, and L. Westphal, pp. 135–56. New York: Academic Press, 1984.

Krueger, A. O. *The Developmental Role of the Foreign Sector and Aid*. Cambridge, Mass.: Harvard University Press, 1979.

Krueger, A. O. *Foreign Trade Regimes and Economic Development: Liberalization Attempts and Consequences*. Cambridge, Mass.: Ballinger Press for the National Bureau of Economic Research, 1978.

Krueger, A. O. "Import Substitution Versus Export Promotion." *Finance and Development* 22, no. 2 (June 1985): 20–23.

Kuo, S. W. Y. "Income Distribution by Size in Taiwan: Changes and Causes." In *Income Distribution, Employment, and Economic Development in Southeast and East Asia*. Papers and proceedings of the seminar sponsored by Japan Economic Research Centers and the Council for Asian Manpower Studies. Tokyo, July 1975.

Kuo, S. W. Y. *The Taiwan Economy in Transition*. Boulder, Colo.: Westview Press, 1983.

Kuo, S. W. Y. *The Taiwan Success Story*. Boulder, Colo.: Westview Press, 1981.

Kuznets, S. "Quantitative Aspects of the Economic Growth of Nations, 1, Levels and Variability of Rates of Growth." *Economic Development and Cultural Change* 5, no. 1 (October 1956): 5–94.

Kuznets, S. "Quantitative Aspects of the Economic Growth of Nations, 10, Level and Structure of Foreign Trade: Long-term Trends." *Economic Development and Cultural Change* 5, pt. 2 (January 1967): 1–140.

Kwack, S. Y. "The Economic Development of the Republic of Korea, 1965–1981." In *Models of Development*, edited by L. J. Lau, pp. 65–134. San Francisco: Institute for Contemporary Studies, 1986.

Lal, D. "Nationalism, Socialism, and Planning: Influential Ideas in the South." *World Development* 13, no. 6 (June 1985): 749–59.

Lappe, F. M., J. Collins, and D. Kinley. *Aid as Obstacle*. San Francisco: Institute for Food and Development Policy, 1980.

Lee, C. H. "On Japanese Macroeconomic Theories of Direct Foreign Investment." *Economic Development and Cultural Change* 32, no. 4 (July 1984): 713–24.

Lee, C. H., and S. Naya. "Trade in East Asian Development with Comparative Reference to Southeast Asian Experience." Paper read at Conference on East Asia, Vanderbilt University, Nashville, Tenn., October 1986.

Lee, J. S. "External Debt Servicing Capacity of Asian Developing Countries." *Asian Development Review* 1, no. 2 (1983): 68–71.

Lee, J. S., and E. Banaria. *Meeting Basic Human Needs in Asian Developing Countries.* Asian Development Bank Economic Staff Paper no. 32. Manila, March 1985.

Leibenstein, H. "Economic Decision Theory and Fertility Behavior." *Population and Development Review* 7, no. 3 (September 1981): 381–400.

Leontief, W. "Technological Advance, Economic Growth, and Income Distribution." *Population and Development Review* 9, no. 3 (September 1983): 403–10.

Lessard, D. R. *International Financing for Developing Countries: The Unfulfilled Promise.* World Bank Staff Working Paper no. 783. Washington, D.C., 1986.

Lewis, W. A. "Economic Development with Unlimited Supplies of Labor." *The Manchester School*, May 1954, pp. 139–91.

Lim, C. P. "Small Enterprises in ASEAN: Need for Regional Cooperation." *ASEAN Economic Bulletin*, November 1984, pp. 89–114.

Lin, C. Y. *Developing Countries in a Turbulent World Economy: Patterns of Adjustment since the Oil Crisis.* New York: Praeger Publishers, 1981.

Lin, T. B., and V. Mok. "Trade, Foreign Investment, and Development in Hong Kong." In *Foreign Trade and Investment: Economic Growth in the Newly Industrializing Asian Countries*, edited by W. Galenson, pp. 219–56. Madison: University of Wisconsin Press, 1985.

Little, I. M. D. *Economic Development: Theory, Policy, and International Relations.* New York: Basic Books, 1982.

Little, I. M. D., T. Scitovsky, and M. Scott. *Industry and Trade in Some Developing Countries.* New York: Oxford University Press, 1971.

Liu, T., and Y. Ho. *Export-Oriented Growth and Industrial Diversification in Hong Kong.* Hong Kong Series Occasional Paper no. 7. Economic Research Center, Chinese University of Hong Kong, 1980.

Lockwood, W. W. *The Economic Development of Japan.* Princeton, N.J.: Princeton University Press, 1963.

Lohani, P. C. "Nepal's Economy in Retrospect and Its Prospects for the 1980s." *Economic Bulletin for Asia and the Pacific*, 1982, pp. 66–93.

Lopez, J. G. "The Post-War Latin American Economies: The End of the Long Boom." *Banca Nazionale Del Lavoro Quarterly Review* 38 (September 1985): 233–60.

Lumbantobing, S. "Small and Medium Industries in Indonesia." Paper presented at the Management Development of Small and Medium Enterprises in Asia Conference, Tokyo, March 1984.

Malaysia, *The Fourth Malaysian Five-Year Plan, 1981–1985*, Kuala Lumpur, 1981.

Marshall, A. *Principles of Economics.* 8th ed. London: Macmillan for the Royal Economic Society, 1930.

McCawley, P. *Industrialization in Indonesia: Developments and Prospects*. Development Studies Center Occasional Paper no. 13. Canberra: Australian National University, 1979.

McKinnon, R. I. *Money and Capital in Economic Development*. New York: Brookings Institution, 1973.

McKinnon, R. I. "Issues and Perspectives: An Overview of Banking Regulations and Monetary Control." In *Pacific Growth and Financial Interdependence*, edited by A. H. H. Tan and B. Kapur, pp. 319–36. Sydney: Allen and Unwin, 1986.

Mears, L. *The New Rice Economy of Indonesia*. Yogyakarta: Gadjah Mada University Press, 1979.

Meerman, J. *Public Expenditure in Malaysia: Who Benefits and Why*. London: Oxford University Press, 1979.

Meesook, O. A. *Income, Consumption, and Poverty in Thailand, 1962/63 and 1975/76*. World Bank Staff Working Paper no. 364. Washington, D.C., November 1979.

Meier, G. M. *Emerging from Poverty: The Economics That Really Matters*. New York and London: Oxford University Press, 1984.

Meier, G. M. *Leading Issues in Economic Development*. 4th ed. New York: Oxford University Press, 1984.

Meier, G. M. "New Export Pessimism." In *Economic Policy and Development: New Perspectives, Essays in Honor of Saburo Okita*, edited by T. Shishido and R. Sato, pp. 21–37. London: Auburn House Publishing Co., 1985.

Mikesell, R. F., and J. E. Zinser. "The Nature of the Savings Function in Developing Countries: A Survey of the Theoretical and Empirical Literature." *Journal of Economic Literature* 11 (March 1973): 1–26.

Morgan, T. "Investment Versus Economic Growth." *Economic Development and Cultural Change* 17 (April 1969): 392–414.

Mujaiton, T. "Factors Affecting Variation in Interest Rates: A Case Study of Rural Thailand," Ph.D. dissertation, University of Hawaii, December 1985.

Myers, R. H. "The Economic Development of the Republic of China in Taiwan, 1965–81." In *Models of Development: A Comparative Study of Economic Growth in South Korea and Taiwan*, edited by L. J. Lau, pp. 13–64. San Francisco: Institute for Contemporary Studies, 1985.

Myint, H. "Inward and Outward-Looking Countries Revisited: The Case of Indonesia." *Bulletin of Indonesian Economic Studies* 20 (August 1984): 39–51.

Myint, H. "Organizational Dualism and Economic Development." *Asian Development Review* 3 (1985): 24–42.

Myint, H. *Southeast Asia's Economy: Development Policies in the 1970s*. New York: Praeger Publishers, 1972.

Myrdal, G. *Asian Drama: An Inquiry Into the Poverty of Nations*. 3 vols. Abridged by S. S. King. New York: Random House, 1971.

Naqvi, S., and A. R. Kemal. *The Structure of Protection in Pakistan, 1980–1981*. 2 vols. Islamabad: Pakistan Institute of Development Economics, 1983.

National Planning Commission. *A Survey of Employment, Income Distribution, and Consumption Patterns in Nepal*. Kathmandu, 1983.

Naya, S. *Resources, Trade, Technology, and Investment—Southeast Asia in the Pacific Cooperative System*. Resource Systems Institute Working Paper 85–5. Honolulu: East-West Center, 1985.

Naya, S. "The Role of Small-Scale Industries in Employment and Exports of Asian Developing Countries." *Hitosubashi Journal of Economics* 26 (December 1985): 147–63.

Naya, S. "Trade and Trade Policies." In *Challenge of Asian Developing Countries: Issues and Analyses*, edited by S. Ichimura, chap 3. Tokyo: Asian Productivity Organization, 1988.

Naya, S., and W. E. James "External Shocks, Policy Responses, and External Debt of Asian Developing Countries." In *Pacific Growth and Financial Interdependence*, edited by A. H. H. Tan and B. Kapur, pp. 292–316. Sydney: Allen and Unwin, 1986.

Naya, S., D. H. Kim, and W. E. James "External Shocks and Policy Responses: The Asian Experience." *Asian Development Review* 2 (1984): 1–22.

Naya, S., et al. *Developing Asia: The Importance of Domestic Policies*. Asian Development Bank Economic Staff Paper no. 9. Manila, May 1982.

Nayyar, D. "International Relocation of Production and Industrialization in LDCs." *Economic and Political Weekly*, July 1983, pp. 13–26.

Nayyar, D. "Transnational Corporations and Manufactured Exports from Poor Countries." *Economic Journal* 88 (March 1978): 59–84.

Nugent, J., and P. Yotopoulos. "What Has Orthodox Development Economics Learned from Recent Experience?" *World Development* 7 (June 1979): 541–54.

Nurkse, R. *Problems of Capital Formation in Underdeveloped Countries*. Reprint. New York: Oxford University Press, 1967.

Okhawa, K. *Dualistic Development and Phases: Possible Relevance of the Japanese Experience to Contemporary Less Developed Countries*. Laxenburg, Austria: International Institute for Applied Systems Analysis, 1980.

Okhawa, K., and H. Rosovsky. *Japanese Economic Growth: Trend Acceleration in the Twentieth Century*. Stanford, Calif.: Stanford University Press, 1973.

Organisation for Economic Co-operation and Development. *Financing and External Debt of Developing Countries*, 1985 Survey. Paris, 1986.

Organisation for Economic Co-operation and Development. *Geographical Distribution of Financial Flows to Developing Countries*. Paris, various years.

Organisation for Economic Co-operation and Development. *National Accounts Statistics*. Paris, various years.

Oshima, H. *Economic Growth of Monsoon Asia: A Comparative Survey*. Tokyo: University of Tokyo Press, 1988.

Oshima, H. "Income Distribution in Selected Asian Countries." In *Challenge of Asian Developing Countries: Issues and Analyses*, edited by S. Ichimura, chap. 8. Tokyo: Asian Productivity Organization, 1988.

Oshima, H. "Manpower Quality in the Differential Growth between East and Southeast Asia." *Philippine Economic Journal* 19 (1980): 380–406.

Oshima, H. "The Significance of Off-Farm Employment and Incomes in Post-War East

Asian Economic Growth." Asian Development Bank Economic Staff Paper no. 21. Manila, January 1984.

Palacpac, A. C. *World Rice Statistics*. Los Banos, Philippines: International Rice Research Institute, 1982.

Panchamukhi, V. R., and K. M. Raipuria. "Productivity and Development Strategy in India: Major Dimensions, Issues, and Trends, 1965/66 to 1982/83." In *Challenge of Asian Developing Countries: Issues and Analyses*, edited by S. Ichimura, chap. 12. Tokyo: Asian Productivity Organization, 1988.

Papenek, G. "Aid, Foreign Private Investment, Savings, and Growth in Less Developed Countries." *Journal of Political Economy* 81 (January/February 1973): 120–30.

Papenek, G. *Development Strategy, Growth, Equity, and the Political Process in Southern Asia*. Washington, D.C.: U.S. Agency for International Development, 1985.

Papenek, G. *Pakistan's Development: Social Goals and Private Incentives*. Cambridge, Mass.: Harvard University Press, 1967.

Papenek, G. "The Poor of Jakarta." *Economic Development and Cultural Change* 24 (October 1975): 1–28.

Papenek, G., ed. *The Indonesian Economy*. New York: Praeger Publishers, 1980.

People's Republic of China, State Statistical Bureau. *Statistical Yearbook of China 1986*. Hong Kong: Economic Information Agency, 1986.

Philippine Tariff Commission. *Tariff Profiles in ASEAN*. Manila, 1979.

Philippine Tariff Commission. *Tariff Profiles in ASEAN: An Update*. Manila, 1985.

Popkin, S. *The Rational Peasant: The Political Economy of Rural Society in Vietnam*. Berkeley and Los Angeles: University of California Press, 1979.

Population Reference Bureau. *1985 World Population Data Sheet*. Washington, D.C., 1985.

Power, J. "The Economics of Keynes." In *Economics and Human Welfare: Essays in Honor of Tibor Scitovsky*, edited by M. Boskin, pp. 321–60. New York: Academic Press, 1980.

Power, J., and G. Sicat. *The Philippines: Industrialization and Trade Policies*. New York and London: OECD Development Center, 1971.

Prebisch, R. "Commercial Policy in the Underdeveloped Countries." *American Economic Review* 49 (May 1959): 251–91.

Raj, K. N., and A. K. Sen. "Alternative Patterns of Growth under Conditions of Stagnant Export Earnings." *Oxford Economic Papers* 13 (February 1961): 43–52.

Rana, P. *The Impact of the Current Exchange Rate System on Trade and Inflation of Selected Developing Member Countries*. Asian Development Bank Economic Staff Paper no. 18. Manila, September 1983.

Ranis, G. "The Dual Economy Framework: Its Relevance to Asian Development." *Asian Development Review* 2 (1984): 39–51.

Ranis, G. "Equity with Growth in Taiwan: How 'Special' is the 'Special Case'?" *World Development* 6 (March 1978): 397–409.

Ranis, G. "Prospective Southeast Asian Strategies in a Changing International Environment." In *New Directions in Asia's Development Strategies*, pp. 1–29. Tokyo: Institute of Developing Economies, 1980.

Ranis, G., J. C. H. Fei, and S. W. Y. Kuo. *Growth with Equity: The Case of Taiwan*. New York: Oxford University Press, 1979.

Rao, D. C. "Economic Growth and Equity in the Republic of Korea." *World Development* 6 (March 1978): 383–96.

Republic of China, Central Bank of China. *Balance of Payments, Taiwan District, Republic of China*. Summary and various issues. Taipei, 1958–82.

Republic of China, Central Bank of China. *Financial Statistics, Taiwan District, Republic of China*. Taipei, various issues.

Republic of China, Council for Economic Planning and Development. *Taiwan Statistical Data Book*. Taipei, various issues.

Republic of China, Department of Statistics, Ministry of Finance. *Monthly Statistics of Exports and Imports*. Taipei, various issues.

Republic of China, Directorate-General of Budget, Accounting, and Statistics. *Statistical Yearbook of the Republic of China*. Taipei, 1984, 1986.

Republic of China, Ministry of Economic Affairs, Investment Commission. *A Survey of Overseas Chinese and Foreign Firms and Their Effects on National Economic Development*. Issues in Chinese. Taipei, 1980–1984.

Republic of Korea, Economic Planning Board. *Major Statistics of Korean Economy*. Korea, 1982–1984.

Republic of Singapore, Department of Statistics. *Report on the Census of Industrial Production*. Singapore, 1975–82.

Reynolds, L. G. *Image and Reality in Economic Development*. New Haven, Conn.: Yale University Press, 1977.

Rhee, H. Y. "Protection Structures of the Developing Countries in South and East Asia." Paper presented at Pacific Cooperative Task Force Workshop on Trade in Manufactured Goods, Seoul, 1983.

Riedel, J. "Trade as an Engine of Growth in Developing Countries Revisted." *Economic Journal* 94 (March 1984): 56–73.

Robinson, S. "Sources of Growth in Less Developed Countries: A Cross-Section Study." *Quarterly Journal of Economics*, August 1971, pp. 391–408.

Rose, B. *Appendix to the Rice Economy of Asia: Rice Statistics by Country*. Washington, D.C.: Resources for the Future, 1985.

Rosenstein-Rodan, P. "Problems of Industrialization of Eastern and Southeastern Europe." *Economic Journal*, June-September 1943. Reprinted in *The Economics of Underdevelopment*, edited by A. N. Agarwala and S. P. Singh, pp. 245–55. New York: Oxford University Press, 1963.

Rosenstein-Rodan, P. *The Theory of Economic Growth*. London: Allen and Unwin, 1955.

Roumasset, J. *Rice and Risk: Decision-Making Among Low-Income Farmers*. Amsterdam: North-Holland Publishing Co., 1976.

Roumasset, J., and J. Smith. "Population, Technological Change, and Landless Workers." *Population and Development Review* 7 (September 1981): 401–20.

Roy, S. "Pricing, Planning, and Politics: A Study of Economic Distortions in India," Institute of Economic Affairs Occasional Paper no. 69. London, 1984.

Ruttan, V. "Induced Institutional Change." In *Induced Innovation: Technology, Institutions, and Development.* H. P. Binswanger and V. Ruttan, pp. 327–57. Baltimore, Md.: Johns Hopkins University, 1978.

Sacay, O., M. Agabin, and C. Tanchoco. *Small Farmer Credit Dilemma.* Manila: National Publishing Cooperative, 1985.

Sachs, J. "The Current Account and Macroeconomic Adjustment in the 1970s." *Brookings Papers on Economic Activity* 1 (1981): 201–82.

Sanguanruang, S. "Small and Medium Manufacturing Enterprises in Thailand." Paper presented at the Management Development of Small and Medium Enterprises in Asia Conference, Tokyo, March 1984.

Santiano, M. A. "Small and Medium Enterprises in the Philippines." Paper presented at the Management Development of Small and Medium Enterprises in Asia Conference, Tokyo, March 1984.

Santikarn, M. *Regionalization of Industrial Growth.* Thai University Research Association, report no. 6. Bangkok, 1980.

Schultz, T. W. *Investing in People.* Berkeley, Calif.: University of California Press, 1981.

Schultz, T. W. "Nobel Lecture: The Economics of Being Poor." *Journal of Political Economy* 88 (August 1980): 639–51.

Schultz, T. W. *Transforming Traditional Agriculture.* New Haven, Conn.: Yale University Press, 1964.

Schultz, T. W. "The Value of the Ability To Deal with Disequilibria." *Journal of Economic Literature* 13 (September 1975): 827–46.

Scitovsky, T. "Economic Development in Taiwan and South Korea, 1965–1981." *Food Research Institute Studies* 19 (1985): 1–26. Reprinted in *Models of Development,* edited by L. J. Lau, pp. 135–96. San Francisco: Institute for Contemporary Studies, 1981.

Sen, A. K. *Poverty and Famines: An Essay on Entitlement and Deprivation.* Oxford: Clarendon Press, 1981.

Shaw, E. S. *Financial Deepening in Economic Development.* New York: Oxford University Press, 1983.

Shinohara, M. *The Japanese Economy and Southeast Asia: In the New International Context.* Institute of Developing Economies, Occasional Papers Series no. 15. Tokyo, 1977.

Solow, R. "Technological Change and the Aggregate Production Function." *Review of Economics and Statistics* 39 (August 1957): 312–20.

Staley, E., and R. Morse. *Modern Small Industry for Developing Countries.* New York: McGraw-Hill, 1965.

Streeten, P., et al. *First Things First.* New York: Oxford University Press, 1981.

Sugitani, S. "International Strategy of Small- and Medium-Sized Enterprises." *Kwansei Gakuin University Annual Studies* 32 (December 1983): 105–19.

Sugitani, S. "Japan's Exports and Small-Scale Industry." *Kwansei Gakuin University Annual Studies* 31 (December 1982): 189–200.

Tan, A. H. H. "Singapore's Economy: Growth and Structural Change." Paper presented at the Singapore and the United States into the 1990s Conference, sponsored by the Fletcher School, The Asia Society, and the Institute of Southeast Asian Studies, Tufts University, 1985.

Tan, A. H. H., and O. C. Hock. "Singapore." In *Development Strategies in Semi-Industrializing Economies*, edited by B. Balassa et al., pp. 280–309. Washington, D.C.: World Bank, 1982.

Timmer, C. P. "Choice of Technique in Rice Milling in Java." *Bulletin of Indonesian Economic Studies* 9 (July 1973): 57–76.

Timmer, C. P. "Energy and Structural Change in the Asia-Pacific Region: The Agricultural Sector." In *Energy and Structural Change in the Asia-Pacific Region*, edited by R. M. Bautista and S. Naya, pp. 51–72. Manila: Philippine Institute for Development Studies and Asian Development Bank, 1984.

Timmer, C. P., and W. P. Falcon. "The Political Economy of Rice Production and Trade in Asia." In *Agriculture in Economic Development*, edited by L. G. Reynolds, pp. 373–410. New Haven, Conn.: Yale University Press, 1975.

Timmer, C. P., W. P. Falcon, and S. R. Pearson. *Food Policy Analysis*. Baltimore, Md.: Johns Hopkins University Press, 1983.

Tinbergen, J. "Development Cooperation as a Learning Process." In *Pioneers in Development*, edited by G. M. Meier and D. Seers, pp. 326–27. New York: Oxford University Press, 1984.

United Nations. *Commodity Trade Statistics*. New York, various years.

United Nations. *Statistical Yearbook*. New York, 1978, 1981.

United Nations. *Yearbook of International Trade Statistics*. Vol. 1. New York, various years.

United Nations Conference on Trade and Development. Computer tapes. Geneva, 1983, 1984.

United Nations Conference on Trade and Development. *Handbook of International Trade and Development Statistics*. New York, 1985.

United Nations Conference on Trade and Development. *Handbook on International Trade and Development Statistics*. Supplement 1986. New York, 1987.

United Nations Economic and Social Commission for Asia and the Pacific. *Economic and Social Survey of Asia and the Pacific 1985*. Bangkok, 1986.

United Nations Economic and Social Commission for Asia and the Pacific (ESCAP). *Policies, Programmes, and Perspectives for the Development of the ESCAP Region: Regional Development Strategy for the 1980s*. Bangkok, January 1980.

United Nations Educational, Scientific, and Cultural Organization. *Statistical Yearbook 1975*. New York, 1975.

United Nations Food and Agriculture Organization. *Agriculture towards 2000: Regional Implications with Special Reference to the Third Development Decade*. Rome, 1979.

United Nations Food and Agriculture Organization. *FAO Fertilizer Yearbook 1984*. Rome, 1985.

United Nations Food and Agriculture Organization. *FAO Production Yearbook, 1979, 1983*. Rome, 1980, 1984.

United Nations Food and Agriculture Organization. *FAO Trade Yearbook*. Rome, various years.

United Nations Food and Agriculture Organization. *Production Yearbook 1972*. Rome.

Unnevehr, L., and A. Balisacan. *Changing Comparative Advantage in Philippine Rice Production*. Philippine Institute for Development Studies, Staff Working Paper. Makati, Philippines, 1983.

U.S. Agency for International Development. *Free Zones in Developing Countries: Expanding Opportunities for the Private Sector*. AID Program Evaluation Discussion Paper no. 18. Washington, D.C.: Sabre Foundation, November 1983.

U.S., Department of Commerce. *Survey of Current Business* 66, no. 8 (August 1986).

U.S., Department of Commerce. *U.S. Direct Investment Abroad 1977*. Washington, D.C., 1981.

U.S., Department of Commerce. *U.S. Direct Investment Abroad, 1982 Benchmark Survey Data*. Washington, D.C., 1981.

Utami, W., and J. Ihalaw. "Some Consequences of Small Farm Size." *Bulletin of Indonesian Economic Studies* 19 (July 1973): 46–56.

Vaidyanathan, A. "Indian Economic Performance and Prospects." Economic and Social Commission for Asia and the Pacific, Development Planning Division Discussion Paper no. 2. Bangkok, 1981.

Von Pischke, J. D., et al. *Rural Financial Markets in Developing Countries*. Baltimore, Md.: Johns Hopkins University Press, 1983.

Vyas, V. S. "Asian Agriculture: Achievements and Challenges." *Asian Development Review* 1 (1983): 27–44.

Vyas, V. S., and W. E. James. "Agricultural Development in Asia: Performance, Issues, and Policy Options." In *Challenge of Asian Developing Countries: Issues and Analyses*, edited by S. Ichimura, chap. 7. Tokyo: Asian Productivity Organization, 1988.

Wade, R. "The Organization and Effects of the Developmental State in East Asia." La Jolla: Center for U.S.-Mexican Studies, University of California, May 1986.

Wade, R. "The Role of Government in Overcoming Market Failure: Taiwan, South Korea, and Japan." Washington, D.C.: World Bank, December 1985.

Watanabe, T. "An Analysis of Economic Interdependence among the Asian NICs, the ASEAN Nations, and Japan." *The Developing Economies* 28 (October 1980): 393–411.

Watanabe, T. "Pacific Manufactured Trade and Japan's Contributions." Japan Association of International Affairs, 30th Conference Proceedings, Yokohama, September 1986.

Watanabe, T., and H. Kajiwara. "Pacific Manufactured Trade and Japan's Options." *The Developing Economies* 31 (December 1983): 313–39.

Weisskopf, T. "The Impact of Foreign Capital Inflows on Domestic Savings in Underdeveloped Countries." *Journal of International Economics* 2 (February 1972): 25–38.

Wells, R. J. G. "The Rural Credit Market in Peninsular Malaysia: A Focus on Informal Lenders." *Asian Economics*, no. 31 (December 1979).

Westphal, L. W. "The Republic of Korea's Experience with Export-Led Industrial Development." *World Development* 6 (March 1978): 347–82.

Wheeler, D. *Human Resource Development and Economic Growth in Developing Coun-*

tries: A Simultaneous Model. World Bank Staff Working Paper no. 407. Washington, D.C., July 1980.

Williamson, O. *Markets and Hierarchies: Analysis and Anti-Trust Implications*. New York: The Free Press, 1975.

Wolf, M. *India's Exports*. London: Oxford University Press, 1982.

World Bank. *Bank Policy on Agricultural Credit*. Washington, D.C., 1974.

World Bank. *Industrial Development Strategy in Thailand*. World Bank Country Study. Washington, D.C., 1980.

World Bank. *World Debt Tables: External Debt of Developing Countries*. Washington, D.C., 1985, 1987.

World Bank. *World Development Report*. New York, Oxford University Press, various years.

World Bank. *World Tables*. 1st, 2d, 3d eds. Baltimore, Md.: Johns Hopkins University Press, 1976, 1980, 1983.

Yamazawa, I., and A. Hirata. "Industrialization and External Relations: Comparative Analysis of Japan's Historical Experience and Contemporary Developing Countries Performance." *Hitotsubashi Journal of Economics* 18 (February 1978): 33–61.

Yamazawa, I., and T. Watanabe. "Industrial Restructuring and Technology Transfer." *Challenge of Asian Developing Countries; Issues and Analyses*, edited by S. Ichimura, chap. 5. Tokyo: Asian Productivity Organization, 1988.

Yamazawa, I., K. Taniguchi, and A. Hirata. "Trade and Industrial Adjustment in Pacific Asian Countries." *The Developing Economies* 31 (December 1983): 282–312.

Young, A. "Increasing Returns and Economic Progress." *Economic Journal* (December 1928): pp. 527–42.

Young, K., W. Bussink, and P. Hasan. *Malaysia: Growth with Equity in a Multiracial Society*. Baltimore, Md.: Johns Hopkins University Press, 1980.

Yudelman, M. *The World Bank and Agricultural Development: An Insider's View*. World Resources Institute Paper no. 1. Washington, D. C., 1985.

Index

ADB (Asian Development Bank)
Loans from, 95, 98, 100
study of financial development by,
19, 80, 83
surveys of Asian agriculture by, 143
Africa
external debt of, 106, 111t, 112
income distribution in, 202
output growth in, 4t, 29fig, 145fig
Aggregate demand management
adjustment to external shocks and, 116
debt-servicing problems and, 119-20
financial development and, 19
Agriculture
credit availability in, 78-79, 166
diversification of, 168-69
employment in, 146-47
environmental problems in, 141-43
exports, 154-58
fertilizer use and, 151, 162-63
fisheries, 156-57
food grains production, 147-52
forestry, 157-58
government intervention in, 159-69 passim
HYVs (high-yielding varieties)
and, 147, 152, 164
irrigation/other infrastructure
investments in, 151, 164-65
land use in, 142-43, 150-51
livestock production, 156-57
macroeconomic policies and, 159-61
population pressure on, 141-42, 171,
205
pricing in, 161-63
research and development in, 164-68

technology transfer in, 164-65
See also Food prices; Food self-sufficiency;
Land reform; Natural resources; Rice
"Aid-fatigue," 105, 110. See also Foreign aid
ASEAN-4 (Association of Southeast Asian
Nations)
agriculture in, 145-58
domestic savings in, 63-67
economic cooperation in, 12-13, 224
economic growth versus social welfare in, 20
education policies in, 190-95
exports of, 5, 23t, 32t, 39-49 passim
external borrowings of, 98-99,
105-14, 219-20
external shocks and adjustments in, 114-19
financial development in, 70t, 76-81
foreign investment in, 93, 96-97, 122-33
GDP of, 6t, 8t, 222
general characteristics of, 3-4, 7-9, 11-13
government saving/investment in, 85-87
health/nutrition in, 143fig, 196-98
income distribution in, 201-4
industrial policies in, 39-49
labor force growth in, 180-82
population of, 8t, 176-78, 187t
protection of domestic producers in, 41-42
savings rates in, 64-67
structural transformation in, 11t, 12t, 13
tariff rates in, 42-43
See also Indonesia; Malaysia; Philippines;
Thailand
Asian ethics, 16
Austerity programs, 120
Australia, 8t, 11t, 12t, 223

273